$\mathcal{W}$OMEN, $\mathcal{F}$AMILY, AND UTOPIA

Utopianism and Communitarianism
LYMAN TOWER SARGENT AND GREGORY CLAEYS
Series Editors

Oneida women engaged in a bag-making bee. A man is reading aloud to the group. Note the distinctive bloomer-style dresses and short hair worn by the community women. *Courtesy Oneida Community Mansion House.*

m278

WOMEN, FAMILY, AND UTOPIA

Communal Experiments of the Shakers,
the Oneida Community, and the Mormons

LAWRENCE FOSTER

SYRACUSE UNIVERSITY PRESS

First Edition 1991
91 92 93 94 95 96 97 98 99   6 5 4 3 2 1

The paper used in this publication meets the minimum requirements of American National Standard for Information Sciences—Permanence of Paper for Printed Library Materials, ANSI Z39.48–1984. ∞™

Library of Congress Cataloging-in-Publication Data

Foster, Lawrence, 1947–
    Women, family, and utopia : communal experiments of the Shakers, the Oneida Community, and the Mormons / Lawrence Foster.—1st ed.
        p.   cm. — (Utopianism and communitarianism)
    Includes bibliographical references and index.
    ISBN 0–8156–2534–0 (alk. paper). — ISBN 0–8156–2535–9 (pbk.)
    1. Sex—Religious aspects—Christianity—History of doctrines—19th century. 2. Sex role—Religious aspects—Christianity—History of doctrines—19th century. 3. Christian communities—United States—History—19th century. 4. Shakers—History—19th century. 5. Oneida Community—History. 6. Church of Jesus Christ of Latter-Day Saints—History—19th century. 7. Mormon Church—United States—History—19th century. 8. Women in Christianity—History of doctrines—19th century. I. Title. II. Series.
    BT708.F67 1991
    307.77′4′0973—dc20   91–8496
                                                               CIP

Manufactured in the United States of America

For Julie, David, Paul, Laura, and Eric

Say not the struggle naught availeth,
    The labor and the wounds are vain,
The enemy faints not nor faileth,
    And as things have been they remain.

If hopes were dupes, fears may be liars;
    It may be, in yon smoke conceal'd,
Your comrades chase e'en now the fliers,
    And, but for you, possess the field.

For while the tired waves, vainly breaking,
    Seem here no painful inch to gain,
Far back, through creeks and inlets making,
    Comes silent, flooding in, the main.

And not by eastern windows only,
    When daylight comes, comes in the light;
In front the sun climbs slow, how slowly.
    But westward, look, the land is bright!
                    —ARTHUR HUGH CLOUGH

LAWRENCE FOSTER is an associate professor of American history at the Georgia Institute of Technology in Atlanta. A former Woodrow Wilson, Ford Foundation, and National Endowment for the Humanities fellow, he has written extensively on American social and religious history. His first book, *Religion and Sexuality* (Oxford University Press, 1981; paperbound edition, University of Illinois Press, 1984), won the Mormon History Association award for "best book of the year in Mormon history." In 1985–86, Foster served as Visiting Fulbright Professor of American History at the University of Sydney in Australia and the University of Auckland in New Zealand.

CONTENTS

ILLUSTRATIONS

Oneida women's bag-making bee   *frontispiece*

PREFACE

My INTEREST in alternative life-styles and communal societies in America developed during the turbulence of the late 1960s. As a student at experimental Antioch College, I felt the full force of the disorder, protest, and social unrest of those years. So many people seemed to be at loose ends, looking for a sense of community and purpose but often not finding it. Was there any way out, I wondered. Had any other periods of American history been similarly confused and uncertain? If so, could we learn anything from the experiences of another time about how to deal constructively with our current concerns?

There *was* one period, I discovered, that seemed to display almost uncanny similarities to my own troubled era. That was the 1830s and 1840s before the Civil War. Especially in New York State, the antebellum equivalent of present-day California, an extraordinary range of religious and reform groups sought to transform society. By far the most extreme of these efforts were made by fanatical new religious movements—groups we might label "cults" today. Three groups in particular stood out—the Shakers, who created a celibate system that gave women full equality with men in religious leadership, the Oneida Perfectionists, who set up a form of group marriage or "free love" that radically changed relations between men and women, and the Mormons, who eventually introduced a form of polygamy based on Old Testament patriarchal models. Why had such groups emerged, attracted a following, and lasted at least thirty years in each case, I wondered. Eventually I became so fascinated by those experiments that I wrote a dissertation and then a book, *Religion and Sexuality*, trying to explain how they worked.

That book, which attempted to present a comprehensive overview of all major aspects of the development of each movement over as much as three-quarters of a century, was widely praised as a lively and insightful analysis. Even Mormons, who frequently have been sensitive about non-Mormons investigating their polygamous past, were enthusiastic about my work and gave it a historical award. The book, however, did not allow me to explore as fully as I wanted many issues of contemporary concern, particularly regarding the implications these groups might have, directly or indirectly, for the changing role of women today. I thus began writing a series of more sharply focused essays that told a story that was in many ways substantially new and different from that of my first book.

This new book has two main goals. Six core chapters (1, 2, 5, 8, 10, and 12) highlight and elaborate on my research regarding relations between men and women in the early Shaker, Oneida Perfectionist, and Mormon movements for those who may never have heard of their experiments. The remaining six chapters (3, 4, 6, 7, 9, and 11), which draw on and go beyond the core pieces, further explore the ways in which these unorthodox experiments in communal living addressed issues of major contemporary concern such as the changing role of women, the nature of the family, and impact of sexuality—in all its complexity—on society. Although many of these chapters first appeared originally in published form elsewhere, almost all of them have been substantially revised for this volume in order to provide a coherent overall perspective that speaks to the most recent popular concerns and scholarship.

Let me add a few words about what I think is new and distinctive about this book and my earlier work. From one perspective, as the author of the book of Ecclesiastes observes, "there is nothing new under the sun." The ideas that one generation finds new and exciting are often only newly discovered or reinterpreted versions of ideas that really are as old as the hills. Both this volume and my earlier study *Religion and Sexuality* might best be described as ventures in historical anthropology that are informed by an effort to combine a special quality of sympathetic understanding of these groups on their own terms with critical analysis that places them into a larger comparative perspective with significance for each of us today.

This approach is not inherently new, but it has not usually been applied to the controversial communal experiments I studied. Until the past several decades, they typically have been caricatured or patronized, treated simply as freaks that failed. My objective, instead, has been to be essentially a historical "participant-observer," inspired by the credo of the philosopher Spinoza: "I have made a ceaseless effort not to ridicule, not to bewail, nor to scorn human actions, but to understand them." What is chiefly new in my work is my effort to see these groups and their sexual experimentation as part of a total gestalt, system, or way of life that is worthy both of respect and of critical attention as we attempt to come to terms with our own era as well.

As part of this attempt at sympathetic reconstruction of a total way of life, I have deliberately avoided developing a highly elaborated theoretical analysis of how these communities functioned. These groups could be and have been analyzed using a variety of Marxist, feminist, sociological, psychological, and other perspectives. Rather than tossing another limited external critique into the dustbin of communitarian history, my chief goal here has been to let the experiences of the groups themselves suggest key issues and concerns. In particular, while I have dealt with the complex interaction of issues connected with women, the family, and sexuality in these groups, I have chosen not to present any highly articulated contemporary feminist critique of these experiments. Instead, I have let these groups speak for themselves about their attitudes toward the role of women in society. I have sought to reconstruct as fully as possible the perspectives and goals expressed by members of these groups and to judge their efforts, fairly and critically, in terms of how well they achieved their own goals.

Although the past decade appears on the surface to have been a much more "conservative" period than the 1960s, which originally got me interested in these groups, many today still feel profound uncertainty about how best to deal with perennial problems in the relations between men and women, between the family and society. One way to approach our current concerns is to limit ourselves exclusively to the present. An alternative is to seek a broader perspective by focusing on individuals in the past who struggled with issues similar to those we face today and see if we can learn from their successes and failures about new possibilities for our own time. Whatever the immediate climate of opinion in America may be, these remarkable communal experimenters will continue to provide a mirror reflecting our hopes and fears, as well as a chance to view our own era from unorthodox and revealing perspectives.

ACKNOWLEDGMENTS

DURING THE COURSE of more than two decades of research and writing on the Shakers, the Oneida Community, and the Mormons, I have incurred a host of debts to individuals too numerous to mention. Here, therefore, only the most exceptional assistance can be acknowledged. By far my most important debt is to Martin E. Marty, my dissertation adviser and mentor at the University of Chicago, a fine critic of my first book, *Religion and Sexuality*, who encouraged me to share my further insights into these groups in this new study. Robert Fogarty, who supervised my earlier B.A. thesis at Antioch College comparing the Shakers and the Oneida Community, also has been a continuing source of inspiration and advice over the past two decades. I shall always be grateful to Donald C. Scott, then at the University of Chicago, for advising me to follow my broad comparative instincts rather than focusing narrowly on any one of these groups. Invaluable assistance, including an incisive critique of the entire manuscript, has been provided by Michael Barkun at Syracuse University and by Howard Page Wood at Lankenau Hospital in Philadelphia.

In the field of Mormon history, Leonard J. Arrington and his associates at the LDS Church Historical Department during the 1970s have proved a continuing source of inspiration and valued criticism. Jan Shipps, who first introduced me to many fine Mormon scholars and showed me how one could be an "inside-outsider" in a faith not one's own, has continued to influence my thinking. Klaus J. Hansen and Robert B. Flanders similarly have provided me with both an intellectual and a personal stimulus for which I can never adequately thank them. I owe a special debt of gratitude to Linda King Newell and Valeen Tippetts Avery for permission to make extensive use of their superb, and in my view definitive, biography of Emma Hale Smith in chapter 8 of this book. In addition, Linda Newell's thorough and perceptive critique of chapter 8 substantially improved its quality, even though I did not always follow her advice.

One of the most enjoyable aspects of my research has been the enthusiasm and support of librarians and archivists. I have been given exceptional assistance by individuals at the Regenstein Library of the University of Chicago; the Newberry Library in Chicago; the Western Reserve Historical Society Library in Cleveland; the Huntington Library in San Marino, California; and the Library and Archives of the Historical Department of the Church of Jesus Christ of Latter-day Saints in Salt Lake City. I also have received valuable help from librarians at the Bancroft Library in Berkeley, California; the Beinecke Library at Yale University in New Haven, Connecticut; the Brigham Young University Special Collections in Provo, Utah; the Chicago Historical Society Library; the Garrett Theological Seminary Library in Evanston, Illinois; the Library and Archives of the Reorganized Church of Jesus Christ of Latter Day Saints in Independence, Missouri; the Library of Congress in Washington, D.C.; the Sabbathday Lake Shaker Community Library at Sabbathday Lake, Maine; the Shaker Museum Library at Old Chatham, New York; the University of Utah Library Special Collections in Salt Lake City; and the Utah State Historical Society Library in Salt Lake City.

Permission to use materials that I first published elsewhere has been generously granted. Special thanks are due to Oxford University Press, which published my first book, *Religion and Sexuality: Three American Communal Experiments of the Nineteenth Century*, Copyright © 1981 by Oxford University Press, for permission to make extensive use of portions of that earlier study. Permission to use previously published articles, often considerably revised for this book, has been granted by the publishers of the following articles: "Shaker Spiritualism and Salem Witchcraft: Social Perspectives on Trance and Possession Phenomena," *Communal Societies* 5 (1985): 176–93; "Had Prophecy Failed?: Contrasting Perspectives of the Millerites and

Shakers," in Ronald L. Numbers and Jonathan M. Butler, eds., *The Disappointed: Millerism and Millenarianism in the Nineteenth Century* (Bloomington: Indiana University Press, 1987), 173–88; "The Psychology of Free Love in the Oneida Community," *Australasian Journal of American Studies* 5 (December 1986): 14–26; "Free Love and Feminism: John Humphrey Noyes and the Oneida Community," *Journal of the Early Republic* 1 (Summer 1981): 165–83; "The Rise and Fall of Utopia: The Oneida Community Crises of 1852 and 1879," *Communal Societies* 8 (1988): 1–17; "James J. Strang: The Prophet Who Failed," *Church History* 50 (June 1981): 182–92; "Polygamy and the Frontier: Mormon Women in Early Utah," *Utah Historical Quarterly* 50 (Summer 1982): 268–89; and "From Frontier Activism to Neo-Victorian Domesticity: Mormon Women in the Nineteenth and Twentieth Centuries," *Journal of Mormon History* 6 (1979): 3–21.

Permission to use the illustrations in this book has been granted by the following institutions (listed in order of the appearance of the first illustration credited to each source): the Library of Congress, Washington, D.C., for the nineteenth-century camp-meeting print; the Newberry Library, Chicago, Illinois, for the title page of *Testimonies of the Life, Character, Revelations and Doctrines of Our Ever Blessed Mother Ann Lee* (1816); the University Press of New England for the map showing the location of Shaker Communities that appeared in Priscilla Brewer's *Shaker Communities, Shaker Lives* (Hanover, N.H.: University Press of New England, 1986); the Winterthur Library: the Edward Deming Andrews Memorial Collection, Winterthur, Delaware, for the stereograph of the New Lebanon Second Family, ca. 1880, and the manuscript version of "Simple Gifts"; Hancock Shaker Village, Inc., Pittsfield, Massachusetts, for the Shaker dining room print from *Frank Leslie's Illustrated Newspaper* and Hannah Cohoon's spirit drawing of "The Tree of Light or Blazing Tree"; the Shaker Museum, Old Chatham, New York, for the print of the Shaker ring dance from *Frank Leslie's Illustrated Newspaper*; Syracuse University Library, for the early photograph of John Humphrey Noyes, and the map showing the location of the Oneida Community; the Oneida Community Mansion House, Kenwood, New York, for the photographs of the quadrangle of the Mansion House, a women's bag bee, a pea-shelling bee, and the entire membership of the Oneida Community; the Library-Archives of the

Reorganized Church of Jesus Christ of Latter Day Saints, the Auditorium, Independence, Missouri, for the painting of Joseph Smith and the photograph of Emma Hale Smith and David Hyrum Smith; MIT Press for the map of Mormon migrations that appeared in Dolores Hayden's *Seven American Utopias: The Architecture of Communitarian Socialism* (Cambridge, Mass.: MIT Press, 1976); the Historical Department of the Church of Jesus Christ of Latter-day Saints, Salt Lake City, Utah, for the early photograph of Nauvoo, the announcement of Joseph Smith's campaign for president of the United States in 1844, the 1887 painting of Joseph Smith addressing the Nauvoo Legion before his martyrdom, and the photographs of Brigham Young, Salt Lake City in the 1860s, Brigham Young's residences, and four leading women of Zion; Carl Landrum, Quincy, Illinois, for the photograph of the Nauvoo Temple sunstone taken by Joe Leisen; the Michigan State Historical Society Library, Ann Arbor, Michigan, for the photograph of James J. Strang; and *Dialogue: A Journal of Mormon Thought* for the photograph of Sonia Johnson by Brenda Schrier.

I am deeply grateful to the Georgia Tech Foundation for granting a subvention to make possible simultaneous publication of this study in a paperbound edition.

It has been a genuine pleasure to work with Cynthia Maude-Gembler, my fine acquisitions editor at Syracuse University Press, and all the other excellent and responsive members of the press. I also am grateful to Lyman Tower Sargent and Gregory Claeys, the editors of the new Syracuse University Press series on Utopianism and Communitarianism, for their decision to include my book among those launching the new series.

Finally, special thanks and appreciation are due to my family, to whom I dedicate this book.

LAWRENCE FOSTER

Atlanta, Georgia
March 1991

Women, Family, and Utopia

INTRODUCTION

1

RELIGION, SEXUALITY, and WOMEN'S ROLES

Alternative Family and Sexual Systems
in Nineteenth-Century America

*D*URING THE TURBULENT DECADES of the 1830s and 1840s
before the Civil War, thousands of Americans joined new
religious movements that rejected existing marriage and sex-role patterns in favor of alternative life-styles. The most colorful and controversial of these unorthodox experiments were conducted by three
groups that were founded or were active in New York State. Like California today, New York in the nineteenth century was an extraordinary hotbed of religious and social diversity. In this area, the Shakers
introduced a celibate, essentially monastic pattern that formally gave
women complete equality with men in religious leadership. The
Oneida Community created a form of "free love" or group marriage
that radically revised traditional forms of sexual expression between
men and women. And the Mormons, who also were founded in the
region, eventually developed a form of polygamy and established it as
the ideal form of marriage for more than one hundred thousand of
their followers in Utah and adjacent areas of the American West.[1]

What was the attraction of such unorthodox religious groups—
groups we probably now would call "cults"? What possible significance could such extraordinary experiments have? For many
years, most historians and popular writers have tended to treat these
groups as though they were colorful freaks in a circus sideshow or
strange natives in some primitive tribe. The dominant tone has been

3

unsympathetic and voyeuristic, caricaturing or making fun of these movements. They were said to have inevitably "failed" because they were out of touch with the developing economic and industrial order, or because their leaders and members were unstable and psychologically maladjusted, or because they were somehow out of touch with the American "mainstream," whatever that may have been.[2]

More interesting than the alleged "failure" of these groups, however, was their considerable degree of "success." How could such remarkable alternative systems of sexual and family organization have been conceived, introduced, and established—lasting for more than a quarter of a century in each case? Why would thousands of Americans, especially those from New York State and other areas of New England expansion, have been so dissatisfied with conventional marriage and sex-role patterns before the Civil War that they would not simply complain about those patterns but would actually join and live in groups that set up radically different systems?

Increasingly I became convinced that the struggles of men and women in these groups could have much meaning for us as we seek to understand more recent periods of turmoil and uncertainty in American life. Like Perry Miller's Puritans, these nineteenth-century religious experimenters could provide "an ideal laboratory"[3] through which the actual process of social change could be seen at both the individual and group levels. Indeed, precisely *because* these groups were so extreme in carrying every idea to its logical conclusion, they might more dramatically highlight underlying issues of religious and sexual expression than would more conventional groups.

The specific *solutions* that these three movements developed for dealing with relations between men and women may not appear particularly appealing to most of us; however, the underlying *issues* with which they struggled are of central importance during times of social unrest and rapid transformation. Perhaps by sympathetically exploring the struggles, successes, and failures of men and women in these three groups, we may better be able to understand the promise and pitfalls of other periods of rapid social change as well.[4]

I

To appreciate the complex challenges faced by the people who organized or joined these three unconventional religious groups, we must first place these movements into their larger social and intellectual context. Our tendency today is to feel that we live in a uniquely turbulent and rapidly changing age; we often think that nineteenth-century America, in particular, was somehow a more "stable," "traditional," "conservative," "Victorian" period. This impression is highly misleading. Not only have there been other periods of uncertainty and rapid transition in American life, but one of the most disruptive of those periods came in the 1830s and 1840s, when Americans were leaving behind earlier, relatively more stable, colonial patterns but had not yet arrived at the newer, Victorian approach.

All the earlier social institutions were being called into question during the first half of the nineteenth century. In religion, the end of state support for churches after the American Revolution required the development of new methods of recruitment and commitment. In politics, earlier deferential forms of political participation had increasingly changed by the Jacksonian era so that all adult white males could vote and hold office. In economics, older subsistence-style agriculture was rapidly giving way to a market economy and the beginning of the industrial revolution in America. And in marriage and family life, earlier, more community-based ways of controlling sexual behavior and deviance were becoming less effective as settlement rapidly expanded into new areas without long-established traditions.[5]

No area of the country was undergoing more rapid transition than western New York following the completion of the Erie Canal in 1825. This "burned-over district," as it was called because of the frequency with which the fires of the revival spirit swept through the region, was a spawning ground for new religious and social movements. Every conceivable mainstream or unorthodox group seemed to be able to find a following in the Burned-over District. Charles Grandison Finney, one of the most prominent revivalists of the pre–Civil War years, got his start and many of his supporters there. So too did many temperance advocates, abolitionists, and crusaders for women's rights. The Millerites attracted attention to their predictions that the world would literally end in 1843 or 1844, while the Fox sisters gained notoriety for their spirit rappings.

Many people in the Burned-over District were at loose ends, seeking for answers to pressing religious questions and for a more satisfying life-style, but none more insistently than the Shakers, Oneida

Perfectionists, and Mormons. In New York, the Shakers set up or enlarged their celibate communities, the Oneida Perfectionists established a free-love colony, and Joseph Smith saw visions, "translated" his golden plates, founded the Mormon church, and may have first considered the idea of polygamy, which he later began to introduce among his followers in Illinois.[6]

Let us look briefly, in turn, at the Shakers, the Oneida Perfectionists, and the Mormons, suggesting the way they developed and some of the key questions that they raised, both for their own time and for us today. Although the Shakers experienced a period of disruptive "spiritual manifestations" and attracted many new members in the 1830s and 1840s, their roots actually went back to England in the mid-1700s. There they were known as "Shaking Quakers," or simply "Shakers," because of their highly emotional religious services in which they literally shook, shouted, danced, and spoke in tongues.

Under the leadership of Ann Lee, a poor but highly intelligent and dynamic Manchester factory woman, the Shakers also developed their distinctive commitment to celibacy. Ann Lee had experienced four traumatic deliveries, losing all four of her children either in infancy, or, in one case, at the age of six. Rather than viewing these terrible experiences as her unique problem, she instead came to the remarkable conclusion that her traumas represented a universal human condition. She argued that only by giving up sexual intercourse entirely and devoting all energies to God could humankind ultimately be redeemed.[7]

This message attracted few converts in England, but in America during the disruptive aftermath of the American Revolution the Shakers developed a highly committed following of several thousand people, many of them teenagers. The unusual Shaker worship services, which by their own admission could sometimes be heard from as far away as two miles, created considerable hostility, as did their demand for celibacy, which many saw as an outrageous assault on normal human relationships and indeed the entire social order.

Following the death of Ann Lee and the other English leaders because of the intense persecution they experienced, American Shaker leaders formally set up essentially monastic communities in which women had complete equality with men in religious leadership. During the pre–Civil War years, there were some sixty semi-autonomous Shaker communities at eighteen different geographical locations, and with as many as four thousand members, scattered from Maine to Ohio, Indiana, and Kentucky. By the Civil War, when the intensity of their proselyting ardor slackened, the Shakers had become increasingly respected and even admired by many of their neighbors. Today the Shakers, who have dwindled to a handful of members in two villages, are best remembered for the quality of their workmanship, especially their functional furniture, and for their hymns such as "Simple Gifts," which provided the chief theme for Aaron Copland's composition "Appalachian Spring."[8]

The development and persistence of a group such as the Shakers, which has now survived in American for more than two hundred years, raises many complex questions. Three issues particularly deserve attention and will be considered in the chapters that follow. One has to do with the Shaker emphasis on equality for women. The Shakers were unique among major religious groups in America in giving total equality to women in religious leadership. Not only were they founded by a woman and led by women at later stages of their development up to the present, but they also set up *formal* religious structures in which women had equal religious authority with men. Why and how was such a system set up? What were the difficulties and advantages inherent in such a system? Why did the Shakers not go further than just giving women religious equality and also do away with differences and inequalities between men and women in other areas of life such as economics?[9]

A second question that the Shakers raise relates to their requirement of celibacy. Americans have great difficulty understanding why any individuals would want to be celibate and devote their whole lives to the worship of God. One Shaker pamphlet asked the question in its colorful title: *A Shaker's Answer to the Oft-Repeated Question, "What Would Become of the World If All Should Become Shakers?"*[10] The author pointed out that the Shakers felt that their primary concern was to do God's will, as they understood it, not simply to survive as a group. With the benefit of hindsight, we may find it ironical that although the Shakers were celibate (and thus totally dependent upon converts for membership), they have survived more than two hundred years, longer than any similar religious

communal group in American history. How did the Shakers' semimonastic model relate to the group's survival? What were the
advantages and disadvantages of such a system? How was celibacy
related to the Shaker emphasis on equality for women and to their
liberalism in many other areas?[11]

A third question highlighted by the Shakers has to do with the
social significance of their highly emotional religious services, which
included singing, shouting, speaking in tongues, and ecstatic dancing. Such activities provoked strong reactions—both positive and
negative. What types of people were attracted by Shaker charismatic
phenomena and why? In particular, did such activities have special
appeal for women who felt constricted by more conventional religious organizations? What was the impact of the decade-long charismatic revival in the Shaker communities during the 1830s and
1840s? And why did the Shakers during the 1840s attract a significant number of disillusioned followers of William Miller after the
world failed to end as he had predicted in 1843 or 1844?[12]

II

At least as complex and remarkable as the Shaker movement was the
community founded by John Humphrey Noyes at Oneida, New York,
in 1848. This "free love" group, which also was based on deep religious conviction, has fascinated journalists, scholars, and the general
public for more than a century. John Humphrey Noyes began as an
intense young theology student at Yale, then wandered quixotically
around New England and New York trying to convert the world to
his highly unorthodox religious beliefs. Failing to achieve that goal,
he turned his sights to establishing a community and spreading his
message via the newspapers he printed.

For over thirty years, first in his hometown of Putney, Vermont,
and then at Oneida in central New York State, Noyes successfully
presided over a communal system of "complex marriage" that the
journalist Charles Nordhoff described as an apparently unprecedented
"combination of polygamy and polyandry with certain religious and
social restraints."[13] The group members, who numbered more than
two hundred adults at the community's peak, considered themselves

all married to each other. Men and women exchanged sexual partners frequently within the community, while breaking up all exclusive romantic attachments, which were described as "special love,"
antisocial behavior threatening communal order.[14]

Associated with this unorthodox system were a number of complex control mechanisms. All members lived together in one large
communal Mansion House, ate together, worked together, had a system of communal child rearing, and shared all but the most basic
property in common. Community government was achieved by having daily religious-and-business meetings which all attended, by using
an informal method of group feedback and control called "mutual
criticism," and by developing an informal status hierarchy known as
"ascending and descending fellowship." A difficult voluntary system
of birth control known as "male continence" was used exclusively
until the final decade of the community, when a "stirpiculture" or
eugenics experiment was introduced for some members.

At Oneida, sex roles were perhaps more radically revised than
in any comparable American group. There was far less role stereotyp-
ing, men and women worked alongside each other, and women
served in positions of authority over men in certain jobs. The system
of complex marriage, which was associated with these practices, existed at Oneida from 1848 until 1879, when it was given up because
of a combination of internal dissatisfaction and external pressure. In
1881 the group also officially gave up its communistic system of economic organization, reorganized as a joint-stock corporation, and
went on to become one of the most successful small businesses in
the United States, best known for its silverware, which is marketed
today throughout the country. Today descendants of the community
are indistinguishable from ordinary Americans; if anything, they are
more conservative in their religious and political orientation.[15]

A host of complex questions are suggested by this extraordinary
community that one member characterized as "a home the like of
which has not been seen since the world began."[16] Three issues especially come to mind. The first has to do with how a complex organization such as this could have been set up and made to work for
more than thirty years. Surely such success was far from accidental; it
was based on careful planning and deep commitment. How were
Oneida's unorthodox institutional arrangements related to the func-

tioning of the community? In particular, what was the role of the system of "mutual criticism" or group criticism, of "male continence" or *coitus reservatus,* and of "complex marriage"? What psychological impact did such practices have on male and female members of the community?[17]

A second question suggested by Oneida is the extent to which sex-role stereotypes and power relations between men and women were changed within the community. For many years, it was fashionable to describe Oneida as part of the vanguard of sexual liberation and women's rights, a prototype for the future with much to say to us today. More recently, many feminists have gone back to the Oneida records and concluded that John Humphrey Noyes was really a male chauvinist and his community a disappointment to those seeking true equality. How can these two seemingly incompatible approaches to Oneida and the role of women be reconciled? Why was Noyes supportive of many women's concerns yet also critical of much of the women's movement of his day? How did Noyes attempt to reorganize relations between men and women, and how successful was he in accomplishing his goals?[18]

A final issue raised by Oneida relates to the reasons for the initial success in setting up a new system of communal living but the inability of the group to sustain that experiment in bringing about a radical transformation of society. In particular, why was the community able to weather early crises such as the one in 1852 but unable to survive a strikingly similar crisis twenty-seven years later in 1879? Did the discontinuance of complex marriage in 1879 and of communal living in 1881 signify the failure of the underlying goals of the experiment or was there another sense in which the more than thirty years of communal living at Oneida can be viewed as a success by all who admire the struggle to achieve a difficult ideal?[19]

III

Larger and more successful than either the Shakers or the Oneida Community—at least in numbers—was the Church of Jesus Christ of Latter-day Saints, or Mormon church, as it is popularly known. The roots of Mormonism go back to Joseph Smith, a precocious, sensitive, and ambitious young farm boy living near Palmyra, New York. Deeply disturbed by the cacophony of ideas and causes that surrounded him, young Joseph began having a series of visions in the early 1820s. He concluded that all existing religions were wrong and that God had specially chosen him to set up a new religious and social synthesis.

Smith began by engaging in what he described as a "translation" "by the gift and power of God" of inscriptions on golden plates he claimed to have found buried in a large hill near his home. Published as the Book of Mormon in 1830, the same year that Smith officially founded the Mormon church, both the book and the Mormon movement were a focus of curiosity and controversy from the very beginning. Fierce persecution developed because many individuals viewed Mormon religious claims as an outrageous hoax and their rapidly growing, close-knit church as a threat to American democratic values. During their first twenty years, the Mormons were forced to move repeatedly—from New York, to Ohio, to Missouri, to Illinois, and eventually to Utah.[20]

An important factor that eventually contributed to the hostility faced by the Mormons was Joseph Smith's decision in the early 1840s to introduce the idea and practice of polygamy secretly among his closest followers living at the Mormon headquarters in Nauvoo, Illinois. In 1843 a revelation was privately promulgated there calling for a restoration among the Mormons of polygamous practices similar to those of the biblical patriarchs Abraham, Isaac, and Jacob. These new standards were set within the larger context of a conception of marriage, growth, and development lasting throughout all eternity. Not surprisingly, many of Joseph's closest followers who were strong supporters of monogamy were outraged by this move. In 1844 Joseph Smith and his brother Hyrum were murdered in a jail in Carthage, Illinois, while awaiting trial on charges arising in part from the dissatisfaction of some of their followers with the new polygamous beliefs and practices.[21]

This tragic denouement might have been expected to cripple the young church and lead it to abandon polygamy. Instead, the reverse occurred. Under Brigham Young's leadership, and following a heroic trek to the Great Basin region, polygamy became fully established among the Mormons. From 1852, when the Mormons in Utah first announced to the world their commitment to plural marriage, until 1890, when intense federal pressure combined with internal Mormon dissatisfaction to force official discontinuance of the practice in the United States, polygamy was accepted as the highest standard of marriage by more than one hundred thousand Mormons in Utah and adjacent areas of the American West. Today the strong family ideal that undergirded polygamy has been transferred by Mormons to an equally strong commitment to the nuclear family as the core of Mormon religious and social life. As memories of polygamy have receded, Mormonism has developed an increasingly positive public image, becoming one of the fastest growing religious movements in the United States and securing more than 7 million members worldwide by 1990.[22]

The development of polygamy and Mormon family patterns raises many complex questions. Three deserve special attention. The first has to do with why and how polygamy was initially conceived, introduced, and successfully established. What were Joseph Smith's motives for attempting to introduce practices so radically divergent from American norms? How did his followers respond to his efforts? In particular, what were the responses of women who accepted plural marriage, women who rejected plural marriage, and Joseph Smith's dynamic and articulate first wife, Emma? And how did the form of plural marriage advocated by Smith differ from polygamy in Mormon splinter groups formed after Smith's death such as James J. Strang's community on Beaver Island in Lake Michigan in the early 1850s?[23]

A second issue suggested by the Mormon experience is how polygamy actually worked in practice. In particular, how did polygamy affect the lives of women in early Utah? During the last half of the nineteenth century, Mormon women in Utah were generally viewed by the outside world as a benighted and oppressed class, victims of a system of institutionalized lust. In fact, the situation was much more complex. Certainly polygamy posed difficult emotional and practical challenges to many women who had been socialized to monogamous norms. Yet somewhat paradoxically, polygamy also was associated in many respects with greater independence and power for women. Utah Mormon women were the first to vote in the United States, had early opportunities at coeducation, were active in teaching and the professions, and published a distinguished women's newspaper.

What accounts for the apparent inconsistencies in women's status in Utah? Why did polygamy in early Utah not only serve as a repressive system but also, at times, allow Mormon women greater freedom and a larger range of options than were available to many of their Victorian contemporaries?[24]

A final set of questions the Mormon experience raises has to do with the current status of Mormon women. After the Mormon church officially stopped sanctioning any further plural marriages in 1890, it gradually developed a more positive public image focused on the close-knit, family-centered values of the group. More recently, however, some Mormon and former Mormon women such as Marilyn Warenski and Sonia Johnson have argued that the extreme family orientation and highly sentimentalized approach to the role of women in Mormonism are stifling women's full development. What accounts for the change in the ideal of Mormon women from the late nineteenth-century emphasis on women's active participation in almost all aspects of society (except the formal governance of the church) to the present more narrow stress on domesticity as almost the sole end of women's lives? How can Mormon women today achieve their full development as persons within a church that appears to be restricting their role and participation?[25]

The experiences of the Shakers, the Oneida Community, and the Mormons raise important issues, both for their time and for our own. The chapters that follow will address some of the most important of these issues. Although the solutions these groups put forward to problems of relations between men and women were idiosyncratic and impermanent in many respects, these serious and sustained efforts to introduce new patterns of religious and social life can help us better understand the process of radical social change, community formation, and sex-role reorganization.

THE SHAKERS

2

CELIBACY and FEMINISM

The Shakers and Equality for Women

*F*EW COMMUNAL EXPERIMENTS in American history have been more complex, long-lived, and culturally influential than that of the Shakers. The Shakers, a revivalistic religious group whose official name was the United Society of Believers in Christ's Second Appearing, first emigrated from England to America in 1774 and began to attract a significant following in New York State and New England following the American Revolution. They aroused much interest and hostility because of their lively religious services, during which they sang, shouted, danced, and literally shook with emotion, as well as because of their requirement of celibacy and their veneration of Ann Lee, their chief early leader.[1]

By the 1830s, when the Shakers reached their peak membership of as many as four thousand individuals living in approximately sixty semimonastic communities at eighteen different sites scattered from Maine to Indiana,[2] they had become increasingly recognized for their successes in communal living, serving as an inspiration to a wide variety of social theorists, including Robert Owen, John Humphrey Noyes, and Friedrich Engels.[3] In the twentieth century, the Shakers, who continued to survive in ever-diminishing numbers until the present, when they now number less than a dozen individuals, became best known for the simplicity of their furniture and other products and for hymns such as "Simple Gifts." In the words of the cultural historian Constance Rourke, "No other community created and sustained its own modes in music, the crafts, and even in architecture as did the Shakers."[4]

17

Perhaps no aspect of Shaker life has attracted more interest than the emphasis on equality for women. A host of recent feminist writers, including Rosemary Radford Ruether, Mary Farrell Bednarowski, Barbara Brown Zikmund, Marjorie Proctor-Smith, Jean Humez, Jeanette and Robert Lauer, D'Ann Campbell, Henri Desroche, Jane Crossthwaite, and Sally L. Kitch, have looked to the Shakers as a precursor and possible prototype for women seeking greater equality with men.[5] Especially valuable is Proctor-Smith's *Women in Shaker Community and Worship*, which constitutes a major step forward from earlier studies.

The emphasis on equality put forward by these writers has much to recommend it at first sight. Ann Lee, the chief founder of the Shakers, was a woman, and women have served as the supreme head of the society at several later stages of Shaker history down to the present. Even God, the Shakers believed, was dual in nature, embodying a complementary and equal expression of male and female elements. Celibacy, the most distinctive feature of Shaker life, was a practice that removed the burden of childbearing and freed women for full participation in the religious system.

Although no feminist movement as such existed when the Shakers first came to America, the group was sensitive to many of the issues that would later attract feminists, particularly the sexual exploitation of women by men. Shaker publications, from the earliest hymn books to the later histories such as the one written by Anna White and Leila S. Taylor, stressed concern for sexual equality as a key part of the effort to attract new members, and numerous capable women did choose to make religious careers with the Shakers. As Rosemary Radford Ruether notes, "The only female-led religion that developed a consistent system of equal empowerment of women was the Shakers."[6]

Yet there are problems with the argument that the Shakers were egalitarian in dealing with relations between men and women. Only in the area of religious leadership did the Shakers make equality between men and women a part of their formal structure, and even that equality existed in the context of an extremely hierarchical, oligarchic structure that opponents described variously as "papist" and "an absolute despotism." Every aspect of Shaker life was regulated, including the time and way one rose in the morning, ate meals, or went to bed. Close personal relationships between any individuals, male or female, were systematically and effectively broken up in order to raise the loyalty of all individuals to the larger group, which was seen as standing in the place of God. In short, the degree of equality that existed between men and women in religious leadership occurred in the context of a tightly controlled, celibate structure that sharply restricted individual freedom. If there was equality between the sexes, it existed within a fundamentally unfree and restrictive system.[7]

Perhaps even more significant, in the area of economic relations between men and women, which is of such importance to present-day feminists, the Shakers were almost wholly traditional, rigidly separating men's and women's spheres of work. Shaker women did typical women's work—cooking, sewing, cleaning, and washing—while Shaker men did traditional male tasks in the fields, shops, and similar locations. Although both sexes changed their primary work tasks periodically, Shaker men were able to do far more varied and interesting work as a whole. Visitors to Shaker communities often commented that women, whose work was primarily indoors, tended to look less healthy and happy than male Shakers.[8] Clearly, although the Shakers increased the possibilities for women in some areas of life, they were far from being feminists in the full, modern senses of the term.

How is one to resolve the apparent dichotomy between a group that appears highly egalitarian in certain respects and highly authoritarian in others? Some writers have ignored the unfree, inegalitarian aspects of Shaker life, preferring instead to highlight the ways in which the Shakers may serve as a model for those seeking equality today. Others, recognizing the egalitarian-authoritarian dichotomy, have suggested that the Shakers were going in the right direction, but just were not as enlightened as we are. Still another approach, the one I shall use here, is to seek to understand what the Shakers themselves were trying to accomplish and how their restructuring of relations between men and women fitted into their overall worldview. Was that worldview consistent, and if not, how did the group successfully hold its apparent inconsistencies in creative tension?

The thesis of this chapter is that only by developing an understanding of and appreciation for the distinctive Shaker religious commitment to celibacy can Shaker egalitarianism in relations between men and women ultimately be understood. Celibacy, both in theory and in practice, had profound ramifications for every aspect of Shaker life, including equality between the sexes. This chapter will explore the roots of the twin Shaker testimonies for celibacy and for equality between the sexes, the interaction between those testimonies before the Civil War, and the implications that those twin commitments raise both for the Shakers and for present-day feminists seeking to transcend elements in relations between the sexes that they find oppressive.[9]

I

Fundamental to understanding the Shaker restructuring of relations between men and women is the realization that all aspects of Shaker social life grew out of the group's underlying religious commitment. The Shakers did not set out to be social reformers. Rather, their primary goal was the millenarian one of setting up religious communities that would help achieve the kingdom of heaven on earth. Only within that millenarian religious ethos did they attempt to transform social relations as well. Central to the Shaker religious message, differentiating the group from a host of similar revivalistic movements throughout history, was their belief that celibacy was essential for salvation. Only by giving up all "carnal" propensities—including sexual intercourse and close family attachments—and devoting oneself wholly to the worship of God within a supportive communal setting could salvation ultimately be achieved.[10]

Other aspects of Shaker theology and practice were explicitly considered subject to change and progressive development. Only the group's celibate commitment within an authoritative religious communal setting remained essentially nonnegotiable through more than two hundred years of Shaker development. Even the group's attitudes toward its founder Ann Lee might vary substantially, but not the Shakers' celibate commitment itself. One colorful anecdote highlights this point. When a rebellious Shaker young man informed the astute Shaker elder Frederick Evans that he had had a trance communication from the deceased Ann Lee that the group should give up celibacy and move into the higher married state, Evans simply replied that the Shakers did not believe in Ann Lee. Rather, they followed her principles. If she had fallen from grace even in the afterlife, they would continue to follow the truth of the basic principles she had taught when she was alive.[11]

The urge to adopt celibate practice as a means of self-purification and devotion to the worship of God has deep roots in the Christian tradition, but this impulse has not always been associated with a parallel concern for equality for women. Indeed, perhaps the most common attitudes leading to male celibacy have been misogynistic. St. Paul, whose comments have most frequently been quoted justifying the superiority of celibacy, told women to keep silent in the churches and wives to be subject to their husbands. Early Christian hermits who went off to live by themselves in the desert often viewed women as temptresses and sought to escape them so that they could recover the purity of Adam before Eve tempted him to eat the forbidden fruit.[12]

Although medieval monasticism eventually allowed for women's orders and did give some women significant opportunities for self-expression and independent development that were not present for most women in the society at large, monasticism as a whole remained male dominated and deeply suspicious of sexuality, especially female sexuality. Similar trends continued and accelerated as Roman Catholicism increasingly moved to enforce celibacy of even the secular clergy. The veneration for an "immaculate" (read celibate) Mary, which eventually became part of Catholic dogma, sometimes only accentuated further the gulf between her and ordinary, "carnal" women. The recent refusal of the Roman Catholic church to approve women's ordination further highlights the patriarchal and sexually inegalitarian attitudes of the dominant wing of the church's celibate leadership today.[13]

When Protestant groups broke with the Church of Rome in the sixteenth century, those like the Anabaptists and Pietists that continued to express recurrent impulses toward asceticism and celibacy did not necessarily do so because of any commitment to greater equality for women. Indeed, most of the Germanic groups with Anabaptist or Pietistic roots that emigrated to the United States, including those that founded the Rappite, Zoarite, and Amana settlements, remained strongly patriarchal, even when they introduced or advocated celibacy. Egalitarian impulses did tend to be associated with some of the more extreme heretical sects of the Middle Ages and with some revivalistic Protestant movements, but even in those movements tendencies toward inequality persisted.[14]

What, then, made the difference for the Shakers? To answer this question, we must go back to the beginnings of Shaker development in England during the mid-1700s. The Shaker movement in England emerged about 1747 out of a fluid revivalistic milieu that was probably most influenced by the Quakers, French Camisard refugees, and early Wesleyan Methodism. As far as can be reconstructed from historical records published more than half a century later, the small initial group near Manchester emphasized the immanence of the millennium, the necessity of repentance, and the value of the free workings of the spirit. Under Jane and James Wardley, the primary early leaders, women played a substantial role, and some members remained celibate because of personal inclination, but neither practice was a part of the group's fundamental beliefs.[15]

It was Ann Lee, an illiterate but highly dynamic and intelligent Manchester working woman who joined the Wardleys' little society in 1758, who eventually helped transform the group. Lee's personal struggles, both religious and sexual, gradually added distinctive elements to Shaker faith, separating Shaker believers from those in many similar revivalistic groups. During approximately nine years following her marriage to Abraham Standerin in 1762, Ann Lee gradually developed her testimony against the evils of humanity's fallen, "carnal" nature. In the process of suffering four painful deliveries and the loss of all her children in infancy or early childhood, Lee became increasingly terrified of all sexual intercourse, avoiding her bed as if it were "made of embers" and spending sleepless nights calling out to God for redemption. Although naturally robust, she wasted away, becoming weak and emaciated.

The climax of this early traumatic period came in the summer of 1770, when the thirty-four-year-old Ann Lee was incarcerated in a jail in Manchester after taking part in noisy religious services that neighbors complained had disturbed the peace. During that difficult time in jail, Ann Lee had a powerful "open vision" of Adam and Eve in carnal intercourse. At last she knew with absolute inner certainty that this act was, indeed, the very transgression that had resulted in the Fall of Man in the Garden of Eden and the entry of sin into the world. Following this traumatic discovery, Lee had another compelling vision in which the Lord Jesus Christ appeared to her in all his glory. He comforted her and confirmed her sense of mission to spread her new knowledge throughout the world. After her release from jail, Ann Lee increasingly became the key leader in the small Shaker group, and its testimony against carnal sin became more pointed.[16]

This message had little appeal in England, where the Shakers never attracted more than about thirty members and were generally ignored. In 1774, therefore, Ann Lee and eight of her followers emigrated to America, where they hoped their message might eventually thrive. After landing in New York City in August 1774, the Shakers, who were extremely poor, separated temporarily to find individual employment. Ann Lee's husband, who had followed his wife to America, finally forced the issue of whether she would live with him in a normal marital relationship. Her adamant refusal, which led to their permanent break, must have been a heartrending experience for both of them. As Ann Lee said, "The man to whom I was married was very kind, according to his nature; he would have been willing to pass through a flaming fire for my sake, if I would but live in the flesh with him, which I refused to do."[17] Freed from her husband at last, Ann Lee joined her followers on some land they had leased at Niskeyuna (now Watervliet) near Albany, New York. There for some six years, often discouraged, they eked out a bare living and continued to hope for the spread of their religious message.

The first major Shaker membership breakthrough came in 1780. As one of the small religious excitements in the aftermath of the Revolutionary War, a revival had broken out in 1779 in New Lebanon, not far from the Shaker settlement at Niskeyuna. The leader of the revival was Joseph Meacham, a "new light" Baptist preacher from Enfield, Connecticut, whose father had been converted by Jonathan Edwards, a key figure in the earlier Great Awakening. Feeling discouraged and looking for further light as the 1779 revival waned, Meacham and some of his followers approached this strange group of foreign religionists that was led by a woman, required celibacy, engaged in ecstatic religious services, and professed to be living "sinlessly" in daily obedience to the will of God. Greatly impressed by what he saw, Meacham converted to the

Shakers. He brought with him many followers, who became the initial American nucleus of the Shaker church. Between 1781 and 1783, the Shakers further engaged in a series of highly successful missionary trips throughout southern New England, attracting several thousand new members, many of them Freewill Baptists and many of them teenagers. The proselytizing effort also generated intense hostility, including mobbings and beatings that may have contributed to the premature deaths of Ann Lee and her brother William in 1784.[18]

Before Ann Lee's death, and indeed for some time thereafter, the Shaker movement remained extremely fluid, both organizationally and doctrinally. Ann Lee may well have acted during her life essentially as "the first among equals," sharing much of her power and responsibility with other English leaders, notably her brother William Lee and her younger associate James Whittaker, who succeeded her as head of the group between her death and his own in 1787. Similarly, before Lee's death the scattered groups of Shaker believers throughout New England and New York State remained loosely organized, without any clearly established communal structure like that which later developed.[19]

Shaker beliefs during this period also remained fluid. At least three key emphases stand out, however. The first was the demand for repentance and for confession of all sins, especially those connected with "carnality." The roots of this twin demand for repentance and confession of sins went back to England under Jane Wardley and the earliest Shakers, but under Ann Lee in America the emphasis on confession of sins was further elaborated, increasingly focusing on sexual sins and emphasizing the necessity for believers to embrace celibacy in order to achieve full repentance. Required confession of sins by all new members was a means of acquainting Shaker leaders with the character and abilities of incoming individuals. Such confession also could have a therapeutic effect, allowing individuals who felt deeply the inadequacies of their earlier experience to rebuild their lives around a new center. As a continuing requirement, confession of all sins to designated elders of the same sex provided an important way to allow the leadership to guide and shape the character of individuals and the whole society. And should individuals be tempted to apostatize and "tell all," they would be likely to have second thoughts, knowing that their personal sins of omission and commission might be fully aired in response.[20]

A second key emphasis in early Shakerism was revivalism, which encompassed an extraordinary variety of activities ranging from shaking and trembling to shouting, leaping, singing, dancing, speaking in tongues, whirling, stamping, rolling on the floor or ground, crying out against sin, and a wide range of even more extreme ecstatic, trance, and possession phenomena that few would believe unless they had seen them with their own eyes. Many of these activities seemed to be beyond any conscious human agency, and thus were seen as manifestations of the supernatural. Disbelievers often attributed the manifestations to the Devil; believers, on the other hand, saw the manifestations as a sign of God's continuing workings in human history and the existence of an authority going beyond the purely man-made.

Shakers argued that their revivalistic activities demonstrated that the old order was being shaken, both literally and metaphorically. Human authorities, whether religious or secular, no longer seemed to have any validity, so a return was made to primary and sometimes undifferentiated emotion within a supportive group. The expression of this emotion was seen as lending supernatural sanction to the new order. As a primary Shaker doctrinal source stated, believers "knew perfectly what those things meant, and felt, therein, the greatest possible order and harmony, it being the work of God for the time then present; and which bore the strongest evidence that the world was actually coming to an end, (at least to those who were the subjects of it,) and the day of judgment commenced."[21]

A third and most distinctive early Shaker emphasis was the deep and unquenchable love believers expressed for Ann Lee. Even her critics agreed that she was a capable, articulate, and dynamic woman, warm and loving to her followers, whom she called her "children." Ann's followers loved her so deeply that they would eventually come to believe that in her the spirit of God had been incarnated in female form, just as they believed that in Jesus the spirit of God had been incarnated in male form. Whether Ann Lee ever claimed such quasi-divinity is open to question. On the one hand, her frequent ecstatic utterances, like those of many other early religious leaders, are open to such interpretation, particularly when she talked of walking with Jesus as her Lord and Lover, or described herself as his Bride.[22]

On the other hand, Ann Lee was also a straightforward, down-to-earth woman who admonished her followers to put their "hands to work and their hearts to God." When an overawed follower came to her, she reportedly said, "Don't kneel to me, but kneel to God; for I am but your fellow servant."[23] Expressing sentiments that many religious leaders must feel, she once confessed that she was afraid to talk with young believers because they assumed that whatever she said came directly from On High. Ann said in frustration that she never claimed to be omniscient in temporal matters. All she knew with certainty was that humanity's recovery to God could be achieved only by giving up all "carnal" desires and practices.[24]

The exact nature and character of the beliefs early members held about Ann Lee also are unclear. She was variously described, either at the time or following her death, as the Elect Lady, the Woman of the Apocalypse with the moon under her feet and a crown of stars on her head, the Bride of Christ, the king's daughter, dressed in wrought gold and "all glorious within," and, above all, as Mother Ann or simply Mother, a title she had inherited from her predecessor Jane Wardley, who had also been addressed as Mother.[25] As Clarke Garrett has suggested, these early millenarian understandings of Ann Lee appear to reflect "the traditional role of the woman who before the Millennium will appear 'clothed with the sun' and will 'bruise the serpent's head' thereby completing the work of redemption undoing Eve's sin."[26] This set of ideas was pervasive in the period, appearing in England, France, and Germany. In England followers of the controversial female prophet Joanna Southcott would most dramatically put forward such ideas at a slightly later date than the Shakers did.[27]

What was the nature of the earliest Shaker expectations of the Second Coming of Christ? Would it occur through the agency of a female prophet or through the collective faith of Christ's church? Both positions appear to have been held, at least in embryonic form, during the fluid early period. The very first apostate pamphlet, written by the theologically sophisticated Valentine Rathbun in December 1780, only one year after the Shakers formally opened their testimony in America, declared: "Some of them say, that the woman called the mother [Ann Lee], has the fullness of the God head dwelling in her, and that she is the queen of heaven, Christ's wife: and that all God's elect must be born through her; yea, that Christ through her is born a second time."[28] Although this statement may best be understood, as Garrett suggests, in the context of seventeenth-century millenarianism,[29] it also may serve as a bridge to the later Shaker quasi-deification of Ann Lee that was first publicly enunciated during the early nineteenth century.

By contrast, in 1782 another apostate, Amos Taylor, argued that Shakers believed that the Second Coming would be a collective one through the church.[30] The astute non-Shaker William Plumer made a similar report after long conversations with the Shaker Ebenezer Cooley in 1783, although Cooley was noted for telling visitors what they wanted to hear.[31] The first published Shaker pamphlet, written by Joseph Meacham in 1790, does not mention Ann Lee and traces the second appearance of Christ to 1747, the date the Wardleys' society was founded, when an outpouring of revivalistic gifts served to provide a sign of God's presence and power among them.

As Priscilla Brewer has noted, it is likely that Meacham's omission of Ann Lee was made for public consumption because, in theological manuscripts written for Shaker readers, Meacham several times discoursed at length on the appropriateness of the appearance of Christ in a female form.[32] Not until approximately the turn of the nineteenth century, when Thomas Brown joined the Shakers, however, is there a clear indication of a widespread Shaker belief that Ann Lee had served as a second embodiment of God's spirit in the same way that Jesus had at first.[33] And not until publication of the first Shaker doctrinal treatise, Benjamin Seth Youngs's *Testimony of Christ's Second Appearing*, in 1808, was the idea of Ann Lee as a female savior enunciated to the world at large.[34]

What can we conclude about the role of women in the Shaker movement while Ann Lee was alive? One obvious point is that Shaker celibacy, millennialism, and revivalism tended to break down conventional patterns of interaction between men and women. The chief leader of the early group was a woman, and other women played leading roles during the fluid early period. Yet it is revealing that even when Ann Lee was at the peak of her charismatic powers, she continued to show deference to more conventional notions of male leadership. Joseph Meacham's last question in 1780 before join-ing the Shakers was how a woman could govern or stand at the head of the church when St. Paul had so expressly forbidden it. Ann Lee's reply to Meacham (significantly, it was conveyed through a male in-termediary) was that "in the natural state the man is first in the government of the family; but when the man is absent the govern-ment belongs to the woman."[35]

So long as the Shakers saw themselves living in an extraordi-nary state associated with the millennium, old rules and restrictions might be ignored. What would happen, however, once Ann Lee had died and the earlier revivalistic euphoria had subsided? Would all things still remain possible, or would Shaker leadership and patterns of interaction gradually revert to those of the world? These were the questions that Ann Lee's American successors would answer in new and creative ways.

II

Although Ann Lee and the English Shakers provided the initial im-petus for the new religious movement, the actual organization of the scattered groups of Shaker believers into functioning celibate com-munities was conducted primarily under the new American leaders, particularly Joseph Meacham and Lucy Wright. James Whittaker ini-tiated the move toward greater organization after Ann Lee's death in 1784, but not until Joseph Meacham acceded to the leadership of the Shakers in 1787 did the shift from a primarily charismatic to a more routinized organization begin in earnest.

The precise factors that influenced the organizational develop-ment of the new Shaker communities cannot be clearly identified. Probably many features of the new system reflect a pragmatic re-sponse to certain characteristic problems any celibate religious group would have to face. Nevertheless, the striking similarities between Shaker structures and some aspects of Roman Catholic dual monastic organization raise the question of whether monastic or other similar communal traditions might have been used as models. Although ex-tant literature does not permit any reliable answer to this question, Meacham, Wright, and other early American leaders of the Shakers were well educated for their time and may well have borrowed from earlier traditions. Certainly, the Christian communism described in Acts 2:44–45, which speaks of the early Christians holding "all things common," would always be a continuing ideal for the Shakers as they sought to restore and revitalize the faith of early Christianity in their own day.[36]

Joseph Meacham's first major action on acceding to the leadership of the scattered bands of Believers in Christ's Second Appearing was to begin—carefully but firmly and decisively—to establish governmental forms that would make women equal to men at all levels of the society.[37] Although Mother Ann had attempted to give women a prominent role in her society, after her death there was a tendency to drift back toward male dominance in the leadership. Meacham sought to counter this tendency. He realized that "there must be a visible parental order to lead the visible spiritual family of Christ," in short, that women must be encouraged to participate fully in the life of the church-community. Marjorie Proctor-Smith observes: "Although it is conceivable that Meacham's decision to appoint eldresses and deaconesses was motivated by a commitment to the principle of equality between the sexes, it is certain that pragmatic requirements of a mixed celibate community demanded a distinct set of leaders for Shaker women."[38]

Toward this end, Meacham appointed Lucy Wright as his co-equal to help establish a women's order of the Shakers that would allow them strict equality with men in their respective spheres and activities. This was a revolutionary departure, "contrary to all earlier rules and views of ecclesiastical Government in the so called Christian world," and many Shakers opposed the move. Shakers may have followed and venerated the charismatic leadership of Mother Ann Lee, but they looked upon the institutionalization of new authority relations between the sexes as another matter. In fact, Meacham's efforts to increase female participation were so controversial that he found it necessary to present by "revelation" his new ecclesiastical organization and Lucy Wright's appointment. With Meacham's encouragement, Childs Hamlin, a moving singer and an impressively spiritual man, declared that "the Order of Mother in Church relation was revealed to him, & that Lucy Wright was the female" prepared by God to assume that role.

Even with this apparent divine sanction, establishment of the new dual order required nearly ten years of strenuous efforts in re-educating believers. Getting the women to assume a more active role was especially difficult. Mother Lucy worked tirelessly to prepare the sisters to "come forward in their proper sphere, & take their share of the burdens and toils in all needful labors & sufferings, unitedly with their Brethren, as well as to be leaders according to their order in every Department of the Church." Wright served as a model of the capable, committed woman the Shakers were laboring to produce. But opposition still remained strong. "In no preceding Dispensation had the Order of spiritual Mother been gained; hence the female portion of humanity never had its due share in the organization & Government of Ecclesiastical Institutions." Quite probably, the so-called "great apostasy" that began in the Shaker orders shortly before Joseph Meacham's death in 1796 was related in part to opposition to the idea of a woman, Lucy Wright, leading the church.

Despite the many problems, the basic order of the Shaker church gradually became fully established during this period.[39] This overall structure would remain largely unchanged throughout the history of the group. Supreme authority was vested in the head ministry at New Lebanon, New York, usually four in number, two of each sex. The head figure of this ministry had the authority, tempered only by the sentiments of the membership, to appoint or replace the other three members, and with them, all the leadership of the various Shaker communities. This was an hierarchical and oligarchical system that critics frequently attacked as "papist," but it worked with great effectiveness throughout most of Shaker history. In their more than two-hundred-year existence in America, the Shakers have never experienced a successful schism.

Each Shaker settlement was divided into smaller communal groups called "families," usually with between thirty and one hundred members. These families included both men and women who lived under the same roof but were strictly separated in their activities. Each family was relatively self-sufficient, both spiritually and economically. Just as each larger Shaker settlement site had its own ministry appointed from New Lebanon, so each family ideally had two elders and eldresses to take care of spiritual affairs and two deacons and deaconesses to run the temporal business. This pattern would prevail throughout all levels of the society after the initial period of organization. All authority was hierarchical, but at each level men and women shared equal responsibility in the work of regeneration.

Shaker celibacy made possible this remarkable system that gave women a degree of equality in leadership that even the most militant socialist advocates of women's rights were unable or unwilling to achieve in practice.[40] Celibacy, when combined with communal child-rearing practices for the children of individuals joining the Shakers and for orphans adopted by the society, freed Shaker women for active leadership at all levels. Shakers justified their arrangements theologically by observing that St. Paul's admonitions to wives to be subject to their husbands, keep silence in the church, and so forth did not apply to women who had given up earthly marriage and were living a life of "virgin purity." In effect, such women were "married to Christ." Their loyalty was directly to God, or, in practice, to the larger community families in which the divine pattern was being realized on earth. Freed from the entanglements of the world, believers could devote themselves fully to God, for, as St. Paul had also said, there is "neither male nor female in the Lord."

In addition to departing radically from traditional ecclesiastical government, the Shakers under Meacham and Wright began to set up a cooperative, communistic form of economic organization to buttress their religious ideals. A "joint united interest" in all things had been an implicit goal under Mother Ann and the English leaders, but not until Joseph Meacham took charge was the new system developed and set up. The details of this temporal side of Shaker life have been discussed at length elsewhere and will only be summarized here, particularly as they relate to Shaker sexual and marital reorganization.

Just as Shaker celibacy had contributed to changes in ecclesiastical relations between men and women in the group, so too it contributed to the possibility of creating a form of Christian communalism in which the good of the individual was subordinated to that of the collectivity. Believers did not look upon productive labor as part of the curse pronounced upon Adam. Rather, they sought to integrate economic and religious life into a harmonious whole, thereby overcoming the exploitative individualism that became increasingly pronounced during the years after the American Revolution. By removing all but the most basic private property and by removing the competing demands inherent in separate nuclear family arrangements, the Shakers were able to devote their entire lives to establishing their ideal of the kingdom of heaven on earth.

Far from stifling economic initiative, the joint united interest set up by the Shakers appears to have been associated with a high level of economic innovation and commitment. The basic economic unit was the single Shaker family of up to a hundred or more individuals working cooperatively. Sometimes several families would unite in an industry or business venture or maintain a common store or a clearinghouse for farm or manufactured items. Throughout New York and New England, Shaker businessmen developed an extensive range of contacts because of the consistently high quality of the many Shaker products. And individual Shakers developed an enormous range of ingenious inventions and devices that were put to good use in their communities.

Edward Deming Andrews, the pioneering scholar of Shaker material culture, notes that Shaker farm enterprises were organized to operate with an almost military precision, with a clear division of labor in which each member had his or her appointed task at an appointed time. "In these early group activities of the Shakers one recognizes a formative chapter in large scale or 'mass production' enterprise, an anticipation of the corporate businesses which rose later in the machine age in this country."[41] Thus the Shakers' "amazingly productive economic system" was by no means out of touch with larger American economic developments. Though its response to nascent industrialism was unusual, the Shaker church contributed in many ways to the successful adjustment of believers to modern economic realities, while mitigating much of the harshness of the competitive and individualistic economic order that was then developing.

Despite their economic progressiveness and their practice of allowing women equal leadership roles in their society, the Shakers left almost totally unchanged the basic economic division of labor between the sexes that prevailed in America at that time. Shaker women worked in kitchen and dairy industries, they engaged in weaving and manufacture of cloth, they washed, cleaned, and cooked for the communities, and they did a variety of other largely indoor tasks typically performed by women of their period. Shaker men were typically engaged in farm labor in heavy agriculture, as well as in blacksmithing, tanning, and the like. The basic American household division of labor in the nuclear family thus remained in force in the larger Shaker families. Only women's disabilities that were connected with their sexual function in childbearing and child rearing were eliminated.

Why did the Shakers maintain this economic division between the sexes while breaking down many other important inequalities in organizational and religious life? The key factor, once again, was celibacy. As Proctor-Smith has suggested, the Shakers "not only accepted the traditional division of labor within the family, they were in a sense *compelled* to practice it in order to maintain the strict segregation required by their system."[42] Shaker men and women who joined the society as adults had been trained in the traditional occupational skills deemed appropriate for their sexes. In the Shaker communities, they worked under direct supervision only of members of the same sex and thus had little opportunity to cross sex boundaries and learn occupational skills typical of the opposite sex. Any cross-sex contacts of this sort were deemed "contrary to order" and were seen as potentially threatening to the Shaker commitment to celibacy. In answer to Charles Nordhoff's question whether a Shaker woman could, if she desired, become a blacksmith, the Shaker elder Frederick Evans replied, "No, because this would bring men and women into relations which we do not think wise."[43]

The Shakers insisted that they did not view either men's or women's work as inherently "superior" but felt instead that all occupations were of equal importance in God's sight. Visitors and critics, however, suggested that Shaker women's work seemed less varied and interesting than that of the men and implied that Shaker women appeared less happy than the men.[44] In any event, though the Shakers eliminated or minimized differences between the sexes that were explicitly connected with sexual intercourse, reproduction, and child rearing, they firmly maintained that sexual distinctions remained both on earth and in heaven. Such differences could hardly be done away with, for even God was composed of a union of male and female attributes—even God was sexual, a fusion of complementary opposites.

III

By 1800 the Shakers in the northeastern communities had passed through both an initial charismatic phase and a period of institutional organization. Rather than relaxing at this point, however, they initiated a third phase in their development. A major missionary venture into the Ohio Valley was begun in an attempt to establish new Shaker communities in the area affected by the Kentucky Revival. Between 1805 and 1820, seven new Shaker community sites were established and began to thrive in Ohio, Kentucky, and Indiana, nearly doubling the membership of the group.[45]

The process of expansion and transformation during this second wave of Shaker settlement was very similar to the first. In the disillusioned aftermath of the Kentucky Revival, as the original euphoria degenerated into fragmentation and excess, Shaker missionaries from the Northeast typically worked with the most highly committed individuals or with small, receptive groups, stressing the inadequacy of individual Bible interpretation alone as the basis for religious and social truth. Instead, individuals were told that a new communal order and basis of authority were necessary for a holy life. Believers must submit themselves to the authority of the new dispensation as mediated by the Shaker elders, who were representatives of the true church of Christ. The adoption of celibacy was emphasized as the key requirement through which believers could fully overcome their sinful carnal natures and achieve salvation.

Perhaps the chief significance of the development of midwestern Shakerism during this period lies in the stimulus it provided for the establishment of Shaker printed literature. In the earliest charismatic and organizational phases of the group's development, little need was felt for printed statements of belief because fundamental principles could be passed on orally and modified as the needs of the group demanded. By the early nineteenth century, however, the effects of time and distance made written formulation of beliefs and practices desirable to supplement the still necessary personal contacts and continuing openness of the group to changing realities. Within less than two decades of the first Shaker book, Richard McNemar's *Kentucky Revival*, initially printed in 1807, came a rich outpouring of histories, doctrinal and polemical works, hymnals, and other writings.[46]

These works provide valuable insights into Shaker attitudes toward celibacy and the relations between the sexes, but perhaps the best summation and defense of Shaker sexual and marital beliefs is found in *A Summary View of the Millennial Church*, by Calvin Green and Seth Y. Wells. First published in 1823, it is the most readable of the three major Shaker doctrinal works published during this period. Throughout the nineteenth century, the *Millennial Church* served as the basis for numerous pamphlet defenses of celibacy and equality for women, some of which used almost verbatim extracts from the work.[47]

Like other Shaker writers, Green and Wells emphasized that in the original Adamic state, human sexuality and the faculty of generation arising from it were positive forces, part of the original creation of God which he had pronounced "very good." It was "as simple and innocent, in itself, as the faculty of eating and drinking." But man's transgression had corrupted the very fountainhead of life itself; the human generative function had become subordinate to the inordinate demands of lust. The Shakers interpreted the story of the Garden of Eden in a symbolic, not a literal sense. They believed that although disobedience to a command of God was the *cause* of man's fall, the specific *act* of disobedience was one of carnal intercourse engaged in out of its proper time and season.

In support of this thesis concerning the origin of human suffering, Green and Wells look at the curse pronounced upon the first woman: "I will greatly multiply thy sorrow and thy conception; in sorrow shalt thou bring forth children; and thy desire shall be to thy husband, and he shall rule over thee." Green and Wells argue that this curse placed by God upon Eve must have been in response to the nature of the transgression. That transgression, therefore, must have been a sexual one. This curse of excessive sexual demands upon the woman is seen as a great social problem in antebellum America as well:

> This same curse has been more or less felt by the fallen daughters of Eve to this day. . . . Thus the woman is not only subjected to the pains and sorrows of childbirth, but even in her conception, she becomes subject to the libidinous passions of her husband; . . . This slavish subjection is often carried to such a shocking extent, that many females have suffered an

unnatural and premature death, in consequence of the unsea-
sonable and excessive indulgence of this passion in the man.
Thousands there are, no doubt, who are able to bear sorrowful
testimony to the truth of this remark.[48]

The marriage ceremony does not alleviate this problem, for lust
corrupts even the marriage bond. Humans, unlike other animals, do
not have a specific period of the year during which they engage in
sexual intercourse. Rather, they indulge this passion at their whim,
inside or outside marriage, irrespective of the law of nature and of
their desire for progeny. As a result, "the lawless passion of lust
knows no bounds, is confined to no limits, and subject to no laws."
Green and Wells bitterly ask why, if sexual intercourse is such a good
thing, those pious divines who try to sanctify the act by a marriage
ceremony should refuse to ask their parishioners to do it in public
before their very eyes! Shame, they assert, is an inseparable part of
the act, proof that it is a work of darkness. The inability to establish
order in the process of generation is both a symbol and a cause of all
other types of social disorder. If sexual behavior could be properly
regulated, all other social problems could be brought under control
as well.

This analysis, only briefly indicated here, provides interesting
perspectives on the tensions between the sexes facing many antebellum Americans. Recent research indicates that, despite the general optimism and expansiveness of the period, serious sexual
problems may have existed before the Civil War, especially for
women. For whatever reasons, it seems indisputable that the desire
for smaller families had begun well before the Civil War. In the
absence of effective means of birth control (other than abortion),
self-control or repression was widely advocated as a means of avoiding the evils of excessive procreation.[49] The Shakers, doubting that
such a halfway approach could ever really handle the problem, went
one step further by advocating the elimination of physical connection between the sexes altogether, in effect a drastic form of birth
control.

But in their practice of celibacy, the Shakers were engaged in
considerably more than simply an early faltering attempt at birth
control. Had their program been only of this character, it could

justly be dismissed as an eccentric attempt to counteract the still prevalent emphasis on having large families. From the Shaker viewpoint, humanity's recovery to God was a positive process involving total commitment to an ideal and a way of life. They felt that the depth of religious commitment they sought was impossible unless men and women could be freed from the inevitable distractions associated with sexual relations and the nuclear family. Thus, with the possible exception of the earliest period, when their millenarian expectations were in the fullest flower, the Shakers never seriously expected that everyone would join their movement. They formally recognized the validity of normal procreative life, insofar as it was well lived, but they felt that they were living according to a higher standard.[50]

IV

The high point of Shaker spiritual and social tensions before the Civil War and the last major effort during the antebellum period to revitalize their society came during approximately a decade of "spiritual manifestations" beginning in 1837. Originating in trance and possession phenomena among young Shaker women in the northeastern communities and spreading rapidly throughout all the closely linked communities in the Northeast and the Midwest, the phenomena brought severe challenges to community order yet also attempts to revive inner Shaker life and commitment to the group's ideals. Hundreds of new hymns and literally thousands of messages of verbal exhortation and verbal gifts purporting to come from departed spirits were announced. As in earlier revivals, the spiritual manifestations of the 1830s and 1840s were attended by violent shaking, speaking in tongues, and other forms of ecstatic dance and trance phenomena that could be seen as providing direct experiential support for the new order, especially among recent converts and younger Shakers who had not known Mother Ann and the early leaders personally.

The overall details of this remarkable period are discussed in the following chapter and are not important to this analysis. What is significant here is the role these revivalistic effusions played in the lives of women in the Shaker communities. As in many other societies throughout the world analyzed by the anthropologist I. M. Lewis, Shaker trance and possession phenomena of this period occurred chiefly among women, the young, and other peripheral members of the group who felt themselves outside the dominant leadership structures of the community.[51] Females predominated among those presenting messages and female imagery also came to predominate among the messages themselves. Even within a group with as strong a feminine emphasis as the Shakers had, patriarchal influence evidently led to tensions for many women.

Although the spiritual manifestations frequently helped to revitalize Shaker spiritual commitment, the phenomena also contained highly disruptive possibilities. Some mediums began attacking prominent Shaker leaders for their alleged failings, and a few even called for the abandonment of celibacy, a cornerstone of Shaker belief and practice. Eventually some of the most disruptive mediums, especially the teenage females, left the society and the leadership reasserted its power, promulgating the Millennial Laws of 1845, the strictest and most rigid in Shaker history.[52]

The power and ambiguity of Shaker female imagery, which reached perhaps its fullest flowering during this period, is highlighted by Proctor-Smith. She notes that the Shakers

> had the rich and complex image of Mother Ann, Daughter of God and Mother of all Believers; and they had the still female Holy Ghost, "Wisdom," who shares the throne of God . . . But it must be noted that the female images employed in Shaker worship and theology are not unambiguous. While images of the Daughter of God and the Mother of the New Creation are both powerful and positive, the image of the Bride of Christ reinforces and justifies patriarchal marriage patterns of dominance and submission, and the image of the "Second Eve" is made powerful at the expense of the rest of womankind, which must bear the onus of causing the Fall. The Daughter of Zion is the one anointed to raise women from their sin and misery to be the second Eve; the Mother of All Living is mother because she is the obedient spouse of her Lord and head Jesus Christ. The inextricability of these complex and contradictory themes testifies to the ambiguity of the Shaker view of women.[53]

V

What, in conclusion, was the relationship between celibacy and Shaker women's lives, especially the emphasis on religious equality for women in the group? Do the experiences of the Shakers before the Civil War offer new perspectives for those seeking a greater degree of equality for women, or was the Shaker experience so extreme that it offers few, if any, useful insights to modern-day feminists?

For the Shakers, as for those in many similar millenarian groups, the primary goal was a total religious transformation. Only within the context of that total transformation could other secondary social goals be sought and achieved. Central to that religious transformation was salvation from sin by confessing and forsaking all "carnal" desires and entanglements. Specifically, only by totally renouncing lust and regenerative sexuality and living a life of "virgin purity" could salvation ultimately be achieved. And such a life could best be lived within a total communal framework that harkened back to the ideals of early Christianity in which "all who believed were together, and had all things common." In such a community, freed from the distractions of lust and of separate family relations, believers could devote their full loyalty to their religious community and, through that community, to God.

The distinctive Shaker commitment to celibacy ultimately proved to be the decisive factor separating them from many similar revivalistic groups. Celibacy allowed the Shakers to institutionalize a high degree of equality between men and women. In a celibate lifestyle that insisted on maintaining male and female believers in close proximity to each other, separate male and female leadership was needed. At the religious level, the Shakers believed that women who were living lives of "virgin purity" were equal with men before God and could share equally in the work of regeneration. In the subsidiary economic sphere, however, the Shakers did not see inequality but only difference in maintaining separate male and female economic roles.

Celibacy for the Shakers was a necessary but not sufficient element leading toward equality. Logically, there was no reason why celibacy should not have been associated with a separate but *unequal* structure of authority, as has existed in so many other celibate orders throughout history. Although surviving evidence is inconclusive, one assumes therefore that something more must have been present in the Shaker case. An egalitarian tendency was no doubt present during the early days, perhaps because of the key leadership role of Ann Lee and the other capable women such as Lucy Wright who were associated with her.

Yet all those early egalitarian tendencies would not have been sufficient to sustain substantial male-female egalitarianism beyond the early charismatic period unless, for whatever reasons, durable institutional arrangements had been created to sustain such an unconventional set of authority relationships between the sexes. That achievement came primarily from the work of two individuals. One was Joseph Meacham, who played a key role in beginning to set up the institutional structures that would sustain religious equality between the sexes throughout two hundred years of subsequent Shaker history. The other was his coequal Lucy Wright, who cooperated with Meacham in overseeing the creation and development of parallel men's and women's orders of the Shakers and then as head figure in the society for more than twenty years saw to it that the new order became firmly established in practice.[54]

The Shakers may have achieved a substantial degree of equality between men and women within their tightly controlled, hierarchical religious communities, but do their experiences suggest any new insights for present-day feminists seeking greater equality and opportunity for women in our modern secular world? From current feminist perspectives, the Shaker approach toward women often may appear both appealing and frustrating. Feminists today typically have emphasized individualism, fuller self-expression, and the need for women to get free from traditional expectations that they should subordinate themselves to others such as their children or husbands rather than have the opportunity to develop their lives as individuals in their own right. A key element in many modern feminist ideologies has been the notion that the underlying problem in the world is male oppression of women and that if women could only be empowered themselves, they would avoid the mistakes that male-dominated societies have made throughout the centuries.

Despite their apparent liberalism toward women, the Shakers would take issue with many of these modern feminist approaches.

Rather than stressing individualism and self-realization as the chief goal, the Shakers emphasized cooperation and the good of the community above any individual interests for either men or women. For the Shakers, as for other religious communitarians, the underlying source of evil in the world was the selfish individualism and self-assertion that distracted *both* men and women from the larger worship of God. In particular, lustful sexual intercourse and its related consequences constituted the root of evil for both men and women. Only by renouncing and rising above carnality and devoting themselves fully to the worship of God could human beings ultimately achieve salvation from sin. The Shakers thus saw true freedom coming, paradoxically, through submission to the will of God as mediated through a holy community rather than through doing whatever the selfish individual—male or female—might wish to do.

The Shakers, then, may challenge as well as support some modern feminist assumptions. They suggest that in order to achieve a substantial degree of equality between the sexes one may have to renounce many other appealing aspects of life in the larger world, especially sexual intercourse. By implication the Shakers raise the disquieting question of whether those who seek full equality for women, in whatever sense equality may be defined, can achieve such equality without giving up other aspects of normal life which most individuals deem of great value. For example, can modern women achieve full parity with men in careers in the outer world of work *and* also have a full and rewarding experience in family life and child rearing? Is maintaining such a dual career possible for anyone except the most exceptional? Or must one who wishes to achieve equality in the public sphere find ways of curtailing sexuality and of giving up conventional patterns of family life as the Shakers did?

The Shaker experience suggests how difficult it can be for even those most committed to equality between the sexes to realize that equality in practice. Despite the inevitable limitations of their experiment, the Shakers nevertheless provide valuable evidence of how much *can* be done to change, and some would say improve, relations between the sexes within a committed group. The costs of those Shaker commitments—celibacy and the renunciation of private personal ties between individuals—were high, but the rewards were also great for individuals of both sexes who sought to participate fully in a close-knit, caring, religious community. The Shakers struggled with complex human problems that have no simple answers, and they managed to set up and sustain a distinctive way of life with much appeal for more than two hundred years. Far less an achievement than this could justly be counted a success.

3

SHAKER SPIRITUALISM and
SALEM WITCHCRAFT

Social Perspectives on Trance and Possession Phenomena

O N AUGUST 16, 1837, a group of ten- to twelve-year-old girls
meeting for worship in the Gathering Order of the Watervliet
Shaker community near Albany, New York, began to exhibit extraordinary behavior. Some shook and whirled, becoming completely
oblivious to their external surroundings. A few fell to the ground,
broke out into beautiful unknown songs, and told of being led by
angels through heavenly places and of seeing Mother Ann Lee, the
founder of the society, who had died more that fifty years earlier.[1]
News of these strange and seemingly inexplicable manifestations
caused a current of intense excitement to run throughout the celibate Shaker communities. Within a year most of the closely linked
northeastern Shaker settlements and a few of the midwestern ones as
well were beginning to experience similar and sometimes bizarre and
frightening physical occurrences. In an extreme example of a group
of young Watervliet boys meeting for worship, "Some were thrown
violently on the floor and all efforts of strong men were unavailing
to raise their stiffened bodies. . . . Sometimes they were with those
in suffering and torment; they seemed suffocated, as by sulphur
fumes; their bodies were distorted and bore every mark of intense
agony, while their screeches were terrible to hear."[2]

Thus in a variety of forms of highly emotional activity began a
complex and tension-ridden decade of "spiritual manifestations,"

43

described at the time by Shakers as "Mother Ann's Work" and some-times later as the "spiritualist period," because many communi-cations were supposedly received from the spirits of departed Shaker leaders.[3] The manifestations brought severe challenges to communal order yet also attempts to revitalize Shaker spiritual life and commit-ment to their ideals. A rich outpouring of creativity in new forms of worship and ecstatic dance resulted, including hundreds of new songs. Numerous new members temporarily came into the Shaker communities and literally hundreds of messages of exhortation and verbal gifts that the Shakers considered "words of comfort, gifts of love" were received from departed spirits.[4]

Nearly 150 years earlier, in 1692, several young girls of Salem Village, Massachusetts, began to grow ill and display alarming symp-toms. Some were racked with convulsive fits so grotesque and violent that eyewitnesses agreed that the girls could not possibly be acting. Loss of hearing, speech, and sight for long periods of time, a choking sensation in the throat, loss of appetite, and, worst of all, terrifying hallucinations in which the girls felt themselves pinched and bitten by demonic persecutors began to occur. Community leaders, baffled by the strange behavior and unable to determine any organic cause for it, concluded that the activity was the work of the Devil. As the afflicted girls began accusing individuals of being witches and persecuting them, paranoia spread throughout the community, trials of alleged witches and their accomplices were held, hundreds were placed in jail, and eventually twenty people were put to death. By that time, as the net of accusations threatened to engulf the en-tire community, including prominent government and religious figures, public revulsion developed at what had occurred, and the witchcraft scare ended almost as abruptly as it had begun. Perry Miller, historian of the New England mind, has suggested that al-though the witchcraft hysteria flared briefly, it had surprisingly little long-term impact and might well have been forgotten today were it not for the fascination that historians have continued to show for the episode.[5]

The phenomena that occurred at Salem Village and at Water-vliet appear strikingly similar in many ways, yet they were perceived very differently by the affected individuals and by the communities in which they lived. One episode was seen as diabolical and threatening; the other, primarily as a sign of divine blessing. What accounts for such differences in response? Why were the Shakers able to channel such phenomena in relatively positive directions, while the Salem villagers failed to do so? This chapter will address such questions by looking first at the complex ways in which the Shaker spiritual manifestations developed. Then the Salem witchcraft episode will be contrasted with the Shaker experiences. Finally, both episodes will be used to highlight broader questions about the social significance of trance and possession phenomena throughout history, especially as they relate to gender issues.

I

The Shaker spiritual manifestations that began in 1837 have long puzzled and challenged scholars. Some have viewed the phenomena as the behavior of quaint eccentrics; others have postulated deliberate fraud; still others have suggested mental disorder.[6] A convincing historical analysis, however, must go beyond such primarily psychological approaches to place the Shaker spiritual manifestations into their larger social context, showing how the phenomena were related to the social challenges and tensions faced by the group. Similar social approaches have already been used effectively to help understand the dynamics of the Salem witchcraft episode.[7] If applied to the Shaker experiences, such perspectives also can help illuminate what has often been viewed simply as bizarre or incomprehensible behavior.

The starting point for the Shaker spiritual manifestations was a sense of crisis and decline in the society. In 1837, exactly fifty years after the formal gathering of the first Shaker community in 1787, most of the believers who had known Mother Ann and the early leaders personally had died or grown old and feeble. A serious gap existed between old and young in many communities. Discipline was becoming lax. Curious visitors would come in to stare with uncomprehending amusement at the strange Shaker worship services. The leaders felt that they were gradually losing control of their communities. There was a pervasive sense of malaise and a longing for some supernatural or unconscious intervention, as in the past, to provide revitalization. If young people were to be inducted successfully into

Shaker life, they would have to undergo a powerful direct experience of the truth of the Shaker message.[8]

Thus, when the spiritual manifestations began in 1837, they attracted enormous interest. Positive Shaker precedents for such phenomena went back to Mother Ann Lee's time, when similar ecstatic and trance activities had played an important role in helping to solidify the faith of believers. Although such phenomena also had produced some excesses and problems, their overall impact was remembered favorably.[9] When 1837 brought both an internal Shaker sense of crisis and a corresponding sense of external economic collapse associated with the Panic of 1837, the time seemed ripe for a new revival. The spiritual manifestations spread rapidly and, with encouragement and some direction from the leadership, rose to a crescendo between 1841 and 1843. Not coincidentally, this was roughly the same time that revivalistic excitements were peaking in the outside world, especially the Millerite expectations of Christ's Second Coming in 1843 or 1844. Eventually, many disillusioned Millerites seeking a more secure faith would join the Shaker communities.[10]

The Shaker manifestations themselves were numerous and varied. As described by the official New Lebanon Shaker account, external actions ranged from those that were "so irresistibly violent that it would seem life was in danger to that which is gentle and scarcely perceptible to the beholder." Most activities took this milder, nontrance form in which the emotions were quickened and faith and fellowship were strengthened. The more extreme actions, however, included violent gyrations such as turning rapidly upon the toes, bowing, bending, or reeling as though drunk. After these activities, individuals would sometimes fall to the floor and lie helpless, stiff and cold as a corpse, sometimes for days. Suddenly they might resuscitate and resume their dance, still abstracted from the world, perhaps speaking with a voice or personality not their own, singing strange and unearthly new songs, or babbling in a euphonious sort of pseudo-language, known popularly as "speaking in tongues." When unwilling to let themselves move freely in these "exercises," individuals might become temporarily blinded, physically contorted, or possessed of seemingly preternatural strength. Understandably, the Shakers concluded that such actions could not be feigned and must be caused by a supernatural agency.[11]

These varied physical activities were associated with two types of verbal communications: first, personal messages of encouragement, comfort, and evidence of spirit concern for individual members, and, second, messages of moral exhortation urging renewed commitment to key Shaker ideals and a strengthening of group solidarity. Average members most frequently received personal messages, while the leadership tended to receive messages of general moral exhortation. Both individual and group concerns found expression through new forms of communal worship. These group activities developed primarily after 1842 and led back over the next few years toward the more patterned forms of worship that characterized the end of the influx from the "spirit world."[12]

Personal messages of encouragement and comfort were the first and most common form of spirit communication. Typically there were accounts of travel to the spirit world and visits with Mother Ann and the early beloved leaders. Various presents, seen in the mind's eye, would be brought back from these "heavenly parents" to show their continuing concern for their "children" in the temporal world. These presents had no physical existence but were obviously highly symbolic, even in the accounts of less sophisticated Shakers. "Spectacles of discernment"; "sparkling balls of love"; lamps "to be kept well trimmed and burning so that the enemy may not impede our progress"; celestial wine; silver sacks filled with the bread of life; priceless gems; "six clusters of white plums from the Angel of Peace, with his love and peace written on the leaves that hang to the stems of the clusters"—these and innumerable other "spiritual" gifts were brought back verbally to strengthen the faith of believers.

Many of the visions were of exquisite loveliness. A medium of Tyringham, Massachusetts, for example, gave this description of her guides to the spirit world: "Some had what seemed like filmy gold; others were clad in garments of rich, changeable colors, glossy, like silk, while some were enveloped in soft, fleece-like drapery, as white as snow; around their heads were crownlike halos of golden light; some were decorated with diamonds, stars, pearls and other precious gems."[13] Paradoxically, this vivid visual imagery was occurring among a people who eschewed all private ownership of property and dressed in drab clothing without jewelry, precisely at the time when increasingly stringent regulations against any worldly possessions were being enforced. Eric Rohmann was led to speculate that a sort of "spiritual materialism" may have been operating in many cases, with the Shakers unconsciously compensating for their repressed worldly longings by having exquisite visions of the spiritual world to come, when they would obtain surcease from all their strivings.[14]

While messages of personal encouragement and comfort were commonly received by average members struggling to overcome the desires of "carnal nature," the larger group concerns of the Shakers were most clearly reflected in exhortations delivered by the leadership. The first direct participation of a leader as a spiritualist "instrument" occurred on April 22, 1838, about a year after the beginning of the manifestations, when Philemon Stewart, an important New Lebanon figure, went into trance. Through him a personality purporting to be Mother Ann Lee spoke at length to an assembled Shaker meeting, exhorting believers to cast off worldly "superfluities," return to the "true order" of initial Shakerism, and obey the leadership.[15]

Brother Philemon's statement provided a focus for earlier, more inchoate messages, suggesting that the leadership may have seen the general spiritual awakening in the societies as a heaven-sent means of helping to restore earlier discipline and commitment. Though some have dismissed such leadership involvement as cynical manipulation, this is an inadequate explanation. Individuals in trance are highly suggestible and have a tendency to objectify their deepest desires, so it is not surprising that Shaker leaders, distraught at the loss of faith in the societies, should have expressed their concerns in trance communications. Even when messages were obviously of a sermonic rather than an involuntary character, no cynicism need be postulated, for the Shakers felt that the connection between the spiritual and temporal was so close as to be almost inseparable, and ordinary sermons could progress almost imperceptibly into trance communications in the surcharged atmosphere of a lively meeting.[16]

A few of the Shaker trance experiences occurred to isolated individuals such as men working in the fields, but the vast majority took place in meetings for worship where emotions could be aroused and channeled within a supportive setting. With the mounting collective excitement, new forms of group worship were developed to give freshness and vitality to spiritual life. As in earlier communications, these new forms of worship had a high symbolic content and often did not distinguish clearly between the temporal world and that of aspirations and dreams.

Although the spiritual manifestations could help revitalize Shaker spiritual commitment, the phenomena also contained highly disruptive possibilities. As early as 1839, three leading Shakers, including the venerable Richard McNemar, who had been a key figure in the founding of the midwestern Shaker communities, were expelled from the Union Village, Ohio, Shaker community at the behest of a young female medium. This medium was perhaps unconsciously acting in support of the leadership of Freegift Wells, who had recently been appointed by the northeastern Shakers and was involved in a power struggle with McNemar and the old guard midwestern leaders. Only belatedly were McNemar and his associates reinstated by a directive from the central office at New Lebanon. This unfortunate incident led to the promulgation of rules for testing the validity of spirit communications: they must not be in conflict with basic Shaker beliefs, and those affecting policy must be cleared with the New Lebanon ministry.[17]

Nevertheless, the problem continued. As tensions increased between 1841 and 1843, potentially anarchic tendencies appeared. Whereas earlier revelations had been primarily from deceased Shaker leaders such as Mother Ann, later revelations began coming from an extraordinary range of historical figures. These included biblical characters such as Jesus, Mary Magdalene, and St. Paul; popular culture heroes such as Christopher Columbus, George Washington, and Napoleon; outstanding women such as Queen Isabella and Queen Elizabeth; martyred saints of the Middle Ages; and others. Following this period was the "gathering of all nations," during which the Shakers claimed to be visited by a motley crew of American Indians, Chinese, Arabs, and so forth, all of whom acted out popular American stereotypes of those cultures.[18] Possessed by the spirits of Indians, for instance, Shaker youths whooped and hollered, war danced, passed the peace pipe, or powwowed.

Such activities began to reduce the spiritual communications to absurdity. In addition, the content of the messages appears to have become more idiosyncratic, chiefly representing the repressed desires of Shaker membership. A tendency toward cynicism about all spiritual truth and a pervasive spirit of infidelity developed. Mediums issued messages attacking prominent Shaker leaders, many visionists experienced the terrors of hell, and only with great difficulty were some of the manifestations contained within the Shaker communal structure.

Faced with such challenges to their leadership and even to celibacy, the only unalterable Shaker tenet, Shaker leaders appear to have recoiled. Rather than seeking to channel the vitality of young believers into renewed external missionary activity or attempting to take advantage of the religious and social ferment of the Burned-over District by setting up new communities there, Shaker leaders turned their attention inward and sought to tighten their control over existing communities. They promulgated the Millennial Laws of 1845, the strictest and most rigid in Shaker history. Unlike the earlier Millennial Laws of 1821 or the later ones of 1860, the 1845 Laws were so extreme as almost to parody the Shaker spirit of progressive change and perfectionism. One item went so far as to declare: "Sisters must not mend, nor set buttons on brethren's clothes while they have them on."[19] Such regulations suggest that laxness in obeying the spirit and the letter of regulations separating the sexes was becoming a serious problem that had to be corrected at all cost.

What was the significance of this remarkable period of spiritual excitement for the Shakers? The faith of many believers was deepened and strengthened, yet the appeal of the society to new members also dropped off sharply. The society would continue to take in many new individuals, but few of them would stay for more than three or four years. The Shakers were rid of many of their most disruptive members because almost all the most severely affected mediums, particularly the young girls, left the society. Yet other capable individuals such as Hervey Elkins, who could have contributed much to the group, also left. Shaker leaders looked back with nostalgia at the spiritual vitality of the period, while feeling that its overall contribution to the group had been mixed.[20]

II

The parallels between the Shaker period of spiritual manifestations and the Salem witchcraft episode are striking. Like the Shaker phenomena, the Salem witchcraft episode occurred during a period of perceived crisis and declension. In 1692 the original Massachusetts Puritan "errand into the wilderness" was more than fifty years old. Although material growth and accomplishment had been substantial, many people were distressed at the corresponding weakening of religious fervor and commitment. Ministers frequently delivered jeremiads from their pulpits, seeing in every current problem or disaster the hand of an angry God calling his people to repentance. In the colony as a whole, perhaps the greatest distress was caused by the revocation of the original Massachusetts Bay Company charter in 1684, the continuing efforts to reach a new accommodation, and the ensuing uncertainty about the colony's ability to control its own political and social destiny. In small Salem Village itself, a sharp rift had developed between the more economically successful villagers, many of whom lived near the larger Salem Town, and the more conservative faction that sought to preserve an older way of life that appeared to be threatened.[21]

This emotionally supercharged atmosphere contributed to the intensity of reactions when a group of young girls began behaving in inexplicable and often disturbing ways in 1692. Initially the villagers did not know what to make of the phenomena. Cotton Mather, a leading Puritan minister with strong medical and scientific interests, sought to find an organic cause for the girls' strange affliction. Unable to do so, however, he and the Salem villagers moved toward the conclusion that the behavior must have been supernaturally induced. Unlike the later Shakers, the Massachusetts Puritans of the seventeenth century lacked a positive way of interpreting extreme revivalistic, trance, or possession phenomena. When the girls and the black slave Tituba, with whom they had been associated, attributed the actions to witchcraft, the villagers thus easily came to believe that the behavior was the result of demonic agency. The disturbing phenomena were seen, within the jeremiad tradition, as just another and more tangible sign of a demonic counterattack on the still godly, but less than fully dedicated, Puritans.

Such an interpretation was hardly surprising. The real surprise was the severity of the trials that ensued at Salem Village. Although England and continental Europe had seen extensive witchcraft trials and executions during the sixteenth and seventeenth centuries, the English colonies in the New World had been relatively free of such persecution, and no other trials in the American colonies even began to compare in scope with those that occurred at Salem Village.[22] Undoubtedly, the Salem situation was so explosive because of the interaction of complex social tensions, both within the village and in the colony as a whole. These tensions have been ably analyzed by Paul Boyer and Stephen Nissenbaum, John Demos, Kai Erikson, Carol F. Karlsen, and others, and need not be discussed again here.[23] For this analysis, it suffices to point out that tacit or direct support of the trials by leaders in the community and by community members themselves was necessary for them to continue. When such support evaporated, as excesses in the trials and the executions discredited them, the persecution stopped abruptly, even though the girls' behavior did not return to normal immediately.

The aftermaths of the Salem and Shaker episodes also are worthy of comparison. The Salem phenomena, which were viewed negatively and which continued for less than a year, had little long-term impact. Cotton Mather attempted to justify the proceedings, but most Puritans preferred to forget the whole unpleasant episode. The trend toward further secularization of the Puritan experiment would continue, largely unaffected by the convulsive events at Salem which briefly had seemed to reaffirm the existence of spiritual forces directly at work within the world.

By comparison, the Shaker phenomena, which were viewed more positively, continued for about a decade and left a mixed legacy for the society. Many Shakers remembered the spiritual manifestations positively, but most also expressed reservations about their value. Like the Salem episode, the Shaker spiritual manifestations failed to reverse an underlying trend already in progress toward secularization and the weakening of earlier spiritual commitment.[24]

III

To appreciate the significance of the Shaker and Salem episodes, one must place them within a broader perspective. The enormous complexity of the underlying phenomena is suggested by the great difficulty that scholars have had in understanding both cases. In seeking to gain a more inclusive understanding of these phenomena, which have occurred repeatedly throughout recorded history, psychologically based interpretations provide a starting point.

From a negative perspective, such behavior was described by the ancient Greeks as "hysteria." Derived from the word for uterus or womb, the term suggests that the phenomena were caused by distinctive disorders of the female reproductive system. Although this explanation cannot be complete because men also exhibit such behavior, the sexual element clearly is an important component of such activities. Supernaturally based interpretations that attribute such phenomena to demonic agency and witchcraft also contain strong sexual overtones. Accused witches have usually been women, and the accusations against them have often included fantastic stories of illicit sexual activity. By far the most influential critical approach to such phenomena was developed by Sigmund Freud in the late nineteenth and early twentieth centuries. In trying to understand the complex dynamics of hysterical patients with whom he worked, Freud developed his concepts of the "unconscious mind" and the role of repressed sexual energies in producing neurosis. [25]

More positive interpretations of such phenomena also abound, both in religious and secular writing. Involuntarily or deliberately induced ecstatic, trance, and possession phenomena occur in all major religious traditions worldwide. Such activities frequently are viewed in extremely positive terms as a means of directly linking the divine and the human. Often too, such activities appear to serve the functional role of sublimating troublesome sexual impulses into channels viewed as supremely positive. Christian mystics and visionaries tell of their rapturous union with Christ. Contemporary revivalistic and charismatic groups engage in lively services that help to release physical and emotional tensions. Even the essentially negative analysis of Sigmund Freud also contains a positive side. Using the Greek concept of catharsis Freud developed the idea that a cathartic release from emotional blockages could be achieved when repressed subconscious elements were brought back into the consciousness of a patient. Another provocative analysis, influenced by Pavlovian theory, was developed by William Sargant in *Battle for the Mind*. He argued that the cathartic release that can occur in a highly emotional religious or secular setting can leave an individual temporarily free of emotional blockages and in a state of remarkable psychological plasticity—able to experience a radical transformation in life or belief.[26]

With these diverse approaches in mind, the psychological factors that triggered the Shaker and Salem events come more clearly into focus. Not surprisingly, both episodes began with young girls near puberty who faced a difficult and often baffling transition in their physical and emotional lives. Such challenges were especially severe in the Shaker communities, which demanded celibacy of their members. The use of lively religious services was an important means of directing such energies positively toward the worship of God. By finding positive channels for such emotions, the Shakers minimized their disruptive possibilities. In contrast, the Salem girls were encouraged to interpret and express their experiences negatively. Although the Salem phenomena did include some experiences that could be viewed positively—described in one account as an expression of natural teenage "high spirits"[27]—the predominantly negative and fearful attitude adopted by the girls and the community encouraged the expression of the phenomena in increasingly destructive ways. Whereas later revivalists often would channel such emotional forces into positive conversion experiences and release of tension, the Salem Puritans blocked the phenomenon, thereby diverting it from its positive potential.[28]

Psychological approaches can help in understanding the initial behavior of the young girls at Salem Village and at Watervliet, but psychological interpretations alone cannot account for the ensuing community reactions in each case. The Shakers, for example, had experienced similar trance behavior by young girls that did not lead to a groupwide revival lasting nearly a decade. Similarly, the Massachusetts Puritans had encountered examples of trance and possession phenomena that had not resulted in major trials and persecutions. To understand the community responses to such phenomena, therefore, sociological and anthropological perspectives also must be used.

Perhaps the most compelling social-anthropological treatment of such phenomena is presented in I. M. Lewis's *Ecstatic Religion: An Anthropological Study of Spirit Possession and Shamanism*. Stripped to its barest essentials, Lewis's argument is that trance and possession phenomena are most likely to occur and be fostered among individuals who are temporarily or permanently outside normal power channels—specifically, women, lower-class men, and teenagers. When individuals in these groups begin experiencing strange involuntary behavior, they gain attention and, in some societies, prestige and influence. Yet such phenomena are almost by their very nature disruptive and may serve as an oblique, if unconscious, aggressive strategy for challenging powerful community leaders and standards. Although community leaders temporarily tolerate or even encourage mild displays of such behavior as a useful safety valve, when affected individuals and their behavior become too disruptive and threatening to the system, community elites eventually will act to put the affected individuals back in their place and reaffirm traditional authority structures. In a society that believes in the supernatural, for example, a woman who purports to be receiving trance communications from God initially may be given a cautiously positive hearing, yet eventually she may be accused of receiving "false revelations" or being a "witch" in league with powerful demonic forces.[29]

Such social-anthropological approaches help in understanding the dynamics of both the Salem and the Shaker episodes. As the work of Demos and of Boyer and Nissenbaum suggests, the witchcraft trials at Salem Village were associated both with generational tensions between young girls (the primary accusers) and older women (those who were primarily accused) and with tensions between supporters of the village minister, Samuel Parris (whose faction provided most of the accusers), and the opponents of Samuel Parris (whose faction provided most of the accused). One could argue that for a time the witchcraft accusations gave additional strength to several interrelated groups that felt their position to be either weak or threatened. Yet when the accusations began to engulf the entire community, the accusers eventually lost credibility and the traditional power structure of the society was reaffirmed.[30]

The Shaker spiritual manifestations that began in 1837 have not yet received quantitative social analysis similar to that done for Salem. Such an analysis could be made using the extensive records of the troubled Union Village community in Ohio, in which a power struggle between community founder Richard McNemar and the aggressive new leader Freegift Wells was reflected in trance communications by a young female medium. Other Shaker communities in the Midwest and Northeast also experienced disruptions that parallel those at Salem. In both the Salem and Shaker cases, trance-related phenomena clearly reflected deeper underlying tensions within the community.[31]

In conclusion, what is one to make of the Salem and Shaker episodes? The ambiguous social potential of such phenomena is highlighted, especially by the experiences of the Shakers. As Giles Avery, a Shaker leader who had himself been severely criticized by the mediums, observed, the phenomena were a "revolutionary element, both in religious and secular society," a two-edged sword with both positive and negative possibilities.[32] For Henry C. Blinn, who wrote a book about the Shaker spiritual manifestations, they were "not a foundation pillar; but rather a helping hand. . . . The better guide is love, 'Love never faileth.' "[33] Catherine Allen, eldress at New Lebanon, succinctly observed that while not in the least doubting the mediums' sincerity, "we agree with the Indian who said: 'Blow breath thro [sic] onion stalk and it smell of onion.' "[34]

Trance phenomena illustrate how fine is the line that divides mental and social disruption from ecstasy and the highest visionary creativity. The Salem witch trials demonstrate the negative side of such phenomena, while the Shaker experiences show that such phenomena may have a positive side as well. By maintaining a supportive emotional framework and seeking always to understand the deeper meaning underlying sometimes bizarre external behavior, the Shakers were able, at least for at time, to channel powerful unconscious forces into the service of individual and communal good, rather than letting such forces degenerate into terrified paranoia as happened in the Salem witchcraft trials.

4

HAD PROPHECY FAILED?

Contrasting Views of the Millerites and Shakers

*W*HY WOULD THOUSANDS OF AMERICANS before the Civil War have joined a highly restrictive, celibate religious movement such as that of the Shakers? Did the Shakers have a special appeal for any particular types of people, and if so, which ones? Which types of converts remained permanently in Shaker communities and which types eventually left them? For many years, scholars have known that the Shaker movement appealed especially to individuals who had been most strongly committed to the great religious revivals of the antebellum period but who had become disillusioned at the almost manic-depressive mood swings they experienced as a result of those revivals. The Shakers and other groups like them that arose out of the great revivals achieved much of their success because they claimed to be able to provide a secure and permanent basis for salvation, both as a result of their ideas and, more important, because they offered a stable, functioning communal environment in which those ideas could be realized in practice.

More recent Shaker community and demographic analyses by writers such as William Sims Bainbridge, Priscilla Brewer, Jean McMahon Humez, Edward Horgan, Lawrence Foster, and others have further emphasized the complex and divergent motivations of individuals who joined the Shakers. Although there has been a tendency to stereotype the Shakers as aged spinsters and bachelors with few sexual impulses or struggles, in fact many of the early Shakers were teenagers, who displayed all the fervor of present-day religious cultists. Others were orphans or children whose parents could not take care of them adequately. Sometimes whole families with as many as ten or more children joined the Shakers. And other converts came in as single, middle-aged men and women after failing to find true religious satisfaction and commitment in more conventional revivalistic groups. Most Shaker communities were in rural areas near small towns, yet there was also a predominantly black Shaker out-family in Philadelphia, and one family of the central New Lebanon community drew much of its membership from New York City and Booklyn.[1]

One way to begin to understand the nature of Shaker appeal is to look closely at why and how Shakers attracted—and lost—members from another group during the antebellum period. One of the largest such influxes of membership into the Shakers came from followers of William Miller who had become disillusioned after Christ failed to come again, as Miller had predicted, in 1843 or 1844. The complex interrelationship between the Millerite and Shaker movements during the 1840s is perhaps best highlighted by the career of the articulate midwestern Adventist leader Enoch Jacobs.

Serving initially as editor of *The Western Midnight Cry!!!*—a newspaper started in Cincinnati, Ohio, in 1841, with Joshua V. Himes as its publisher—Enoch Jacobs tirelessly sought to spread Miller's message that Christians must repent and prepare for Christ's literal return to earth in 1843. Following the failure of the 1843 predictions and of the prediction of October 1844 as well, Jacobs, like many others who experienced the Great Disappointment, struggled to understand what had gone wrong. The number of exclamation points in the title of the *Western Midnight Cry* was reduced from three to one, and on February 18, 1845, the newspaper title was changed to *The Day-Star* with Jacobs as the sole editor and publisher. The name change reflected a significant change of emphasis: "The day-star must arise *before* the Sun of Righteousness: The Resurrection must take place before Christ can come with '*all* his saints.' "[2]

Jacobs increasingly found himself attracted to the United Society of Believers in Christ's Second Appearing, better-known as Shakers, who were convinced that the second coming of Christ's spirit had already taken place in 1770 through the person of their foundress, Ann Lee. Shakers argued that the kingdom of heaven was now being realized on earth in their closely knit communities, which shared all things in common like the primitive Christian church and practiced celibacy as a sign of their participation in the resurrected state in which "they neither marry nor are given in marriage." Jacobs opened the columns of the *Day-Star* to spirited letters for and against Shaker claims. An editorial observed, "None should think that the 'Day-Star' is the instrument of a sect or party: it is God's instrument; and God's children ALL have right to talk through it to each other, and speak aloud the praises of God in the language of Christ."[3]

By May 23, 1846, Jacobs had converted to Shakerism. He began publishing extracts from Shaker doctrinal works, as well as lengthy argumentation on the necessity of celibacy as tangible proof of the overcoming of carnal propensities separating humanity from God. Jacobs repeatedly visited and reported on his visits to the Shaker villages at Whitewater and at Union Village in Ohio. That latter community, near Lebanon, Ohio, was the first and largest Shaker settlement in the Midwest, with some four hundred members in the 1840s. Jacobs worked closely with prominent Shaker leaders seeking to convert disaffected Millerites, and he was instrumental in eventually attracting more than two hundred persons to Shakerism in the Midwest.[4] In the summer of 1846, Jacobs traveled throughout the northeastern United States on a proselytizing mission. During that time, the *Day-Star* appeared irregularly, with two issues from New York City and one from the Shaker village at Canterbury, New Hampshire, where on September 19, 1846, thirteen hundred copies were issued, the Shakers assisting with typesetting and presswork and also contributing $20 toward expenses.[5] A large and inconclusive meeting between Millerites and Shakers near Enfield, Connecticut, was thoroughly reported in the *Day-Star*.[6]

Following Jacobs's return to Ohio, he and his wife, Electa, and family lived at Union Village, Ohio, publishing the *Day-Star* from that community beginning on November 7, 1846. In all probability, the press used was that of Richard McNemar, founder of the major Shaker communities in the Midwest and author of *The Kentucky Revival*, the first published Shaker book.[7] Articles from Union Village increasingly reflected Shaker concerns. Jacobs took vigorous exception to the Millerites who criticized his conversion to Shakerism in a short-lived Adventist publication, *The Day-Dawn*, that was self-consciously modeled on Jacobs's newspaper.[8] Publication of Jacobs's own *Day-Star* ceased abruptly and without explanation following the issue of July 1, 1847, about the time that Jacobs left the Shakers. A letter from Jacobs published in the Shaker newspaper *The Manifesto* in November 1891 showed that he had subsequently been influenced by the Spiritualist movement and that he still retained fond memories of the Shakers.[9]

Enoch Jacobs's curious odyssey raises a host of complex questions. How and to what extent were his experiences representative of those of other Millerites following the Great Disappointment? Why did Shakerism come to have special appeal for some of these distraught Millerites? What was the impact of the sudden infusion of Millerites into the Shaker communities, which had themselves already been suffering great disruption as a result of the "spiritual manifestations" that had begun in 1837? Why did Jacobs, like so many other Millerites who briefly joined the Shakers in the late 1840s, eventually become dissatisfied with the group and move on to continue searching for other, more appealing ways of interpreting his experiences? And from a larger perspective, can the experiences of individuals in these two highly unconventional movements shed light on more general questions of religious development, especially how millenarian movements may be able most effectively to deal with the apparent failure of prophecy? This chapter will address these and other questions relating to how millenarian movements handle problems of apparent failure or disconfirmation of their claims.

I

Both the theological and social aspects of early Shakerism show a remarkable degree of sophistication that would later help account for the appeal of the Shaker movement to disaffected Millerites. Although Shaker and Millerite views of the nature of Christ's second advent initially were in sharp opposition, individuals attracted to both groups shared many common dissatisfactions with established religious and social practice. Shaker unorthodoxy and theological liberalism is suggested by the story that Thomas Jefferson was sent a copy of *The Testimony of Christ's Second Appearing* (1808), the first published Shaker doctrinal treatise, and that this freethinker and devotee of "natural religion" pronounced it the best ecclesiastical history he had ever encountered, declaring he had read it through "three times three."[10] Jefferson's letter has not survived and the entire story may well be apocryphal, yet in all probability he would have been impressed by Shaker theology had he read it. The brilliant nineteenth-century freethinker and social reformer Frederick W. Evans was only the most noteworthy of the liberal religious figures who were attracted to Shakerism and rose to prominence within the movement. Such figures were counterbalanced be equally articulate theological conservatives such as Hervey L. Eads, who spent much of the nineteenth century debating Shaker theology with Evans. Within Shakerism, with its emphasis on continuing revelation, there was much room for religious seekers of all varieties.

Looking back, the scholar of American cultural history Constance Rourke notes in her sensitive appreciation "The Shakers" that Shaker theology, breaking with Calvinism, had a remarkably "modern" cast, with its emphasis on secular progress, functionalism, and equality for women. Indeed, she asserts, Shaker views would have been quite appealing to the likes of Thomas Paine.[11] Another scholar of the early Shakers, Stephen Marini, links their appeal following the American Revolution to that of groups such as the Freewill Baptists and the Universalists.[12] And Whitney Cross, dean of scholars of the Burned-over District and enthusiastic religion in western New York State from 1800 to 1850, sees Shakerism throughout this period as "a kind of ultimate among enthusiastic movements." It incorporated many ideas that would become characteristic of the other major enthusiasms of the area and provided a temporal as well as a spiritual refuge for the most earnest seekers who became disturbed by the vagaries of revivalistic religion.[13]

Shaker theology used a spiritualized rather than a literalistic approach to biblical interpretation from an early date, perhaps from the very beginning of the movement. Three themes are worthy of special emphasis here. First was the call for repentance and confession of sin, specifically the demand that celibacy be practiced as a tangible sign of the realization of the kingdom of heaven on earth. Shaker theological writings, discussed more fully in chapter 2, developed a symbolic rather than a literalistic interpretation of the story of the fall of man in the Garden of Eden, arguing that the cause of the fall was not an act of disobedience involving eating an actual fruit but rather an act of disobedience involving a sexual transgression. Only by renouncing all carnal propensities and devoting oneself wholly to the worship of God could humankind ultimately achieve salvation.[14]

A second theme in Shaker theology related to the role of Ann Lee and the nature of the millennium. Although it is difficult to be certain how Ann Lee viewed her role or how believers during her lifetime viewed her, later Shaker theological writers argued that Ann Lee had been infused by God's spirit in the same way that Jesus had previously been infused by God's spirit. Ann Lee was, therefore, Christ's Second Appearing—using the term *Christ* not to refer to the man Jesus but rather the Divine Spirit that had similarly animated Jesus. With this second coming of Christ's spirit to earth, realization of the millennium, the kingdom of heaven on earth, was now under way. Christ's second advent had not occurred instantly in literal "clouds of glory," as so many expected it would, but was rather "gradual and progressive like the rising of the Sun." The first coming had been through a male; the second, to maintain balance, was through a female. Reflected in this notion of restoring a true balance between the sexes was the Shaker rejection of the Trinity, which they took to be an exclusively male conception of God. Instead, the Shakers argued that God, like the whole of creation, was dual, a combination of male and female elements harmoniously related to each other.[15]

A third element in Shaker theology was a restorationist effort to return to the spirit of early Christianity, the "primitive Christian church," in which believers truly loved each other and held "all things common," sharing not only their spiritual commitment but all aspects of life. As in their dealings with other issues, the Shakers did not slavishly attempt simply to copy the specific forms that had been used by early Christians. Instead, believing that a progressive revelation and elaboration of truth was going on in their own as well as in biblical days, they sought to infuse the spirit of early Christianity into new forms appropriate for their time. All aspects of life would ultimately come to form a unified spiritual and temporal whole within a distinctive community devoting itself, like a monastery, to the service of God. The Shakers' success in linking spiritual and temporal life would ultimately prove a key factor in their appeal to dissatisfied individuals seeking a secure spiritual home that would free them from the emotional rollercoaster of revivalistic religion.[16]

Although Shaker restorationism was present from the very beginning of the movement, the precise forms that Shaker communal life would take did not become established until after Ann Lee's death. The first "gathered" Shaker community was established in 1787 at New Lebanon, New York, and by the close of the 1790s, eleven communal centers, each composed of numerous smaller "families" of thirty to a hundred individuals, had been established in New York State and in New England and were thriving with a total of sixteen hundred members.[17] As early as 1803, two Shaker communities were sufficiently well established that they could give away thousands of dollars of specie, livestock, and produce to help feed the starving poor who were suffering from cholera in New York City.[18] A second wave of expansion in the Midwest, growing out of the Kentucky Revival of the early 1800s, and a lesser revival in 1827, brought the Shakers to eighteen communal centers across New England, New York, and the Midwest, with as many as four thousand members by 1830, the date at which the Shakers felt they had reached the peak of their spiritual and temporal strength.[19]

Visitors to Shaker communities during the period were struck by the order, serenity, and simplicity of Shaker life and the impressive degree of fellow feeling that was manifested. One observer noted, "The people are like their village . . . soft in speech, demure in bearing, gentle in face; a people seeming to be at peace not only with themselves, but with nature and with heaven."[20] John Humphrey Noyes, founder of the Oneida Community, also praised the Shakers as an inspiration for later communal ventures.[21]

In summary, the Shakers had numerous strengths, both theologically and socially. Theologically, the Shakers began with a sophisticated and largely spiritualized understanding of the basis of their movement, which could easily be modified to deal with changing circumstances. Socially, the Shakers had achieved recognized excellence in communal living, and even their critics were forced to admit that the fruits of Shaker spirituality appeared to be good. Although celibacy and closely knit communal living were demanding practices, they also called forth a high degree of commitment which initially strengthened the group. The Shakers might have been expected to look toward the future with confidence.

Yet by the late 1830s the Shakers clearly were experiencing a decline. In 1837, exactly fifty years after the formal gathering of the first Shaker community in 1787, the Shakers were experiencing a subtle but profound sense of malaise. Astute leaders sensed a growing loss of control over their communities. Even though Shaker theological beliefs remained remarkably flexible, the loss of spiritual dynamism in the group was calling into question whether the Shakers would be able to continue to see themselves as key movers in setting up the kingdom of heaven on earth. [22]

In response to the growing Shaker internal tensions and loss of nerve—which coincided with the Panic of 1837 and ensuing depression in the outer world—a remarkable decade of spiritual manifestations began among the Shakers in 1837 and rapidly spread throughout all the closely knit Shaker communities. The details of this upwelling of fervor and its impact on the group have been discussed in the preceding chapter and need not be recounted here. Suffice it to note that the manifestations helped to revitalize the spiritual commitment of some believers, but they also provided an opportunity for others—especially teenage females—to challenge the authority of Shaker leadership. Many Shaker leaders initially were cautiously supportive of the phenomena, seeing them as a means of strengthening the group by encouraging young Shakers and other flagging believers to undergo a powerful direct experience of the truth of the Shaker message. Eventually, however, the anarchic potential implicit in individual revelation coming from all members of the group forced the leadership to restrict the spiritual manifestations and reassert full control over the societies. [23]

The dramatic Shaker spiritual phenomena peaked at approximately the same time during the early 1840s that Millerite tensions were beginning to rise to a crescendo, By the time the Millerite Great Disappointment took place in October 1844, the Shakers had largely reestablished order in their communities and were able to supply a seemingly secure and appealing alternative for some Millerites who were seeking further light to help them understand their difficult experiences. In curious and very different ways, both groups during this period were struggling to come to terms with an apparent failure of prophecy. Alert Shakers could sense that their communities, the visible sign of Christ's second appearance on earth, were beginning to experience a temporal decline, while dedicated Millerites were painfully aware that Christ had not returned to earth a second time when they had expected him.

III

The reasons that some Millerites became converted to Shakerism and that many of those same converts eventually left the movement can clearly be seen by looking at the heated argumentation that took place in the pages of the *Day-Star* between 1845 and 1847. The final failure of the Millerite prediction of the specific date for Christ's literal Second Coming was emotionally shattering to many in the movement. Shock, grief, and perplexity were widespread. Derided by outsiders and unsure themselves of what had gone wrong, second advent believers desperately sought to salvage something out of the commitment they had so sincerely devoted to the cause. Some individuals fell apart emotionally, at least for a time, because of the "tribulations deep" which they experienced, or else become completely cynical about all religion and morality. Some continued, though in ever-decreasing numbers and with less and less enthusiasm or success, to set new dates for Christ's second advent, each of which eventually would prove false. And some returned to orthodoxy.[24]

But for those who had been thoroughly convinced, a return to orthodoxy offered no solution. Rather than "go back," they felt that they must "go on" to a new and fuller understanding of God's will and plan for their lives. The Shakers had much to offer these more committed believers. In the first place, the Shakers, too, were devout second adventists, who, it seemed, had already gone through many of the same thought processes that disappointed Millerites were now experiencing. Enoch Jacobs spoke approvingly of how the Shakers, unlike so many others, took his second-advent concerns seriously. He was astonished to discover Shaker accounts going back to the Kentucky Revival of the early 1800s that were almost uncanny in the degree to which they seemed to illustrate emotional and thought processes he was experiencing, as though for the first time, many years later.[25] Jacobs was impressed to discover that a Shaker poem composed in 1807 or 1808, "The Midnight Cry," could speak so clearly to his present condition.[26] Articulate Shaker leaders worked with him as an individual, encouraging him to "go on" to develop a deeper spiritual insight. Given these circumstances, Jacobs was at least open to considering that the Shakers might have something to teach him.

The most appealing aspect of Shakerism for Jacobs and other Millerites like him was not so much theological as social. The Shakers really seemed to be living their faith successfully, unlike so many Millerites. Even Millerites who were most critical of the Shakers in the columns of the *Day-Star* could not restrain their grudging admiration for the well-ordered, loving communities that the Shakers appeared to have created.[27] Jacobs commented on how impressed he was by the Shakers' stress on works, not on mere talk. Though Jacobs initially had difficulty accepting the Shakers' contention that their organization was the true representative of the "body" of Christ on earth, he noted that "the spirit of the Shakers is much more like Christ, than the spirit that opposes them."[28] If the test by which one was to know truth was by its fruits, then the Shakers scored high marks, especially for those individuals who had been so badly burned by the revival fires and were seeking true religious security.

Henry B. Bear, a Millerite who joined the Shakers and wrote a reflective account of his advent experience, exhorted his brethren: "O come and be gathered. . . . I know there can be no happiness in being thus scattered."[29] Even more eloquent was Enoch Jacobs's peroration:

> O what an ocean of contradictory theories is that upon which the multitudes have been floating for the last 18 months. Do you not long for rest from these conflicting elements? Do you want to find a place where Advent *work* takes the place of Advent *talk*—where "I" is no longer the prominent *idea* in any theory—where the purity of wives and husbands is the purity of heaven, and where your little children are protected from the poisonous influence of the world.[30]

The Shaker symbolic rather than literal interpretation of Christ's second advent was in sharp opposition to Millerite literalism, yet a symbolic approach appeared much more appealing follow-

ing the Great Disappointment. Shaker doctrinal works going back to
The Testimony of Christ's Second Appearing in 1808 presented an extremely persuasive case for seeing Christ's second advent as an internal, not an external, phenomenon. In the wake of the failure of
Christ to make a literal return as they had anticipated, Millerites
searching the Scriptures for guidance could come to the conclusion
that the error had been in their *own* understanding and not in the
Lord's word.

Enoch Jacobs again articulated the Shaker alternative to Millerite literalism:

> Have you found salvation? It was that for which we looked in
> 1843, and in the autumn of 1844. On the 10th day of the 7th
> month of the last named year, we were all placed in a situation
> to receive it, if it had come in *our way*. George Storrs told me
> that he felt just as completely dead to the world as though he
> had been laid in his coffin—buried under ground and waiting
> for a resurrection. This was the feeling of thousands. It was
> mine. Earthly ties were as completely sundered, for the time be-
> ing, as though they had never been known. Thus we waited, but
> Salvation did not come: We thought the fault was all without—
> sad mistake!! It was *within*. This out of doors salvation has al-
> ways been a precarious thing.[31]

And a stanza from a poem by the Shaker Charles Main also made
the same point:

> So stand no longer waiting, ye men of Gallilee,
> Into the literal heavens, your Savior there to see;
> But listen to his teaching, and cleanse your soul
>   from sin,
> The everlasting kingdom must be set up within.[32]

There were problems, of course, with the specifics of Shaker
adventist theology. Why, for example, should Christ's second advent
have been through a woman? And even if one were to accept such a
possibility, why should one conclude that Ann Lee was that woman?
Yet in the face of great need for a new understanding of their experience, even the unorthodoxy of Shaker theology was not an insur-

mountable stumbling block to devoted Millerites who found the Shakers otherwise attractive.[33]

The great stumbling block, instead, was celibacy. This, not Shaker theology per se, had always been the ultimate limiting factor in the growth of the group. Not only did celibacy make Shakerism entirely dependent upon a continuing supply of converts from the outer world for its survival and growth, but celibacy was also a powerful test of whether the dedication of new converts was sufficiently great that they were prepared to give up "all" for Christ. By demanding an extreme degree of loyalty and the severing of normal earthly relationships, Shaker celibacy could have considerable appeal to the most devoted believers in the great revivals who sought to commit their lives wholly to God without any carnal distractions. Millerites who had been eagerly awaiting Christ's second advent, living with husbands or wives, following St. Paul's advice, as though they had none, could understand the need for such a sacrifice, at least for a time.[34]

Yet when Christ did not literally appear in clouds of glory in 1844, even devout Millerites must have reassessed the desirability of continued celibacy. As a lifelong practice rather than a prelude to eternal glory, the demands must have seemed excessive to most. Enoch Jacobs himself struggled with his impulses and with those of his wife, who initially opposed Shakerism because of that demand.[35] Again and again, Jacobs emphasized how difficult the commitment to celibacy was:

> I now ask if there is one Advent believer in the land, who would not gladly share the peaceful home they [the Shakers] enjoy, were it not for the cross [celibacy]? Excuse after excuse is brought forward, while the real one is hidden. You wish to reserve the privilege of gratifying the lusts of the flesh, which you know you cannot do under any circumstances, in the dispensation in which we live, appealing to God that you do it for his glory.[36]

Some Millerite converts to Shakerism did accept the Shaker celibate cross permanently. Henry B. Bear and his family, for example, remained committed members of the group throughout the remainder of their lives. Yet far more Millerite converts to Shakerism appear to have "turned off" from the movement than remained. Although Shaker membership figures still have not been completely analyzed, the work done to date is suggestive. The membership records of the New Lebanon Second Family between 1830 and the dissolution of the community in 1896 show, for example, that only slightly more than 10 percent of all converts during the entire period remained in that community for the rest of their lives.[37] The percentage of converts who stayed faithful dropped precipitously at the beginning of the decades of the 1830s and 1840s.[38] The fluidity of membership was even greater in the Sodus Bay, New York, community from 1826 to 1838, where more than 50 percent of the group changed in some years.[39] Although we do not yet know the reasons why Millerites who joined the Shakers in the 1840s often subsequently failed to stay, celibacy must have been an important factor. The story is that Enoch Jacobs himself left the Shakers after declaring that he would "rather go to hell with Electa his wife than live among the Shakers without her."[40]

If some Millerites were influenced for a time by Shakerism, then how, correspondingly, were Shakers influenced by Millerites? Only a few hypotheses can be raised here. The impact of significant numbers of Millerite converts joining some Shaker communities, particularly in the Midwest, and then subsequently leaving the group must have been considerable. In the former case, the Shakers must have been enthusiastic at the infusion of new converts and may well have modified the emphasis of their group in order to retain the Millerites. In the extreme case of the Shaker village at Whitewater, Ohio, in 1845, for example, 80 out of a total of 144 members were former Millerites, and their influence on the direction of the group must have been profound.[41] At Union Village, Ohio, the largest and one of the most internally troubled Shaker communities during the 1830s and 1840s, thirty Millerites were added to one family alone in the course of six months.[42] Even if no direct changes in Shaker theology or practice were made, such an infusion of converts must have affected which aspects of Shakerism were emphasized at the time.

Direct Millerite influence on the Shakers is difficult to establish, based on available evidence, but experimentation with new forms of ritual may well have been one activity stimulated by the

Millerite influx. One of the most colorful of the new forms of group worship that the Shakers introduced during the 1840s, for example, was called the "Midnight Cry." A group of Shaker mediums—six male and six female, with two elders in the lead carrying lighted lamps in their right hands—marched through all the community buildings at midnight every night for a period of two weeks. "Every medium wore upon the right wrist, a scrap of scarlet flannel, some two and one half inches wide, and attached to this a written inscription as follows—'War hath been declared by the God of heaven, against all sin, and with the help of the Saints on earth, it shall be slain.' "[43] These activities were interpreted as the actualization of the "searching as with candles" foretold at the beginning of the manifestations. At midnight on the last night, the brothers and sisters were awakened with singing:

> Awake from your slumbers, for the Lord of Hosts
>   Is going through the land,
> He will sweep, he will clean his holy sanctuary.
> Search ye your Camps, yea read and understand
> For the Lord of Hosts holds the Lamps in his
>   hand.[44]

All the believers dressed quickly and hurried out to join in the marching and singing, before repairing to the meetinghouse for an hour of active worship. "This strange alarm had a wonderful effect on the minds of those thus suddenly aroused."[45]

If a new spirit and enthusiasm was imparted to Shakerism by the Millerite influx, then the subsequent departure of many of those same Millerite converts a few years or decades later must have undercut Shaker morale, contributing to the deep pessimism apparent in so many of the Shaker writings of the 1850s and 1860s. Although difficulty in retaining converts can be traced to the decade of the 1830s, before the Millerite infusion, the length of time the Shakers were able to keep their converts became progressively shorter for individuals who entered during the 1840s and 1850s. Thoughtful Shakers must have wondered if their own efforts had also "failed," not theologically but socially.

Ultimately the most appealing answer to the apparent failure of Millerite prophecy of the 1840s was provided not by the spiritualized second advent beliefs and practices of the Shakers but by the beliefs and practices introduced by Ellen G. White and others, who argued that, on October 22, 1844, Christ had entered the most holy compartment of the heavenly sanctuary to begin the "investigative judgment" preliminary to the Second Coming. In effect, belief in a heavenly event that could not immediately be confirmed or discon-firmed was substituted for Millerite belief in an earthly event that had not occurred as anticipated. On the foundation of this new belief, as well as other distinctive beliefs and practices, would rise the Seventh-day Adventist movement, a classic example of a success-ful group that developed out of the ashes of an apparently failed prophecy.[46]

THE ONEIDA COMMUNITY

5

THE PSYCHOLOGY of FREE LOVE

Sexuality in the Oneida Community

*F*EW COMMUNAL EXPERIMENTS IN AMERICA have attracted more attention than the Oneida Community, founded in nineteenth-century New York State by the eccentric Vermont-born genius John Humphrey Noyes. Historians, sociologists, psychologists, literary scholars, and popular writers alike have continued to be intrigued by the "complex marriage" system at Oneida, which both Noyes and his critics somewhat misleadingly referred to as "free love."[1] Virtually every treatment of utopian communities or alternative marriage and sexual patterns in America includes the obligatory chapter on the Oneida "free love" colony.[2]

Despite this widespread interest, most analyses of Oneida have been superficial or sensational, simply retelling once again the external arrangements of complex marriage, male continence, mutual criticism, stirpiculture, and other distinctive community practices. Writers have found in the Oneida Community a mirror that reflects their own concerns and preoccupations. John Humphrey Noyes has been variously described as a "Yankee saint," whose sexual attitudes and practices can serve as a model for "liberated" present-day lifestyles, as a "Vermont Casanova," with sick and exploitative attitudes toward women, and even as a prototype for Hitler, because Noyes's stirpiculture or eugenics experiment could be seen as prefiguring some of the most repressive and threatening human-engineering experiments of the twentieth century.[3] Seldom have scholars or the general public attempted to understand Noyes and his experiments in communal living on their own terms, considering both their strengths and weaknesses.

Studies of the psychology of Oneida sexuality have been particularly biased and idiosyncratic, suggesting little more than a Rorschach test might. This is true in part because of the enormous complexity of Noyes's ideas and practices. If presented selectively, they can be analyzed convincingly using almost any psychological framework, from classic Freudian, Jungian, or behaviorist approaches to more modern perspectives found in gestalt psychology, transactional analysis, or ego psychology. With rare exceptions, writers who have attempted to analyze Noyes's psychology have failed to read more than a handful of the many books and pamphlets published by the community before confidently asserting that he perfectly exemplifies their pet psychological theories. Virtually no use has been made of the revealing newspapers that Noyes and his associates published (eventually on a daily basis) between 1834 and 1879, of the interviews with leading Oneida members after the community's breakup, which are now held at the Kinsey Institute, or of the community diaries and records that were not burned in the late 1940s and are now held at the Syracuse University Library in Syracuse, New York.[4]

This chapter is a preliminary attempt to reconstruct, more thoroughly than has heretofore been possible, the sexual ideology and attitudes that underlay the Oneida experiment and the way in which sexual expression occurred and was channeled at Oneida. After focusing on the complex sexual ideology and practices introduced by John Humphrey Noyes, the chapter also will briefly consider the backgrounds and experiences of the approximately two hundred adults who joined the community in the 1840s and 1850s and the factors that led to the breakup of the community in 1879–81.

Before launching into this ambitious analysis, let me emphasize three points. First is the enormous complexity of human sexuality, by which I mean not simply coitus itself but also the broader interrelationships between men and women that occur both between individuals and in society. Oneida tested the outer limits of human behavior in this area during more than thirty years of the community's existence. Even sexually sophisticated individuals today can learn much about the range of possible sexual expression by paying close attention to the Oneida experiment. A second, closely related point is that no single psychological theory alone convincingly explains the Oneida Community. Noyes formulated, both in theory and in practice, a distinctive approach to understanding and revitalizing relations between men and women. Although insights from various psychological theories inform this analysis, I shall be trying to understand the Oneida Community on its own terms rather than forcing its experience into the procrustean bed of any single theory. A final caveat, lest anyone be disappointed, is that when I speak of "free love" in this essay, I am referring to the system used at Oneida, not to what anyone else may have fantasized free love to be like. Oneida free love was in many ways anything but free. Although the range of adult heterosexual contacts within the community was greatly extended, any exclusive romantic attachments were rigorously broken up as a threat to community stability. In this as in other respects, a convincing analysis of Oneida must first see the community on its own terms.[5]

I

To understand the Oneida Community, both its theoretical underpinnings and its practice, one must first understand its founder, John Humphrey Noyes. To a large extent, Oneida is best understood as the lengthened shadow of this one extraordinary man, reflecting his complex personality and concerns. Noyes struggled with unusual intensity to overcome his religious and sexual problems. Unlike most individuals, who simply seek to reach an accommodation with the larger world, Noyes adopted a prophetic stance, arguing that his insights provided a universally valid model for setting the world straight. Possessed by this extraordinary and compelling idea, unable or unwilling to work within what he considered to be an unstable and inconsistent value framework, Noyes sought "to initiate, both in himself as well as in others, a process of moral regeneration."[6] He projected his ego strengths and weaknesses onto the world. He was one of those individuals about whom William James wrote in whom a "superior intellect" and a "psychopathic temperament" coalesce, thereby creating "the best possible condition for the kind of effective genius that gets into biographical dictionaries. Such figures do not remain mere critics and understanders with their intellect. Their ideas possess them, they inflict them, for better or worse, upon their companions or their age."[7]

The world into which John Humphrey Noyes was born in southern Vermont in 1811 was one which was undergoing disquieting social, political, and religious changes as the young American republic gradually left behind elements of its more cohesive colonial past and moved into the rough-and-tumble world of nineteenth-century capitalist individualism. Like many of the people who would later join his communities, Noyes grew up in a family of higher than average intellectual and social attainments. His father, John, was a successful businessman who served in the United States House of Representatives, while his strong-willed and deeply religious mother, Polly Hayes, was a second cousin to Rutherford B. Hayes, who later became the nineteenth president of the United States.

The close-knit family environment in which young John grew up on the family holdings in Putney, Vermont, would later be reflected in many of the features of the organizational life of the Putney and Oneida communities. The family was emotionally ingrown yet strongly aware of its distinctive talents and capabilities. All four of Noyes's father's brothers had, apparently because of shyness, married close cousins. The elder John Noyes himself had married Polly Hayes only after a long and desultory courtship when he was forty. Throughout his life young John shared his father's intense shyness around women, as well as the related tendency to intellectualize relations with the opposite sex. The complex marriage system that John Humphrey Noyes would eventually institute among his followers at Putney and Oneida would reflect the curious combination of intimacy and distance he had first experienced in his own family.[8]

Young John Noyes first began to move out into the world on his own as a result of his conversion in a religious revival in 1831. That conversion sent him off to Andover and then to Yale theological seminaries to study to become a minister. Noyes was an intense and driven young man who seemed to expect absolute perfection of himself. He compulsively read his Bible as much as twelve to sixteen hours a day, trying to discover God's will for his life. Finally, after an intellectual breakthrough in 1834, he realized that God could not expect the impossible of him. The total perfection that God demanded of all true Christians must be achieved through a right attitude and an inner sense of salvation from sin, not by any outward acts per se. When Noyes publicly announced that he was "perfect" in this sense, he was viewed as crazy by his colleagues, and he lost his license to preach. For three emotionally tumultuous years until 1837, he wandered quixotically throughout New England and New York State trying to convert the world to his highly idiosyncratic, perfectionist religious beliefs. He was determined to establish "right relations with God," a common value framework for the world, but instead he found his message either ignored or ridiculed. On several occasions, he experienced such intense psychic turmoil that his family and close associates feared he was temporarily deranged.[9]

During this difficult period, when all religious and social truth seemed uncertain, Noyes also began to question and rethink the basis for relations between the sexes. He struggled to understand his sexual impulses and to determine why so many of the perfectionists with whom he was associated were engaged in such erratic and often self-destructive sexual experimentation. Eventually Noyes applied the same principles to sexual relations that he had to understanding religious truth. He concluded that if one had the right attitude, sexual relations, like other activities in life, would be expressed in an outward manner that would be pleasing to God. The sexual impulse was basically a good one, but it needed to be expressed through proper channels. Noyes rejected the extremes of Shaker celibacy, on the one hand, or spiritualist promiscuity, on the other. In his words,

> The Shaker and the licentious spiritualist are alike in their fundamental error, which is an over-emphasis of the importance of the outward act of sexual union. The Shaker, with a prurient swollen imagination of the importance of the act, pronounces it a damnable abomination prohibited to the saints. The licentious spiritualist, with the same morbid imagination, thinks it right and necessary in the face of all human regulations, to perform it at the bidding of impulse.

Noyes declared that neither the act of sexual union nor abstinence from it had any importance in itself. The goal, rather, was "a

healthy development and faithful subordination of the sexual susceptibility."[10] As early as 1837, he argued that eventually in the holy
community of Christians, love, including sexual love, would be expressed freely among all God's saints.[11]

Public announcement of the latter views temporarily lost Noyes
virtually all of his remaining supporters. In attempting to justify
himself and rehabilitate his reputation, he began during the late
1830s to settle down and establish the organizational forms that
would eventually allow his principles to be realized in functioning
community life. After returning home to Putney, Vermont, Noyes
started first a Bible School, then a Society of Inquiry, and finally the
full-scale Putney Community, which ultimately, after its relocation to
Oneida, New York in 1848, would become the Oneida Community
and last for more than thirty additional years. The process of development was a gradual one, part of an attempt to find the best way of
expressing the group's religious convictions in practice.[12]

At the core of Noyes's religious beliefs was a millenarian expec-
tation that the ideal patterns of the kingdom of heaven could literally be realized on earth in his communal experiments. Noyes argued
that he and his followers were returning to the ideals of early Christianity, the "primitive Christian church." Following his hero St.
Paul, Noyes argued that the spirit not the letter of the law was what
really mattered. Noyes and his followers did not slavishly seek to follow the *forms* of early Christianity but instead attempted to realize
the *spirit* of early Christianity in their particular nineteenth-century
setting. Perfection, not in externals but in internal attitudes and a
sense of salvation from sin, was required by God of all true Christians on earth.

The complex and highly unorthodox religious beliefs around
which Noyes's perfectionists eventually organized their communities
at Oneida and its smaller branches[13] were most fully presented and
elaborated in Noyes's articles in the community newspapers and in
the compendium of those articles published in 1847 as *The Berean: A
Manual for the Help of Those Who Seek the Faith of the Primitive
Church*. Theologically, the core of Noyes's heresies was his belief that
the Second Coming of Christ had occurred in 70 A.D. when the
Temple in Jerusalem was destroyed and the great Diaspora began.
Noyes argued that at that time there was a primary resurrection and

judgment in the spiritual world which marked the beginning of the Kingdom of God in the heavens. A second and final resurrection judgment was now approaching: "The church on earth is now rising to meet the approaching kingdom in the heavens, and to become its duplicate and representative on earth."[14]

Associated with Noyes's millenarian conviction that the kingdom of heaven could literally be realized on earth was his intense desire to overcome the disruptive individualism of nineteenth-century America by instituting among his followers a new set of religious and social values. Those values stressed the subordination of individuals and their private, selfish interests to the good of the larger community, as interpreted by Noyes. The goal, most briefly stated, was to move beyond the "egotism for two" implicit in monogamous family life to create "an enlarged family" in which all loyalties, including sexual loyalties, would eventually be raised to the level of the entire community.[15] These new values were introduced and internalized during the decade at Putney through the practice of male continence, mutual criticism, and complex marriage.

Male continence, the extraordinary method of birth control used at Putney and Oneida, was developed initially in response to the problems of Noyes's wife, Harriet. During the first six years of their married life, Harriet was traumatized by five difficult childbirths, four of which resulted in the death of the child. Noyes's attempt to spare Harriet such agony in the future led him to develop the distinction between sexual intercourse for "amative" and "propagative" purposes. The primary concern of sexual intercourse was social or "amative"—to allow the sexes to communicate and express affection for each other. Noyes argued that such intercourse could be separated from propagative intercourse in practice, and without artificial aids, by "male continence," the practice that is technically known as *coitus reservatus*. Under male continence, a couple would engage in sexual congress without the man ever ejaculating, either during intercourse or after withdrawal.[16] Noyes saw this practice, which required substantial male self-control, as a logical outgrowth of his principles. In his view, regular intercourse is wasteful, sowing the seed where one does not want or expect it to grow. "Yet it is equally manifest that the natural instinct of our nature demands frequent congress of the sexes, not for propagative, but for social and spiritual purposes. It results from this that simple congress of the sexes, without the propagative crisis, is the order of nature for the gratification of ordinary amative instincts."[17]

Recognizing the controversial nature of male continence, Noyes used several intriguing analogies to explain and defend his unorthodox method of birth control. He denied that male continence was "unnatural." If it was, then "cooking, wearing clothes, living in houses, and almost everything else done by civilized man, is unnatural in the same sense. . . . Every instance of self-denial is an interruption of some natural act. The man who virtuously contents himself with a look at a beautiful woman is conscious of such an interruption. The lover who stops at a kiss denies himself a natural progression." Noyes was merely drawing the line further along than a group such as the Shakers, which had only resorted to "the most imposing of human contrivances for avoiding the woes of undesired propagation."[18]

To describe the process of male continence, Noyes used a striking analogy:

> The situation may be compared to a stream in three conditions, viz., 1, a fall; 2, a course of rapids above the fall; and 3, still water above the rapids. The skillful boatman may choose whether he will remain in the still water, or venture more or less down the rapids, or run his boat over the fall. But there is a point on the verge of the fall where he has no control over his course; and just above that there is a point where he will have to struggle with the current in a way which will give his nerves a severe trial, even though he may escape the fall. If he is willing to learn, experience will teach him the wisdom of confining his excursions to the region of easy rowing, unless he has an object in view that is worth the cost of going over the falls.[19]

How well did such an unusual system work? Initial experimentation by Noyes and his followers at Putney in the early 1840s suggested that the procedure was effective in curtailing pregnancies. And during the twenty years between 1848 and 1868, when male continence was almost the sole sanctioned method of sexual intercourse at Oneida, community records show only twelve unplanned births in a group numbering approximately two hundred adults, equally balanced between the sexes and having frequent sexual congress with a variety of partners during that time.[20] Undoubtedly that low birth rate can be traced in part to the practice of having women past the menopause induct young men into male continence and having older, more experienced men induct young women. But the effectiveness of male continence as a means of birth control in a regulated community setting is incontestable.

The psychological effects of the system are more ambiguous. Unfortunately, approximately forty years ago an extensive body of diaries, journals, and other personal papers of community members which might have shed light on this matter was destroyed. And the items that were fortuitously saved are only now in the process of becoming available to outside scholarship at Syracuse University Library, under various restrictions. As a result, the analysis that follows is based primarily on other sources, including a close reading of the first twenty-one years of the newspapers published by Noyes and his associates and of every book and pamphlet published by the Oneida Community throughout its existence, as well as on the interviews with the community members after the breakup, now held at the Kinsey Institute.[21] These sources are often remarkably candid in discussing ideals and problems of all sorts.

These sources suggest that there were indeed serious problems associated with both the introduction and dissolution of community life, but that at other times throughout most of the community's existence male continence and other forms of community control do not appear to have been perceived as especially burdensome. Even during the troubled late stages of Oneida's history, a careful medical study of the health of the community by Noyes's son Theodore showed less incidence of "nervous disorders" than in the society at large, although the relationship of such disorders to male continence is not clear.[22] Noyes himself felt that a slightly higher than average level of sexual tension was not necessarily harmful.[23] His son Pierrepont dimly recalled a quality of restrained romantic excitement pervading and invigorating community life, an atmosphere that Abel Easton described as a sort of "continuous courtship."[24] Finally, the practice of male continence for many years evidently did not lead to impotence. When Noyes instituted his experiment in "scientific

propagation" in 1868, many men who had long practiced male continence deliberately sired children.

Despite the disclaimers, it is difficult to believe that there were
no significant problems associated with male continence. Probably
even with unusually strong religious commitment, proper training,
and stringent enforcement procedures, few men could have found the
technique "easy," as Noyes declared it was for "spiritual men." Hints
in Noyes's writings, for instance, suggest that masturbation, and associated antisocial withdrawal from community life, may have been a
problem at times, but the record is inconclusive. Whatever the difficulties associated with male continence, most Oneida men evidently preferred it to celibacy, the only other option, which seems to
have been practiced by a few men of the community.[25]

However men may have reacted, women at Oneida evidently
found the practice an improvement. In describing his early experimentation with male continence, Noyes observed, "My wife's experience was very satisfactory, as it had never been before."[26] The
medical historian Norman Himes opined "that the Oneida Community stands out historically as perhaps the only group experiment, at
least in the Western World, placing great emphasis on the full
satisfaction of the woman, and this in a culture dominated by male attitudes."[27] And the sex researcher Havelock Ellis concluded that some
women did reach orgasm when male continence was practiced.[28]

Male continence can be viewed as an accentuation and synthesis of certain characteristic Victorian sexual attitudes that sought internalized control of sexual expression.[29] The primary importance of
the technique was practical, however. Noyes declared that the
"Oneida Community in an important sense owed its existence to the
discovery of Male Continence" and that the principle underlying its
practice "has been the very soul of its working constitution."[30] Male
continence undercut the emotional and physical exclusiveness of
couples. It prevented the complications having children would have
posed to establishing the primary loyalty to the community in all
things. And it allowed a degree of sexual pleasure, coupled with
stringent self-control and self-denial, not found in artificial methods
of birth control. Few would be tempted simply to make a "hobby" of
the practice and withdraw from the normal round of community life
into exclusive emotional and sexual attachments.

The second form of social control that helped to prepare the way for complex marriage and the close community life associated with it was the practice of "mutual criticism."[31] Under this special form of group feedback and control, which has parallels with a variety of modern techniques, from gestalt therapy to Chinese thought control, the person to receive criticism would be openly and honestly evaluated by other members of the group to encourage his or her character development. Usually criticism sessions at Oneida were conducted by groups of ten to fifteen members, with an approximately equal balance between the sexes. The person to receive criticism would remain silent while other members of the group, in turn, discussed his or her strengths and weaknesses. The process brought faults and irritating personality characteristics into the open, rather than letting the problems fester in secret. Topics brought up in the sessions could range from ideological issues to the most private personal and sexual matters. In the absence of a formal governmental structure at Oneida, mutual criticism served as the chief means of informally establishing and sustaining community cohesion and norms.

Institutionalization of male continence and mutual criticism among Noyes's followers preceded his further action at Putney in 1846 to move out from traditional monogamous marriage into a new group form called complex marriage. The details of this difficult transition, which was not completed until the early 1850s at Oneida, are discussed at length in chapter 7 and are not important to this analysis.[32] Suffice it to note that the essence of the complex marriage system Noyes eventually introduced among his followers was the elimination of "selfishness"—the subordination of individual self-interest to the interests of the community, which in turn was dedicated to achieving God's will. Even individual sexual loyalties had to be given up, raised instead to the level of the community, to the "enlarged family."

Noyes argued that the resulting ties were at least as binding and as demanding as those of ordinary marriage. In the words of the community handbook, "The honor and faithfulness that constitutes an ideal marriage, may exist between two hundred as well as two; while the guarantees for women and children are much greater in the Community that they can be in any private family."[33] To sustain such larger ties, any tendencies toward "special love" (exclusive romantic attachments) were rigorously discouraged. Special individual attachments to offspring or close friendships between members of the same sex were similarly broken up. The enlarged family at Oneida eventually all lived under one roof in a large Mansion House, ate together, worked together, gathered daily for religious-and-business meetings of the whole group, and shared all but the most basic personal property in common.[34]

It is interesting to speculate about the psychological motives that led Noyes to set up a community in which intense loyalty to the group was required, but all exclusive sexual and social attachments were discouraged. The sociologist Maren Lockwood Carden makes the acute, if only partially correct, observation that Noyes was never able "to commit himself fully to any idea, action, or person."[35] A more accurate statement might be, instead, that Noyes always was firmly committed to his own sense of mission and core ideas, but he was never willing to open himself up to close personal relationships, either with men or with women. Until Noyes was able to find followers willing to acknowledge his unique, God-given leadership, he remained intensely shy and insecure. Once his supreme authority was accepted, however, he was able to relax somewhat and benevolently delegate authority to his loyal subordinates who, in turn, showed great flexibility in putting his ideas into practice.[36] As Robert David Thomas has suggested in *The Man Who Would Be Perfect*, Noyes was a man whose great ego strengths and weaknesses were reflected in a sharp ambivalence about his competing drives for autonomy and for dependence.[37] In effect, Noyes skillfully used his communities, with their institutionalized combination of emotional distance and closeness, to overcome his inner divisions and establish a sense of worth and power.

II

John Humphrey Noyes was far more than an isolated individual propounding idiosyncratic, if very interesting, social and sexual theories. He was also the founder of a community that at its peak numbered some three hundred members at Oneida and its branch communities and successfully put his theories into practice for more than thirty years. One wonders, therefore, what kinds of people were attracted to Oneida and why. Did individuals who joined the group, as Maren Lockwood Carden suggests, have an unusual "psychological makeup" that led them to want to participate in the complex system at Oneida?[38] And, whatever their backgrounds, how did Oneida members adapt successfully to the social and sexual system there that broke up all exclusive personal relationships to focus primary attention on larger communal goals?

Fortunately, extensive primary and secondary records help us to begin to answer these questions. Robert Fogarty's analysis of the Oneida Community as an experiment in "conservative Christian utopianism" provides a particularly valuable starting point for such an analysis.[39] Fogarty uses the Oneida Family Register, a manuscript giving names and personal data on the first 111 people who joined the community, as well as U.S. census data from 1850 to 1880 and annual reports and newspapers printed at Oneida, to reconstruct backgrounds and histories of the members. From his work and from other sources, it becomes apparent that individuals were not attracted to the group because of any narrow social or psychological factors.

The most striking features of Oneida Community members were the careful process by which selection occurred and the extraordinarily high rate of retention. Although a few accessions to the group and a few defections from it would occur throughout the community's existence, 84 of the 109 adults who joined during the first two years at Oneida either died in the community or lived there until its breakup.[40] This impressive degree of membership stability was connected with the carefully selected character of the group. Members were deliberately chosen on the basis of complete loyalty to Noyes's leadership and to his perfectionist ideals. Members represented a wide range of occupational backgrounds, personality types, and special interests that could contribute to the success of the community. They came from most of the areas of New York and New England where sizable pockets of Noyes's perfectionist followers lived, and many of them were relatively affluent.[41] By 1857, for example, the members had invested almost $108,000 in the Oneida Community and its branches. Only such a large capital backing allowed the community to continue to function despite a loss of $40,000 during the initial decade before Oneida finally began to achieve financial stability.[42]

The psychological attraction of Oneida to new members can be briefly summarized. Most individuals for whom we have data were in an emotionally unsettled state when they joined the community. Usually they had been religious "seekers," distressed at repeatedly experiencing the emotional ups and downs of revivalistic religion. They yearned for release from this emotional roller coaster and thus were attracted by Noyes's promise to provide "salvation from sin" within a stable, supportive, and authoritative communal structure.[43] Interestingly, Oneida's sexual system does not appear to have been the major attraction for new members; indeed, in some cases it proved a deterrent to joining the group.[44] Despite the emotionally unsettled state of individuals when they entered Oneida, they do not appear to have had any special "character structure" that could differentiate them from the generality of Americans of their day. The detailed psychological critiques of Oneida Community members that were given in mutual criticism sessions and reported in the community newspaper from 1850 onward show the full range of human types, with almost every conceivable character strength and weakness. Oneidans, like converts to any religious or secular ideology which attempts a radical restructuring of the lives of its adherents, found Noyes's system appealing because it helped them to overcome the disorder they experienced and to become resocialized to a more secure and satisfying way of life.

How well did individuals at Oneida adjust to the constraints of the group's social and sexual system, especially the deliberate breaking up of all exclusive emotional relationships? Available evidence does suggest that the initial transition to complex marriage was turbulent. Once the initial transition was completed, however, individuals generally appear to have adapted well to communal living. Tendencies to return to "worldly" patterns were countered by the control mechanisms of male continence, mutual criticism, and ascending and descending fellowship. Even with its constraints, the community was anything but dour, gloomy, and ascetic. A wide variety of expressions of cultural and intellectual life were encouraged. Special activities ranged from spirited dancing to community-produced plays, musical events, and skits that helped to vary the normal routine and keep the community lively.[45] Noyes's son Pierrepont recalled: "The grown folks seemed almost as bent on being happy as they did on being good. Everyone worked; almost everyone seemed to have time for play, or perhaps I should say recreation."[48] For more than two decades, life at Oneida would continue to follow a basically tranquil course.

III

Despite its many strengths, the Oneida Community eventually experienced sufficient internal and external tension that it terminated both its complex marriage and its communistic economic systems by the early 1880s. What were the chief factors contributing to the end of complex marriage and the breakup of the community? This complicated but fascinating question is analyzed more fully in chapter 7, so here I shall present only the briefest possible summary before discussing the larger significance of the Oneida experiment.

The Oneida Community can in many ways be considered as the lengthened shadow of one man—John Humphrey Noyes. So long as Noyes retained his ability to lead, the community prospered. By the late 1870s, however, Noyes's leadership was faltering, and no other individuals were able to pull together an increasingly divided community. Thus, when an external campaign against the community was launched in the mid-1870s, the Oneida Community was no longer confident of its mission and the loyalty of its members. Rather than risk an externally induced breakdown of the community, leaders of the group acted skillfully in August 1879 to terminate their distinctive sexual arrangements while they could still be counted a success. Little more than a year later, on January 1, 1881, the community formally ended its communal economic system, reorganizing as a joint-stock corporation in which former community members held shares. Thus ended the communal phase of one of the most remarkable religious and economic experiments in American history.

What, in conclusion, is the larger significance of John Humphrey Noyes and his Oneida Community from a psychological perspective? The major interest of the experiment lies in the interplay between the experiences and perceptions of Noyes, the eccentric genius who founded and inspired the group, and the ideology and practices he introduced at Oneida. Because Noyes was in many respects fundamentally outside the normative world of the 1830s and 1840s, he was able to experience that world freshly, avoiding many of the easy assumptions about human sexuality made both by his contemporaries and by individuals today. Nevertheless, Noyes was deeply influenced by many prevailing attitudes and beliefs of his time, and he sometimes accentuated tendencies such as the developing Victorian emphasis on male self-control in sexual relations.

Ultimately, however, Noyes sought to achieve a balance between opposing tendencies of his time. He attempted to develop a wholesome and unified form of communal life that would demonstrate the validity of his views in practice. By gathering a loyal following and setting up a community that put his new synthesis of truth into practice, Noyes was able to overcome his personal insecurities and project onto the world a creative vision of human potentialities that still deserves attention today.

6

FREE LOVE and FEMINISM

John Humphrey Noyes and the Oneida Community

*A*S ONE OF THE VERY FEW EXAMPLES in human history of a long-lived system of group marriage (somewhat misleadingly described both by community founder John Humphrey Noyes and by his critics as "free love"), the Oneida Community in central New York State has provoked continuing curiosity and lively discussion. Certainly no question has been more hotly debated than Noyes's attitudes toward sexual expression and women's role.

One popular approach has been to portray Noyes as part of the vanguard of sexual liberation and women's rights—a man ahead of his time whose efforts have much to say to us today. This approach seems plausible at first view. Oneida did represent one of the most radical institutional efforts to change relations between the sexes and improve women's status in America. Women at Oneida were freed from the fear of unwanted pregnancies through elaborate birth control practices called male continence, and they were liberated from the strains of child care through a system of communal child rearing. They wore a functional, Bloomer-type outfit, cut their hair short, and were able to engage in virtually any type of community work they wished. They participated in the daily religious-and-business meetings at Oneida and actively helped shape communal policy. And through a system of "complex" or group marriage, they were freed from the double standard and given basic equality in sexual expression with men of the community. From such a perspective, Oneida appears as a sort of idyllic utopia which successfully solved many of the problems of women's role and relations between the sexes that still trouble us today.[1]

In contrast to this highly positive view, much of the recent literature on Oneida has seen Noyes as a seriously disturbed individual who vacillated between extreme license and excessive concerns for sexual control. The community at Oneida, far from being part of the vanguard of sexual liberation, was repressive and definitely unfree. Important but seriously flawed studies of Oneida from contemporary feminist perspectives conclude that, in the last analysis, Noyes was a male chauvinist and his community a disappointment to those seeking true equality.[2]

This viewpoint, too, has much to recommend it at first sight. While it is true that Noyes was concerned to improve relations between the sexes, he certainly was no feminist. On numerous occasions, he bluntly and unambiguously stated that he believed men were superior to women. Indeed, he went so far as to argue that the superiority of masculine to feminine principles was inherent in the nature of the universe. He declared, for example, that in his dual godhead, composed of the Father and the Son, the Son stood in a relationship of cooperative subordination to the Father similar to the relationship that should exist between men and women.[3] Noyes's Bloomer outfit was instituted, against the wishes of many community women, to "crucify the dress spirit," as he put it, and to contribute to the realization of his ultimate ideal that woman would become "what she ought to be, a *female man*" (emphasis in original).[4] Noyes's eugenics experiment, involving selective breeding of members within his community, was justified in terms that would cause any feminist to cringe.[5] And in his newspapers, Noyes clearly and articulately criticized the contemporary women's rights movement. Though he felt that the movement had identified real problems, he was convinced that its approach to changing relations between the sexes was wrong.[6]

How is one to account for such widely divergent interpretations of Noyes and his relationship to women's issues? Was Noyes a chauvinist, a liberator of women, or perhaps both? The frequent appearance of these two interpretations of Noyes in the literature suggests that there is probably some valid basis for each of them, but the very existence of two such seemingly contradictory views also suggests

that a vital element is being left out of each analysis. Both the interpretations of Noyes as liberator and as chauvinist fail because they
take into account only a fragment of the evidence. They judge Noyes
from external perspectives that do not fully apply to his experiment,
instead of trying to understand what he himself was attempting to do
and how well he succeeded in his own terms.

This analysis began with the assumption that any community as
unconventional as Oneida could not have survived and prospered for
more than thirty years by accident. A functioning system as demanding as complex marriage must have been based on some coherent
philosophy and the ability to realize that philosophy in practice. A
close reading of Noyes's thoughtful and well-formulated critique of
his society suggests that he was not a Dr. Jekyll and Mr. Hyde character, but rather a man who eventually combined many contradictory elements of his culture into a new and effective synthesis. As
Whitney Cross, foremost interpreter of turbulent western New York
before the Civil War, has noted, the Oneida Community represents
"the keystone in the arch of Burned-over District history, demonstrating the connection between enthusiasms of the right and those
of the left."[7]

I

Underlying Noyes's whole life and sense of mission was a deep-seated
concern to overcome the social and intellectual disorder that he experienced both in his own life and in the world around him. The
areas of New England and western New York where Noyes had his
formative emotional and intellectual experiences were undergoing
rapid economic growth, unstable social conditions, and sharply conflicting religious movements. John Humphrey Noyes, a precocious
and strong-willed yet socially maladept and painfully shy child, was
particularly jarred by the cacophony of ideas and causes that surrounded him. Ultimately he reached the extraordinary conclusion
that he was uniquely responsible for achieving a new religious and
social synthesis—both for himself and for others. As he declared in a
letter in 1837, "God has set me to cast up a highway across this

chaos, and I am gathering out the stones and grading the track as fast as possible."[8]

How was this new order to be achieved? Like many millennial revivalists of his day, Noyes felt that the old order was so radically diseased and corrupt that no external social, economic, or political palliatives by themselves would suffice to set things straight. The underlying problem was a crisis in values. The first priority, therefore, was to establish a new set of common values, to achieve "right relations with God," as Noyes put it.[9] Toward this end, Noyes developed a complex set of religious perfectionist principles and then wandered throughout New York and New England with the aim of eventually converting the entire world to his idiosyncratic and heretical views. The effort, predictably, was a failure. Noyes therefore decided to retrench. He returned to his home in Putney, Vermont, and there started first a Bible School, then a Society of Inquiry, and finally a full-scale community, which ultimately would become the Oneida Community. Beginning at Putney, Noyes sought to get his followers to internalize his new values that stressed the subordination of the individual and his or her private, selfish interests to the good of the larger community as interpreted by Noyes. The greed, individualism, and conflict that threatened to tear the broader society apart must be overcome by developing a cooperative, Gemeinschaft-type community, which Noyes envisioned as essentially an enlarged family. Only after such basic communal harmony was established could other pressing social problems be addressed effectively.[10]

If reestablishing "right relations with God," or a sense of common values, was the first priority for Noyes, then a second, closely related goal was reestablishing "right relations between the sexes."[11] As a painfully shy young adult, Noyes had struggled to understand his own impulses and to determine why so many of the perfectionists with whom he associated were engaged in such erratic and often self-destructive sexual experimentation. The existing marriage system was unsatisfactory, he concluded; "the law of marriage worketh wrath."[12] Unrealistic and unnatural restrictions were being placed on relations between the sexes. In marriage, women were held in a form of slavelike domestic bondage, while their husbands toiled away in an uncertain and highly competitive external world.[13] Romantic love and the monogamous family merely accentuated the disruptive individualism present in other areas of social life. In a sort of "egotism for two," monogamous family interests were pitted against those of the larger society.[14] Most serious of all, men acted as though they owned their wives, as though their wives were a form of property. Noyes felt, instead, that sexual and emotional exclusiveness between the sexes should be done away with. Cooperation should replace disruptive conflict. Within the ideal order he was attempting to set up, sexual relations should be fundamentally restructured so that loyalty could be raised to the level of the entire community.[15]

The details of this remarkable effort at reorganizing marriage and family relations have been treated in many accounts and need not concern us again here. What does need to be stressed, however, is both the systematic and the institutionally radical character of Noyes's innovations. Noyes first conceived the idea of complex marriage a full nine years before beginning to put it into practice in 1846.[16] With a strong sense of responsibility for the social consequences of his ideas, he was unwilling to break down the old order until he was certain that he had something better to put in its place and that he stood a reasonable chance of getting the new ways adopted. Thus measures such as group-criticism sessions and a system of birth control through *coitus reservatus* were developed to ensure that complex marriage, when it was instituted, would not lead to private experimentation and a reduction in loyalty to the community. Once basic community loyalty and the necessary institutional supports had been established, Noyes proceeded to introduce the practice of complex marriage and a variety of other radical changes that attempted to do away with all nonintrinsic distinctions between the sexes.[17] Women were formally freed to participate in almost all aspects of community religious, economic, and social life, in contrast to the far greater restrictions that they faced in the outside world. Within the limits necessary to maintain the primary loyalty to the larger communal order, all individuals were encouraged to develop their highest capacities. Few societies in human history have done more to break down arbitrary distinctions between the sexes than did Oneida.[18]

It might initially seem paradoxical that this significant revision of sex roles and rise in women's status at Oneida should have been accomplished in the face of John Humphrey Noyes's formal belief in the superiority of men over women. The chief reason this could occur was that Noyes's primary concern was not with male and female authority patterns per se, but rather with establishing his own personal authority over all his followers, both men and women. So long as Noyes's male and female followers unquestioningly acknowledged his paternalistic, God-like authority, he was prepared to be flexible in delegating that authority and making major changes in the interests of both sexes.[19] No one way of organizing relations between the sexes was sacrosanct; the underlying spirit rather than any specific external forms was Noyes's concern.[20]

In effect, therefore, both men and women at Oneida shared a common personal and religious commitment that radically undercut normal social restrictions. Woman's primary responsibility was not to her husband or to her children, but to God—and all souls were ultimately equal before God.[21] While it was true that St. Paul had said that wives should be subject to their husbands in this life, he had also said that there is "neither male nor female in the Lord."[22] Because the Oneida Community was attempting to realize a heavenly pattern on earth, the conventional juxtaposition of male superiority and female inferiority no longer had much significance for them. If some women were, in fact, spiritually superior to some men—as they recognizably were—then they should exercise more authority at Oneida than *those* men.

Thus, instead of stressing gender as the basis for authority at Oneida, life in the community gradually came to be governed by a philosophy of "ascending and descending fellowship," in which those of higher "spirituality" exercised more authority than those of lesser attainments. Noyes was at the top, along with a handful of the most spiritual men, who oversaw most major decisions. These men cooperated closely with the most spiritual women, who in turn were above the less spiritual men, who were above the less spiritual women, and so forth. Those who were seen as more spiritual generally were older than the less spiritual, so there was an implicit age factor operating in determining community status. Because it was considered desirable to associate with those higher in the ascending fellowship, higher-status individuals had access to a larger range of sexual contacts than did lower-status members. Children appear to have entered into this hierarchy of ascending and descending fellowship at puberty and sexual initiation, and at least during their teens and twenties they were expected to associate sexually with older, more spiritual men and women.[23] In these and other ways, authority relations between men and women were restructured at Oneida.

II

Even though Noyes may have succeeded in resolving problems that he and his followers faced by setting up an experimental community, the question still remains whether his activities had anything to say to the larger society and its concerns. Was the Oneida Community simply a "utopian retreat," a way of avoiding serious consideration of the complex problems of American society?[24] Noyes did not think so. In the first place, he was a communitarian reformer, who viewed his efforts as a sort of pilot project that might provide a model for the regeneration of the larger society. "Great oaks from little acorns grow," and similarly a relatively small community like Oneida could well have an influence far larger than its size might indicate.[25] Moreover, even when Noyes began to realize that his specific community model would never be accepted by American society, he still felt that the *philosophy* underlying his approach to social change was the best one. Difficult social issues should be solved by cooperative means—by finding a synthesis that would serve the interests of all groups— rather than by seeking further to polarize class, sex, or political factions against each other. Although he recognized that both an inner change of attitude and an outer change of institutions were essential for successful reform, Noyes felt that a change of attitude, a restoration of mutual confidence in the basic goodwill of all parties must come first.[26]

Noyes reached out to the world with these ideas by means of his newspapers, which he viewed as even more important than his communal efforts. From his conversion to perfectionism in 1834 until his formal retirement as head of the Oneida Community in 1877, he was almost continually involved in publishing his views to the world. During the troubled early days at Oneida, Noyes made it clear that if he were forced to sacrifice either his newspaper or his community, he would sacrifice the latter so that he could continue to issue his paper.[27] And when he finally gave up direct control over Oneida, Noyes chose to continue as editor of his all-important newspaper.

Noyes always retained an avid and well-informed interest in the events of the outer world. He commented shrewdly and incisively on the many pressing issues of his day, including the women's rights movement. The following paragraphs suggest how Noyes's overall approach to social reform was reflected in his attitudes toward antebellum feminism.

Two main points should be stressed about Noyes's response to the contemporary women's rights movement. In the first place, Noyes was genuinely sympathetic to many of the basic goals of antebellum feminists. He not only agreed that relations between the sexes were out of joint, but he also felt that a major reason for that disruption was the restricted role assigned to women. As a former abolitionist with ties to William Lloyd Garrison, he explicitly compared a woman's status to that of a slave and used other language as vivid as that of the most militant feminists. Women's rights concerns and activities, both before and after the 1848 Seneca Falls conference, were reported in an essentially sympathetic fashion in his newspapers.[28] Such writing was more than mere rhetoric unsupported by action. Noyes saw himself as a figure with a mission to free women (as well as men) from servitude to stereotyped behaviors and attitudes, and he made specific and often highly controversial changes at every level of community life to end discrimination against women, encourage their participation, and reestablish harmonious relations between the sexes.

Yet although Noyes was in general agreement with much of the feminist diagnosis of the illness affecting relations between men and women, he was in sharp disagreement with its prescription for the cure. Feminist stridency and emphasis on conflict between the sexes as a method of social change particularly repelled him and his followers. A note in the community newspaper in 1850, for example, mentioned a women's rights convention in Ohio at which Elizabeth Cady Stanton spoke and compared married women's legal status to that of slaves. The paper editorialized: "There is an oblique pointing at the truth in this statement, but it is far from probing the real depths of the case. . . . What is really wanted is to be able to live under the government of God, to establish mutually satisfying relations between the sexes."[29] Elsewhere, in an article entitled "Woman-Suppression," Noyes made clear that he was as strongly opposed to the current legal restrictions on women as any feminist: "Woman needs surely to be emancipated—to be permitted to stand up as a responsible individual in society; and any statute or institution that denies this privilege cannot long stand before the scrutiny of the age."[30] The point was to achieve the necessary and desirable changes in the right manner, one that would contribute to restoring harmonious relations between all parties involved in the conflict.

Like conservatives such as Catharine Beecher, who helped to articulate and establish the Victorian synthesis, with its emphasis on the family, domesticity, and women's power in the home sphere, Noyes felt that the whole social order was threatening to come apart. New and more satisfying roles for men and women must be established, but this should be done in such a way that the divisiveness and conflict that were already so rampant in society could be minimized. Noyes achieved such a new synthesis for himself and his followers by creating a communal family at Oneida. The larger society, in the meantime, achieved much the same effect by making use of the nuclear family in conjunction with larger institutional agencies for social control such as churches, schools, and asylums. The specifics of their programs might differ, but in a curious way both Noyes and the larger Victorian society were alike in seeking to use essentially conservative means to achieve ways of life that differed greatly from those that had come before.[31]

Thus, although John Humphrey Noyes chose an unorthodox *form* for his new social order, the *methods* that he used had much in common with those of the larger society. Any functioning social order, Noyes declared, must seek to maintain a harmonious balance between "the two great principles of human existence"—"solidarity," on the one hand, and "liberty," on the other. Though at times these principles may appear antagonistic, "like the centripetal and centrifugal forces in nature," they are, in fact, "designed to act upon human life in equilibrium."[32] Put another way, a period of rapid social change leads to centrifugal tendencies—complaints and cries for reform by crusading minorities—yet, in a healthy society, such "useful fanatics" (as one writer described them) eventually find their main ideas absorbed and integrated into a new social and intellectual consensus.[33] Depending on the sensitivity and skill of the leadership, fundamental social change thus can sometimes be achieved—either in small-scale communities or in the larger society—by individuals like Noyes who consider themselves essentially conservative.

III

What, then, was the larger significance of Noyes's effort to reorganize male and female sex roles at Oneida? To what extent did he succeed in embodying his ideals in practice? The ambivalence expressed in many recent feminist attempts to address these questions does not appear to result primarily from lack of factual information, but seems instead to be connected with ambivalence among feminists about what, in fact, they really want today. Is contemporary "liberation" for women to be achieved by women simply taking on the same roles and activities as men? Or does such liberation primarily involve freeing women to choose whatever they really want to do, including, in some cases, assume domestic roles? Or is liberation to be based on other criteria which either combine or go beyond these? Until feminists can consciously and consistently address such questions, their attempts to evaluate how successful Oneida was from a feminist perspective are likely to continue to prove inconclusive.

One brilliant attempt to understand the status and self-perception of women at Oneida from a new perspective that resolves some of the above dichotomies is presented in a recent article by Ellen Wayland-Smith.[34] She begins with Carol Gilligan's psychological perspectives,[35] which suggest that women's early developmental experiences stress connection or an ongoing relationship while men's stress individuation and separation. These differing early experiences incline men to try to resolve moral dilemmas using a doctrine of individual rights or noninterference, while women are more concerned with response and a preservation of connection. Ironically, women's emphasis on connection and inclusion becomes both a strength and a weakness. The traditionally lauded "feminine" virtues of self-sacrifice and care are simultaneously the very qualities that militate against women's "development" into adults by male standards of separation. As Gilligan characterizes the conflict, "The exercise of. . . . choice brings her [the woman] privately into conflict with the conventions of femininity, particularly the moral equation of goodness with self-sacrifice. Although independent assertion in judgment and action is considered to be the hallmark of adulthood, it is rather in their care and concern for others that women have both judged themselves and judged others."[36]

Wayland-Smith argues that when John Humphrey Noyes emphasized that the "liberty of unity" was superior to the "liberty of independence" at Oneida, "he phrased the moral problem in feminine language."[37] The model he held up for both his male and female followers was essentially a feminine one. In contrast to the dominant nineteenth-century American emphasis on "rights" and "individual liberties," Noyes argued that only those who had overcome personal selfishness and subordinated themselves to the good of the whole could be truly "free" and happy. "Thus, it is possible that Noyes's system helped women resolve this conflict [between individualism and connection]."[38] Wayland-Smith suggests, using extensive primary writings by women at Oneida, that by putting into practice a society emphasizing an ethic of connection and self-sacrifice to maintain the good of the group, Noyes helped to bolster women's self-perceptions, allowing them a richer and more fully integrated experience than most women in the outer world found possible.

Whether Wayland-Smith's analysis is correct or not,[39] perhaps the greatest value of Oneida for contemporary feminists is that it highlights a host of important questions about how best to organize relations between the sexes—without providing any definitive answers to them. For more than thirty years at Oneida, John Humphrey Noyes and his followers struggled with complex issues of social organization, not simply in theory but also in practice. They made attempts to modify extremely deep-seated sexual attitudes and behavior patterns, and they made important (if ultimately temporary) changes in the relations between men and women. But Noyes and his followers certainly did not achieve an egalitarian millennium (nor was that their intention). Those historians who would treat the Oneida experiment as a "failure" simply because it did not achieve absolute perfection (in whatever sense perfection is being judged) are unrealistic in their expectations and in their understanding of the way in which social change takes place. Noyes was a doer as well as a thinker. He sought, as much as possible, to approximate his ideal community, but

he was also aware of the limitations and strengths of the human beings with whom he was working.

In conclusion, therefore, a full understanding of John Humphrey Noyes's attitudes toward women and the women's movement
must place those views within the larger context of his overall concerns for social order and the effective change of social institutions.
Restoring right relations between the sexes was an important goal for
Noyes, but it was always secondary to his broader concerns for
achieving religious and social revitalization.[40] Perhaps Noyes's evaluation of his mission as that of a true conservative seeking fundamental social change may serve as a fitting summary of the significance
of his work. He wrote:

> The truth is, all present institutions are growths from an imper-
> fect society and are adapted only to a transition state. This is
> true of religious as well as political institutions, marriage as well
> as slavery. The spirit of heaven in order to fulfill its full devel-
> opment in this world requires that we be ready to forsake all
> institutions adapted to the selfish state of society, and to expect
> something new and better. A truly conservative man therefore
> will be ready for change. He will not violently or unwisely at-
> tack any present institutions, but he will be ready and on the
> lookout for change.[41]

John Humphrey Noyes, his communities, and his philosophy deserve
the serious scholarly attention that they have only recently begun
to receive.

7

THE RISE and FALL of UTOPIA

The Oneida Community Crises of 1852 and 1879

O N MARCH 7, 1852, the four-year-old Oneida Community in central New York State made an unexpected announcement in response to internal and external pressure against its controversial complex-marriage system. The community declared that it still believed that its system was vindicated "in reason and in conscience" but that to avoid giving offense to the surrounding society, the community and its branches "have receded from the practical assertion of their views, and formally resumed the marriage morality of the world, submitting themselves to all ordinances and restrictions of society and law on this subject." The community went on to say that it viewed this step as only a temporary one which would last until there was a "change of public feeling" that would gradually extend the "area of freedom tolerated." Yet the announcement also conveyed a sense that one chapter of the group's story had been completed; the community had let "its previous activities pass into history." Nevertheless, six months later, on August 29, 1852, the community announced that it was resuming all its distinctive practices, including complex marriage. For more than a quarter of a century, the Oneida Community would successfully practice its extraordinary marriage system.[1]

Twenty-seven years later, on August 28, 1879, the Oneida Community made an announcement that was remarkably similar to that of 1852. In the face of rising internal dissension and external pressure against complex marriage, the community declared once again that it would discontinue the practice of complex marriage, "not as renouncing belief in the principles and prospective finality of that institution, but in deference to the public sentiment which is evidently rising against it." In a further statement on September 4, the community also declared that "its present social position and its future course, whatever they may be, have no power to change the facts of the past; and the more these are studied, the more remarkable they will appear."[2] Despite such announced uncertainty about the "future course" of the community's "social" (i.e., sexual) practices and the desire of many members to continue complex marriage, this second discontinuance of complex marriage proved permanent. Indeed, only sixteen months later, on January 1, 1881, the community underwent a total dissolution, giving up its system of communal living entirely and reorganizing as a joint-stock corporation.

The tone and substance of these two announcements in 1852 and 1879 were much alike, yet the results in practice were strikingly dissimilar. In the first case, the Oneida Community was able to re-establish its sense of mission and cohesion, going on to experience a distinguished career as one of the best-known and most controversial communal experiments in American history. In the second case, the announcement served primarily as an epitaph for this extraordinary venture in communal living. What accounts for these different outcomes in the same group twenty-seven years apart? Why did the community weather its crisis in one case and fail to do so in the other?

The issue of why so-called utopian communities "succeed" or "fail" has long fascinated both scholars and the general public. John Humphrey Noyes, the founder of the Oneida Community, himself discussed this issue perceptively and at length in his 1870 *History of American Socialisms*. In the wake of the revival of interest in communal experimentation in the 1960s, Rosabeth Kanter and others put forward influential sociological explanations for the success and failure of ventures in communal living. Most recently, the anthropologist Jon Wagner has suggested in a provocative article that most scholarly attempts to determine the success or failure of communal experiments have been unconvincing, begging the most interesting philosophical questions about how such judgments can or should be made.[3]

This chapter will not focus on the most common question raised by scholars—the differences *between* groups, why some groups last longer or are more successful than others. Instead, I shall high-light the factors *within* one group that allowed it to sustain its distinc-tive life-style in one instance but caused it to give up that life-style permanently in the other. I shall try to analyze these complex devel-opments from the perspective of the Oneida Community itself, judg-ing the degree of success or failure of the group primarily in terms of its own goals rather than the goals that scholars may argue the group *ought* to have pursued. More than most communal experiment-ers, members of the Oneida Community were exceptionally self-conscious about what they were trying to do and how well they were doing it. Far from seeing their efforts as a static, unchanging, uto-pian attempt to achieve embalmed perfection, the Oneida perfec-tionists always stressed the necessity for progressive change and a never-ending process of development to achieve their goals. The ex-periences at Oneida thus suggest larger issues and concerns of signif-icance to all those desiring to achieve radical social change or create a "permanent revolution."

I

Crisis was nothing new to John Humphrey Noyes or his followers at Oneida in 1852. Indeed, crisis had been an almost constant part of Noyes's life since his conversion in February 1834 to perfectionism, the belief that a progressive process of achieving "perfect holiness" was possible on earth. Faced with his inability to convince others of the truth of his new convictions, Noyes in May 1834 experienced three emotionally devastating weeks in New York City, during which he plumbed the depths of suffering and came to the verge of total mental collapse. Although he partially recovered from this psychic distress, Noyes found the succeeding three years exceptionally diffi-cult as he wandered erratically around New York State and New En-gland, trying unsuccessfully to convert the world to his highly unorthodox religious beliefs. The unauthorized publication in 1837 of portions of a private letter in which Noyes advocated sexual freedom in the holy Christian community caused him temporarily to lose vir-tually all his remaining followers. Nevertheless, in the succeeding decade Noyes rebounded by publishing a series of newspapers defend-ing his views and by establishing a small core group of nearly forty followers in his hometown of Putney, Vermont.[4]

The Putney Community, as the group came to be known, experienced a modest degree of success, despite continuing internal and external tensions. By the mid-1840s, the group was moving toward communism of property—and of persons. The first recorded practice of complex marriage on a limited scale began in 1846. The formal announcement in 1847 of the group's sexual experimentation (even though that announcement was couched in veiled terms) outraged some members of the group and of the town of Putney. Noyes was indicted on two specific counts of adultery, and rather than face a possible lynching or a conviction, he left the state, forfeiting his $2,000 bond. Early in 1848, Noyes and his Putney loyalists started over again on a farm owned by one of his supporters in Oneida, New York. Noyes, optimistic about the future despite the recent setbacks, also at that time wrote his extraordinary manifesto presenting his social and sexual theories, which he published and sent out to leading public figures in New York and New England. Despite all the turmoil, Oneida grew rapidly. By January 1849, the original nucleus of Putney perfectionists had expanded to 87; by February 1850, the number had risen to 172; and by February 1851, the total reached 205. No one at the time, however, could have predicted that this little group and its sister community founded at Wallingford, Connecticut, in 1851, would survive for nearly thirty more years with a core group of some 300 individuals participating in its controversial religious and social system.[5]

Before we can understand the 1852 crisis that followed, we must first understand Noyes's key religious and social beliefs, the means by which he was attempting to spread those beliefs, and the initial controversies resulting from attempts to implement those beliefs in community living. Fundamentally, Noyes's religious and social experiments represented an attempt to overcome the religious and social disorder that he and his followers had experienced in the rapidly expanding America of his day. Noyes had three underlying objectives. They were to achieve: (1) "right relations with God," a common set of religious values for himself and for his followers; (2) "right relations between the sexes" that would allow men and women to live together harmoniously; and (3) "right economic relations" that would overcome the disruptive "dog-eat-dog" capitalism of early nineteenth-century America. The achievement of these three objectives, Noyes argued, was a precondition for the realization of a fourth goal, the full establishment of the millennium, the literal kingdom of heaven on earth. The stages leading to that final goal were not static, but progressive and ever-changing. Perfection of spirit, the correct inner attitude demanded by God, might be basically unchanging once one had achieved "salvation from sin," but the external social arrangements necessary to implement that perfection of attitude in practice were constantly changing and would continue to change, even after the establishment of the millennium.[6]

How did Noyes hope to achieve these ambitious goals? He had two chief means. The first was to spread his ideas through the newspapers he published, and the second was to establish his ideas in practice among a community or communities of his followers. Although the communitarian side of Noyes's experimentation has attracted the greatest attention, he himself always gave primacy to the publication of his newspapers as a means of getting his ideas before the world. As the Oneida Community declared in its *Third Annual Report* in 1852, "the publication of truth shall be our central business objective around which all other industrial interests shall organize."[7] Noyes's communities were thus in his mind chiefly important as the vehicle by which publication of truth as he understood it was possible. In addition, however, the communities were profoundly important in themselves. They provided a laboratory through which Noyes's ideals could be realized in practice and a core group of followers who directly affirmed Noyes's key role as God's chief spokesman on earth.[8]

Because the social practices implemented at Oneida were so controversial and demanding, a word must be said about them if we are to understand the 1852 crisis. As part of his effort to reestablish a holy community of Christians on earth, Noyes argued that such a community would eliminate exclusive sexual relations. Instead, his followers would consider themselves married to the entire group in a "complex marriage" in which love, including heterosexual love among adults, could be expressed freely among the entire community. The specific arrangements that made possible this complex marriage—including birth control by *coitus reservatus*, group criticism sessions, and an informal status hierarchy known as "ascending and descending fellowship"—were developed gradually during the decade at Putney and only began to be fully implemented in 1847, shortly before the departure for Oneida.[9]

The effort to implement these controversial new beliefs in practice caused many difficulties. That all was not well at Putney and Oneida between 1846 and 1852 is suggested by numerous exhortations in the community newspapers during these years to unquestioning obedience, unity, love, harmony, right devotion, and the like. Psychosomatic illnesses and faith cures were frequently discussed, and several cases of temporary insanity and suicidal tendencies were mentioned. In 1849, about a year after the founding of the Oneida Community, Noyes—who typically tried to absent himself from conflict situations he could not handle—moved with the nucleus of his most loyal Putney followers to a small community outpost in Brooklyn, New York. He lived there for most of the time between 1849 and 1854, when John Miller, who had been the primary leader at Oneida, died. During those years, and particularly once he formally resumed editorship of his newspaper in 1851, Noyes wrote with a surprising degree of distance from his communal ventures. In his column "Ideas from the Communes," for instance, he seemed to write with an observer's detachment about his own "associated communities" at Oneida, New York; Wallingford, Connecticut; Newark, New Jersey; and Cambridge and Putney, Vermont.[10]

One has the sense that in this period, Noyes, deeply afraid of failure or loss of control, was hedging his bets. Faced with uncertainty in his communal ventures, he seemed to be returning to his first concern—getting his ideas before the public through his newspapers. He left the difficult task of translating those values into communal life to capable subordinates who had internalized his values. This pattern would persist throughout the life of the Oneida Community. Between 1842 and 1880, Noyes spent only about half his time at Putney and Oneida, and he typically left at times of major stress.[11] In retrospect, this appears to have been the best thing he could have done. Few prophets have sufficient wisdom to know when to step partially aside after they have established the value foundations of their communities and leave the pragmatic problems of implementing their ideals to capable subordinates. As a distant figure above the battle, Noyes and his ideas could serve as a unifying force in times of conflict.

External pressures also contributed to community tensions during this period. In 1850 and 1851, grand juries in Oneida and Madison counties, on whose boundaries the community was located, heard complaints about the perfectionists from their enemies, probably including seceders. The exemplary deportment of community members, who answered highly personal questions freely and honestly, helped defuse the hostility, and influential local power figures also interceded on their behalf.[12] The success of the community in weathering this crisis was partly attributable to its circumspectness in not actively seeking new members at Oneida and thereby avoiding the explosive hostilities that the vigorous search for local members at Putney had entailed. The exigencies of successfully establishing as difficult a system as complex marriage thus necessitated a move away from Noyes's desire to convert the entire world toward a more restricted goal of establishing a tightly knit, internally unified community. Such an order could not be established if there were too many new people joining the community or leaving it all the time.[13]

Even in a small and tightly knit community, however, establishing a radical alternative to monogamous marriage was no easy task. On October 3, 1850, a letter published from a perfectionist in Wisconsin bitterly asked "from the depths of my soul" why the Oneida Community should insist on maintaining unorthodox sexual practices that alienated many potential converts to holiness. In reply, John Miller simply asserted that their sexual theory was a part of the demands of God; it could not be accepted or rejected on opportunistic grounds.[14] This unprecedented newspaper airing of opposition to Noyes's sexual theories among his following suggests deep divisions within his community. It is quite possible that Noyes's decision to resume formal editorship of his newspaper in 1851 was in part an attempt to avoid losing control over *both* his newspaper and his communities in the face of deep-seated opposition to his policies.

II

The peak of the early difficulties over the institutionalization of complex marriage, and the beginning of the resolution of those problems, apparently came between March and August 1852. There is compelling evidence that during those six months complex marriage was temporarily discontinued at Oneida. The obvious external reason for this abrupt change was an all-out newspaper crusade launched by the New York religious paper *The Observer* and supported by other papers. On March 7, 1852, evidently in response to this pressure, the Oneida *Circular* made the surprise announcement that despite its continuing commitment to its system, the community was temporarily discontinuing the practice of complex marriage until public feeling moderated. By this action, the community declared, it was graphically demonstrating that it was "not attached to forms," even to its own. "To be able to conform to *any* circumstances, and *any* institutions, and still preserve spiritual freedom" was the goal of the perfectionists. The community's new efforts would be devoted to the establishment of a free press and to what must appear a most puzzling objective indeed—the "abolition of death."[15]

What is one to make of this remarkable announcement? To begin with, there is every reason to believe that the practice of complex marriage was, in fact, discontinued during this period. Although "Bible Secretiveness" might sanction speaking in a sort of code language or not telling a hostile public the whole truth, Noyes and his followers were invariably honest when they made direct, factual assertions. Furthermore, numerous articles over the next six months either directly or indirectly support the contention that complex marriage was temporarily discontinued at this time.[16] Had it continued to be secretly practiced, community dissidents probably would have passed on that information to a hostile press. And it is significant that in looking back at the final discontinuance of complex marriage in 1879, which was said at the time to be only a temporary move as well, Abel Easton noted that "on more than one occasion previously, in the presence of sickness in the family or of persecution or other causes, John H. Noyes proposed that the Community as a body consider itself under criticism, and proclaim a fast from conjugal freedom. . . . Such seasons of fasting sometimes lasted a few days or *six months*, and they were strictly observed by all."[17] The six months between early March and late August 1852 is the only period when there is any indication of such a lengthy suspension of complex marriage at Oneida. And if a six-month suspension in fact took place in 1852, it would appear to have been both a response to external pressure and a reaction to a sense of internal malaise for which communal penance was necessary.

A further key to the motivation behind this apparent retreat from complex marriage is Noyes's enigmatic observation that for a time the primary efforts of the community would be devoted to the "abolition of death" rather than to marriage reform. A later article reasserts this primary concern, clearly indicating that "death" was being used in a special sense: If this attack on "death" be madness, yet there is a method to it.[18] In fact, when Noyes speaks of trying to "abolish death," he usually is referring to his efforts to overcome sickness and ill health, especially mental and emotional disorders. Such psychologically related ailments are the first that must be eliminated if the "King of Terrors" is eventually to lose his hold over the mind and spirit of man.[19]

Thus what Noyes may be saying here, in his own special code language to be understood by his followers but not by the outside world, is that for a time, the severe mental and emotional problems (many of them associated with the introduction of complex marriage) are to be the primary concern of the community. This interpretation also is supported by the number of articles appearing during this period on topics such as nervousness, faith and unbelief, insanity, spiritualist excesses, inattention, the uselessness of self-condemnation, problems of insubordination, and the like. The Oneida Community appears to have been deliberately retrenching, performing an internal and external penance that would prepare a solid foundation for a second and successful effort to reintroduce the practice of complex marriage later.

Noyes was also faced with the threat of internal insubordination and even apostasy during this period. The problems of "bridling sensuality" and placing such drives at the service of the larger purposes of the community are discussed in numerous articles. Noyes himself did not always appear to be contributing to the solution of such problems when he wrote in enthusiastic terms of God being "married to matter" and the like.[20] A concrete threat of outright apostasy also existed. In late March and early April 1852, two articles appeared on Judas Iscariot, who "was not merely an unprincipled traitor, but a positive rival of Christ." The articles make it clear that a high community member was seen as playing the role of Judas.[21]

In these articles, the community Judas is portrayed as one whose sin was that of "covetousness"—of affections. His character is contrasted with that of the Mary who impulsively anointed Christ with expensive ointment. This Mary, and her community counterpart, "had little worldly prudence. Her love exceeded her discretion, She was found at Jesus' feet, absorbed in his discoursing," abandoned "to the attractions of her heart—a dangerous susceptibility in the case of misplaced affections, but her glory as a follower of Christ. This led her, at the loss of dignity, into that wonderful gratitude and love, which Christ promised should be recorded of her as a memorial of praise to all generations." But Judas, with his base, uncomprehending heart, could not appreciate Mary's "tribute of affection," and so betrayed Christ for a paltry thirty pieces of silver to the public authorities.

There can be little doubt as to the identity of the community members whose relationship was obliquely discussed in these articles. Almost certainly, George Cragin, a member of the central committee and one of Noyes's earliest followers, stood in the place of Judas; his wife, Mary Cragin, who first inspired Noyes in 1846 to begin the actual practice of complex marriage, was represented by the wayward Mary whose devotion to Christ brought her everlasting glory; and, of course, John Humphrey Noyes, God's special representative, served symbolically as Christ. Full documentation of this complex triangular relationship of Noyes and the Cragins, which apparently led to George Cragin's temporary estrangement from Noyes, will not be provided here. Some of the probable general outlines can be indicated, however.

John Humphrey Noyes's relationship with Mary Cragin had always had strong overtones of idolatry, the sort of selfish "special love" which he so discouraged in his followers. It must have been galling to George Cragin to be for all intents and purposes supplanted by Noyes in his wife's affections, especially when both the Noyeses and Cragins were living together in Brooklyn between 1849 and 1851. After Mary Cragin died in a boat accident in July 1851, Noyes proved almost inconsolable. For more than a year, nearly every issue of his newspaper contained fulsome tributes to her character, examples of her writing, and the like. In 1853, Noyes's *Bible Communism*, the final important summation of his sexual and marriage theories, was dedicated obliquely to her memory. "To Mary of Nazareth, the blessed of all generations, who so beautifully yielded to the will of heaven, though it contravened the fashion of this world, and, at the hazard of her good name, and of all earthly affections and interests, became the mother of Christ, and so the mother of Christianity, this work is respectfully and loyally dedicated."[22]

The recognition that Noyes continued to be emotionally involved with Mary Cragin, even after her death, could certainly have disturbed George Cragin. Furthermore, there were also clear conflicts between the small, relatively comfortable, elite Brooklyn group that printed the newspaper, and the larger group of struggling perfectionists at Oneida that provided their financial support. That Noyes apparently slipped his emotional moorings after Mary Cragin died did little to maintain community confidence in him or his ideas. Noyes, however, was extremely sensitive to external conditions and needed to validate the truth of his own ideas by seeing them accepted by his followers. Thus his emotional instability at this time could also be seen primarily as a reflection of the disorder then present in his communities, rather than as simply his individual problem.

In an attempt to overcome these personal and communal conflicts, Noyes launched a wholehearted effort to reestablish common values among his following—values that could provide a rationale for their existence. His newspaper printed repeated exhortations to unity and also systematically reprinted articles from the mid-1840s which he had originally written to prepare the minds of his supporters for closer communal living and complex marriage at Putney. Individual and communal purification was stressed as part of a larger effort to achieve God's objectives on earth.

These and other measures apparently proved effective. On August 1, 1852, an article by George Cragin reaffirmed his total submission to God's will (as mediated through Noyes).[23] In the next issue, an article titled "The Character of Peter"[24] noted that although Peter's denial of Christ might appear culpable, Peter had nevertheless come back to become Christ's "devoted follower." Throughout August a new optimism was evident in the newspaper. The tone rose to a radiant crescendo in the August 29 issue, with articles such as "The Resurrection King," "The Light Shineth in Darkness," and

"The Heart Satisfied." Most important, that issue contained Noyes's "Theocratic Platform," which apparently served to announce to the world the reestablishment of complex marriage and close communal life at Oneida. Among the planks of the platform were "Abandonment of the entire fashion of this world—especially marriage and involuntary propagation," "Cultivation of free love," and "Dwelling together in association or complex families."[25]

Although emotional tensions within the group continued to exist, by the end of 1852 the worse was over, both for Noyes and for Oneida. With the basic value premises and marital forms established, the primary effort of the community was increasingly directed toward developing successful and satisfying economic arrangements. After the death of the overworked and exhausted John Miller in June 1854, Noyes returned to Oneida to take personal charge. Recognizing that he had overextended himself in attempting so many different communal ventures, Noyes consolidated the six associated groups into two communities at Oneida and Wallingford.

This action, and the development of a successful line of animal traps for sale, succeeded in putting Oneida firmly on its financial feet by 1857. An increasingly secular and relaxed tone prevailed in the community newspaper. In place of the interminable abstruse theological essays of earlier years, the newspaper broadened its coverage to include numerous chatty articles on community life; discussions of economic matters, including articles such as "Christ: A Business Character";[26] and accounts of Noyes's extraordinarily diversified interests, ranging from botany to world politics and social life. The transition process at Oneida was largely complete. Noyes and his followers had passed "from the restrictions of martial law, to the conditions of permanent civilized life," and were now free to enjoy the fruits of their labors.

III

Despite more than a quarter-century of successful communal living after 1852, the Oneida Community eventually experienced sufficient internal and external tension that it gave up complex marriage in 1879 and discontinued its communal form of economic life as well in 1881. What were the chief factors contributing to the end of complex marriage and to the breakup of the community? This difficult yet fascinating issue has been explored in many studies, most notably Constance Noyes Robertson's model analysis *Oneida Community: The Breakup, 1876–1881*.[27] Only the basic outlines of that complex story will be suggested here.

The primary factor that brought individuals to Oneida and kept them there was loyalty to John Humphrey Noyes and his ideas. That loyalty—and the implementation of Oneida ideals in common life— was sufficiently strong that for more than two decades it convinced members to override personal desires in favor of larger group goals. By the 1870s, however, a series of subtle but significant changes were occurring that undercut community cohesiveness. The declining ability of the aging and increasingly deaf John Humphrey Noyes to lead the community set the stage for the breakup. No other leaders emerged who were able to fill Noyes's place. Noyes's efforts to ap- point his agnostic and less socially skillful son Theodore to be his successor repeatedly failed to satisfy the community. Eventually, a faction challenging the old order and calling for reform coalesced around James William Towner, a capable leader who had joined Oneida along with a small group of his followers during the mid- 1870s, but he too was unable to secure enough support to replace the still present John Humphrey Noyes.

Associated with this leadership vacuum and underlying it was the decline in commitment of the group to its original religious ideals. A younger generation lacking direct experience of the early struggles of the group on behalf of its ideals showed an ever more skeptical and secular bent. Without a strong commitment to com- mon values, it became more and more difficult to justify the intense self-sacrifice necessary to make the community's distinctive organiza- tion work. Actions by the governing central committee members came to be viewed as arbitrary and lacking any other rationale than self-interest.

As leadership and common values broke down, specific sexual tensions that had always been present began to be very divisive. Young people and community members of lower status began to chafe under the system of ascending and descending fellowship, which lim- ited the sexual contacts of those with lower status. One issue that created special controversy among key leaders had to do with who should have the responsibility of initiating young women into the community's sexual system. A related concern, especially among young women, who felt growing uncertainty about the stability of Oneida, was the increasing desire to form an exclusive, committed sexual relationship. Further complications were introduced by the stirpiculture or eugenics experiment which Noyes had initiated in 1868.[28] Only certain individuals were deemed good enough to have children. And once children were born, tendencies toward "special affection" began to emerge, even when children were reared communally. With a high degree of commitment to basic ideals, these and other tensions could perhaps have been minimized. In the absence of such commitment, however, factionalization resulted. When an external campaign against the community by the Reverend John W. Mears and other religious leaders heated up in the mid-1870s, the weakened community was no longer confident of its mission and the loyalty of its members.

In the face of an increasingly uncertain internal and external situation, the community leaders in August 1879 acted gracefully to terminate their distinctive sexual arrangements while their venture could still be counted a success. In discontinuing more than thirty years of unorthodox marital practice, the community announced that it was placing itself "not on the platform of the Shakers, on the one hand, nor of the world on the other, but on Paul's platform which allows marriage but prefers celibacy." The community also stated, in what may well prove a fitting epitaph:

> The past history of the Oneida Community is at least secure. Its present social position and its future course, whatever they may be, have no power to change the facts of the past; and the more these things are studied, the more remarkable they will appear. These things prove, as does also their present course in giving up that phase of their communal life which has caused offense, that the Communists have not been the reckless bacchanalians a few have represented them. The truth is, as the world will one day see and acknowledge, that they have not been pleasure-seekers and sensualists but social architects, with high religious and moral aims, whose experiments and discoveries they have sincerely believed would prove of value to mankind.[29]

As part of the process of ending complex marriage, a major effort was made to disentangle the complex web of relationships that had developed and to formalize new relationships between men and women of the community. Provision was also made for the care of children, even through some were unable to remain with both of their natural parents because their parents were married to different spouses. Although many Oneidans still hoped to continue communal living following the termination of complex marriage, the group had lost its focus. Increasingly, individuals wanted to return to private property and the institutions of the world. Leaders of the group realized that a reorganization of the entire system would be necessary. After careful planning in consultation with the entire membership, on January 1, 1881, the Oneida Community was legally transformed into a joint-stock company, the Oneida Community, Limited, thus ending the communal phase of one of the most extraordinary religious and social experiments in American history.

IV

What accounts for the success of the Oneida Community in sustaining its unorthodox sexual and communal system in 1852 but not in 1879? What larger significance does the experience of the Oneida Community have for understanding issues of success or failure of other experiments in communal living?

The 1852 and 1879 Oneida crisis had both external and internal aspects. The external component was clearly less important. The external attacks began, in both instances, not primarily as an assault on Oneida but as part of a larger upwelling of hostility against sexual deviation, specifically that embodied in Mormon polygamy, which was a focus of widespread opprobrium in both years. In both cases, the external attacks by themselves posed little difficulty to Oneida because the community's immediate neighbors viewed the group as composed of responsible citizens who deserved to be let alone. External crusaders against Oneida in both years found frustratingly little public sympathy for their cause. In 1879, for example, the satirical journal *Puck* printed a cartoon on its front cover that skewered the critics of Oneida. It showed a band of self-righteous ministers pointing at Oneida and declaring "Oh, dreadful! They dwell in peace and harmony and have no church scandals. They must be wiped out."[30]

Such negative reactions to attacks on Oneida were common among those who had closest contact with the community and who were in the most direct position to aid or hurt the group. Thus, external attacks proved the occasion but not the cause of the Oneida crises of 1852 and 1879.

Internal tensions, instead, were the key to the Oneida crises in both years. In each case, a significant minority of the community's members were dissatisfied with the way the community was being run. In both cases, a major aspect of that dissatisfaction focused on the community's controversial sexual system. Both in 1852 and 1879 there was a possibility that community dissidents might go outside the group and "tell all" to the press or to legal authorities, thereby making possible direct external interference in the group's functioning. So long as the community remained strong, such external threats posed a minimal problem, a minor annoyance at worst. If internal and external opposition coalesced, however, the result could conceivably have brought about the termination of the community. Both in 1852 and 1879, Noyes and other politically astute community leaders headed off any such possible direct external action by themselves discontinuing the group's most vulnerable and externally objectionable feature, complex marriage.

The question still remains, however, why in 1852 the group was eventually able to regain its cohesion, whereas in 1879 it could not. Several considerations stand out. In 1852 Noyes and his leadership cadre were in their thirties and forties, ready and able to take risks for a cause in which they profoundly believed. In 1879, many of those same leaders, who still dominated the community, were in their fifties and sixties, less energetic and less in touch with the younger generation, which had not experienced the trials and triumphs of the early years. In any organization, one would expect problems of leadership transfer to arise at such a stage. In the case of Oneida, the stress was even more intense because of the unusual, highly demanding nature of the group's social system and because the community remained to a large extent part of the "lengthened shadow" of its founder and still surviving patriarch, John Humphrey Noyes.

Noyes, an astute judge of character and a shrewd practical leader, even in his declining years, was well aware of the succession problem that he had in part created. So long as he lived and retained the loyalty of the preponderance of his followers, the group would not die but neither could it reorient itself to deal with the new conditions its members faced. The very influence of Noyes, who like a great tree shaded out any other great trees from growing up, thus limited the group's potential for change. James William Towner, a capable outsider who had the potential to lead the community in new directions, was unable to do so while Noyes was still present. At most, Towner and capable community dissidents such as William Hinds could have caused a schism within the community that would have opened up the group to dissolution by outside forces.

Faced with this difficult "no-win" situation, Noyes and his loyal lieutenants did the best they could do under the circumstances to salvage the lives of their followers. They first, in 1879, called for the dissolution of complex marriage, thereby defusing external pressure on the group. Then, when that action merely accelerated rather than staunched the internal breakdown, they skillfully worked out a plan for the dissolution of the community itself and turned it into a joint-stock corporation in 1881. In taking those two steps, they were realistically assessing their circumstances and trying to work out the best possible arrangements to deal with the temporal and spiritual needs of the group. Eventually, after Noyes's death in 1886 and nearly a decade of further uncertainty, Noyes's son Pierrepont would return to Oneida, offering new guidance as the descendants of the community transformed their group into a primarily economic rather than spiritual enterprise.[31]

Did the dissolution of complex marriage in 1879 and the abandonment of the group's system of communal living in 1881 constitute the failure of the Oneida Community? I think not. Noyes himself had no notion that his communal experiments would produce static, unchanging utopian perfection. Throughout his life, he stressed the need for flexibility in developing the changing forms through which his ideals would be expressed in practice. Noyes had a keen sense of the responsibility of the intellectual or creative person for the social consequences of his ideas. He tried to break down old and outmoded beliefs and ways of action, but he did not leave his followers to drift without guidelines. He provided new, if highly unconventional, standards and practices, and he took responsibility for seeing that they worked or else that they were discarded or modified.[32] Viewed from such a perspective, the Oneida crises of 1852 and 1879 reflect a triumph of the human spirit rather than a failure. No human organization is or can be permanent or unchanging. But "say not the struggle naught availeth."[33] There is inestimable value in the great game of life, with all its variety, richness, and struggle.

Fig. 1. Women played a key role in the great religious revivals of the early nineteenth century, as is suggested by this 1829 lithograph of a camp meeting. Although the Shakers, Oneida Perfectionists, and Mormons reacted against some of the excesses of the great revivals, they also encouraged women to take on new roles and responsibilities in their communal experiments. *Courtesy The Library of Congress.*

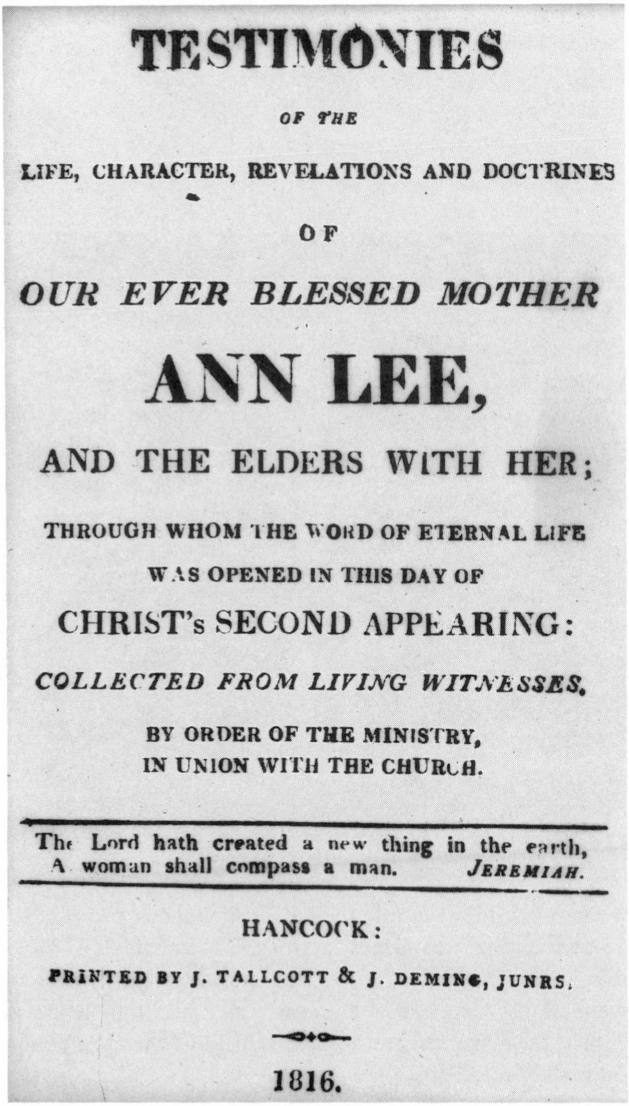

TESTIMONIES

OF THE

LIFE, CHARACTER, REVELATIONS AND DOCTRINES

OF

OUR EVER BLESSED MOTHER

ANN LEE,

AND THE ELDERS WITH HER;

THROUGH WHOM THE WORD OF ETERNAL LIFE
WAS OPENED IN THIS DAY OF

CHRIST's SECOND APPEARING:

COLLECTED FROM LIVING WITNESSES,

BY ORDER OF THE MINISTRY,
IN UNION WITH THE CHURCH.

The Lord hath created a new thing in the earth,
A woman shall compass a man.   *JEREMIAH.*

HANCOCK:

PRINTED BY J. TALLCOTT & J. DEMING, JUNRS.

1816.

Fig. 2. Ann Lee, the chief founder of the Shakers, remained a powerful spiritual force in the movement during more than two hundred years following her death. Although there are no historically accurate likenesses of Lee, this rare 1816 book with testimonies of her followers suggests why she had such a profound impact. *Courtesy The Newberry Library.*

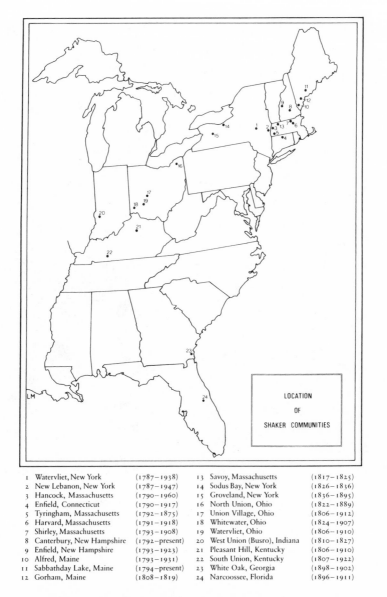

1	Watervliet, New York	(1787–1938)
2	New Lebanon, New York	(1787–1947)
3	Hancock, Massachusetts	(1790–1960)
4	Enfield, Connecticut	(1790–1917)
5	Tyringham, Massachusetts	(1792–1875)
6	Harvard, Massachusetts	(1791–1918)
7	Shirley, Massachusetts	(1793–1908)
8	Canterbury, New Hampshire	(1792–present)
9	Enfield, New Hampshire	(1793–1923)
10	Alfred, Maine	(1793–1931)
11	Sabbathday Lake, Maine	(1794–present)
12	Gorham, Maine	(1808–1819)
13	Savoy, Massachusetts	(1817–1825)
14	Sodus Bay, New York	(1826–1836)
15	Groveland, New York	(1836–1895)
16	North Union, Ohio	(1822–1889)
17	Union Village, Ohio	(1806–1912)
18	Whitewater, Ohio	(1824–1907)
19	Watervliet, Ohio	(1806–1910)
20	West Union (Busro), Indiana	(1810–1827)
21	Pleasant Hill, Kentucky	(1806–1910)
22	South Union, Kentucky	(1807–1922)
23	White Oak, Georgia	(1898–1902)
24	Narcoossee, Florida	(1896–1911)

Fig. 3. Map of the major and minor Shaker communities, showing the primary community concentrations in the Northeast and Midwest. From Priscilla J. Brewer, *Shaker Communities, Shaker Lives* (Hanover, N.H.: University Press of New England, 1986). *Used by permission.*

Fig. 4. The New Lebanon Shaker Second Family, about 1880. Note the large, plain, well-built communal buildings characteristic of Shaker architecture. *Courtesy The Winterthur Library: The Edward Deming Andrews Memorial Shaker Collection.*

Fig. 6 (*opposite*). An elaborate ring dance in the New Lebanon Shaker community, about 1870, with men and women dancing together but in separate circles. Note the large, high-roofed meetinghouse and the benches along the side of the room. From *Frank Leslie's Illustrated Newspaper*, November 1, 1873. *Courtesy The Shaker Museum, Old Chatham, New York.*

Fig. 5. The communal dining hall of the New Lebanon, New York, North Family in the 1870s, with men and women eating at separate tables. From *Frank Leslie's Illustrated Newspaper*, September 1, 1878. *Courtesy Hancock Shaker Village, Inc., Pittsfield, Massachusetts.*

Fig. 7. Satirical print of a Shaker dance, the square-order shuffle. The artist portrays Shaker women as indistinguishable nonentities, Shaker men (including one black Shaker) as grotesquely varied in size and body build, and an overdressed visitor on the edge of the room watching the performance.

Fig. 8. "The Whirling Gift," from David Lamson's *Two Years' Experience Among the Shakers* (1848), shows the extreme Shaker charismatic activities that characterized the spiritual manifestations of the early 1840s. Note that one woman who had been whirling has fallen on the floor in a trance.

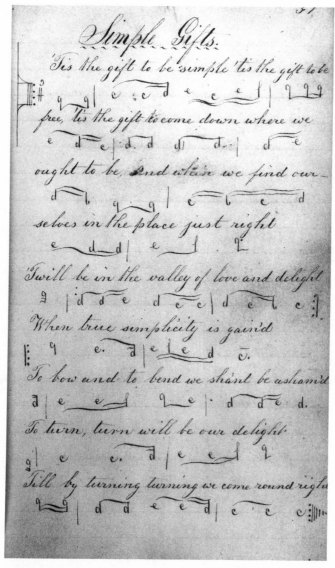

Fig. 9. Manuscript version of "Simple Gifts" (1848), the best-known of more than ten thousand Shaker songs, many of which were received during the spiritual manifestations of the 1840s. Note the distinctive form of musical notation developed by the Shakers. *Courtesy The Winterthur Library: The Edward Deming Andrews Memorial Shaker Collection.*

Fig. 10. "The Tree of Light or Blazing Tree" (1845) by Hannah Cohoon. This was one of the colorful "spirit drawings" from the aftermath of the period of spiritual manifestations of the 1840s. *Courtesy Hancock Shaker Village, Inc., Pittsfield, Massachusetts.*

Fig. 11. This photograph of John Humphrey Noyes about 1850 suggests his almost demonic intensity during the period when he founded the Oneida Community. *Courtesy Syracuse University Library.*

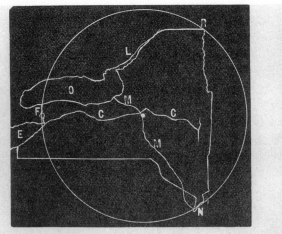

In this diagram *N* stands for New York City, *R* for Rouse's Point, *L* for St. Lawrence River, *O* for Lake Ontario, *E* for Lake Erie, *F* for Niagara Falls, *C* for New York Central Railroad, *M* for N. Y. & Oswego Midland Railroad, and the white dot near the intersection of the two railroads for the Oneida Community. It will be noticed that the circle struck with this dot as a center touches New York City, Niagara Falls and Rouse's Point, the three principal extremities of the State.

Fig. 12. Map from *Oneida Community Handbook* (1875) shows the Oneida community's location near the geographic center of New York State. *Courtesy Syracuse University Library.*

Fig. 14. Oneida men and women engaged in a pea-shelling bee. Note the men's costumes, which suggest styles of some communes of the 1960s. John Humphrey Noyes is in the left background behind the woman with glasses. *Courtesy Oneida Community Mansion House.*

Fig. 13 *(opposite).* Oneida Community men and women in the 1870s posed on the quadrangle with wings of the great Mansion House in the background. Note the women dressed in the distinctive Bloomer-style outfits and short hair worn at Oneida. *Courtesy Oneida Community Mansion House.*

Fig. 15. Women at work in the Oneida print shop (above) and bakery (below). By showing the man and woman in the print shop who have stopped work to chat, the artist may be suggesting subtly that when both sexes work alongside each other, less is accomplished. From *Frank Leslie's Illustrated Newspaper*, April 2, 1870.

OUT OF THE FOLD

"Oh, dreadful! They dwell in peace and harmony, and have no church scandals. They must be wiped out."

Fig. 16. Satirical cover of *Puck* on February 26, 1879, shows self-righteous clergymen in the late 1870s denouncing the Oneida Community.

Fig. 17. Oneida Community photograph from the 1870s, with John Humphrey Noyes in the right foreground as the patriarch of the community. *Courtesy Oneida Community Mansion House.*

Fig. 18. *(opposite, above)*. Joseph Smith, founder of the Mormon movement, was an unusually handsome and dynamic leader. *Courtesy Library-Archives, Reorganized Church of Jesus Christ of Latter Day Saints.*

Fig. 19 *(opposite, below)*. Emma Hale Smith, a powerful figure in her own right, holds her son David Hyrum Smith, born after Joseph Smith's martyrdom in 1844. *Courtesy Library-Archives, Reorganized Church of Jesus Christ of Latter Day Saints.*

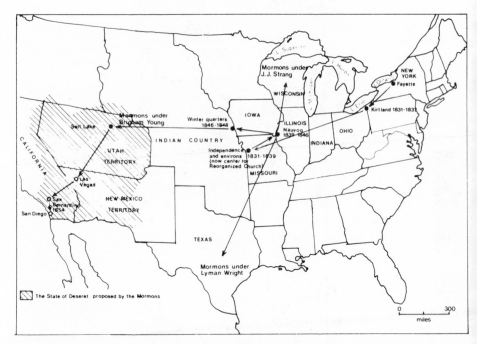

Fig. 20. Map showing some of the extensive Mormon migrations during the pre–Civil War years. From Dolores Hayden, *Seven American Utopias: The Architecture of Communitarian Socialism, 1790–1975* (Cambridge, Mass.: MIT Press, 1976). *Used by permission.*

Fig. 21. Rare photograph of Nauvoo in the early 1840s illustrates the extremes of wealth and poverty in the city. Shacks and outhouses occupy the foreground, while the imposing Temple on the hill dominates the background. *Courtesy Historical Department, Church of Jesus Christ of Latter-day Saints.*

Fig. 22. Sunstone from the Nauvoo Temple, where plural marriages were solemnized, suggests the millennial themes that played such a key role in the development of Mormon Nauvoo. Photograph by Joe Leisen. *Courtesy of Carl Landrum, Quincy, Illinois.*

Fig. 23. *(opposite).* This advertisement announcing Joseph Smith's candidacy for president of the United States in 1844, which appeared in the New York City Mormon newspaper *The Prophet,* highlights the millenarian quality of the Mormon prophet's ambition during the last years of his life. Note that the words "Error vis Veritas" appear in the clouds. *Courtesy Historical Department, Church of Jesus Christ of Latter-day Saints.*

THE PROPHET.

SATURDAY MORNING, JUNE 22, 1844

SUPER HANC PETRAM ÆDIFICABO.

FOR PRESIDENT,

GEN. JOSEPH SMITH,

OF NAUVOO, ILLINOIS.

FOR VICE PRESIDENT,

SIDNEY RIGDON,

OF PENNSYLVANIA.

Fig. 24. This 1887 painting by John Hafen, which shows Joseph Smith addressing the Nauvoo Legion prior to his martyrdom in 1844, illustrates the Mormon prophet's dynamism, even grandiosity, during his final days. The painting idealizes the Nauvoo period and incorporates historical inaccuracies, such as the Nauvoo Legion in full uniform and a tower that was not erected on the Temple until after Joseph Smith's death. *Courtesy Historical Department, Church of Jesus Christ of Latter-day Saints.*

Fig. 25. James J. Strang, the most important challenger to Brigham Young after Joseph Smith's death, was a powerful leader who founded a community on Beaver Island in Lake Michigan in the late 1840s. *Courtesy Library, Michigan State Historical Society.*

Fig. 26. Brigham Young in 1847, at the time he led the main group of Mormons west to Utah. Young was a dynamic leader who directed the establishment of more than three hundred Mormon settlements in the American West before his death in 1877. *Courtesy Historical Department, Church of Jesus Christ of Latter-day Saints.*

Fig. 28 *(opposite)*. Although most of Brigham Young's plural wives lived in two large residences built in the 1850s, the Lion House and the Beehive House (far left and far right), a more common pattern, when possible, was for plural wives to have their own homes. Young conducted much of the Mormon church's business from the President's Office, located between the two residences. *Courtesy Historical Department, Church of Jesus Christ of Latter-day Saints.*

Fig. 27. Photograph of Main Street in Salt Lake City in the early 1860s suggests the orderliness of Mormon settlement patterns. Note the wide streets and the irrigation ditches that run alongside the street. *Courtesy, Historical Department, Church of Jesus Christ of Latter-day Saints.*

Fig. 29. Four leading women of Zion, Zina D. H. Young, Bathsheba W. Smith, Emily P. Young, and Eliza R. Snow, the most powerful woman in the history of the Mormon church. Note the conventional Victorian styles of dress worn by these leading plural wives. All the women except Bathsheba W. Smith had been plural wives of Joseph Smith and had subsequently married Brigham Young. *Courtesy Historical Department, Church of Jesus Christ of Latter-day Saints.*

Fig. 30. Sonia Johnson, a feminist supporter of Mormons for ERA, was excommunicated in 1979 for challenging restrictive Mormon church policies toward women. Photograph by Brenda Schrier. *Courtesy* Dialogue: A Journal of Mormon Thought.

THE MORMONS

8

BETWEEN TWO WORLDS

Plural Marriage and the Experiences of Mormon Women
in Illinois During the Early 1840s

$\mathcal{E}$ FFORTS TO INTRODUCE a form of polygamy among the Mormons
at their primary church settlement in Nauvoo, Illinois, during
the early 1840s created intense controversy, both at the time and
subsequently. Records of the main body of the Church of Jesus Christ
of Latter-day Saints indicate that the first plural marriage sanctioned
by a ceremony occurred there on April 5, 1841, between the
church's thirty-five-year-old prophet-founder, Joseph Smith, Jr., and
the twenty-six-year-old Louisa Beaman. On July 12, 1843, formal
written sanction was given to the practice when Smith privately dictated a revelation calling for a restoration among the Latter-day
Saints of polygamous marriage practices similar to those of the Old
Testament patriarchs Abraham, Isaac, and Jacob. These new practices were set within the context of a conception of marriage,
growth, and development—a "new and everlasting covenant"—
which was to continue throughout all eternity. Presentation of this
revelation within the following month to many in the church's leadership cadre led to a crisis in the young church. Little more than a
year later, on June 27, 1844, Joseph Smith and his brother Hyrum
were murdered in a jail in Carthage, Illinois, while awaiting trial on
charges arising in part from the dissatisfaction of some of their followers with the new polygamous beliefs and practices.[1]

This brief and turbulent effort by Joseph Smith and some of his
associates in Nauvoo to introduce plural marriage among the Latter-

day Saints has led to bitter and often unproductive debate for more than a century. Critical accounts generally have attacked Joseph Smith and his alleged failings, while apologetic treatments have represented the practice as a response to divine command and have attempted to downplay apparent inconsistencies in early polygamy practice. Until the past several decades, few scholarly analyses have attempted to place this period of Mormon development in Nauvoo into its larger social and cultural context. Even fewer studies have systematically addressed the responses of Mormon women to the controversial new beliefs and practices.[2]

This chapter suggests the larger social and intellectual context within which polygamy in Nauvoo developed, and then explores the differing responses of Mormon women to these developments. Special attention is devoted to the complex and ambivalent reactions of Joseph Smith's first wife, Emma, which have been reconstructed in a major biography by Linda King Newell and Valeen Tippetts Avery.[3] During this period, Smith and many of his followers were caught "between two worlds," between an old order that was dying and a new order that was yet to be born. The result—particularly for those who could not bring themselves to accept the sincerity of Smith's efforts to introduce the new order, including polygamy—was often intense anguish and bitterness. The early Mormon experience suggests new insights about both the promise and the pitfalls of efforts to achieve radical social change.[4]

I

Before the origins of Mormon polygamy can be understood in context, we must briefly consider the early development of the Mormon movement and four partially inadequate earlier efforts to explain the later development of polygamy practice in the 1840s. At the outset, it must be emphasized that the Church of Jesus Christ of Latter-day Saints was one of the most complex and extraordinary of all the religious groups to develop in the Burned-over District of western New York State. Joseph Smith, though poor and largely unlettered, was by any estimation a religious and organizational genius who evoked strong reactions, both positive and negative, from those with whom he came in contact. His supporters became convinced that he had discovered and "translated" an ancient Scripture, the Book of Mormon, that supplemented and went beyond the Old and New Testaments, and that he had been specially chosen by God to "restore" true Christianity and, indeed, produce a synthesis of all previously valid human truth in preparation for the coming of the millennium.

Critics were equally convinced that Smith had fabricated the Book of Mormon as a hoax and that he was a dangerous megalomaniac and con man who took advantage of his gullible followers. Critics were particularly disturbed that Smith claimed to be receiving continuing revelation from God, as had the biblical prophets, and that his well-organized church was attracting so many people away from more established denominations. Mormon economic and political cohesiveness also proved threatening to their neighbors, contributing to tensions that forced the Mormons during less than a decade to move from New York to Kirtland, Ohio, and thence to two locations in Missouri, and finally to Nauvoo, Illinois.

Although many people assume that polygamy was the major element leading to early persecution of the Mormons, for the first decade of the movement's development, the issue of polygamy was of little importance in the controversies that swirled around the young church. Only during the early 1840s, when Joseph Smith had established a secure power base in Nauvoo, Illinois, did allegations of plural marriage become a major disruptive factor *within* the Mormon movement. And not until after Smith's death, the exodus to Utah, and the public announcement of the practice in 1852 in Salt Lake City did plural marriage become a major focus of non-Mormon hostility toward the group.

After that public announcement of the controversial new practice, four major approaches were put forward to attempt to explain why it had developed. Those four approaches have continued to dominate explanations of polygamy to the present. To those who hold these views, each provides *the* obvious and complete explanation for the development of the practice. Yet none of these hypotheses alone can explain all the phenomena associated with the introduction of polygamy among the Mormons.

Most obviously inadequate is the view, held by the smaller Re-organized Church of Jesus Christ of Latter Day Saints (RLDS), with headquarters in Independence, Missouri, that polygamy was not in-troduced into the Mormon church by Joseph Smith at all but was instead a corruption of the church resulting from actions by Brigham Young or by other unspecified individuals after Smith's death. Over-whelming and historically conclusive evidence refutes this argument. Available historical records leave no doubt that Joseph Smith not only introduced polygamous beliefs into the Mormon church but that he also engaged in polygamous practice himself.[5]

Also partially inadequate is the "commonsense" non-Mormon view that polygamy was introduced because Joseph Smith was an oversexed individual—a lusty, good-natured libertine, perhaps—who was simply trying to rationalize his amorous propensities. Al-though sexual impulses undoubtedly were a part of the reason for the introduction of polygamy, the sexual-impulses argument fails to ex-plain why formal polygamous relationships rather than informal ex-tramarital relationships should have been introduced by Smith, or why his formulation of polygamous beliefs as early as 1831 should have preceded by a decade any clear attempts to introduce the practice.[6]

Similarly incomplete is the believing Latter-day Saint viewpoint that Joseph Smith was commanded by God to introduce plural mar-riage and that he was just being obedient in carrying out the inscru-table will of the Lord. Even if one accepts such a belief in divine revelation, one still is faced with the question of why Smith came to the Lord with a question about polygamy when he did—what the social and intellectual context was for his revelatory process.[7]

A final limited approach suggests that Joseph Smith was a psy-chologically disturbed individual and that his psychological problems were a key factor contributing to his attempt to introduce polygamy. Although a case can and will be made for a sophisticated variant of this argument later in this chapter, most previous arguments for psychopathology have tended to be reductionistic. They generally have presumed that no sane, rational person could possibly want to introduce polygamous practice as the norm for a society. Such a view might have seemed convincing in a more ethnocentric envi-ronment, but in our pluralistic modern world one cannot casually assume, without a careful consideration of evidence, that efforts to introduce alternative ways of life into a society are necessarily a sign of psychopathology.[8]

II

If none of these four approaches appears fully adequate to account for the origin of Mormon polygamy, then how can its introduction best be explained? Rather than attempting to find *the* explanation for Joseph Smith's introduction of polygamy, let us instead consider three closely interrelated preconditions that help account for the development of the practice.

The first necessary-but-not-sufficient factor contributing to the introduction of polygamy was Joseph Smith's strong sex drive. Surely it is hard to imagine polygamy being introduced and practiced by a eunuch, and Smith was definitely no eunuch. He was a handsome, dynamic leader with great physical and intellectual vitality—a man not afraid to break with convention. Many of his statements reveal a basically positive attitude toward sexual expression, as well as the difficulty he sometimes had in keeping his impulses in check. He was idolized by many of his followers as a prophet of God, and he had to deal with a host of personal and practical problems he and his followers faced. Like any public figure under such circumstances, he faced a greater than average number of temptations that might have made him susceptible to unorthodoxy in personal behavior. Yet men respond in a variety of ways to strong sex drives. Many resist or find socially acceptable channels for such impulses. Very few individuals attempt to deal with those impulses by introducing a formal system of polygamy among their followers. Something more was obviously necessary.[9]

A second precondition for the introduction of polygamy was religious. Central to Joseph Smith's sense of mission was his millennial vision of a corrupt, diseased old order tottering inevitably toward destruction. That corrupt old order would eventually be replaced by a glorious restoration of the true religious and social practices of the veritable kingdom of heaven on earth. The Bible provided the key model for this restored order. Like many of his contemporaries, Smith immersed himself in the Bible and conceived of the whole of human history within the context established by the biblical record. Under the circumstances, he could hardly have helped but wonder why the Lord apparently approved of the taking of plural wives by the Hebrew patriarchs whom he admired so much. If the millennial dispensation was to be a "restoration of all things," might it not also include a restoration of polygamous marriage? Although the biblical and prophetic concerns reflected in early Mormon writings certainly did not make the reintroduction of polygamy inevitable, such concerns did provide a context within which the possibility became at least intellectually conceivable.[10]

A final key precondition for the introduction of Mormon polygamy was related to the social disorder with which Joseph Smith had to try to deal. The poverty and high mobility of many Mormons before they joined the church was exacerbated by intense persecution that led Mormons to move repeatedly during the decade that followed the founding of the movement. Active missionary efforts also brought in numerous new converts who had to be integrated somehow into the new society that was being created. At least as early as 1835, the Mormon church began to take responsibility for the marriage and divorce practices of its members, increasingly ignoring the plethora of contradictory state laws on the subject and sometimes even directly violating those external regulations.

Not feeling able to achieve redress of their grievances from the larger society, Mormons, in attempting to create their "new Israel," increasingly turned in on themselves and depended on family and kinship ties to secure loyalty to the group. Polygamy could make possible a far greater extension of such ties than could monogamy. For example, by the time of his death at age eighty-eight, the Mormon patriarch Benjamin F. Johnson was related by blood or by marriage to more than eight hundred people and presumably had greater power and security than those with less extensive kinship networks. The Mormon concern for extending family ties and for controlling their own marriage practices was part of a larger effort to establish an autonomous, self-sufficient organization separate from an evil and corrupt world, an effort to create a "political kingdom of God." Church autonomy in supervising the marriage and divorce practices of its members did not necessarily lead to polygamy, but such independent control clearly was a prerequisite if marriage and kinship practices such as polygamy—which violated existing moral and legal standards—were to be introduced.[11]

III

The contradictory tensions and potential of the Mormon movement came to a head during the crucial transition years between 1839 and 1844 that the Mormons spent in Nauvoo, Illinois, under Joseph Smith's leadership. Nauvoo marked the climax of an earlier phase of Mormon development and set the pattern for new doctrinal, social, and political approaches that would be further developed and tested in Utah. In Nauvoo, Smith made his most concerted effort to realize his conception of the kingdom of heaven on earth. No aspect of life was left untouched.[12]

A variety of factors made possible the introduction of plural marriage on a limited scale in Nauvoo. The key emotional thread running throughout the period, without which events cannot be understood, was a sense of increasing tension and imminent crisis. This emotional atmosphere encouraged self-sacrifice, intellectual and practical isolation conducive to excess, and an almost compulsive emphasis on unquestioning loyalty to the Mormon priesthood as the cardinal virtue. The Mormons started over again in Illinois after fleeing attacks in Missouri that surpassed in brutality even the outrages that would later be perpetrated on "Bleeding Kansas."

Determined not to be pushed around any more, the Mormons secured a city charter that, if freely interpreted, made Nauvoo almost autonomous from the state. An all-Mormon militia of more than two thousand men called the Nauvoo Legion was established, provoking fears in nearby non-Mormon areas. And a tightly organized church, presiding over a city second in Illinois only to Chicago in size and appearing to hold the balance of power in the state, managed to alienate both political parties. Within this context of increasing tension and experienced separateness, the inhibitions that normally discourage radical innovation in the larger society became less significant and major doctrinal and social changes could occur.[13]

Social tensions within Mormon Nauvoo also added to the volatile mixture there. Nauvoo was a boom town, growing within five years from a sleepy backwater settlement of a few hundred people to a city of more than eleven thousand inhabitants. Like many such boom towns, it was plagued by a host of problems attendant upon rapid growth. Visitors commented on the extremes of wealth and poverty in the city, as well as on Mormon efforts to overcome those problems.[14] Inducting thousands of new immigrants into Mormon cultural and social patterns also posed a major challenge. In addition, the city was close to the marshy malarial bottoms along the Mississippi, and according to one historian as many as fifteen hundred to two thousand people may have died during the six years that the Mormons lived in Nauvoo. Although this estimate is undoubtedly too high, few families in the area were not intimately acquainted with disease and death.[15]

The most important dislocations probably were the unintended side effects of the Mormon missionary effort itself. While bringing in vitally needed convert-settlers and capital, this program placed great strains on marital relationships. On the one hand, men were frequently called with little or no notice to go "without purse or scrip" on extended missionary trips that amounted to long periods of voluntary celibacy. The emotions of many such men were expressed by Parley P. Pratt when he wrote his wife, Mary Ann, from England in 1840: "Why must we live separate? Why must I be forever deprived of your Society and my dear little Children? I cannot endure it, and yet I must." Only extreme personal commitment to the larger Mormon enterprise could make possible such sacrifice.[16]

Wives of absent missionaries faced even more severe problems. Of necessity they were left behind, often pregnant or with young children to care for, and faced the problem of trying to support themselves. The trials and hardships of such women were typified by the case of Eunice Shurtliff. She wrote her husband, Luman, in 1842 that she was four months pregnant, had been severely sick for three months, and could not get credit to purchase food at the store. "I have no husband to talk with or comfort me these long nights. . . . You know when Jane was born and you were gone from home . . . I had to get along the best I could. Luman, I do not think it is your duty to leave me under such circumstances. Come without fail."[17]

The plight of yet another woman, whose husband was absent for the exceptionally long period of five years, was tellingly described as a period of temporary "widowhood."[18] Under such conditions, the marital and sexual dissatisfactions of both men and women must have pressed for resolution.

Thus there may well have been a relationship between the significant expansion of the Mormon missionary program, represented by the founding of the English mission in 1837 and by revived and expanded missionary activities from Nauvoo, and the subsequent effort under Joseph Smith's leadership to introduce new marriage and family beliefs and practices. Nor is it surprising that the major leadership faction that supported Smith in these efforts and that eventually oversaw the introduction of polygamy into the Mormon church was the twelve apostles, who ran the missionary program. Faced with long separations from their wives and families, such leaders might understandably have been attracted to the idea of eventually formalizing and consummating other emotional attachments that they had made with the young women they had encountered in their work. They also may well have idealized marriage and been attracted to the idea of establishing permanent family ties that would survive throughout eternity, a concept that would become a key element in the beliefs that were used to introduce polygamy.

Likewise, the dissatisfied wives of missionaries must also have felt frustrated at having absentee husbands. Many wives must have longed for permanent and satisfying marital relationships with their husbands, while others may have wanted to abrogate unsatisfactory relationships and start over again. The "new and everlasting covenant" that Joseph Smith formally introduced to his closest followers in July 1843, partly as a justification for plural marriage, indicated, on the one hand, that marriages that were properly "sealed" under the authority of the Mormon priesthood would continue for "eternity." On the other hand, the revelation also included the corollary idea that existing temporal arrangements were not binding *until* sealed for eternity and that such unsealed temporal arrangements could, if unsatisfactory, be terminated and replaced by other, more desirable "eternal" ones with new partners. Whether as a result of such logic or as part of more pragmatic efforts to resolve marital dissatisfactions, a substantial number of individuals in Nauvoo eventually found new marital partners during the last turbulent years there or during the exodus to Utah.[19]

IV

All the contradictory pressures in Nauvoo eventually seemed to become fused within Joseph Smith as he sought to deal with the complex problems of the city. Uncertain of the loyalty and reliability of even some of his closest associates, especially after the devastating apostasy of his close associate John C. Bennett in 1842, Smith increasingly attempted to concentrate all positions of power in his own hands. He served simultaneously as prophet and president of his church, mayor of the city, head of the Nauvoo Legion, chief economic planner for the church, and in many other capacities. He was also faced with problems of counseling and trying to help provide economic support for many women whose husbands were away on missions.

During this period, Smith moved vigorously to present new doctrines that had long been germinating in his mind, doctrines designed to reestablish social cohesion not only on earth, but also throughout all eternity.[20] Basic to these new doctrines was an elaboration of church authority through ceremonies believed to link indissolubly the living and the dead. Smith claimed the keys of St. Peter, with the power to bind and to loose, on earth and in heaven. This was the basis for the doctrine of baptism for the dead, which was designed to allow dead relatives to accept the Mormon gospel in the afterlife. The material and spiritual worlds were described as a closely linked continuum. God was seen in anthropomorphic terms— once a man, he had progressed to godhood, as men could too.

Perhaps most important were special marriage-sealing ceremonies designed to give permanence to earthly marriage after death. Marriage and the social cohesion provided by family and kinship ties were declared to be the basis for all progression in the afterlife. Earthly marriage was an ephemeral state; unless marriages were properly sealed by the Mormon priesthood in the light of eternity, they would not continue after death. Those who were not married for eternity would be the lowest class in the afterlife—solitary "minister-

ing angels," a sort of perpetual servant class unable to progress further. Sealings for eternity, by contrast, made possible progression
toward godhood, as men became great patriarchs who ruled over an
ever-increasing posterity and moved on to settle whole new worlds.
There was a sense of the awesome power of sexuality and procreation
in human development.

This much was known, at least in embryonic form, to many of
the knowledgeable Mormons who worked so hard to build the Temple, where the sealing ceremonies would be conducted. Only to his
most trusted associates, however, did Smith convey the final corol-
laries to these sealing doctrines. To them he explained that polygamous marriage was a particularly exalted form of eternal or celestial
marriage. If marriage with one wife, sealed for eternity under the
authority of the Mormon priesthood, could bring ultimate godhood
for men, then having more than one wife merely accentuated the
process, in line with God's promise to Abraham that his seed eventually would be as numerous as the stars in the sky or the sand on
the seashore. Furthermore, polygamy made possible the reuniting of
all family members around their patriarchal leaders in the afterlife.
Even if a man had lost his wife and remarried, she would be his
again after he died.

Although little was said about exactly how polygamy was to be
practiced on earth, the revelation on plural and celestial marriage
repeatedly stressed that any liaisons outside the bounds of churchly
supervised law were heinously sinful and required drastic measures for
atonement. Total loyalty to the church was emphasized repeatedly as
the supreme principle.[21]

V

Joseph Smith may have developed an internally consistent rationale
for plural marriage, but the practical development and workings of
the new polygamous system were much more problematic, both for
men and for women. Even under ideal circumstances, polygamous
practices could hardly have been introduced into nineteenth-century
Illinois without provoking severe misunderstandings and conflicts.

Most people were already suspicious of individual immorality or deviance. To go farther and claim that a deviant practice such as polygamy, which was illegal in Illinois, was authorized and indeed commanded by God seemed to undercut the very basis of moral authority itself.

The complex political controversies over polygamy in Nauvoo need not be treated in detail here. Suffice it to note that the opposition to polygamy was formidable. That opposition included not only Joseph Smith's capable and strong-willed wife, Emma, who bitterly hated polygamy and almost left her husband several times because of its practice, but also many of Smith's closest associates, who came to the reluctant conclusion that he had become a "fallen prophet," unfit to lead the church he had founded. Perhaps most devastating of all was the defection of the colorful adventurer John C. Bennett. In his meteoric eighteen-month career with the Mormons between 1840 and 1842, Bennett rose from the rank of a virtual nobody to become mayor of Nauvoo and Joseph Smith's right-hand man, only to fall from favor and write a lurid 1842 book exposing alleged Mormon misdeeds, including polygamy.[22]

The defection of the second-best-known Mormon in Nauvoo, an intimate friend of Joseph Smith, precipitated a severe crisis for the young church. Bennett charged the Mormon hierarchy with almost every imaginable sin and presented a detailed and highly inflated account of the problems of the early development of polygamy, the first such to appear. Convinced that Smith had threatened to kill him if he would not publicly make statements about the purity of Smith's character that he felt to be false, Bennett devoted the next two years of his life, in turn, to trying systematically to expose and secure the death of his former friend. Not only did he continue to maintain contact with Mormon leaders such as Orson Pratt and Sidney Rigdon who were disaffected with polygamy, but he also cooperated closely with hostile external sources such as *The Warsaw Signal,* an anti-Mormon newspaper that delighted in printing gossip and allegations from disaffected Mormons. Only Bennett's own equivocal character and tendency for polemical exaggeration, together with a carefully orchestrated church campaign to blacken his reputation and neutralize his influence, enabled the Mormons to weather the storm his apostasy stirred up.[23]

More revealing than such predictable opposition were the reactions of individuals who accepted polygamy. Even the leading men who eventually supported the practice most vigorously stated that they initially expressed shock when introduced to the idea. Brigham Young, who oversaw the introduction of plural marriage after Smith's death in Nauvoo and in Utah, declared that when he first heard the revelation and thought of all the troubles that would ensue, "it was the first time in my life that I desired the grave."[24] Heber C. Kimball, always implicitly loyal, was so distraught after receiving the command to take another wife without the knowledge of his first wife, Vilate, that he begged Smith to remove the requirement lest he apostatize and forfeit his salvation.[25] And Benjamin F. Johnson, later patriarch of an extensive plural family in Utah, said that he had been horrified when Smith explained plural marriage to him and told Johnson to ask his sister Almera to become Smith's plural wife. Recovering from the shock, Johnson remembered telling Smith that he would try to do as he had been asked but that "if ever I know you do this to degrade my sister I will kill you, as the Lord lives."[26] As we shall see below, women who received polygamous overtures faced an even more difficult and essentially untenable situation than did men.

The acceptance and practice of plural marriage increasingly represented one of the chief tests of the total loyalty that Smith was coming to demand of his closest followers. Men or women who engaged in polygamous practice were in no position to apostatize because if they did so the air would be made blue with stories of their supposedly licentious behavior. Likewise, if a man's sister or daughter were sealed as a plural wife to Joseph Smith or another leader of the church, effective opposition to the practice became exceedingly difficult. To oppose polygamy under such circumstances would be tantamount to disowning one's own children or relatives, as well as everything to which one had previously committed one's whole life.

VI

Women faced by far the greatest emotional and practical difficulties in coming to terms with the new polygamous beliefs and practices, yet seldom have women's responses to early polygamy been systematically explored. Until recently, most attention has focused on Joseph Smith's relationships, with much of that simply an effort to make head counts of his alleged plural wives. The Mormon historian Andrew Jenson listed twenty-seven probable plural wives, Fawn Brodie claimed forty-eight, and Stanley S. Ivins identified eighty-four possibilities. These speculative lists do not adequately distinguish between different types of wives, particularly between those who actually sustained connubial relations with Joseph Smith and those who probably were only sealed to him for "eternity."

To go beyond such head counts and begin to reconstruct the human dimension behind early polygamy, the remainder of this chapter will look at three different types of women's perspectives on polygamy. The first is that of the women who accepted plural marriage overtures. The second is that of the women who rejected such overtures. And the last is the complex and ambivalent case of Joseph Smith's first wife, Emma Hale Smith, whose love for her husband and hostility toward his polygamy posed severe problems for his efforts to introduce the practice.[27]

The frank and detailed personal statement of Lucy Walker, who became a plural wife of Joseph Smith and later of Heber C. Kimball, shows many of the characteristic features of Smith's relationships for which we have extensive information.[28] Lucy was born on April 30, 1826, in Peacham, Vermont. Her family joined the Latter-day Saints shortly after the church was founded, moved frequently with the Mormons, suffered intense persecution in Missouri, and eventually settled in Nauvoo. The family developed a close personal relationship with Joseph Smith. When Lucy's mother died in Nauvoo in 1842 leaving ten motherless children, Lucy's father's health seemed to give way under the strain. Joseph Smith stepped in, suggesting the father seek a change of environment. Then Smith temporarily adopted the four eldest children as part of his own family and household, going out of his way to help them in any way he could.

Early in 1843, when Lucy was a lively and attractive sixteen-year-old, Joseph Smith had a private interview with her. He told her that God had commanded him to take her as a plural wife. Her "astonishment knew no bounds." She felt that he was insulting her. Smith asked her if she believed him to be a prophet of God. She said that she did. He explained "the principle of plural or celestial marriage" to her. He said that it was being restored for the good of the human family and that it would "prove an everlasting blessing to my father's house, and form a chain that could never be broken, worlds without end." Lucy was told to pray and that she would receive a personal testimony of the correctness of the principle, but her mind was filled with darkness. She had no father or mother to give her counsel, and she was deeply distraught.

Joseph Smith could see her unhappiness. He said that although under the present circumstance he could not publicly acknowledge her as his wife, she would eventually be "acknowledged and honored as my wife." He also told her that if she rejected this message "the gate will be closed forever against you." This threat made her angry. Lucy felt that she was being asked "to place myself upon the alter a living sacrifice—perhaps to brook the world in disgrace and incur the displeasure and contempt of my youthful companions." Unless she knew that God approved her course of action, she would rather die. Smith said she would receive a personal testimony of the truth of the principle. Lucy earnestly desired such a testimony. Shortly before dawn, after a sleepless night of fervent prayer, she felt as though her room were "lighted up by a heavenly influence." "Supreme happiness took possession of me, and I received a powerful and irresistable testimony of the truth of plural marriage." On May 1, 1843, she was sealed to Joseph Smith "for time and all eternity" by Elder William Clayton, Smith's personal secretary.[29]

Even more telling as a description of the pressures and emotional disturbance that Smith's plural marriage overtures could bring to women who accepted them is the account of Helen Mar Kimball, daughter of Heber C. Kimball. Although Helen supported plural marriage strongly in books such as *Why We Practice Plural Marriage*, privately she vividly recalled the emotional strain that the introduction of plural marriage caused her and her mother, Vilate, when she became Joseph Smith's plural wife at age fourteen (in her "fifteenth summer"):

> Just previous to my father's starting upon his last mission but one, to the Eastern States, he taught me the principle of Celestial marriage, & having a great desire to be connected with the Prophet, Joseph, he offered me to him; this I afterwards learned

from the Prophet's own mouth. My father had but one Eue Lamb but willingly laid her upon the alter: how cruel this seemed to the mother whose heart strings were already stretched untill they were ready to snap asunder, for he had taken Sarah Moon to wife & she thought she had made sufficient sacrifise but the Lord required more. I will pass over the temptations which I had during the twenty four hours after my father introduced me to this principle & asked me if I would be sealed to Joseph who came next morning & with my parents I heard him teach and explain the principle of Celestial marriage—after which he said to me, "If you will take this step, it will insure your eternal salvation & exaltation and that of your father's household & all of your kindred." This promise was so great that I willingly gave myself to purchase so glorious a reward. None but God & his angels could see my mother's bleeding heart—when Joseph asked her if she was willing, she replied "If Helen is willing I have nothing more to say." She had witnessed the sufferings of others, who were older & who better understood the step they were taking, & to see her child, who had scarcely seen her fifteenth summer, following in the same thorny path, in her mind she saw the misery which was sure to come as the sun was to rise and set; but it was all hidden from me.[30]

The backgrounds and experiences of Lucy Walker and Helen Mar Kimball are typical of those of many of Joseph Smith's other plural wives. Women who were approached by Smith or his close associates to become plural wives usually were of proven personal and family loyalty to the church. Frequently they were dependent upon the church for economic support and had a variety of strong ties to Smith and other leaders. Enormous pressure—including, in Helen Mar Kimball's case, the promise that simply by marrying Joseph Smith she would secure salvation for herself, her ancestry, and her posterity—was used in many of the known cases. In an analysis of various relationships among Smith's wives, Vesta Crawford noted that at least eleven of Smith's plural wives were related to prominent church leaders, five were orphans or otherwise dependent, and seven lived at some time in Smith's home, with some overlapping among these categories.[31]

In almost all recorded cases, initial presentation of the belief in plural marriage to either men or women produced shock, horror, disbelief, or general emotional confusion. Those who eventually accepted the principle almost invariably went through a period of inner turmoil lasting from several days to several months. During this period, they might go without adequate sleep, food, or normal social contacts, fervently praying that God would reveal the truth of the new beliefs to them. Those who eventually accepted plural marriage almost invariably had a compelling personal experience revealing the truth of the new standards. Such a drastic step away from established norms demanded more than purely intellectual assent.[32]

Few contemporary documents have survived that show the reactions of supporters of plural marriage within the Mormon community before Joseph Smith's death. One is found in a postscript of a letter of Vilate Kimball to her husband, Heber C. Kimball, dated "Nauvoo June 24th 1843." She wrote:

> June 27th Since writing the above, I have had a visit from brother Parley [Pratt] and his wife, they are truly converted   it appears that J. . . . h has taught him some principles and told him his privilege, and even appointed one for him, I dare not tell you who it is, you would be astonished and I guess some tried. She has ben to me for council, I told her I did not wish to advise in such matters. Sister Pratt has ben rageing against these things, she told me her self that the devel had been in her until within a few days past, she said the Lord had shown her it was all right. She wants Parley to go ahead, says she will do all in her power to help him; they are so ingagued I fear they will run to fast. they asked me many questions on principle   I told them I did not know much and I rather they would go to those that had authority to teach. Parley said he and J were interrupted before he got what instruction he wanted, and now he did not know when he should have an oppertunity. he seamed unwilling to wate, I told him these were sacred things and he better not make a move until he got more instruction. —I have a secret to tell you, but I am almost afrade, it was committed to Sarah and she was requested not to tell me, but she said she considered me a part of her self and she would tell me, and I might tell you for it was just what you had prophecyed would come to pass. now if you know what you have said about Sarah Ally then you have got the secret, for it is even so, and she is

tickled about it. and they all apear in better spirits than they
did before. how they will carry it out, is more than I know, I
hope they have got more faith than I have. Brother nobles folks
all send love to you.

In her concluding remarks, Vilate wrote, "I think you had better
burn this, as soon as you can after reading it. I should not dare to
send it by mail, but I trust it will go safe. if Brigham should go I will
write by him. I am as ever your affectionate wife Vilate Kimball."[33]

This letter clarifies a number of important points suggested by
other sources. It shows clearly that polygamy was taught and practiced before the formal recording of the revelation on plural and celestial marriage, as the revelation itself also indicates. As late as
1843, however, polygamy was practiced only on a very restricted
scale, even in the top echelons of the church, with the exception of
Joseph Smith himself, who may eventually have had as many as fifteen or more women with whom he sustained connubial relations.
Research by D. Michael Quinn and others on wives of church leaders suggests that before Smith's death only about thirty of the top
male leaders were polygamously married with Smith's sanction and
that most leaders had taken at most two or three additional wives.[34]
The taking of large numbers of wives by a few of the early Mormon
leaders would occur largely between Smith's death and the exodus to
Utah that began in 1846. This was a complex period when the transition to plural marriage was beginning to take place in the church as
a whole.

As Vilate's letter also indicates, a tendency to go to extremes
could easily develop once earlier patterns of behavior were broken
down. Furthermore, the impossibility of finding time and privacy to
give detailed instructions even to the twelve apostles, Smith's closest
associates, suggests how difficult it must have been for the general
membership to translate such beliefs into practice. Excesses and confusion were almost certain to follow. Interestingly, the letter hints
that one of the plural wives, Sarah Ally, was pregnant. Her child,
George Omer Noble, was born on February 2, 1844, and is generally
described as the first child born into Mormon polygamy.[35] Finally,
there is the concluding suggestion that the letter should be burned.
Probably most such documents actually were.

One controversial issue suggested by the letter is the question of how pregnancies of plural wives and children born to plural wives was handled in Nauvoo. Although many of Joseph Smith's plural wives testified explicitly that they had had full sexual relations with him,[36] most women who claimed to have been married to him consistently refused, in the face of repeated questioning, to affirm or deny that they or other women had borne his children.[37] Such reticence was entirely understandable. If information about Smith's children by plural wives were brought into the open, the line of questioning adopted by often hostile interrogators would have been even more insulting, and other individuals' names would have been dragged into the discussion. Even if children by Smith's plural wives lived in Utah—as oral and written traditions there suggest—they probably would have borne the names of the family who reared them.[38] Detailed demographic work in progress on the Nauvoo and early Utah periods suggests that some children became part of families in which they were not born, under puzzling circumstances.[39]

Evidence for children Smith may have had by plural wives is based largely on oral and family traditions. Mary Rollins Lightner, one of the most articulate and knowledgeable of Smith's plural wives, said: "I know he had six wives and I have known some of them from childhood up. I know he had three children. They told me. I think two are living today but they are not known as his children as they go by other names."[40] Lucy Meserve Smith recalled that her husband, George A. Smith, told her of going to see Joseph Smith and finding him washing his hands after he had helped Emma—who had served as the midwife—deliver a child by one of his plural wives.[41] Josephine R. Fisher signed an affidavit in 1915 that, when her mother was on her deathbed, she told her she was Joseph's child, but admonished her to keep her knowledge a secret.[42] Persistent but probably embellished family tradition suggests that Eliza R. Snow conceived a child by Joseph Smith and suffered a miscarriage.[43] The Nauvoo Expositor of June 7, 1844, published by a schismatic faction of the church which was attempting to oust Smith from power, alleged that "in order to avoid public exposition from the common course of things," pregnant plural wives "are sent away for a time until all is well; after which they return, as from a long visit."[44]

It is less difficult to explain the apparent lack of children born to the plural wives of Joseph Smith's followers before his death because most of them were married for a shorter time and to fewer women during this period. One account of how pregnancies of high church officials were handled was given by Kimball Young, the late sociologist of Mormon polygamy and a descendant of Oscar Young, the first acknowledged child by any of Brigham Young's plural wives. According to Kimball Young, plural wives who became pregnant, including Oscar Young's mother, Harriet Cook, went into seclusion in the second floor of the Erastus Snow home in Nauvoo. The second floor had an entrance that was separate from the rest of the house. The Snow family was small enough to live entirely on the first floor. Food and other necessities were discreetly brought to the wives who lived on the second floor.[45]

The original construction of the Erastus Snow house does correspond with this account of Kimball Young's. In addition, the fact that an unusual 1846 holograph letter from Brigham Young to "Mrs. Hariot Cook" was sent in care of the Erastus Snow home suggests that she may have been living there at the time as well.[46] Quite possibly other arrangements were made in cases of other plural wives, but these examples at least suggest some of the possibilities. Even under the best of circumstances, the acceptance and practice of plural marriage by some women in Nauvoo must have caused exceptional emotional and practical difficulties for them.

VII

At least as interesting as the cases of women who accepted polygamy in Nauvoo are the cases of women who rejected polygamous overtures by Smith and his associates. No doubt many women simply refused such proposals and remained silent. For example, when Smith approached Hiram Kimball's wife, Sarah Melissa Granger, she rejected his request. "I asked him to teach it to someone else." She kept her own counsel in the matter except to warn a friend, who then refused to meet with him.[47] Other women who refused Smith's proposals, such as Sidney Ridgon's daughter Nancy and Orson Pratt's wife Sarah, had the misfortune to find their cases publicized in the apostate John C. Bennett's 1842 exposé of polygamy.[48] Although these women appear to have been highly respected before the exposé appeared, they soon found their names and reputations thoroughly blackened as part of an effort to discredit Bennett and protect the reputation of the Mormon prophet.

By far the most detailed and straightforward account from a Mormon woman who rejected polygamous overtures in Nauvoo was furnished by Martha Brotherton, an attractive young English convert, whose detailed affidavit of her experiences, dated July 13, 1842, was published in the *St. Louis Bulletin* on July 15, 1842, and in the *Sangamo Journal* on July 22, 1842, and was subsequently reprinted in Bennett's exposé.[49] Brotherton and her family had been in Nauvoo only three weeks when Brigham Young approached her to become his plural wife. She stalled him and then at the earliest possible time left Nauvoo and swore out an affidavit describing her experiences. Her account is particularly valuable as a basis for comparison with later reminiscences of women like Lucy Walker and Helen Mar Kimball, who had accepted such overtures. It also provides one of very few statements written in the immediate aftermath of the proposal that gives a woman's personal reactions to such an experience.

According to Brotherton's affidavit, on the day that the proposal occurred she had joined Brigham Young and Heber C. Kimball, at their request, for the day. After some intervening activities, she and Kimball walked together to Joseph Smith's store, ostensibly to allow her to meet the prophet Joseph Smith for the first time. En route Kimball asked her:

> "Sister Martha, are you willing to do all that the Prophet requires you to do?" I said I believed I was, thinking of course he would require nothing wrong. . . . "Well," said he, "there are many things in these last days that the world would laugh and scoff at, but unto us is given to know the mysteries of the kingdom." He further observed, "Martha, you must learn to hold your tongue, and it will be well with you. You will see Joseph, and very likely have some conversation with him, and he will tell you what you shall do."

After arriving at the store, Martha eventually was taken to an upper room by Joseph Smith, Brigham Young, and Heber C. Kimball. After she was seated, Smith and Kimball soon left, leaving her alone with Brigham Young, who rose, locked the door, and drew the curtain. He first observed, "This is our private room, Martha." Then he said he wanted to ask her a few questions, and he requested that she promise not to mention them to anyone. She agreed. He asked her what her feelings were toward him, and she replied, "My feelings are just the same towards you that they ever were, sir." He replied, "But to come to the point more closely, have not you an affection for me, that, if it were lawful and right you could accept of me for your husband and companion." Martha's feelings at that moment were "indescribable"; she wondered if these men she had admired so much were base deceivers. But how was she to get out of the fix she was in? She decided that the best strategy would be to ask for time to think and pray about the matter, so she replied, "If it were lawful and right, perhaps I might; but you know, sir, it is not."

Young's response was that

> brother Joseph has had a revelation from God that it is lawful and right for a man to have two wives; for as it was in the days of Abraham, so it shall be in these last days, and whoever is the first that is willing to take up the cross will receive the greatest blessing; and if you will accept me I will take you straight to the celestial kingdom; and if you will have me in this world, I will have you in that which is to come, and brother Joseph will marry us here today, and you can go home this evening and your parents will not know anything about it.

Martha said she was not interested in doing anything without her parents' knowledge. The conversation with Brigham Young continued, with more pressure for Martha to make an immediate decision. Young then unlocked the door, went out, and locked Martha back up. Ten minutes later, he returned with Joseph Smith.

> "Well, Martha," said Joseph, "it is lawful and right before God—I know it is. Look here sister, don't you believe me?" . . .
> "I know it is lawful and right before God, and if there is any sin in it, I will answer for it before God; and I have the keys of the Kingdom, and whatever I bind on earth is bound in heaven, and whatever I loose on earth is loosed in heaven—and if you

will accept Brigham, you will be blessed—God shall bless you, and my blessing shall rest upon you, and if you will be led by him you will do well; for I know Brigham will take care of you, and if he don't do his duty to you, come to me and I will make him—and if you do not like it in a month or two, come to me and I will make you free again; and if he turns you off I will take you on."

Martha responded rather warmly, "Sir, it will be too late to think a month or two after. I want to think first." Considerable pressure was then placed on her again to make an immediate decision. Young asked he if she had ever seen him "act in any way wrong in England," and Martha said no. "Well, then," Joseph Smith said, "what are you afraid of, sis?—come let me do the business for you." "Sir," Martha said, "do let me have a little time to think about it, and I will promise not to mention it to anyone." Eventually they seemed willing to let her go, and she rose, whereupon Joseph Smith "commenced to beg of me again—he said it was the best opportunity they might have for months, for the room was often engaged." She finally was allowed to go. "The next day being Sunday, I sat down, instead of going to meeting, and wrote the conversation and read it to my sister, who was not a little surprised." As soon as she could, Martha left Nauvoo for the nearby town of Warsaw, and thence she went to St. Louis, where she swore to her full statement before DuBouffay Fremon, justice of the peace for St. Louis County, on July 13, 1842.

This affidavit by Martha Brotherton is exceptionally valuable, both because of its striking similarities with later detailed reminiscences from women such as Lucy Walker, Helen Mar Kimball, and others who became plural wives of Joseph Smith and because Brotherton's statement also includes other information that was generally excluded from or downplayed in accounts from women who had committed themselves to living in plural marriage. Both the Lucy Walker and Martha Brotherton statements show that an appeal to the revelatory authority of Joseph Smith was the key factor used in trying to get women to accept polygamous overtures. In both instances, the women involved experienced shock and wondered at first if their commitment to the Mormon faith had been misguided. Furthermore, in these and other cases, direct and indirect coercive pressures were placed on the women to become plural wives. They were told that to become a plural wife would link them indissolubly with the new order and to fail to accept the proposal would lead to their being cast into the outer darkness.

The differences suggested by the Brotherton case and other cases of women who rejected plural marriage also are revealing. At the most obvious level, a key reason that Martha Brotherton was able to reject the polygamous overtures and make public her experience was that she was not yet so firmly committed to the Mormon cause that even as a seventeen-year-old female in a strange environment she felt she had no other options. Interestingly, her sister Elizabeth remained in Nauvoo and eventually became a plural wife of Parley P. Pratt, a situation that was alluded to in Vilate Kimball's note of June 27, 1843.[50] Martha clearly had a mind of her own and was not afraid to go public about a situation she found outrageous.

Two other aspects of the Brotherton report differentiate it from most testimonies believing Mormons gave of their introduction to plural marriage. One is the suggestion that Joseph Smith himself may have had some doubts about the correctness of his course in introducing polygamy. Brotherton quotes Smith as declaring decisively, "I know it is lawful and right before God," but in the next breath he appears to qualify that statement by saying "*if* there is any sin in it, I will answer for it before God" (emphasis added), suggesting that the thought had at least occurred to him that God might not fully approve his actions. Although most believing Mormon accounts did not convey such ambivalence, Joseph Lee Robinson, a devout supporter of the Mormon cause, recalled Smith saying to him "that God had revealed unto him that any Man that Ever Committed Adultery in Either of his Probations that that man could never be raised to the highest Exaltation in the Celestial Glory, and that he felt anxious with regard to himself that he enquired of the Lord, that the Lord told him that he Joseph had never committed Adultery."[51]

Perhaps the most striking element in Brotherton's affidavit and in other accounts from women who rejected polygamous overtures is the almost casual tone with which Mormon leaders are represented as tendering their offers of plural marriage. This tone is suggested throughout the Brotherton affidavit but is most evident in Smith's alleged statement that he would make other arrangements for

Martha in a few months if Brigham Young did not do his duty by her or if she found she did not like being his wife. Smith in these reported statements seems to imply that he would be prepared to take her on as a plural wife in such a situation if she so desired.

The apparent casualness of some of the early polygamous overtures is suggested over and over again by other accounts from Mormons, both male and female, who rejected plural marriage in Nauvoo. Perhaps the most vivid example is the statement, acknowledged by Latter-day Saints as coming from Joseph Smith, which can all but conclusively be identified as a letter sent from Smith to Nancy Rigdon, pressing his suit to her after she had initially rejected his overtures. That statement, which was originally published in Bennett's exposé but which also subsequently was printed in volume 5 of the *History of the Church*,[52] begins by saying that "Happiness is the object and design of our existence" but that this can only be achieved through "virtue, uprightness, holiness, and keeping all the commandments of God. But we cannot keep all the commandments without first knowing them. . . . That which is wrong under one circumstance, may be, and often is, right under another."

The letter continues:

A parent may whip a child, and justly too, because he stole an apple; whereas if the child had asked for the apple, and the parent had given it, the child would have eaten it with a better appetite; there would have been no stripes; all the pleasure of the apple would have been secured, all the misery of stealing lost.

This principle will justly apply to all of God's dealings with his children. Everything that God gives is lawful and right; and it is proper that we should enjoy his gifts and blessings whenever and wherever his is disposed to bestow; but if we should seize upon those same blessings and enjoyments without law, without revelation, without commandment, those blessings and enjoyments would prove cursings in the end. . . . Our heavenly Father is more liberal in His views, and boundless in His mercies and blessings, than we are ready to believe or receive; and, at the same time, is more terrible to the workers of iniquity, more awful in the executions of his punishments, and more ready to detect every false way, than we are apt to suppose Him to be. . . . He says: ". . . no good thing will I withhold from them

who walk uprightly before me, and do my will in all things—
who will listen to my voice and the voice of the servant whom
I have sent; . . . for all things shall be made known unto them
in mine own due time, and in the end they shall have joy."

Such statements usually were viewed as pure sophistry by opponents of plural marriage. Even more disturbing to such critics were
allegations that Joseph Smith asked already married women to become his plural wives. The most controversial such allegation, also
reported initially by Bennett, involved Sarah Pratt, wife of the Mormon apostle and intellectual leader Orson Pratt, who served as a
missionary to England during 1841 and 1842. According to Bennett's
account, Joseph Smith wanted Sarah Pratt to become his spiritual
wife, and he tried to seduce her while her husband was away on that
mission. Bennett indicated that Smith had asked him to serve as his
go-between with Sarah and that he warned her of the intrigue. Mrs.
Pratt would not believe such a thing, but he told her that Smith's
true character would soon be revealed. Thereafter, Smith allegedly
took Bennett to the Pratt home and immediately broached the subject with her. Sarah was outraged at his advances, and when he persisted she finally threatened to tell her husband. According to
Bennett, Smith begged not to be exposed.[53]

This explosively controversial allegation and others like it have
seldom been convincingly analyzed and placed into context by scholars. Most Mormon writers have either ignored such charges or denied
their accuracy. Others have focused primary attention on the supposed
unreliability of those making the charges. And still other writers
such as Fawn Brodie and Richard S. Van Wagoner, who apparently
accept some of the charges, have rather naively suggested that a form
of "polyandry" was practiced in Nauvoo.[54] Danel Bachman also re-
fers to Smith's ties to "previously married women" as "polyandrous,"
although his analysis suggests the existence of a much more complex
phenomenon.

What is one to make of such statements? Published Latter-day
Saints accounts, in the first place, document beyond cavil that,
whatever his motives, Joseph Smith did ask some of his followers'
wives to become his plural wives.[55] According to these sources,
Smith's goal in such cases was simply to test the loyalty of the women

and of their husbands (if the husbands knew of the proposal). Such an argument cannot explain all reported cases, however. Most of the remainder could be accounted for if one keeps in mind that, at some level at least, Joseph Smith and his closest associates in Nauvoo believed that no earthly marriage was fully valid unless it had been sealed by the Mormon priesthood, then led by Joseph Smith, for "eternity" as well as for "time." In effect, therefore, wives who had not yet been married under those ceremonies could still be seen as being in some sense eligible to become plural wives of someone else.[56]

Nevertheless, some cases remain that cannot be explained by this line of argument either. In a careful analysis of the data in *Religion and Sexuality*, I suggest that in early Mormonism there may well have been a very limited practice of appointing "proxy husbands" for wives of absent or infertile husbands. Such a practice was clearly sanctioned (without the use of the term *proxy husband*) by Brigham Young in a letter of March 5, 1857, and the practice may well have dated back to Joseph Smith himself. Such a practice, if it existed in Nauvoo, would not have been viewed as polyandrous by its practitioners but rather as part of the developing patriarchal polygamous system.[57]

On this point, the comment of Mary E. Rollins Lightner, wife of Adam Lightner and a plural wife of Joseph Smith, is tantalizing. In a letter to John A. Smith in 1892, she wrote: "I could explain some things in regard to my living with Mr. L. after becoming the *Wife of another*, which would throw light, on what *now* seems mysterious—and you would be perfectly satisfied with me. I write this; because I have heard that it had been commented on to my injury."[58]

Whatever the rationale behind Joseph Smith's requests that women already married to his associates become his plural wives, such actions were extremely controversial when they were reported publicly to Mormons, most of whom did not even know about the church leadership's commitment to plural marriage. The leadership felt that at all costs the Prophet's name must be kept unbesmirched and thus they resorted to extraordinary measures of "damage control." To destroy the credibility of the stories of women such as Martha Brotherton, Nancy Rigdon, and Sarah Pratt, their characters were verbally dragged through the mud, using remarkably similar allegations. *The Wasp*, one of the church's newspapers in Nauvoo, referred to Martha Brotherton as a "harlot" associated with John C.

Bennett, while her sisters Mary and Elizabeth (who later became a plural wife), as well as her brother-in-law John McIlwrick, swore to an affidavit indicating that Martha was a liar and had been seen in a compromising situation with a young man.[59] Stephen Markham swore to an affidavit that he had seen Nancy Rigdon and John C. Bennett in a compromising situation and was convinced that they were "guilty of unlawful and illicit intercourse with each other."[60] And Mormon stalwarts suggested that John C. Bennett, not Joseph Smith, had been having an affair with Sarah Pratt. Zeruiah Goddard claimed that he had once caught Bennett "taking his hands out of her [Mrs. Pratt's] bosom" as they lay on a bed.[61]

The publication of literally hundreds of such scurrilous allegations and counterallegations in Mormon and anti-Mormon newspapers and pamphlets between 1842 and 1844 can cause even the most hardened scholar to feel sickened by the bitterness the exchanges reveal. Furthermore, some of these allegations are demonstrably false. For example, Zeruiah Goddard's affidavit stated that Bennett had visited Sarah Pratt every night with one exception for a period of nearly a month in October 1840, yet during that same time Bennett was living almost one hundred miles away in Springfield, where he was fully occupied in lobbying for measures desired by the Mormons.[62] Even if some of the other allegations against individuals such as Martha Brotherton, Nancy Rigdon, and Sarah Pratt should have been true (which this author feels is unlikely), it is very disturbing that the characters of the daughter of Joseph Smith's first counselor Sidney Rigdon or of the wife of his apostle Orson Pratt (who then stood next only to Brigham Young in seniority in the Quorum of the Twelve Apostles) should have been publicly defamed in such an explicit manner. Joseph Smith also appears to have been deeply disturbed by the bitterness that resulted. He declared in a speech on February 21, 1843, "This biting and devouring each other I cannot endure. Away with it. For God's sake stop it."[63]

One indication of the level of bitterness associated with these events and of the success of the Mormon leadership's efforts at damage control during this period is the confusion surrounding the phrases *spiritual wives* and *spiritual wife system*, which were widely used in discussions of polygamy in Nauvoo. As part of their skillful efforts, so ably analyzed in Charles Shook's *True Origin of Mormon*

Polygamy, to avoid premature public exposure of their polygamous beliefs and practices, leaders of the Mormon church, both at the time and subsequently, vigorously denied that it ever advocated or practiced "spiritual wifery." That terminology is, instead, used to refer to the corruptions introduced by John C. Bennett and other licentious individuals who were thrown out of the church.

Although this line of argument has been almost universally accepted by subsequent Mormon scholars, it is almost certainly false. As Helen Mar Kimball Whitney, a plural wife of Joseph Smith, declared in her 1882 pamphlet *Plural Marriage as Taught by the Prophet Joseph,* "At that time [in Nauvoo] spiritual wife was the title by which every woman who entered into the order was called, for it was taught and practiced as a spiritual order and not a temporal one though it was always spoken of sneeringly by those who did not believe in it."[64] The events at Nauvoo were so painful that many individuals subsequently experienced what amounted to a kind of partial amnesia. When the Mormon church finally admitted in 1852 that it had been practicing polygamy (which it had vehemently denied earlier), the church evidently decided to replace the terms *spiritual wife* and *spiritual wife system* with *celestial marriage,* which also had a spiritual sound but lacked the intense negative baggage associated with the earlier expressions.

VIII

The complex and ambivalent reactions toward polygamy of Joseph Smith's first wife, Emma Hale Smith, provide exceptionally revealing insights into plural marriage at Nauvoo and women's reactions to it. Until the appearance in 1984 of *Mormon Enigma,* the first full-length scholarly biography of Emma, written by Linda King Newell and Valeen Tippetts Avery, many doubted that her full story and reactions could ever be convincingly reconstructed. Now, based on this important biography and on other sources, it is possible to know with considerable confidence precisely how and why Emma reacted in certain ways to her husband's polygamous beliefs and practices. Her story also sheds new light on the overall development of plural marriage. Here only the outlines of her experiences can be suggested. Those interested in further details should consult the biography itself or turn to the longer manuscript version of the biography, which provides the most comprehensive discussion of the relationship between Joseph and Emma now available.[65]

At the outset, it must be emphasized that Emma was in many ways every bit as remarkable a person as her better-known husband. She was, as the authors of *Mormon Enigma* note,

> a capable, articulate, and influential individual in her own right who profoundly affected the development of the religious movements with which she was associated. From her initial elopement with the young would-be prophet Joseph Smith in 1827, through seventeen years of marriage and repeated moves through five states, she became a force to be reckoned with, especially in financial and other practical matters affecting the Mormon church. Deeply in love with her husband, she quietly but vigorously opposed the polygamous beliefs and practices which he sought to introduce into Mormon practice in Illinois in the early 1840s. Following her husband's assassination in 1844 and the migration westward of the main body of Mormons under Brigham Young in 1846, Emma remained behind in the nearly deserted town of Nauvoo, Illinois. There she continued to live thirty-two more years as the wife of Lewis C. Bidamon, who never embraced Mormon doctrines. When a group of individuals dissatisfied with Brigham Young and polygamy founded a church which Emma's son Joseph Smith III would lead after 1860, she gained new status.[66]

Ultimately only one factor weakened and threatened to destroy the powerful bond between Emma and Joseph. That was Joseph's tendency toward polygamy. Hints that a problem might exist date back to the early days of their marriage, when, after Joseph and Emma left Pennsylvania in 1830, Emma's cousin Hiel Lewis, accused Joseph of improper conduct with a woman whom, fifty years later, he identified as "E. W. [Eliza Winters]."[67] Joseph was also connected in some manner with indiscreet behavior toward Nancy Marinda Johnson during the period when he lived with her father and mother in Kirtland, Ohio. Her brothers joined the mob that tarred, feathered, and apparently threatened to castrate him in March 1832, and their anger appears to have been kindled by concerns about Joseph and their sister.[68] A letter from Oliver Cowdery, one of Joseph's closest early associates, accuses him of improper conduct with a servant girl named Fanny Alger in 1836.[69] And a gossip in Kirtland commented about Joseph and Vienna Jacques.[70] Finally, the names of Lucinda Huntington Buell and Lucinda Morgan Harris were linked to Joseph's at some point during the period of time the Mormons were in Missouri.[71]

Not until after 1839, when the displaced members of the church arrived in Illinois to settle the town that would become Nauvoo, however, would Joseph begin to take clear steps to begin to introduce polygamous ideas and practices. Although there is evidence that he may have thought about the possibility of introducing polygamy among his followers as early as July 17, 1831,[72] and although rumors of such practices go back at least as early as 1835, when the first edition of the Doctrine and Covenants made a point of denying that the church sanctioned "polygamy,"[73] no solid evidence of polygamous relationships sanctioned by a formal marriage ceremony survive before Joseph's marriage to Louisa Beaman on April 5, 1841. The majority of Joseph's identifiable polygamous unions, and his problems with polygamy, occurred during the years between 1842 and 1844. George A. Smith estimated that before the formal dictation of the revelation on polygamy on July 12, 1843, probably no more than one to two hundred individuals in Nauvoo (out of a population then numbering more than seven thousand) were aware that the church's leaders privately taught and engaged in the practice.[74]

Although Emma never knew the full extent of her husband's polygamous activities, she had inklings of his leanings in that direction at least as early as the spring of 1841, when Joseph gave a public speech that was recognized and attacked by Emma and other women at the time as implying the possibility that polygamy might be practiced in the future.[75] According to *Mormon Enigma*, Emma's eventual knowledge of at least seven of her husband's plural wives can be documented conclusively.[76] Eliza R. Snow asserted that it was a *"fact* that Sister Emma, of her own free will and choice, gave her husband four wives . . . [and] she not only gave them to her husband, but she taught them the doctrine."[77] Emma felt profoundly ambivalent about the situation she was in. Repeatedly, she would try to resign herself to support her husband, hoping evidently to contain his activities, but almost immediately she would regret her cooperation and give vent to her anger at the situation. As Orson Pratt recalled, Emma "at times fought against him [Joseph] with all her heart; and then again she would break down in her feelings . . . and would then lead forth ladies and place their hands in the hands of Joseph."[78]

To understand Emma's reactions, perhaps the best approach is briefly to identify how her knowledge of Joseph's polygamy practice gradually developed and how she reacted at each stage of her growing knowledge. Emma's first clear knowledge of her husband's polygamy practice in Nauvoo came in April 1842 as the opportunistic and licentious John C. Bennett was being eased out of the church. Someone evidently told her about Joseph's plural marriages. She was furious, and he had to spend the better part of a day to calm her down, perhaps by saying that he had neither sanctioned nor participated in Bennett's spiritual wife doctrine.[79] In the meantime, the Nauvoo Female Relief Society, the rapidly growing women's organization in the church, increasingly became the forum for a subtle sparring between Emma and Joseph over the polygamy issue. Emma would speak strongly against sin and iniquity, while Joseph would warn the women equally strongly against excessive zeal or meddling in matters about which they did not know. Women in the Relief Society who, unbeknownst to Emma, were already plural wives of Joseph or of his associates found themselves in the middle of a curious and disconcerting verbal crossfire.[80]

Matters became substantially more complicated early in February 1843, when Emma discovered that Eliza Snow, her close friend, who had lived in the large Smith mansion house-hotel for seven months, was a plural wife of Joseph's. Emma was furious at what she took to be a personal betrayal, and some sort of physical confrontation evidently ensued between the two women, causing Eliza to move out on February 11.[81] At this point, Emma could no longer believe that Joseph was not involved with polygamy, and he could no longer deny it. He nevertheless continued secretly to pursue the establishment of polygamy in spite of Emma's strong negative feelings. In March 1843, unbeknownst to Emma, he married two sisters, Emily and Eliza Partridge, who were then living in his home.[82] At the same time, he continued to try to prepare the way to introduce new endowment ceremonies, which he taught were essential for exaltation, to women as well as to the select men who had first participated in the ceremonies nearly a year earlier. Joseph wanted Emma to serve as a model to other women and to lead the way in introducing the ceremonies to other women, but he would not let her do so until she became obedient to him and agreed to give him plural wives.[83]

By the spring of 1843, Emma finally came around, briefly, to an acceptance of plural marriage. Apparently convinced that the practice was necessary for her salvation and essential to their continued relationship, she agreed in May 1843 to give Joseph other wives if she could choose them.[84] (At this point, Joseph Smith's plural wives numbered at least sixteen.[85]) Emma chose two sets of sisters then living in their house, Emily and Eliza Partridge and Sarah and Maria Lawrence. Although the Partridge sisters had already been married to Joseph two months earlier, Emily indicated that "to save family trouble Brother Joseph thought it best to have another ceremony performed."[86] This was done in Emma's presence on May 23, 1843. Almost immediately, however, Emma regretted her action and became even more bitter than before "and kept Joseph up till very late in the night talking with him."[87] Thereafter, Emma showed exceptional vigilance in trying to prevent Joseph from meeting with his plural wives. The situation was difficult for all concerned. As Emily wrote, Emma "had, as it were, bound us to the ship and carried us to mid ocean, then threw us overboard to sink or swim as the case might be."[88]

As Newell and Avery note:

Joseph's choice of women as plural wives gradually put a wedge between Emma and her friends as long as she remained either ignorant of the practice or opposed it. By late summer 1843 most of Emma's friends had either married Joseph or had given their daughters to him. Her sister-in-law, Agnes Coolbrith, was married to Joseph; another sister-in-law, Mary Fielding, had consented to the marriage of her husband Hyrum Smith and her sister Mercy. At least five women in her own household were Joseph's plural wives. Whether Emma knew about them or not, the women would not have been sympathetic to Emma while she opposed plural marriage. As a result, she became isolated from her friends and associates, and through the next four years this isolation would become more and more acute.[89]

A major turning point in the development of polygamy and in Joseph's relationship with Emma came on July 12, 1843, when, at the request of his brother Hyrum, Joseph dictated the revelation on plural and celestial marriage, while his personal secretary William Clayton took it down sentence by sentence. Hyrum then took the revelation to Emma, saying, "I believe I can convince her of [the] truth, and you will thereafter have peace." When he returned, he reported "that he had never received a more severe talking to in his life, that Emma was very bitter and full of resentment and anger." Joseph quietly replied, "I told you you did not know Emma as I did." He spent the better part of the following day in conversation with Emma.[90]

Although much of the revelation may have dated back to the Kirtland period of 1830–31, fifteen of the sixty-six verses are clearly directed to Emma and relate to his immediate problems with her.[91] It declared, for instance, "Let my handmaid, Emma Smith, receive all those that have been given unto my servant Joseph, and who are virtuous and pure before me." It went on, asserting that Joseph would receive from the Lord "an hundred-fold of this world, of wives" if she would not obey. Under the "law of the priesthood" a man "cannot commit adultery with that that belongeth to him and to no one else. And if he have ten virgins given unto him by this law, he cannot commit adultery, for they belong to him." "If any man have a wife . . . and he teaches unto her the law of my priesthood, as pertaining unto these things, then she shall believe and administer unto him, or she shall be destroyed, saith the Lord your God."

And what if the wife refused to allow other wives under such circumstances? "It shall be lawful in me, if she receive not this law, for him to receive all things whatsoever I, the Lord his God, will give unto him, because she did not believe and administer unto him." The revelation thus exempted a man from the "law of Sarah," which apparently required a husband to ask his wife for permission to take another wife. If the first withheld her consent for *any* plural marriage, the revelation authorized the husband to proceed without it.[92]

The formal recording of the revelation and its subsequent presentation by Hyrum Smith before the High Council of the church on August 12, 1843, caused the lines of division on the issue to harden. It now became obvious to Joseph Smith's associates that he was intent on carrying through with his policy on polygamy, and they

would either have to support or oppose him.[93] Emma, in the mean
time, remained deeply ambivalent about the entire situation. Perhaps in part to assuage her anxiety that his support of polygamy
might result in his death and leave her and her family unprotected,
on July 14, 1843, Joseph deeded to Emma half his share in the
steamboat *Maid of Iowa* and also sixty city lots.[94] He also may have
destroyed or allowed Emma to destroy the original dictated version of
the revelation, although an exact copy of that revelation upon which
the published form is based had previously been made by Joseph C.
Kingsbury.[95]

Matters became further complicated by August 16, 1843, when
William Clayton recorded in a diary entry: "This A.M. Joseph told
me that sin[c]e Emma came back from St. Louis, she had resisted the
P[rinciple] in toto, and he had to tell her he would relinquish all for
her sake. She said she would give him E[liza] and E[mily] P[artridge]
but he knew if he took them she would pitch on him, & obtain a
divorce & leave him. He however told me he should not relinquish
anything."[96] As the authors of *Mormon Enigma* note: "In the most
serious crisis of their marriage, Joseph backed down. But he confided
to Clayton that he did not intend to keep his word."[97]

By the end of the summer, matters seemed to ease somewhat.
Several accounts suggest that Emma temporarily resigned herself to
the situation. Perhaps this was connected, in part, with her receiving her endowments sometime between May 28 and September 28,
1843, when she received the highest ordinance of the church, the
second anointing. "In the language of the ordinance, she was Joseph's queen. She was the first woman to receive the ordinances and
Joseph administered them to her. Emma then initiated other women,
who in turn initiated others, until Mormon women today trace their
own endowments back to Emma Smith."[98] It must be noted that neither Joseph nor Emma linked the endowment directly with plural
marriage. Because opponents of plural marriage such as William
Marks and Sidney Rigdon were included in the inner circle of
Smith's followers who experienced the early endowments, the issue of
polygamy was not raised directly in that context.[99]

Despite the many tensions, Emma and Joseph maintained an
outwardly warm and loving relationship. Privately, however, matters
soon became stormy again. Emma worked vigorously within the Relief

Society to try to get it to oppose plural marriage. George A. Smith's wife, Bathsheba, remembered Emma saying, "Your husbands are going to take more wives, and unless you consent to it, you must put your foot down and keep it there."[100] A young woman who visited Nauvoo from nearby Carthage asked, "Mrs. Smith, where does your church get this doctrine of spiritual wives?" Emma's face flushed scarlet, and her eyes blazed as she replied, "Straight from hell, madam."[101]

Matters came to a head at the Relief Society meeting of March 16, 1844, when Emma read the "Voice of Innocence,' a statement defending the women of Nauvoo against allegations of loose morals, which had been passed unanimously at the March 9 meeting. Emma also read the church presidency's original letter to the Relief Society, written in 1842, stating, "We therefore warn you, and forewarn you . . . we do not want anyone to believe anything as coming from us contrary to the old established morals & virtues, & scriptural laws . . . all persons pretending to be authorized by us . . . are and will be *liars and base imposters* & you are authorized . . . to denounce them as such . . . whether they are prophets, Seers, or revelators, patriarchs, twelve apostles . . . you are alike culpable and shall be damned for such evil practices." Emma went on to emphasize the importance of searching out iniquity, and she urged women to follow the teachings of Joseph Smith as he taught them "from the stand," implying that his private teachings should be disregarded.[102]

As Newell and Avery observe:

> The "Voice of Innocence" was published in the Nauvoo *Neighbor* March 20, but the Relief Society did not meet again in Nauvoo. In those last meetings Emma had reaffirmed the traditional Christian standards of marriage, using Joseph's public denials of polygamy, his own letter, and the "Voice of Innocence" to give every woman present a valid reason for avoiding plural marriage. When Emma had the women take a public oath with their hands raised in support of virtue, she caused enough consternation in the men's councils to stop the Relief Society meetings. The women would not have their own organization again for more than a decade.[103]

Outside sources soon began to gossip in print about Emma and Joseph's domestic difficulties. When Emma left alone on a steamboat for St. Louis on April 19, 1844, Joseph wrote that she had gone to purchase goods, but the *St. Louis Republican* announced that "the Mormon prophet Joe Smith has turned his wife out of doors for being in communication with a gentleman of the sect which she hesitated or refused to disclose."[104] Upon her return after a five-day visit to St. Louis, Emma was shocked to enter the main room of their mansion house/hotel and discover a bar, complete with counter, shelves, and glasses for serving liquor. She asked Joseph to explain himself, and he indicated that it was only a temporary arrangement for the benefit of his friend Porter Rockwell, who needed a place until a new building across the street was constructed to house his bar and barbershop. Emma told Joseph that either the bar must go or she and the children would move out. Faced with this ultimatum he did not want to accept, Joseph acquiesced and had the bar removed immediately.[105]

The authors of *Mormon Enigma* ask whether Joseph may have similarly acquiesed to halting plural marriages:

He apparently did not take additional wives after November 1843, but evidence is conflicting as to whether he intended to abandon the practice, as Emma believed, or whether he found it expedient to let his opponents *think* he was abandoning it. William Marks, who had never embraced the principle, said that Joseph approached him one day in the spring [of 1844] and invited him to a secluded place to talk. "We are a ruined people." Marks quoted Joseph as saying. "This doctrine of polygamy or Spiritual-wife System, that has been taught and practiced among us, will prove our destruction and overthrow. I have been deceived, in reference to its practice; it is wrong; it is a curse to mankind, and we shall have to leave the United States soon, unless it can be put down." Marks further stated that Joseph asked him to go to the High Council and prefer charges against all who practiced the doctrine, while Joseph would "preach against it, with all my might, and in this way we may rid the church of this damnable heresy." But when Marks told others about these conversations with Joseph, rumors surfaced that he "was about to apostatize." His statements "were pronounced false by the Twelve, and disbelieved."

The minutes of an 1867 meeting within the Reorganized Church refer to this issue. A man named Hugh Herringshaw had "heard Joseph tell the 12 that they must abandon polygamy and turned to Brigham Young and asked if he was willing to do so. Young said he had been asleep. Then Joseph spoke upon the matter as only he could talk denouncing the doctrine of polygamy. Brigham replied that he and Taylor had determined what course they would pursue." A year earlier, in 1866, Brigham Young had conceded, "Joseph was worn out with it, but as to his denying any such thing I never knew that he denied the doctrine of polygamy. Some have said that he did, but I do not believe he ever did." Joseph's niece said he finally "awoke to a realization of the whole miserable affair [and] . . . tried to withdraw from and put dow[n] the Evil into which he had fallen." Sarah Scott, a young immigrant from Massachusetts, wrote home to her mother about the situation. "Mr. Haven [her brother-in-law] told me . . . that those doctrines tried his faith very much till he heard Hyrum Smith explain them and now or then he thought it was right. But . . . [in late May or early June] Hyrum denied that he and Joseph had the revelation concerning it but said that it referred to ancient times; and was published so in the *Neighbor.* After I saw it I said to Mr. Haven: 'What do you think of that?' . . . He said that he supposed Hyrum saw what a disturbance it was making and thought he would say it on account of there being such excitement."[106]

Whatever Joseph Smith may have intended, events began to move rapidly toward their tragic denouement on June 7, 1844, when a group of disaffected Mormons—including William and Wilson Law, Robert D. Foster, Austin Cowles, and Charles and Francis Higbee—published a newspaper, *The Nauvoo Expositor,* that decried polygamy and included a number of straightforward affidavits about the practice in Nauvoo that were difficult to dismiss as mere slander. Knowing that the publication and circulation of such reports would undercut the faith of many members who were as yet unaware that the church sanctioned and advocated the new practices, Smith acted quickly to have the press of the *Expositor* and any remaining copies of the paper destroyed. Almost immediately this action brought outside hostility against the Mormons to a fever pitch. Rather than see outright civil war erupt, Joseph Smith eventually surrendered himself to the authorities in Carthage, Illinois, to stand trial. There, on

June 27, 1844, a mob in collusion with local militiamen entered the jail, shooting and killing Joseph and his brother Hyrum.[107]

IX

Two knotty questions remain before the story of Joseph Smith and the polygamy he introduced in Nauvoo can be concluded. One is the perennial issue of what Joseph Smith's motivations could have been for devoting so much time and energy during his last years to introducing this highly controversial practice. Any simple explanation is probably impossible. The complexity of human genius and the psychological states associated with such genius should not be dismissed by reductionistic arguments. Yet there is one approach, which I shall suggest only as a hypothesis, that may help us come closer to understanding Joseph Smith's remarkable actions.

Before considering this hypothesis, we need to recall William James's discussion of the psychology of religious genius, as it occurs in individuals for whom "religion exists not as a dull habit, but as an acute fever." Genius in such individuals, according to James, is frequently associated with "symptoms of nervous instability."

> Even more perhaps than other kinds of genius, religious leaders have been subject to abnormal psychic visitations. . . . Often they have led a discordant inner life, and had melancholy during part of their career. They have known no measure, been liable to obsessions and fixed ideas; and frequently they have fallen into trances, heard voices, seen visions, and presented all sorts of peculiarities which are ordinarily classed as pathological. Often, moreover, these pathological features in their career have helped to give them their religious authority and influence.[108]

James goes on to emphasize that even if religious inspiration may often occur in psychologically unstable or disordered individuals, that fact does not necessarily discredit the *fruits* of such inspiration. He quotes Dr. Henry Maudsley's statement:

> What right have we to believe Nature under any obligation to work by means of complete minds only? She may find an incomplete mind a more suitable instrument for a particular purpose.

It is the work that is done, and the quality in the worker by
which it is done, that is alone of moment; and it may be no
great matter from a cosmical standpoint, if in other qualities of
character he was singularly defective—if indeed he were a hyp-
ocrite, adulterer, eccentric or lunatic.[109]

James argues that the only ultimate test of the validity of religious
inspiration is practical—in Jesus' words, "By their fruits ye shall
know them." He concludes: "If there were such a thing as inspiration
from a higher realm, it might well be that the neurotic temperament
would furnish the chief condition of the requisite receptivity."[110]

One further caveat needs to be added before we briefly explore
one possible approach to understanding Joseph Smith's psychological
states. The line between health and illness, between normal mood
swings and those that might be described as extreme, is very fine
indeed. It is often difficult for a contemporary psychiatrist who has
worked closely with a patient to make an accurate diagnosis. To di-
agnose with confidence someone long dead, even when extensive
records exist on his or her life, is far more difficult and speculative.
The observations that follow are therefore intended to be suggestive,
not definitive. These observations will have served their purpose if
they open up new possibilities for better understanding aspects of Joseph Smith's beliefs and behavior that might otherwise appear
opaque or incomprehensible.

The psychological interpretation of Joseph Smith that I am pro-
posing was first mentioned to me by a Mormon psychiatrist, Dr. Jess
Groesbeck.[111] He suggested that Joseph Smith's behavior, especially
during the last years of his life, is strikingly similar to behavior that
psychiatrists associate with manic-depressive syndromes. Although
one could understand that any individual under the pressures Joseph
Smith faced might experience substantial mood swings, in the Mormon prophet's case those mood swings appear so severe that they
may be clinically significant.

Groesbeck also pointed out that there is substantial evidence
that tendencies toward manic-depression often are inherited. Although many people are aware that one of Joseph Smith's brightest
and most appealing sons, David Hyrum, tragically lapsed into insanity and spent the last years of his life in a mental institution, few

realize that at least six other male descendants of the Mormon prophet also suffered from psychological disorders, including manic-depression.[112] The possibility that Joseph Smith himself may also have been subject to similar tendencies cannot be discounted.

What are some of the characteristics of psychological mania and how do such states reflect themselves in behavior? According to Harold I. Kaplan and Benjamin J. Sadock's *Comprehensive Textbook of Psychiatry/IV*:

> The critical clinical feature for a manic episode is a mood that is elevated, expansive, or irritable. The associated symptoms include hyperactivity, pressure of speech, flight of ideas, diminished need for sleep, increased self-esteem to the point of grandiosity, extreme distractibility, short attention span, and extraordinarily poor judgment in the interpersonal and social areas. . . .
>
> The person speaks more rapidly, thinks more rapidly, or moves more rapidly. The person frequently requires much less sleep and has apparently limitless energy. Many people with a manic illness feel that they are highly creative during these attacks. The reason, in part, is because there is a flooding of consciousness with ideas and associations that at times are imaginative and creative but that at other times are idiosyncratic and of little artistic merit. . . .
>
> Although the elevated mood is often described as euphoric and cheerful and having an infectious quality, it is characterized by an absence of selectivity and an unceasing driven quality. Mania is also characterized by an extremely poor frustration tolerance, with resulting heightened irritability. A manic patient may be quite humorous, good natured, and friendly until frustrated in some trivial way. The good humor then promptly disappears and is replaced by anger and even rage. . . .
>
> The increased activity often takes the form of sexual promiscuity, political involvement, and religious concern. . . .
>
> The manic episode may or may not include psychotic symptoms. The impairment of judgment may not be sufficiently severe to justify a psychotic diagnosis. Delusions and hallucinations are not unusual. The context is usually consistent with the dominant mood. It is quite common for the person to communicate with God and to have it revealed that he or she has a spe-

cial purpose or mission. Patients frequently describe themselves as an "organ" of God through whom God speaks to the world.[113]

How do such characteristics of psychological mania square with Joseph Smith's actions during the last three years of his life in Nauvoo between 1841 and 1844? To anyone who has worked closely with the records of the Mormon prophet's life during those final years, the parallels are striking. Only a few key elements can be highlighted here, especially as they relate to his efforts to introduce both the belief and practice of polygamy among his most trusted followers.

Most obvious is the Mormon prophet's extraordinary expansiveness and grandiosity during this period. During the last year of his life, to mention only the most well-known examples, Smith served as mayor of Nauvoo and head of his own private army, became "king" of his secret Kingdom of God that he anticipated would eventually encompass all of North and South America, ran for president of the United States (that effort was cut short by his martyrdom), and was the "husband" in some sense of dozens of wives.[114] He commented during that period that excitement had become the very core of his life. Those who supported him during the period were impressed by his sense of divine mission and feeling that he was discovering the very secrets of the universe. Those who opposed him, including some of his previously most loyal lieutenants such as William Marks and William Law, thought instead that he had slipped his moorings and become a "fallen prophet," unfit to lead the church he had founded.

In no area were Joseph Smith's manic qualities more evident than in his efforts to introduce and practice polygamy during the last three years of his life. The point at which Joseph Smith began systematically to introduce polygamy to his closest associates has strong suggestions of mania. As Danel Bachman, summarizing the account by Helen Mar Kimball Whitney, wrote:

> Brigham Young, Heber C. Kimball, and John Taylor [key members of the Quorum of the Twelve Apostles who were returning from England] arrived in Nauvoo on July 1, 1841. . . . Joseph Smith was waiting at the landing with a company of horsemen. As soon as the missionaries disembarked from the boat, he

rushed them to dinner at his home, not even giving them time to visit their own families. Vilate Kimball thought that this discourtesy continued after dinner when Smith brought the entire party to the Kimball Home. The Prophet, wrote Helen Kimball, "seemed unwilling to part with my father and from that time kept the Twelve in Council early and late." Helen said her mother "never dreamed that he was during those times revealing to them the principles of Celestial Marriage" or that her trials were about to begin.[115]

If the initial systematic attempt to introduce the concept of plural marriage among his closest associates bespeaks possible manic enthusiasm on Joseph Smith's part, his subsequent surge of sexual activity with the fifteen or more women with whom he may have sustained sexual relations as plural wives (the full number may have been much greater) is even more suggestive of the hypersexuality that often accompanies manic periods. Some earlier writers such as Fawn Brodie, who have closely investigated the evidence on Joseph Smith's plural relationships, have suggested that he was in effect essentially a lusty, good-natured libertine giving vent to impulses that more cautious individuals keep under better control. I have increasingly come to the conclusion, however, as did Brodie upon later reflection, that this argument cannot adequately explain the extent of Smith's sexual relationships and activities. Something more, surely, was involved.[116]

Clinically significant manic episodes often alternate with correspondingly deep states of depression.[117] Once again, it must be noted that many individuals experience mild depression and that such states of mind are not uncommon during periods of severe stress. Whether such periods of depression were clinically significant in Joseph Smith's case remains debatable. That he *did* have periods of severe depression and discouragement during the last years of his life is, however, indisputable.

One such period was described by one of his plural wives, Mary Rollins Lightner. She recalled Smith saying:

I am tired, I have been mobbed, I have suffered so much, from outsiders and from my own family. Some of the brethren think they can carry this work on better than I can, far better. I have asked the Lord to take me away. I have to seal my testimony to this generation with my blood. I have to do it for this work will never progress until I am gone for the testimony is of no force until the testator is dead. People little know who I am when they talk about me, and they will never know until they see me weighed in the balance in the Kingdom of God. Then they will know who I am, and see me as I am. I dare not tell them, and they do not know me.[118]

Although this was recounted many years later, it seems accurately to reflect the spirit of many of Joseph Smith's private statements during his last days. His sermon of April 7, 1844, at the funeral of Elder King Follett may appropriately serve as his own epitaph. In this sermon, he described his glorious vision of men progressing to the achievement of full godlike powers. He declared in his conclusion, which George A. Smith said referred to plural marriage, "You never knew my heart; no man knows my history; I cannot tell it. I shall never undertake it. If I had not experienced what I have, I should not have known it myself. . . . When I am called at the trump of the archangel, and weighed in the balance, you will all know me then."[119]

Here, it seems to me, was a profoundly lonely man, poignantly aware of the inability of the world (or even himself) to understand the underlying significance of his ideas and mission and seeing with stark clarity that he was about to be overwhelmed by forces he had helped set loose but which were beyond his control. Throughout his life, Joseph Smith was painfully aware of his singularity and never able to escape it.

Where does all this leave us with regard to understanding the dynamics of Joseph Smith's psychology and its impact on his beliefs and practices? I must emphasize again that the analysis presented here about Joseph Smith's possible tendencies toward manic-depressive mental states is not intended as anything but a hypothesis. It is in no way intended to reduce the mystery—and the greatness—of Joseph Smith's accomplishments. Even if this hypothesis be true, the ultimate question remains not the *origin* of Smith's genius but the *fruits* of that genius.

To restate one of William James's observations, "If there were such a thing as inspiration from a higher realm, it might well be that the neurotic temperament would furnish the chief condition of the requisite receptivity."[120] It may well be that only individuals whose inhibitions are bypassed by various forms of mania may able to convince themselves and others that their insights emanate directly from God or other higher spiritual powers. In this context, it is very interesting to note that both John Humphrey Noyes and Ann Lee also showed strong manic-depressive tendencies. Noyes's case could be described as an almost classic example of the syndrome, and Lee's extraordinary mood swings also are well documented.[121] For Noyes and Lee, the self-assurance that accompanied the sense of direct communication with the divine contributed much to their ability to introduce new ideas to their followers.

It must further be emphasized that individuals with manic-depressive tendencies can be extremely effective leaders, especially during times of crisis. One striking example is Oliver Cromwell, the great Puritan general and leader of England during the 1640s and 1650s, who dealt with a host of issues that would have destroyed any lesser person.[122] Thus, even if manic-depressive psychological states may have provided much of the *occasion* for Joseph Smith's remarkable creativity, the validity of the *product* of that inspiration must be judged on its own merits. Nonbelievers no doubt will still see Joseph Smith's creativity as a product of his own fertile mind, but devout Saints may equally well see that creativity as emanation from the Divine.

One final question still remains, namely, how Emma Smith dealt with her husband's polygamy as she lived out the last thirty-five years of her life until 1879. The brief answer is that, with rare exceptions, she remained both publicly and privately silent on the topic, although she clearly believed polygamy was wrong. A proud and self-controlled woman with a strong sense of propriety and a hatred of scandal and notoriety, she maintained a dignified exterior even as controversies over Mormon polygamy continued to swirl, both within the two main branches of the Mormon church and between the Utah Mormons and the government of the United States, which increasingly attacked the practice.[123]

Shortly before Emma died in 1879, her eldest son, Joseph Smith III, then the head of the antipolygamous Reorganized Church of Jesus Christ of Latter Day Saints, talked with her and finally, for the first time in his life, directly broached the topic with his mother. The statement, printed after Emma's death as "Last Testimony of Sister Emma" in the *Saints' Herald* of October 1, 1879, raises more questions than it answers. Apparently the questions had been carefully prepared in advance, with ambiguities in wording that, whether deliberate or not, allowed for "deniability." Before asking her the questions for the record, her son apologized for bringing up the matter.[124]

Emma clearly faced conflicting loyalties to truth and to her sons. Her answers indicate that she chose her words carefully in an attempt to satisfy both. For example, when asked whether there had been a "revelation on polygamy" and about "spiritual wifery," she stated: "There was no revelation on either polygamy or spiritual wives," thus denying the old John C. Bennett terms. The question had not asked about "patriarchal marriage" or the "new and everlasting covenant" or any of the other code words for the system that early church leaders had used.

Significantly, Emma's comments that followed this apparent denial of a "revelation on polygamy" did admit that Joseph had talked with her about the idea: "There were some rumors of something of the sort which I asked my husband. He assured me that all there was of it was, that, in a chat about plural wives, he had said, 'Well such a system might possibly be, if everybody was agreed to it, and would behave as they should.' " Emma then went on to assert that "He had no other wife but me," which was true in a legal sense, for no plural marriage could have been legal under Illinois law.

Pressed further as to whether Joseph might nevertheless have had "marital relations with women other than yourself," she appears to have adroitly sidestepped the issue by saying, "he did not have improper relations with any woman that ever came to my knowledge." As the authors of *Mormon Enigma* note: "Years earlier Emma had established that she did not pretend to have knowledge of anything that she had not witnessed herself."[125]

A month after the interview, the son of Thomas B. Marsh, an early leader of the church, stopped to see Emma. When he asked her if Joseph had been a polygamist, Emma "broke down and wept, and excused herself from answering directly, assigning as a reason . . . that her son Joseph was the leader of the Reorganized church." Marsh interpreted Emma's response as a "tacit acknowledgment to him that her husband was a polygamist."[126] Two months later she died.

There is genuine pathos in the story of this capable and dynamic woman, deeply in love with her husband, yet dead set against the polygamy that was such a preoccupation of the last three years of his life. The emotional strain polygamy caused for Emma and for other Mormon women in Nauvoo, whether they accepted or rejected the practice, must have been enormous. The experiences of such women highlight in stark relief the terrible human cost inherent in efforts to introduce radically new ways of life.

Women who could bring themselves to accept the new practices as divinely ordained could at least have the solace of the sense of power, camaraderie, and closeness of "true believers" committed fully to a cause they were convinced was of cosmic importance. But women such as Emma, who struggled to accept the new practices but could not, experienced a profound sense of ambivalence and revulsion. In a sense they were both emotionally and socially outcasts, feeling most painfully the strains of being caught in limbo between an older order that was coming to an end and a new order they could not accept.

Whatever the initial motivation and form of plural marriage may have been, it did not die with Joseph Smith in 1844. Instead, during the chaotic final years in Nauvoo, the exodus to the West, and the early years in Utah up to 1852, what had been largely one man's private vision was introduced as the ideal model for family life in the whole Mormon church in the Great Basin region, creating a series of new challenges and problems.

9

JAMES J. STRANG

The Prophet Who Failed

𝒯HE POWERFUL IMPACT that Joseph Smith had on the minds and lives of his closest followers is tellingly indicated by the fact that almost every branch of the Mormon church immediately after his death introduced some form of plural marriage. In addition to the polygamy developed by Brigham Young and the Twelve Apostles among the main group of the Latter-day Saints that migrated to Utah, polygamous practice was also found, at least briefly, among the Mormon factions associated with William Smith, Lyman Wight, Alpheus Cutler, and James J. Strang, among others. There even were allegations that a remnant of the followers of Sidney Rigdon, who had emphatically denounced polygamy in his newspapers following Joseph Smith's death, briefly practiced a form of polygamy or marital experimentation in the late 1840s.[1]

In almost all of these instances, the practice of polygamy was short-lived and found primarily among the leadership. In most cases, too, it is difficult to do much more than document that plural marriage was practiced for some period of time and identify the children born to plural wives. A partial exception is provided by the case of James J. Strang, the brilliant would-be Mormon prophet who mounted the most serious and sustained challenge to Brigham Young and the Twelve in the immediate aftermath of Joseph Smith's death. Strang was without doubt the greatest of the early Mormon schismatics, a man of passionate idealism and driving ambition, whom the Mormon historian Klaus J. Hansen has ranked with Joseph Smith as

170

quite possibly one of the two "most creative individuals in Mormon history."[2] Although Strang initially issued scathing denunciations of polygamy, he eventually introduced and defended the largest and longest-lived polygamous system among the Mormons who did not go west. His life raises fundamental questions about the promise and pitfalls inherent in prophetic leadership and the impact of such leadership on the creation of alternative life-styles, not simply in early Mormonism but in many similar movements as well.[3]

Like so many other would-be prophets, Strang was a colorful yet enigmatic character whose underlying motives and drives are difficult to fathom. First appearing on the Mormon scene as a thirty-one-year-old unknown in 1844, he was baptized a Latter-day Saint just four months before Joseph Smith's assassination. Yet only a month after that martyrdom, Strang produced a letter he claimed Smith had written to him shortly before dying. With considerable eloquence, Strang argued that the letter, in conjunction with an angelic ordination he had received, made him Joseph Smith's true successor. To buttress these claims, Strang proceeded to deliver revelations in Smith's "Thus saith the Lord" style. He denounced polygamy as an utter abomination. He called for Mormons to gather to his headquarters at Voree, Wisconsin, rather than undertake a foolhardy migration westward. Under the watchful eyes of four witnesses in the autumn of 1845, Strang dug up brass plates near Voree, which he then "translated." Later he would "translate" a brilliant elaboration and extension of Mosaic Law he called the *Book of the Law of the Lord*, a work that Strang's skeptical, non-Mormon biographer Milo M. Quaife has described as "a complete framework of government . . . applicable to any population, however great, and laying down regulations for the most important relations of human society."[4]

In short, Strang appeared to represent everything that the caretaker, committee-type government of Brigham Young and the Twelve initially did not. He effectively presented himself as a single legal successor to Joseph Smith, a prophet and a charismatic leader, an antipolygamist carrying on the purity of the early Mormon message, and a supporter of the Mormon gathering, who nevertheless opposed the idea of going west. For a newcomer to the Mormon faith, Strang showed an extraordinary knowledge of Mormon beliefs and an almost uncanny sensitivity to Mormon thought patterns.

Even though Strang was new to the Mormon faith and began without any organizational base whatsoever, he soon managed through force of personality, rhetoric, gimmickry, and organizational skill to attract most of the dissenters from the policies of Brigham Young and the Twelve. The founders of the Reorganized Church, James C. Brewster's church, William Smith's church, and many other early Mormon factions were first associated with James J. Strang. In the summer of 1846, Strang's highly successful missionary trip to the eastern United States threatened to undercut the essential sources of support for the Mormon trek westward.

By the 1850s, with the main body of the Mormons securely established in the Great Basin, Strang no longer posed a significant threat to Brigham Young and the Twelve; but in spite of his somewhat narrowed scope of operations, by 1855 he had established a community of more than five hundred followers in his "kingdom" on Beaver Island in Lake Michigan. Contrary to his earlier stance, he had also introduced a form of polygamy into his community. Yet when Strang was assassinated by disgruntled followers in 1856, most of his support melted away. Today only a tiny remnant of Strang's followers still preserve the memory of this tragic figure, a classic example of a prophet who failed.

What nerved this remarkable man and his decade-long career as a Mormon prophet? How can one explain his early success and his eventual failure? Why did he initially denounce and then embrace polygamy? And what larger issues does his career suggest for an understanding of the role of charismatic leadership in early Mormonism and other new religious movements?

I

James J. Strang was born on March 21, 1813, at Scipio, New York, in the heart of the Burned-over District. He showed himself to be an intellectually and emotionally precocious child, painfully attuned to the conflicting issues and events of his time. His remarkable diary, written between the ages of nineteen and twenty-four, records the complex relationship between his passionate idealism and his overweening ambition. On the one hand, he could write, "I am resolved to devote my life to the service of mankind." On the other, he could speak in cipher of his ambition to "rival Caesar or Napoleon," to be "a priest, a Lawyer, a Conqueror, and a Legislator," or to contrive some means of marrying the heiress to the English crown (later Queen Victoria).[5]

Perhaps the key to Strang's character and the emotional power that pulses through his life is the passage that followed his vivid imaginative description of "all the horrors of anarchy and civil war" that he saw growing out of the South Carolina nullification crisis of 1832. That event was, of course, a precursor to the similar South Carolina crisis that triggered the Civil War. Writing in cipher, Strang initially toyed with the idea of forming some sort of prankster club. Then he came to the core of his concerns. He wrote: "Amidst all the ev[i]ls of the disturbances of our national affairs there is one consolation: that if our government is overthrown some master spirit may form another. May I be the one. I tremble when I write but it is true."[6] Like the founders of so many of the religious and social movements of the antebellum period, Strang appears to have felt deeply the hopes, fears, and ambitions that were characteristic of the lack of institutional supports in the period. He could not trust his social world; he would have to create another.

Strang's driving sense of mission to reconstruct a new social order runs throughout his career and gives his words extraordinary emotional power. So great was the cause that almost any methods were justified in its pursuit. Strang therefore appears to have been willing self-consciously to manipulate the credulity of his followers to achieve his larger ends. The meticulous research of the non-Mormon historian Dale Morgan has established beyond any reasonable doubt that Strang's letter of appointment from Joseph Smith was forged, almost surely by Strang himself.[7] Evidence that cannot be detailed here also suggests self-conscious manipulation in many of Strang's other ventures, including his revelations, translations, and reversals of position on issues such as polygamy.

Yet Strang was far more than a simple charlatan. One cannot account plausibly for the sustained dedication that he showed in the face of all the hardships, poverty, and opposition he experienced, or the generally well-thought-out and humane quality of his ideals as the result of simple fraud or psychopathology. Dale Morgan's reflections on the Strang papers at Yale could as well apply to Strang himself. "They are so full of human hope, fear, mistrust, and anger, often sad and as often exalted, that to read them is to be given fresh understanding of Mormonism, what it brought into the lives of its believers, and what they suffered in the cause."[8] Surely Strang was a brilliant and talented human being of rare worth; why, then, did he apparently feel compelled to forge his credentials for authority?

The most obvious answer is a pragmatic one. Strang was an unknown and was fully aware of that fact. He had an intense desire to achieve greatness by attracting a following among whom he could realize his goals. Evidently he saw the potential of the Mormon organization to be a vehicle for obtaining those objectives, particularly after Joseph Smith's death. Yet he had to find some way of attracting attention and legitimating his authority. Brigham Young and the Twelve had control of the core of the Mormon organization in Nauvoo, and no other Mormon faction before 1860 even began to offer them a viable organizational challenge. Strang thus was forced to improvise with every means at hand. In his own life and activities he attempted to embody the spirit of Joseph Smith more fully than even the prophet himself had, and he reached out to dissidents, both the best and the worst. Through his own charisma, dedication, and iron will, he sought to fuse all the disparate elements into a new whole. It was a daring gamble, but ultimately it was too great a task for any one man, no matter how brilliant. While Strang lived, he managed to hold a strong core of followers together, but after his death his personally based organization simply disintegrated.[9]

II

In no area were the problems and inherent inconsistences of Strang's approach more evident than in his response to polygamy. Throughout the mid-1840s, Strang inveighed publicly and privately with telling effect against polygamy, stressing his "unchanged" and "unchangeable" opposition to "spiritual wifery" or anything of the kind.[10] His stinging denunciations of the Twelve for supporting such iniquities were, in fact, one of his primary points of attraction for dissident Mormons. Yet in July 1849, Strang reversed his position in practice by privately taking as his first plural wife the nineteen-year-old Elvira Field. Dressing in a page boy's garb and posing as Strang's private male secretary "Charles J. Douglass," Elvira accompanied Strang east on a major missionary trip in 1849–50 to try to attract Mormons to the community that Strang was attempting to organize on Beaver Island in Lake Michigan. Throughout the next six years before his assassination in 1856, Strang and a small group of his followers quietly engaged in the limited practice of polygamy, eventually defending plural marriage in principle while sidestepping the question of whether they practiced it themselves. [11]

What accounts for Strang's reversal of his position on polygamy, and how does it reflect on the nature of his leadership and motives? Certainly Strang's personal attraction to Elvira Field played an important part in his decision. Moreover, Strang undoubtedly had learned by this time of Joseph Smith's own practice of polygamy, and he may have sought to replicate at least the external form of those activities. [12] But Strang's primary public argument for polygamy was based neither on his personal desires nor on Mormon precedent but on a sophisticated social argument. In his community newspaper— as part of a defense of Utah polygamy—Strang eloquently argued for plural marriage primarily as a means of alleviating the problems that women faced in finding husbands and making satisfactory marriages. [13] He noted that although the monogamous practices of his day supposedly granted women their free choice of a husband, in fact women who wanted to marry at all were usually placed under intolerable pressure to take any man they could get. "In consequence many talented women find themselves tied for life to puerile men whom they cannot but despise; and just and amiable women to selfish men, whom they are compelled to dread; and they set about preaching women's rights in the hope of finding some relief by relaxing the matrimonial bond as much as possible."

Strang argued that the popular remedy of "making marriage so near nothing at all, that it shall be only a partnership at will, for propagating the human species," was not the solution to women's problems in marriage. He did not favor borrowing a husband "for the occasion" or hiring him out as "a lackey or personal attendant," any more than he would favor casual sex with a woman or hiring a prostitute. Rather, his goal was the best possibility for a marriage relationship of commitment between whole human beings. Polygamy would have the effect of giving women "a wider range for the selection of husbands" and more bargaining power.

> Consequently they will accept only such as suit them. Higher talent, purer virtues, more constant kindness, more enterprise, better business capacities, a larger share of everything that makes the man the gentleman is then requisite to get wives at all. . . .
>
> Women admire and love manly excellence, and they are fond of each other's society. Take away the feeling of degradation, and shame, and a half dozen intellectual, amiable and beautiful women would spend their lives far more happily with one man, such as either would really choose, than separately with the same number of men, such as they can get, in the existing state of society.

Men, too, would benefit if women were given greater freedom of choice in husbands.

> The worst fault of the system is, that wives being generally mated rather than matched to their husbands, treat them without affection, and those men who have any degree of kindness acquiesce, because they feel that it would be cruel to exact more than the heart can feel. Desolate in the want of love, they seek that affection in vile places, which is denied them at home, and too often their deliquencies are returned upon them, and the household made a desolation. The few that are really well matched, are carried away by the prevailing custom, and virtuous women are ashamed to show their affection for their husbands. It is an unpardonable *weakness*. Thus connubial felicity is denied the good and the evil, the well and the ill matched.

Was this defense of polygamy simply a debater's ploy, or did it represent a serious attempt to deal with pressing social problems? How well did Strang's system work out in practice? Because of the limited extent and documentation of Strang's polygamy system, these questions are almost impossible to answer in detail. In 1856, out of a Mormon population numbering more than five hundred, there never were more than eighteen to twenty polygamous families on Beaver Island. Strang had four wives in addition to his first, L. D. Hickey had three, and all other polygamous families had but two wives. The limited practice of polygamy appears to have been the result of personal disinclination, simple poverty, lack of eligible females, and the more elite character of Strang's system than that which existed in the Great Basin.[14]

Strang's own family lived together in the same house, with separate rooms for each wife. One wife described Strang as judicious and mild, yet a firm leader.[15] Given the crowded circumstances and the other difficulties they faced, Strang's wives appear to have maintained as good relations among themselves as could be expected. Strang did not pretend that his marriages to his plural wives were legal; he said simply that his wives were women "whom I would marry if the law permitted me."[16] Strang's polygamy belief and practice did not hinder him from giving his wives considerable powers. He introduced a Bloomer outfit for women, made his first wife, Mary Perce, a member of his Governing Council in 1851, and repeatedly emphasized the importance of a relationship of mutual love between husband and wife, rather than more pragmatic property and kinship considerations.

As the only Mormon polygamy system outside the main branch of the Latter-day Saint movement for which anything more than the most superficial documentation exists, the marriage ideals and practices of James J. Strang are of considerable intrinsic and comparative interest. Nevertheless, the primary historic importance of Strang's adoption of polygamy lay in its political impact. That step formally signaled Strang's inability or unwillingness to provide a true alternative to the policies of the Great Basin Mormons under Brigham Young. The most devoted and capable of the disaffected Mormons who followed Strang—including William Marks, Zenos Gurley, and Jason Briggs—left him when he followed Joseph Smith's lead in introducing secret societies and polygamy. Marks, Gurley, Briggs, and others would continue to "wander in the wilderness" until the formal establishment of the antipolygamist Reorganized Church in 1860. To be sure, Strang could not have threatened the survival of the Utah

Mormons effectively after the late 1840s in any case. Yet had he not introduced polygamy among his own followers, he might well have been able to establish the nucleus of a successful nonpolygamous branch of the Mormon church. Instead, Strang retreated to his isolated Beaver Island Kingdom and increasingly became simply a curiosity rather than a dynamic force in history.

III

The core of the Strang problem, however, still remains unanswered: What is the significance of the prophetic pretensions that underlay the career of James J. Strang? Can this remarkable man's motives be untangled, and if so, can his career shed light on the prophetic experience in Mormonism and the problem of prophetic creativity in other contexts as well? I would argue that available evidence strongly suggests that Strang deliberately manipulated the credulity of his followers and self-consciously and knowingly forged his chief credentials for power. How are such actions to be reconciled with a career that one can hardly help but conclude shows elements of true greatness and a sincere dedication to a cause in which Strang believed with all his heart? Is it possible that Strang could have been, in some paradoxical sense, a sincere charlatan, and if so, how?

This was a question with which Strang's own family and some of his most sensitive followers also struggled. On hearing of Strang's early claims, his sister Myraetta A. Losee wrote him on May 5, 1846: "I know not how to address you. I have nothing to say in regard to the motives which may have actuated you—but I entreat, I beg you, in the name of all that is near and dear to you, all that is sacred; pause, and think of the fearful responsibility you have taken upon you."[17]

Even more telling were the reflections of the remarkable Louisa Sanger, whom Dale Morgan characterizes in a rare and justified burst of hyperbole as "a superb woman."[18] In three moving letters to Strang between 1846 and 1849, Sanger reflected at length on her effort to understand Strang's mission, Mormonism, and her place in the world. "You know that my only object in life is to know and obey the truth with a perfect heart, and this I am determined to do as far as I can understand it without regard to the consequences. But I find it very difficult to decide which of the contending parties really holds authority from God. So much can be said against both that I am sometimes half tempted not to believe in either." Reviewing her doubts about Strang and some of his less savory associates and policies, she eventually burst out, almost as a premonition, "Oh it is a fearful thing to give up the very last hope, especially one that has been cherished through long bitter years of affliction and sorrow."[19]

Ultimately, however, Louisa Sanger did give up her faith in Strang. Convinced at last that he was indeed guilty of self-conscious duplicity, she wrote him on August 19, 1849, that she must therefore break with him. She told him sadly that it was not Reuben Miller's influence, but "your own actions, your own writings, that destroyed my confidence in you. . . . One grain after another was thrown into the scale against you until it finally turned." She concluded, still reserving final judgment, that if Strang was a "wilful religious imposter" he was beneath contempt, but that she was willing to leave him and all the other parties in the hands of God.[20] Even in this final letter breaking with Strang, Louisa Sanger still expressed her warm regard for him and could hardly bring herself to accept what her intellect told her to be true. What, then—more than one hundred years later and even further from direct contact with Strang— can we reasonably conclude?

To begin to break the riddle of James J. Strang, we must place his career within the context of the religious prophet or great creative synthesizer in any field. Religious prophets as I have come to understand them have two chief characteristics. First, they create or attempt to create a unitary vision of the world. Far more than most individuals, prophets are disturbed by uncertainty in basic value premises, and they therefore struggle with unusual intensity to achieve a resolution of their own religious and social conflicts. Unlike most persons, who simply try to reach an accommodation with the larger world, prophets ultimately come to the conclusion that the world itself is wrong and that their own experience and insights provide a universally valid model for setting the world straight. Possessed by this extraordinary and compelling idea, unable or unwilling to work within what appears to be an unstable or inconsistent value environment, the prophet therefore seeks to create a new value system and "to initiate, both in himself as well as in others, a process of moral regeneration."[21] By attracting a following to their new ideals and life-styles, prophetic figures feel that they have validated their lives and messages. And so compelling is the need to get across the message that strict literal accuracy or total scrupulousness of means may sometimes become of secondary importance.

A second characteristic of prophets is their realization that al-though truth is ultimately a unitary phenomenon which they have a special mission to convey, truth nevertheless cannot be fully commu-nicated in words. The prophets' experiences are deeper and richer than that of their followers, yet if prophetic figures are to be effective forces rather than otherworldly recluses, they must find some way of expressing their prophetic insights so that others can at least partly understand them. That process of communicating experience will in-evitably distort it; the greater must be described in terms of the lesser. In some sense, therefore, prophets or any individuals who at-tempt to convey a higher truth ultimately are—and realize that they are—in some degree at least charlatans, persons making implied promises on which they cannot fully deliver. Lesser minds expect prophets to have the whole truth, the answer to every problem. Prophets realize that this is not possible; full truth can be known only by God, not by God's representatives.[22] Prophets are reaching toward ideals that inevitably elude their grasp to some extent.

How do such characteristics bear on the complex character of James J. Strang and his career as a would-be Mormon prophet? Strang certainly had the intensity of commitment to his vision of a new order that underlies the prophetic approach. Likewise, his awareness of the complexity and the ultimately incommunicable na-ture of his deepest insights also is clear in works such as his *Book of the Law of the Lord*. Yet Strang's apparently conscious decision to mis-represent his credentials would seem to place his career in a special class and raise difficult questions of interpretation.

Perhaps the nature of Strang's prophetic mission, both its strengths and its weaknesses, may best be suggested by comparing his career with the very different yet related careers of two other key early Mormon leaders—Joseph Smith and John C. Bennett. It could be argued that a large part of Joseph Smith's success can be attrib-uted to his formative visionary experiences that convinced him be-yond any possible doubt of the divine nature of his mission. Even though in some instances Smith may have knowingly presented his own personal desires as though they were revelations from God, his core sense of prophetic mission—his conviction that a power greater than himself alone was speaking through him—appears never to have weakened.

At the opposite end of the spectrum was the opportunistic John C. Bennett, a man who never spoke for anyone but himself and his own narrowly conceived self-interest. Bennett never knew what he really wanted in life, and he never had any higher goal than personal self-aggrandizement. As a result, he could never work for long with anyone else, and he never was able to carry any long-term project involving other people to a successful conclusion.[23]

James J. Strang appears to have fallen midway on the prophetic spectrum between Smith and Bennett. Although Strang possessed an intense sense of personal mission, he appears never to have had Joseph Smith's sense of having his life taken over by a higher power. Yet Strang's ambition was more than Bennett's crude self-interest. Strang sought to achieve personal fame and immortality by creating an appealing and humane community that would embody his ideals. The reason that Strang chose to make explicitly revelatory claims rather than resting his authority on the force of his own ideas must inevitably remain something of a puzzle to us, as it did to Louisa Sanger. Such a self-consciously contrived role, particularly when it was reflected in inconsistencies in action, program, and claims, hardly could have the effectiveness of real belief.

In the final analysis, however, Strang's chief significance may lie not so much in the claims to authority that he put forward as in the way his career illustrates the complex nature of prophetic creativity. Whether as saint or charlatan, prophet or fraud, James J. Strang struggled deeply with his own impulses and ideals. He remains a man well worth knowing as we attempt to come to terms with the heights and depths of human experience, the extraordinary passion that has burned so brightly in many new religious movements.

10

POLYGAMY and the FRONTIER

Mormon Women in Early Utah

HE MORMON ATTEMPT to establish a form of polygamy in Utah and adjacent areas of the Intermountain West during the last half of the nineteenth century constitutes the largest, best-organized, and most controversial venture in radically restructuring marriage and family life in nineteenth-century America. Although other alternatives to monogamy in this period, such as the systems of the celibate Shakers and the free-love Oneida Perfectionists, directly affected only a few thousand individuals at most, plural marriage ultimately became the family ideal for more than one hundred thousand Latter-day Saints who placed their indelible cultural imprint on much of the American West. In setting up their Great Basin kingdom, the Mormons skillfully and systematically sought to create an autonomous religious and cultural order based on American and biblical models. Polygamy became an integral part of that larger effort between 1852, when the Mormons in Utah first publicly announced that they were practicing it, and 1890, when, under intense federal pressure, they began to give up the practice.[1]

Few aspects of Mormon polygamy have been more controversial than its impact on women. During the nineteenth century, hostile external observers attacked the practice as a "relic of barbarism," a system of institutionalized lust that degraded women, destroyed the unity of the family, and led inevitably to unhappiness, debaucheries, and excesses of all kinds. Nineteenth-century Latter-day Saints were equally vigorous in defending their marital practices, arguing that
182

plural marriage and the Old Testament patriarchal model on which it was based actually strengthened family and kinship ties, led to the rearing of righteous children in the best families, and allowed women greater freedom in choosing the men they wanted to marry. More recently, both Mormon and non-Mormon scholars have attempted to treat polygamy with greater objectivity, to show how it functioned in pioneer Utah and what it meant to the people who participated in it. Through the use of demographic studies, literary analyses, oral histories, group biographies, and a variety of other methods, these writers have highlighted key questions raised by this extraordinary effort to introduce new forms of marriage and family relations in nineteenth-century America.[2]

Based on current research and available manuscript materials, it is now possible to move beyond simple polemics and begin to understand the complex ways in which polygamy affected relationships between men and women in the Great Basin region. Although polygamy had been secretly taught and practiced by Mormons at least as early as 1841 in Nauvoo, Illinois, not until the difficult exodus to the relative isolation of the Intermountain West were the Latter-day Saints free to set up their unorthodox marriage system without constant external interference. During the years between 1847, when the Mormons first arrived in Utah, and 1877, when Brigham Young died, polygamy became an integral part of Mormon life in the Great Basin region and profoundly influenced the experiences and activities of women there.

I

The problems and challenges of life under polygamy in Utah are described in numerous diaries, journals, letters, and other firsthand accounts by Mormon women.[3] Perhaps the finest presentation of the range of women's experiences under polygamy is found in the reflections of Jane Snyder Richards, first wife of the Mormon apostle Franklin D. Richards and herself active in many capacities on behalf of her family and the women of Utah. In 1880 in an interview entitled "The Inner Facts of Social Life in Utah," Mrs. Richards spoke candidly about her experiences and feelings with the non-Mormon

Mrs. Hubert Howe Bancroft, who was helping her husband collect information for his monumental history of Utah. Although Mrs. Richards was far from a typical Mormon wife and mother, her interview and other writings sensitively portray many of the characteristic features of early polygamy, as well as the complex adjustments necessary to make polygamy work even in an unusually good relationship. Observing Mr. and Mrs. Richards together, Mrs. Bancroft wrote, "He seems remarkably considerate and kind and speaks of her with gratitude and pride, and that he wanted her to enjoy this little visit to California for she has suffered so much affliction and so many hardships. . . . His attentions and kind consideration for her are very marked. She is certainly very devoted to him, and I am imagining this trip and the one they have just returned from in the East, as a sort of honey-moon in middle life."[4]

Before abstracting out some of the characteristic aspects of polygamy illustrated by the Richards case, a brief look at their relationship and experience is in order. Jane Snyder was born on January 31, 1823, in Pamelia, New York, one of the youngest of eleven children of a prosperous farmer and stock raiser. Her father had not belonged to any church before joining the Mormons, while her mother had been a devout Methodist. Jane showed her strength of will at age seventeen, when, upon deciding to join the Mormon church in midwinter, she insisted on undergoing a proper baptism by immersion out-of-doors in a lake near her home in La Porte, Illinois.[5]

Franklin D. Richards was born in Richmond, Massachusetts, on April 2, 1821. The fourth of nine children, he grew up accustomed to hard manual labor on his father's farm, but in his spare time he loved to read and discuss issues of the day. At age ten Franklin left home and traveled about as an itinerant worker until he joined the Mormon church in 1838. He rose rapidly in the hierarchy as he demonstrated his remarkable organizational and proselytizing skills.

Jane Snyder and Franklin Richards met through their mutual involvement in the Mormon church. Robert Snyder, Jane's father, was one of Franklin's traveling missionary companions. When Franklin became seriously ill on one occasion, Jane nursed him back to health in the Snyder family home in La Porte. Thereafter, he became a frequent visitor to La Porte, eventually marrying Jane in December 1842. Their first child was born in November 1843, and in the spring of the following year Franklin was called on a mission to England.

As an increasingly prominent member of the Mormon church, Franklin soon learned of the new belief in polygamous marriage as a necessity for the highest exaltation in the afterlife. About eight months after their marriage, when Jane was in the advanced stages of pregnancy, he approached her about the possibility of taking another wife. She was deeply hurt at this suggestion, and her opposition may have been largely responsible for his waiting nearly three years before finally taking the seventeen-year-old Elizabeth McFate as a plural wife in January 1846, eight days after he and Jane had been sealed together for "time and eternity" in the temple.

Although Jane Richards had severe misgivings about polygamy, she found that she and Elizabeth could get on well together. Aware of the awkwardness of the situation, Elizabeth was deferential to Jane and tried to be especially kind and considerate. Jane lived in the lower half of the house, while Elizabeth was assigned to the upper story. They divided the labor between them. If Elizabeth did the cooking, for instance, Jane did the washing, and vice versa. To those who knew that the Mormons were practicing polygamy, Jane Richards spoke of Elizabeth as Mrs. Elizabeth Richards.

In May 1846 the Richardses reluctantly sold for a mere pittance the house for which they had sacrificed so much to build. Along with the other Mormons who were fleeing the anti-Mormon mobs in Illinois, Jane and Elizabeth Richards began an incredibly difficult journey west. The two women had to take almost complete responsibility for the difficult move because Franklin Richards was called away on another mission at the time of their departure from Illinois. During the trip west, Jane gave birth to a second child, who promptly died. She also lost her first daughter. Elizabeth, whose health had never been robust, died of "consumption" en route. During the trip Jane was so sick at times that, in her own words, "I only lived because I could not die." Seeing her pitiable state when the Mormons stopped for the winter in Nebraska, Brigham Young expressed special concern for her, saying that if he had known her situation, he would not have required her husband to go on a mission at that time.

Conditions improved somewhat after Jane's arrival in Salt Lake, but life was still exceptionally difficult for her. In 1849, after

Franklin had been back only a short time, he was appointed one of Brigham Young's twelve apostles and shortly thereafter was called to undertake yet another mission to England. There he was playing an increasingly important role in originating and developing the remarkable Mormon emigration system. Before he left, he was married to Sarah Snyder, a sister of his wife Jane. Sarah had been deserted by her first husband while she was coming west, and she was having considerable difficulty managing alone with five small children. Also in 1849, Franklin took Charlotte Fox as a plural wife.

The succeeding fifteen years were marked by Franklin's repeated missionary and church appointments and by his resulting long absences from home. Following a highly successful term as president of the British mission from 1850 to 1852, during which time sixteen thousand people joined the Mormon church, Franklin Richards returned home to the Great Basin, taking three additional wives, Susan S. Pierson in 1853, Laura A. Snyder in 1854, and Josephine de la Harpe in 1857. After Willard Richards died in 1854, Franklin was counseled by Brigham Young—following the Mormon variant on the Mosaic practice of the levirate—to marry his uncle's widows. As a result, four more women, Nancy Longstroth, Mary Thompson, Susannah Bayliss, and Rodah H. Foss, were sealed to him by Brigham Young in March 1857.[6]

Living conditions for the various wives differed greatly during the course of their marriages to Franklin Richards. The early years were the hardest. When Franklin was called to go to England in October 1849, for instance, Jane Richards was left temporarily in a one-room, floorless, almost roofless house. As soon as possible, she and the other women who married Franklin took steps to improve their condition. To a considerable extent they were on their own resources, at least until 1869, when Franklin finally came back permanently to live in the Great Basin region after the last of his four major missionary trips to England. Jane Richards eventually established a house in Ogden, while the other wives lived in different cities in Utah. During this period Jane played an active role in the Relief Society, the women's organization in the church, as well as in national women's organizations, while Franklin served variously as judge, church historian, and president of the Council of the Twelve Apostles, one of the highest positions in the church. Though his work still called him away from home much of the time, many of the greatest pressures from the early period were gone after he had finally completed his missionary activities abroad.

Underlying the entire interview between Mrs. Bancroft and Mrs. Richards was an awareness of the intense personal commitment and the difficult personal renunciations involved in the practice of polygamy, especially for women, and most especially for the first wife. Romantic love was sharply undercut by the new arrangements. Jane Richards spoke of her initial "repugnance" when she first learned of polygamy in Illinois; how "crushed" she felt when her husband first approached her about the possibility of taking another wife; and of her unhappiness when he married three new wives in Utah after he had returned from an extended mission to England. Like many other Mormon women, Mrs. Richards was able to accept polygamy only because she convinced herself that it was essential to her salvation and to that of her husband. She found that in practice polygamy "was not such a trial as she had feared" and that she and the other wives were able to cooperate effectively. On several occasions during the interview Mrs. Richards appeared to be trying to reassure herself that her husband was motivated by a sense of religious duty and not by any lustful desires. Mrs. Bancroft concluded her record of the interview by observing that on the whole it seemed to her that Mormon women considered polygamy "as a religious duty and schooled themselves to bear its discomforts as a sort of religious penance, and that it was a matter of pride to make everybody believe they lived happily and to persuade themselves and others that was not a trial; and that a long life of such discipline makes the trial lighter."[7]

Other diary and journal accounts, interviews with individuals who lived in polygamous families, and recent quantitative analyses show that religious commitment was, indeed, the primary reason that most Mormon women—and most men as well—gave for entering into plural marriage. Only a sense of the cosmic importance of their endeavor was enough to convince thousands of individuals to accept or adopt practices radically at variance with all that they had ever been taught. As the Mormon mother Annie Clark Tanner, who grew up in a polygamous household and became a plural wife herself, declared:

I am sure that women would never have accepted polygamy had it not been for their religion. No woman ever consented to its practice without great sacrifice on her part. There is something so sacred about the relationship of husband and wife that a third party in the family is sure to disturb the confidence and security that formerly existed.

The principle of Celestial Marriage was considered the capstone of the Mormon religion. Only by practicing it would the highest exaltation in the Celestial Kingdom of God be obtained. According to the founders of the Mormon Church, the great purpose of this life is to prepare for the Celestial Kingdom in the world to come. The tremendous sacrifices of the Mormon people can only be understood if one keeps in mind this basic other-world philosophy.[8]

Although polygamy was especially difficult for women, it also required significant renunciations from the men who took on the responsibility of marrying plural wives. Polygamists such as Franklin Richards were typically of a higher religious and economic status than the average member, and they were frequently called away from home on church business for extended periods of time so that they had relatively little opportunity to be with their families. Furthermore, even when such Mormon polygamists were at home, they faced complex problems of family management that made significant expression of romantic love difficult. Like other serious polygamists, Franklin Richards had to try to avoid favoritism toward his plural wives if he were to maintain family harmony; he had to try to make an equitable distribution of his time, money, and affections when he was not away on church business. Jane Richards remembered how even her husband's most sincere efforts to treat his wives equally led to frustration and heartache.[9] Even with the best of will, individuals who had been socialized into monogamous norms found the necessary transition to the new patterns of relationships in polygamy difficult.

Given the complexities of polygamy and the renunciations that it entailed, it is not surprising to find that plural marriage was far from universally practiced in the Great Basin. Using a sample of more than six thousand prominent Mormon families, Stanley Snow

Ivins estimated that at most only 15 to 20 percent were polygamous. Using a subsample of 1,784 polygamous men, Ivins found that a large majority, 66.3 percent, married only the one extra wife considered necessary for the highest exaltation in the celestial kingdom. Another 21.2 percent married three wives, and 6.7 percent went so far as to take four wives. The remaining group of less than 6 percent married five or more women. The limited incidence of polygamy may also have been the result of the limited number of available women. At no time during Utah's territorial history did the total number of women outnumber the men. Finally, according to Ivins's figures, the rate at which new polygamous marriages were established was always in an overall decline after the early 1856–57 peak. Sporadic increases in the rate of entry into polygamous marriages occurred during times of internal or external crisis, when polygamy served as a rallying point through which Mormons could prove their loyalty to the church, but continued exhortation and group pressure appear to have been necessary to sustain the practice.[10]

Although plural marriage may well have been less than appealing to many men and women, such arrangements can be viewed in context as part of the necessary subordination of individual desires to long-term group goals that underlay Mormon success in the rapid settlement and development of the Intermountain West. Sexual impulses were sublimated into the arduous group enterprise of settling Utah and building up a Zion in the wilderness. As the historian Leonard Arrington has observed, "Only a high degree of religious devotion and discipline, superb organization and planning, made survival possible" in early Utah.[11] Mormon men, particularly the leading ones, who were most often polygamists, had to be willing to move flexibly on church assignments as the demands of the group required. By partially breaking down exclusive bonds between a husband and wife and by undercutting direct emotional involvement in family affairs in favor of church business, polygamy may well have contributed significantly to the long-range demands of centralized planning and the rapid establishment of a new religious and communal order.

Polygamy obviously required difficult renunciations and tended to undercut, though by no means to eliminate, emotional attachments based on romantic love. Yet polygamy also had certain positive features that gave it staying power. In a rather impressionistic survey of 110 plural marriages, the sociologist Kimball Young concluded that 53 percent were highly or reasonably successful, 25 percent were of moderate to doubtful success, and 23 percent were unsuccessful.[12] Other evidence also suggests positive features that could be present in polygamous marriages. What were some of the possible compensatory aspects of plural marriage for women, and how did they adapt to the demands of the new arrangements? How did polygamy in some instances encourage women to develop self-reliance and independence?

The status advantages of being a plural wife have seldom been seriously considered. Non-Mormon critics of polygamy have almost invariably assumed that because they would have felt degraded under plural marriage, plural wives must also have felt degraded. Plausible though this might seem, little internal Mormon evidence supports such a view. Life certainly did hold special trials for plural wives, but at least until the 1880s, being a plural wife also brought higher status through association with the most influential men and through a sense of serving as a religious and social model for others. First wives such as Jane Richards who married under monogamous expectations often had considerable difficulty in adjusting, but many plural wives had other reactions. In some cases, first wives actively encouraged a reluctant husband to take a plural wife so that they could both reach the highest state of exaltation in the afterlife or for other more pragmatic economic or personal considerations. Viewed as an honorable and desirable practice, plural marriage could give women a sense of pride and significance within the Mormon community.[13]

The almost cosmic importance attached to home and family life was a major factor determining women's status in the Great Basin region. Children were highly valued by Mormons. Like outside converts, children provided an essential work force to help in settling the new land and in building up an essentially agrarian economy in Utah. One polygamous wife emphasized the extreme importance that Mormons placed on childbearing and child rearing:

> Our children are considered stars in a mother's crown, and the more there are, if righteous, the more glory they will add to her and their father's eternal kingdom, for their parents on earth, if

they continue righteous, will eventually become as Gods to reign in glory. Nothing but this, and a desire to please our Father in heaven, could tempt the majority of Mormon men or women either, to take upon themselves the burdens and responsibilities of plural marriage.[14]

In terms strikingly similar to those used by their Victorian contemporaries, Mormons stressed the positive and vital social role that women could play in the family and, by extension, in the larger community, which in the Mormon case was generally coterminous with the family. As the non-Mormon historian Gail Farr Casterline has noted, "Polygamy seemed to introduce no outstanding change in how Mormon women viewed themselves in their home role; the family was often treated in the same sentimental tones used by those who lauded the monogamous family."[15]

The Mormon emphasis on the mother-child relationship served compensatory emotional functions for women whose husbands were often absent. Jane Richards, like many other plural wives, indicated that her primary emotional involvement was with her children, rather than her husband. Similarly, Mrs. S. A. Cooks, who became a Mormon despite her aversion to polygamy, described how Heber C. Kimball's first wife, Vilate, had advised an unhappy plural wife that "her comfort must be wholly in her children; that she must lay aside wholly all interest or thought in what her husband was doing while he was away from her" and simply be as "pleased to see him when he came in as she was pleased to see any friend." In short, the woman was advised to maintain an emotional distance from her husband to avoid psychic hurt. Mrs. Cooks concluded: "Mrs. Kimball interested herself very much in the welfare of others' wives and their children to see that there was plenty of homespun clothing etc. for all; and set a noble example to others situated as she was."[16]

The strong stress on ties of sisterhood between plural wives also served an important compensatory emotional function when the husband was absent. Informal female support networks and cooperation among women developed, especially during crisis periods such as those associated with childbirth, economic hardship, and bereavement. Mormon "sister-wives," as they were sometimes called, often literally were blood sisters. Of Vicky Burgess-Olson's sample, for instance, 31.2 percent of the plural marriages included at least one pair of sisters. Although such sororal polygamy was a departure from Old Testament standards and led to erroneous allegations that the Mormons practiced incest, such arrangements made much practical sense. If two sisters were married to the same man, they could more easily adjust to each other in the marriage than total strangers could.[17]

The popular seminovelistic American stereotype of the plural wife as living in a Mormon "harem" had almost no basis in fact. Far from secluding women from the world, polygamy and the cohesive Mormon village community with which it was associated could lead some women to participate actively in the larger society. Casterline notes:

> As in New England colonial families, the Mormon wife seemed to move with relative ease and frequency between home, neighborhood, and church; the Mormon village plan of settlement allowed a variety of social contacts outside the immediate family. Wives were not cloistered or excluded from the larger society as in a harem, although husbands did seem to have a possessive attitude on the issue of their womenfolk associating with Gentiles.[18]

Women's independence was stimulated in a variety of ways by the social conditions of frontier Utah and by the practice of polygamy. With husbands frequently away on church missions, wives and their children tended to be thrown back on their own resources and on those of their immediate relatives and friends. Jane Richards said that her husband "was away so much she learned to live comfortably without him, as she would tell him to tease him sometimes; and even now he is away two thirds of the time as she is the only wife in Ogden, so that she often forgets when he is home, and has even sat down at meals forgetting to call him. She says she always feels very badly about it when it happens, but that he was more necessary to her in her early life." Mrs. Bancroft added: "And yet she is a very devoted wife, and he is remarkably attentive to her. To see them together I would never imagine either had a thought but the other shared."[19]

Other accounts also stressed this same tendency of polygamy practice to encourage women's independence. After stating, "Plural marriage destroys the oneness of course" and it "is a great trial of feelings," Mary Horne noted that the practice got her away from being "so bound and so united to her husband that she could do nothing without him." She became "freer and can do herself individually things she never could have attempted before; and work out her individual character as separate from her husband."[20] Evidently in some cases women also were grateful for the possibility polygamy offered for freedom from male sexual demands; as Mary J. Tanner noted: "It is a physical blessing to weakly women."[21] And the feisty Martha Hughes Cannon, who was the first woman state senator in the United States and the fourth wife of a polygamist, argued that a plural wife was in a better position than a single wife: "If her husband has four wives, she had three weeks of freedom every single month."[22]

While this might be the kind of "freedom" that some wives would wish to be freed from, it does suggest how polygamy and the exigencies of life in the Great Basin region could force women into new roles and break down certain sex stereotypes, at least temporarily. In the absence of their husbands, women and their children ran farms and businesses. Some early census reports even went so far as to identify plural wives as "heads of households." Burgess-Olson's sample showed that in polygamous marriages, husbands and wives exercised approximately equal responsibilities in financial management, while in her monogomous sample, men held greater control. By the late nineteenth century a relatively large class of professional women, many of them plural wives, had developed in Utah. Women dominated the medical profession, for instance, and a sizable number worked as teachers and writers.[23]

Brigham Young and other early church leaders recognized the necessity of making use of female talent in establishing and maintaining the group in the sometimes hostile environment of the Great Basin. Mormon leaders encouraged education for women from the very early settlement period, as indicated by the establishment of the University of Deseret as a coeducational institution in 1850. Women voted earlier in Utah than in any other state or territory in the United States, including Wyoming. And, somewhat ironically in view of the non-Mormon attacks on the degradation polygamy supposedly caused women, the efforts of Mormon women in the 1870s and 1880s to organize themselves to support plural marriage against external attacks served as a significant means of increasing their political awareness and involvement.[24]

One major forum for women's expression in the church was the Relief Society. Originally founded in 1842, the Relief Society was organized "under the priesthood after a pattern of the priesthood" to support a variety of activities, including the building of a temple, charitable work, and cultural betterment. During the troubled period that followed Joseph Smith's death, the Relief Society became largely inactive, but with the reestablishment of the society in the mid-1850s under the leadership of Eliza R. Snow, it went on to play an important role in Utah economic, social, and cultural life.[25]

Perhaps the most impressive achievement of the women in Utah during the late nineteenth century was the publication of the *Woman's Exponent*. Although it was not officially sponsored or financed by the church, this largely woman-managed, supported, and produced newspaper served as the major voice for Mormon women's concerns during its publication between 1872 and 1914. The *Exponent* was the second periodical expressly for women to appear in the trans-Mississippi West. A respectable and well-produced periodical by any standards, the *Exponent* spoke highly for the literacy and intelligence of its women contributors and designers. The wide-ranging historical and literary concerns of this publication were by no means limited to sectarian matters.[26]

As suggested by its masthead slogan, "The Rights of the Women of Zion, The Rights of the Women of All Nations," the *Woman's Exponent* provided an important forum for the discussion of many problems of "woman's sphere." Expressing an almost feminist awareness at times, the *Exponent* devoted much attention to the universally inequitable position of women in politics, education, and the professions. Even marriage was not put forward as an absolute imperative for women. In the *Exponent*'s wide-ranging discussion of issues, only polygamy, then one of the key elements of Mormon self-definition as a group, failed to receive a critique. Overall, the *Woman's Exponent* portrayed Mormon women as individuals of character, intelligence, and high aspirations. It served an important identity-building function and helped to reinforce pride and unity among the women of the church.

As Casterline observed:

The reinstitution of the ancient custom of polygamy may have
in its own subtle ways served as a liberating force for women.
This may have occurred by default, with restless or dissatisfied
plural wives looking for places to direct their energies, or it may
have occurred through the necessity of a wife's supporting her
family. Some women may have welcomed polygamy as a great
boon, as it decreased some of the demands and divided the duties of the wife role, allowing them more time to develop personal talents. By these quirks in its machinery, plural marriage
did in some cases provide a working method for women to
achieve independence from men.[27]

III

Despite certain positive or at least mitigating features, polygamy was
obviously a more demanding way to organize marriage than monogamy. Even under the best of circumstances, developing and sustaining an optimal relationship among husband, wives, and children in
polygamous families was difficult. How did Mormon families deal
with the inevitable tensions that arose in plural marriages? Although
the studies of James E. Hulett, Jr., Kimball Young, Vicky Burgess-
Olson, and Jessie L. Embry reveal great differences in the ways conflict situations were managed in both monogamous and polygamous
families, the general rule was to try to deal with problems within the
home as much as possible.[28] As Jane Richards noted, "It is making
confidants of other women in their domestic disturbances that has
brought about most of the trouble in polygamy, and the less people
gossip, the better off they are."[29] In the practice of polygamy, as in
other aspects of social life in Utah, great stress was placed on unity
and consensus, on the avoidance of public expressions of hostility.
This emphasis may well help account for the impressive degree of
external order and social harmony described by many of the more
open-minded visitors to Utah during the nineteenth century.[30]

Even with goodwill and sincere effort, attempts to salvage a relationship could fail. In such cases the possibility of separation or
divorce always remained. Jane Richards was frank in noting, for in-

stance, that when her husband first talked with her in Illinois about the possibility of taking another wife, she told him that he should do what he felt he had to do and that "if she found they [she and the new wife] could not live without quarreling, she should leave him." This never became necessary for her, but she noted that others had taken such steps: "If a marriage is unhappy, the parties can go to any of the council and present their difficulties and are readily granted a divorce."[31]

How representative were Jane Richard's informal observations on nineteenth-century Mormon attitudes toward divorce? This topic has only recently begun to be investigated, but a few preliminary observations may be made. One initial point of reference is Utah territorial divorce policy. The Utah divorce law of February 4, 1852, was one of the most liberal in the country. For instance, a divorce could be granted not only to a person who "is a resident of the Territory" but also to a person who "wishes to become one." Presumably this proviso allowed the Mormon church flexibility in dealing rapidly with converts who had separated from an unbelieving spouse and who needed to be reintegrated as quickly as possible into the new Mormon society. In addition to the usual causes, a divorce could be granted to the plaintiff in cases in which the defendant was guilty of "absenting himself without reasonable cause for more than one year." If liberally applied, such a provision could be used to terminate unsatisfactory relationships in which missionaries were gone for extended periods of time. Finally, the territorial law contained an omnibus clause allowing divorce "when it shall be made to appear to the satisfaction of the court, that the parties cannot live in peace and union together, and that their welfare requires a separation."[32]

The Utah divorce law cannot necessarily be assumed to represent Mormon church policy because marriage and divorce—particularly polygamous marriage and divorce, which were not directly recognized in territorial law—were handled primarily though church courts and procedures. Instead, the primary function of the divorce law probably was to provide maximum flexibility for Mormons in handling their own unorthodox arrangements. What, then, was the Mormon church's policy on divorce? The official stand was highly complex. In theory, divorce was strongly discouraged. Marriage was viewed in the light of eternity as a vital part of life that brought out the finest aspects of human relationships. Brigham Young and other early leaders repeatedly inveighed against divorce, particularly when requested by the man. Using rather salty language, Young could suggest, for example, that one man had made his bed and would have to lie in it. Declarations such as the following were typical: "It is not right for men to divorce their wives the way they do. I am determined that if men do not stop divorcing their wives, I will stop sealing."[33]

Yet if men were discouraged from divorcing their wives, women were given remarkable freedom in seeking a divorce for themselves in unsatisfactory situations. Young himself once publicly offered to give a divorce to any of his wives who did not want to live with him any longer. He could declare that "he liked a woman to live with her husband as long as she could bear with him and if her life became too burdensome than leave and get a divorce." In an important sermon in the Salt Lake Tabernacle on October 8, 1861, Brigham Young further developed the argument about when a women could leave a man lawfully. He said that if a woman became alienated in her feelings and affections from her husband, then it was his duty to give her a bill of divorce and set her free. Men must not have sexual relations with their wives when they were thus alienated. Children born of such alienated unions were properly seen as "bastards," not the product of a full marriage relationship.[34]

This line of argument is strikingly similar to the 1842 argument put out in Illinois in *The Peace Maker*, the first defense of polygamy ever printed under Mormon auspices. According to that pamphlet, whose authorship and significance have been hotly debated, the only "biblical" (i.e., legitimate) ground for divorce was the alienation of a wife's affections from her husband. If a man became dissatisfied with his wife he could not legitimately divorce her if she remained loyal to him, because that would be an irresponsible shirking of family duties. Instead, his option in such a case was to take additional wives, while maintaining the first and her children.

This approach is essentially the same as early Utah practice. Women had the primary initiative in determining when to terminate a relationship, while the husband could not easily divorce his wife if she were opposed. No stigma was attached to the remarriage of a divorced woman; indeed, such remarriage was normally assumed. Thus, in Utah, women could find through easy divorce and remarriage the opportunity for what amounted to a sort of de facto serial polygamy (though Mormon writings never spoke in such terms), while their husbands were allowed to take additional wives if they wished.[35]

The relationship between polygamy and divorce in early Utah may also be easier to understand as a result of the recovery of records of 1,645 divorces granted during the Brigham Young period (1847–77). Although these records have not yet been thoroughly analyzed, the bulk of the cases appear to have involved plural marriages. The entire population of Utah numbered only 86,786 in 1870 (with a high percentage consisting of unmarried children and youths), so the divorce rate might appear rather high. Support for such a conclusion is also suggested by D. Michael Quinn's listing of Mormon church leaders and their wives between 1832 and 1932. A simple analysis of his data shows that the 72 church leaders who practiced plural marriage had a total of 391 wives, with 54 divorces, 26 separations, and 1 annulment. For perspective, one should note that at least some of these divorces were those of apparently nonconjugal wives whose marital ties were only symbolic. The extent to which the divorce situation in Utah and surrounding areas of Mormon settlement differed from that of other frontier areas also needs to be investigated.[36]

To understand the significance of these data on divorce, they must be placed within the larger context of the development of plural marriage and other early Mormon social institutions. Plural marriage appears never to have become fully institutionalized during the relatively brief period when it was publicly practiced in Utah. Joseph Smith's revelatory mandate promulgating polygamy in 1843 had required that polygamy be introduced, but it did not specify exactly how it was to be practiced after it was introduced. Later Mormon leaders apparently also claimed no special inspiration on exactly how the system was to be regulated, except to continue to insist, as Joseph Smith had, that all plural marriages must be sanctioned and sealed by the central church authorities.

The wide variation in polygamy practice has been noted by scholars. James E. Hulett, Jr., one of the earliest serious students of Mormon polygamy, observed that he had "expected to find a variety of behavior but not so great a variety." No fully standardized patterns of handling the needs of polygamous families for things such as shelter, food, clothing, and amusement appear to have developed, although there were tendencies toward such standardization. For example, plural wives sometimes lived together under one roof, sometimes had separate houses adjoining each other, and sometimes lived in entirely different locations. Hulett argued that Mormon society of the period continued to remain basically monogamous in its norms and that "except for the broad outlines, the local culture provided no efficient and detailed techniques for control of the polygamous family; each family in a sense had to develop its own culture." Although Hulett's sample was primarily taken from the period of extreme stress in the late nineteenth century, when polygamy was under heavy attack, scholars who have focused on the period when polygamy was more openly practiced have also found significant variation in the ways polygamous families were organized.[37]

The primary reason that polygamy never became fully standardized in Utah was the short period of time that it existed before the intense antipolygamy persecution of the late nineteenth century led the Mormon church to discontinue the practice. Had there been greater time for the new cultural patterns to develop free of external pressure, plural marriage probably would have continued to adapt itself to the changing conditions of the Great Basin region. Just how the new marriage practices would eventually have stabilized will now never be known, however. After the mainstream of the Mormon church broke decisively with polygamy practice at the turn of the century, a small number of dissidents did continue to practice polygamy, but the church as a whole moved on to find new ways of expressing its underlying family ideals through monogamous marriage. Today, somewhat paradoxically, Mormons are among the most "traditional" of any group in their attitudes toward family life and the role of women.[38]

IV

What is the significance of this extraordinary nineteen-century Mormon experiment with plural marriage? Was the effort simply a freakish American sideshow, a rather unpleasant and unappealing aberration, or does it raise larger issues that are of concern today? As the largest and best sustained attempt in nineteenth-century America to create an alternative to monogamous marriage and family life, Mormon polygamy does suggest larger issues worthy of further exploration. At the most basic level, investigations such as those of Ivins, Burgess-Olson, Smith and Kunz, Embry, and others are needed to show how monogamous and polygamous Mormon marriages in early Utah differed from each other. To what extent were the distinctive features of nineteenth-century Mormon family life the result of the existence of polygamy and to what extent were they a product of the broader Mormon drive for cultural and religious autonomy? How did the life experiences of monogamous wives differ from those of first wives or of subsequent wives in polygamous families?

A second area worthy of further investigation is a comparison of the experiences of Mormon plural wives with the experiences of other women on the frontier or in the larger Victorian society. Research by Maureen Ursenbach Beecher, for instance, suggests that at least in the economic sphere, Mormon women were largely indistinguishable from other women in the frontier West.[39] Similarly, Mormon women appear to have been remarkably closely in touch with general currents of thought and practice in Victorian society. At times, in fact, they seem to have been in advance of popular trends. In what ways were Mormon women in contact with the larger society, and what role did polygamy play in that contact?

Finally, Mormon polygamy of the nineteenth century raises comparative and cross-cultural questions of much significance for the present. The problems of women acting as heads of single-parent families, for example, bear much resemblance to the problems of women in some polygamous families. The issues of easy divorce and its effect on family life are also worthy of comparison. And, of course, the Mormon experience provides an American example of polygamy that could be compared with polygamy as it functions in non-Western societies today, as studied by anthropologists such as Remi Clignet.[40]

These and other questions may be fruitfully investigated by using the nineteenth-century Mormon experience as a reference point. Perry Miller could as easily have been speaking of Mormons as of the New England Puritans when he wrote of their experiment as an "ideal laboratory": "It was relatively isolated, the people were comparatively homogenous and the forces of history played upon it in ways that can more satisfactorily be traced than in more complex societies. Here is an opportunity, as nearly perfect as the student is apt to find, for extracting certain generalizations about the relationship of thought or ideas to communal experience."[41] Scholars have only begun to make use of the rich Mormon experience in their attempts to understand the nature and significance of women's varied experiences in nineteenth-century America.

11

FROM ACTIVISM to DOMESTICITY

The Changing Role of Mormon Women in the

Nineteenth and Twentieth Centuries

HE ROLE OF WOMEN in Mormonism has always been a paradoxical one, the subject of intense interest and controversy both in the larger culture and within Mormon society itself. During the last half of the nineteenth century, when polygamy became an integral part of Mormon life in the Intermountain West, women of the Church of Jesus Christ of Latter-day Saints were viewed by the outer world as a benighted and oppressed class, the victims of a system of institutionalized lust perpetrated by a wicked and unscrupulous male Mormon priesthood. In fact, however, despite this negative public image, Mormon women in frontier Utah enjoyed a remarkable degree of real power, influence, and independence. Utah Mormons were leaders in coeducation, woman's suffrage, women in medicine and teaching, and women's publications. Nineteenth-century women's rights and suffrage advocates such as Elizabeth Cady Stanton spoke to large and enthusiastic Mormon audiences whose participation in such meetings was accepted if not actively encouraged by church authorities.

Nearly a hundred years later, in the latter half of the twentieth century, the image and the reality of life for women in Mormonism has become roughly reversed from that of the nineteenth century. Despite continuing ambivalence reflected in Sonia Johnson's highly publicized criticisms of Mormon church opposition to the Equal

Rights Amendment (ERA) during the late 1970s, the popular image of Mormon women has become much more favorable, influenced by the church's emphasis on close-knit, well-run families and idealizing the important role that women play in Mormon family-oriented culture. In fact, however, despite this basically positive image, the activities and personal options for women in the Mormon church may never have been so narrowly circumscribed as in the present. During the past thirty years, Mormon women lost control over the financing of their organization, the Relief Society; they lost their *Relief Society Magazine;* and they faced what appears to be an almost monolithic church front that encourages them to stay out of public life and the job market. Far from being in the forefront of women's rights activities, the present-day Mormon church and its women were a major factor in defeating efforts to ratify the Equal Rights Amendment, operating by such means as church-funded anti-ERA front organizations and large, carefully staged anti-ERA rallies. Although Mormon women today continue to play an essential role in the home and in grass-roots church activities, their participation in the larger society is discouraged in many ways, both by direct exhortation and by subtle community sanctions against deviance from the church-approved ideal that women should try to be perfect wives and mothers in an almost neo-Victorian sense.

What accounts for this apparent shift from the late nineteenth-century Mormon emphasis on women's active participation in almost all aspects of society (except the formal governance of their church) to the present, more narrow stress on domesticity as almost the sole end of woman's life? Some have suggested that the shift is only illusory; the underlying Mormon stress on authority and obedience to the church, they say, has remained a constant despite shifts in the particular issues to which the church addresses itself. According to this argument, the basic Mormon stress on the importance of the family has remained the same, with continuing emphasis on large families, opposition to birth control, and the conviction that, in the final analysis, women ideally should remain in the home whenever possible. Mormonism looks more conservative today only by comparison with the larger society, which has undergone fundamental transformations during the past century.

This argument has much to recommend it, but it needs to be qualified if it is to help explain the profound changes that do appear to have occurred in the role of Mormon women during the past century. Even if such changes are only apparent, they deserve explanation and analysis. The gap between ideal and practice may well be a most revealing indicator of the underlying dynamics of a culture. Although church policies and practices ultimately have been developed and controlled by men, Mormon women also have played an important role in shaping the policies that have affected them. The Mormon church has never acted in a social and intellectual vacuum; it has always had to take into account both its own internal concerns and those of the larger society. Thus to understand the changing role of Mormon women, one must view their experiences within the total gestalt of the Mormon culture within which they have lived.

This chapter is a preliminary reflection on some of the most important issues that must be addressed if one is to understand the varied experiences of Mormon women during the past century. It focuses, first, on women's status in late nineteenth-century Utah, particularly the ways in which the frontier and polygamy may have contributed to women's independence. This nineteenth-century period is then contrasted with the recent past and with some of the factors leading to increasing restrictions on women's sphere of influence within Mormonism. Finally, some broader perspectives on present and future prospects for Mormon women are suggested.[1]

I

To understand the role of Mormon women in nineteenth-century Utah, one must first attempt to understand the relationship between women and Mormonism as a whole. Mormonism is both a religion and a culture system. Seeing itself as a church not a sect, it attempts to encompass the whole of life. Although Mormonism appears quintessentially American in so many ways, it has, nevertheless, since its founding in 1830 set itself in radical opposition to the prevailing American religious and social pluralism. Latter-day Saints believe that they belong to the one true church, restored through the agency of their prophet-founder Joseph Smith and embodying a synthesis of all previously valid human truth. Facing highly disruptive religious and social conditions in his home in the Burned-over District of central New York State, Smith sought to set up a totally cohesive new order which in spirit had much in common with the high medieval Roman Catholic synthesis. Selfish individual interests were always to be subordinated to the good of the community as a whole. Hierarchy and control were essential parts of the effort literally to realize the kingdom of heaven on earth.[2]

In few areas of life were Mormon concerns for social order and control more evident than in their efforts to revitalize the family. Faced with the marital and familial disorders of central New York, Smith dreamed of "turning the hearts of the children of the fathers" before the coming of the millennium. As part of his attempt to establish cohesive Mormon community life in the 1830s and 1840s, Smith increasingly took over responsibility for overseeing the marriage and divorce practices of members of his church. Elsewhere a detailed discussion has been provided of how this increasing autonomy of the Mormon group from the larger society and the intense identification with the Old Testament Hebrew patriarchs as role models helped make possible the introduction of a polygamous marriage system under Joseph Smith's guidance in the early 1840s.[3] Here it is enough to note that polygamy was envisioned, in part at least, as a means of expanding kinship ties and social solidarity among Mormons.[4] For a heavily persecuted group such as the Mormons, the possibility of expanded kinship linkages proved enormously appealing. According to the elaborate and internally consistent religious ideology developed by Smith, marriage and family ties (including polygamy) were the basis for all social order and development, not only in this life but also throughout eternity, which he envisioned essentially as this life writ large.[5] The Mormons viewed themselves as part of a literal New Israel, restoring the polygamous practices of the Hebrew patriarchs and dedicating themselves to the group with an almost tribal quality of total loyalty.

The role of women within this developing family- and kinship-oriented Mormon culture underwent some expansion during the 1830s and 1840s, although that expansion was always less than, and subordinate to, the expansion in the role of men. For males, Mormonism took literally the concept of the "priesthood of all believers," setting up a hierarchial structure in which all worthy adult male members had some leadership or direct participatory role within the lay structure of governance of the church. Although women participated only indirectly in this structure of church governance through association with their husbands, they did gain new rights in related areas. In the 1830s and 1840s, women secured the right to participate in the public meetings of the church, to vote on important proposals brought before the group, to conduct their own women's organization (albeit under the ultimate direction of the male priesthood), and to receive various spiritual gifts and be "ordained" to administer to the sick. Significantly, the greatest liberalism toward women surfaced between 1842 and 1844 during the height of Joseph Smith's efforts to introduce polygamy into the Mormon church. The temple ceremonies that Smith set up in part to support and validate plural marriage stressed that a reciprocal relationship between men and women was necessary for salvation. No man or woman could ultimately reach the highest exaltation in the afterlife alone, without being sealed in celestial marriage to a worthy spouse. By emphasizing that the family and related kinship ties were the key to all growth and development, not only in this life but also throughout all eternity, Mormon ideology gave new status and dignity to women's role in the family.[6]

How was the changing status of women within Mormonism related to the changing status of women in other religious organizations and in antebellum society as a whole? Religiously, early Mormonism fell midway between the most conservative confessional churches such as the Episcopalians, in which women were almost totally excluded from leadership, and the extreme wing of the revivalistic and sectarian movements such as the Shakers, which permitted a high degree of equality for women. If new elements such as polygamy and temple marriage, which were only beginning to be introduced by 1844, are excluded from consideration, Mormon women's activities closely resembled those in many mainstream Protestant groups such as the Methodists and Baptists. Church women's organizations, benevolent societies, and educational efforts were found not only in Mormonism but in many other groups as well.[7] Moreover, the idealization of woman's role as wife and mother had much in common with the "cult of true womanhood," the nascent Victorian concern for home and family life.[8] Nevertheless, the extraordinary fluidity of Mormon belief and practice immediately preceding Smith's assassination and the exodus to Utah makes any secure generalizations about women's status in early Mormonism impressionistic at best. Only following the Mormon arrival in the Great Basin region in 1847 was the church able to set up and develop its own distinctive way of life to the fullest extent.

In Utah and other Mormon areas of the Intermountain West during the last half of the nineteenth century, at least four factors contributed to the development of a relatively egalitarian role for Mormon women in practice. First in importance undoubtedly was the frontier itself and the challenges that it posed for both men and women. Sheer survival in the arid and inhospitable Great Basin region initially demanded that all available talents and energies of both sexes be mobilized effectively for the good of the group. Brigham Young and his advisers were well aware of the vital role that women could play in the economic, social, and intellectual life of their communities.[9] Women were encouraged to do any work that they could do and were needed to do, and many of the conventional American sex role divisions in economics and other areas of life were temporarily deemphasized.[10]

Closely related to the frontier as a factor contributing to women's independence and equality in the Mormon West was, rather paradoxically, the practice of polygamy itself. Polygamy, of course, has conventionally been viewed as a blight on Mormon women, and certainly it was a difficult system for women, both emotionally and in other respects. Nevertheless, in the frontier environment of early Utah the new marriage system actually tended to encourage greater autonomy of women from men. In the absence of their husbands, who could often be gone for extended periods of time, plural wives ran farms and businesses and became of necessity the acting heads of households, as some early federal census reports so identified them. Plural wives could and often did cooperate with each other in handling child care and other work or in freeing an ambitious or talented wife to pursue a professional career. Many of the most active and influential women in late nineteenth-century Utah were wives of polygamists.[11] Moreover, the intense antipolygamy persecutions of the 1870s and 1880s caused many women who were unhappy with polygamy to subordinate their personal feelings and pull together in vigorous support of their husbands, their church, and their whole way of life, politicizing them to a degree never seen before or since.[12] In short, indirectly and almost in spite of itself, Mormon polygamy in the late nineteenth century contributed to a greater degree of autonomy and political activism among women of the church.[13]

A third factor besides the frontier and polygamy that contributed to women's influence in the Mormon church was the development of both a vigorous and effective women's organization, the Relief Society, and a popular women's newspaper, the *Woman's Exponent*. As reorganized under the dynamic direction of Eliza R. Snow, the most powerful woman in the history of the Mormon church, the Relief Society not only participated in and directed many complex economic and cultural projects of its own in Utah, but it also helped set up the educational programs for youth of both sexes that would serve as the foundation for the comprehensive church educational system of the twentieth century.[14] Similarly important was the *Woman's Exponent*, a lively and well-written women's newspaper that served as the major voice for Mormon women's concerns during its publication between 1872 and 1914.[15] The Relief Society and the *Woman's Exponent* served important identity-building functions and helped to reinforce a sense of pride and unity among women of the church.

A final factor contributing to the independence of Mormon women and their active participation in many aspects of Utah life in the nineteenth century was the issue of woman's suffrage. Although supporters of this key women's issue in the nation at large were still having relatively little success by the late nineteenth century, in Utah (and in adjacent areas of the West, for a variety of complex reasons) a different attitude prevailed. In Utah, influential Mormon figures such as George Q. Cannon and Orson F. Whitney did not see the vote for women as a threat that might undermine the social order and family stability. Instead, they anticipated the later progressive arguments that if women had the vote they could more effectively aid in constructive reform and strengthening the family—and, not unimportant, also strengthen Mormon control in Utah. Quietly and almost half a century earlier than the rest of the nation, the Utah legislature, with the tacit blessing of the Mormon hierarchy, therefore extended the vote to women in 1870.[16] Somewhat ironically, Mormon women not only participated actively in national woman's suffrage organizations and rallies but they also organized thousands of church women in mass meetings supporting polygamy against what they perceived as the efforts of the outside world to destroy the Mormon family system.[17] Eventually, antipolygamy forces, frustrated at the failure of Mormon women to rise up and throw off the chains of polygamy, joined with some supporters of woman's suffrage who hated polygamy to stop women from voting in Utah in 1887. After Utah statehood was achieved in 1896 (following a strategic retreat from polygamy that partially mollified national public opinion), however, woman's suffrage was once again introduced into the Utah constitution, twenty-five years in advance of most of the rest of the country.

In short, despite their negative public image in the late nineteenth century, Mormon women exercised a remarkable degree of real power and influence in Utah society. The frontier, polygamy, women's organizations and publications, and the woman's suffrage movement itself contributed in varied and sometimes contradictory ways to the creation of a considerable degree of freedom and autonomy for women in Mormon society.

II

The contrast between the late nineteenth-century Mormon efforts to encourage women to participate in almost all aspects of society and the present-day stress on domesticity as the only important role for women could hardly be more stark. Non-Mormons visiting Utah today often feel as though they have stumbled into another era, into a scene from a mid-Victorian advice manual. Almost everywhere, the ideal that is held up for women today conveys the gush and cloying sentimentality of the "cult of true womanhood." As in Victorian America, ideals and practices in present-day Mormon society seem in tension at many points.[18] For example, while approximately half of married Mormon women work at least part time outside the home to help make ends meet, the church criticizes women who work and thereby neglect their families.[19] Few voices within Utah Mormonism today appear to be effective in challenging the prevailing ideology of domesticity as the only legitimate role for women.

What accounts for this shift from the ideal of the sturdy pioneer woman to that of the neo-Victorian wife and mother? Certainly the transition has been a complex one, and both ideals continue, to some extent, to be present in Mormonism today. At least four factors, however, have been particularly influential in bringing about a shift in emphasis. First was the gradual end of frontier conditions in turn-of-the-century Utah and the corresponding rise to prominence of Victorian notions of culture and refinement. As Edward Geary has suggested in a brilliant interpretive essay on the genteel tradition in Mormondom, Mormons, like other western Americans, often cherish the image of the pioneer wife and mother who triumphed over the adverse conditions of the frontier to transform a rough cabin or musty dugout into a "real home."[20] The symbols of civilization in the genteel tradition, as represented in the sentimental novels of the nineteenth century, had as their object not high culture, not great achievements of the mind or the arts, but rather the little decencies of life such as lacy curtains and vases of flowers. Significantly, Brigham Young and other early Mormon leaders frequently inveighed against such tendencies within the church. Young's support of the functional Bloomer-style Deseret costume so unpopular among church women, his criticism of sentimentalized Victorian novels as trash, and his forthrightness in bluntly and directly dealing in public with family and sexual issues that polite Victorian society thought should be kept strictly private, if discussed at all, show his concern that the genteel ideal threatened even within Mormonism to divert attention from the austerities and sacrifices necessary for the building up of the kingdom. As conditions in Utah eased and such superhuman dedication was no longer required for simple survival, however, such suppressed urges for culture and refinement became increasingly prominent among Mormon women.[21]

In addition to the end of the frontier, the effort of Mormons at the turn of the century to transform and improve their relations with the larger American society served as a second factor that strengthened the ideal of gentility and contributed to a far-reaching constriction in the role of women. After persecution so intense that the very existence of the church was called into question, the Mormons in

1890 reluctantly began to put an end to polygamy, the major overt cause of conflict with the outer society. Concurrently, in an even more fundamental change, the church also began to withdraw from political life as a monolithic force and to allow greater pluralism within its areas of influence. This "Americanization of Utah for statehood," as Gustive O. Larson has characterized it, is strikingly similar to the acculturation of other ethnic groups in this country. [22] First-generation Mormon leaders such as Brigham Young had tenaciously attempted to maintain distinctive ideals and practices that were in conflict with those acceptable in American society. By the turn of the century, however, these original leaders were giving way to a second generation with different priorities. Reacting against the ways of their fathers, which had created so many problems for them, these new leaders gave up polygamy, overt political control, and other distinctive features of their background and attempted in many respects to become more American than the most American. By the 1930s, the harshest persecution of recalcitrant polygamists came from the Mormon church itself, and upper levels of the hierarchy could seriously consider giving up other practices that set Mormons apart from mainstream Americans. During this period, when so many Mormons were attempting to become "two hundred per cent Americans," Mormon society deeply internalized the dominant Victorian ideals of domesticity and women's role, even as the larger society began to give up such ideals. Today, the leaders of the church are men whose formative intellectual and emotional experiences occurred during this transitional pre–World War I era. Because of the strong authority structure of the Mormon church, these men are able to do much to preserve a style of life that many in the rest of America now view as a relic of a bygone age. [23]

In addition to the end of the frontier and the efforts of Mormons to acculturate, a third factor contributing to the constriction of women's role in the Mormon church has been the effort to establish uniformity among, or correlate, all church programs. Although the effort to establish order and consistency in church programs has been ongoing since the founding of the Mormon church, only since World War II, and especially since 1960, has correlation become an overriding concern among Mormons. The basic causes of this concern are simply stated: Since World War II, the church has experienced a phenomenal sevenfold growth from 1 to 7 million members. Even for a group with an effective, centralized leadership and an unusually sophisticated grasp of organizational dynamics, coping with such a staggering increase in membership in forty-five years has posed complex new problems. In the process of cutting back on duplication of magazines, establishing a uniform educational curriculum, and reorganizing channels of authority, women's activities have been especially hard hit. Since 1969–70, the Relief Society has lost its independent funding and now is forced to justify its budget items to a male hierarchy that may sometimes be unsympathetic to some programs that women feel are especially important. The *Relief Society Magazine* has been discontinued, and its replacement by women's columns in the *Ensign* and a single *Ensign* issue each year devoted to women fails to provide a satisfactory substitute. Some Mormon women, particularly at the upper levels of leadership, have privately expressed deep frustrations with the new policy developments and with women's loss of control over their church organizations and activities.[24]

A final factor contributing to increasing restrictions in the sphere of women in Mormonism has been the church's fear of recent changes in American society, notably the feminist movement and efforts to ratify the Equal Rights Amendment during the 1970s and early 1980s. These developments have been viewed by most Mormons as being potentially at variance with basic Mormon principles of hierarchy and the maintenance of strong sex role distinctions, tending to polarize the sexes and disrupt the family. In addition, the ERA, if it had been passed, could have posed the same sorts of legal challenges to twentieth-century Mormon social practice that the antipolygamy crusade did for the church in the nineteenth century.[25] In 1976, therefore, the church officially went so far as to condemn the ERA as an inappropriate method of dealing with the legitimate aspirations of women.[26] The following year, in an operation that provoked intense controversy in Utah, figures in the church orchestrated the attendance of thousands of Mormon women at International Women's Year meetings throughout the state to block all feminist resolutions and send a "conservative" slate to the national meetings.[27] Most sensational—and destructive to Mormon efforts to be seen as taking a positive stance toward women—the

Mormon church in 1979 excommunicated Sonia Johnson because of her highly publicized activities in Mormons for ERA.[28]

Thus, during the past century the role of women in Mormonism appears to have become increasingly narrowly defined. The end of the frontier, the efforts at acculturation, the concern with correlation, and the opposition to the ERA and other manifestations of feminism have all combined to produce what may well be a more constricted role for women within the Mormon church than at any other time in its history.

III

Where do Mormon women go from here? How can women within Mormonism gain the broadest range of options and the opportunity to develop and use their full talents in the future?

At the outset, it must be emphasized that the more militant types of feminism that stress individualism and full equality for women are fundamentally antithetical to the hierarchical ideology underlying Mormonism. Neither now nor in the foreseeable future is militant feminism likely to be a viable option within the Mormon church.[29] For Mormons, order and hierarchy are fundamental values. All members of the church are viewed as part of a cooperative network of family and kinship ties in which the good of the whole community is always more important than the good of any of the component members in isolation. This does not mean that change in the status of women is impossible, but rather that such change, when it comes, will be part of the broader process of change within the entire organization.

The way in which change may take place in the Mormon church is highlighted by one noteworthy development during the late 1970s that was not directly connected with women, namely, elimination of the policy denying full participation in the church to blacks of African descent. This policy, which went back at least a century to the days of Brigham Young, appeared set in stone, despite the many compelling arguments that were raised against it during the years since World War II. Yet in June 1978 that policy was indeed ended, in part because of the spiritual sensitivity of the church's president, Spencer W. Kimball, the pragmatic demands of the world-wide missionary program, particularly in Brazil, where limiting membership based on racial antecedents ultimately proved too complex to be practical, and the church's desire to improve its public image and alleviate the distress the policy caused thoughtful members.[30]

Despite certain obvious similarities between excluding blacks and women from full participation, women's role in Mormonism will be much more difficult to change than that of blacks. Formally allowing a few thousand black Mormons in the United States to participate in their church on a basis of full equality is much less disruptive than formally allowing women—who comprise more than half the church membership and are closely associated with the dominant males—similarly to participate more equally and fully in the church. The entire nature and character of Mormon family culture would be called into question by allowing women formal participation through the priesthood. The intense ambivalence and concern many Mormon men feel about this possibility was most vividly expressed by Harmon Rector, Jr., a mission president from southern California, who made clear that he felt that "belligerant sisters" such as Sonia Johnson "were no longer Mormons," and that "in order for males and females to be somewhere near even, the Heavenly Father gave him the priesthood or directing authority for the Church and home. Without this bequeath, males would be so far below females in power and influence that there would be little or no purpose for his existence in fact [sic] would probably be eaten by the female as is the case with the black widow spider."[31]

As this statement suggests, Sonia Johnson's case highlights the strong emotions that the women's issue has aroused, not only for non-Mormons but especially for Latter-day Saints. A brief look at the basis for this controversy and at the subsequent impact Sonia Johnson's excommunication has had on Mormon women thus may provide one way of understanding developments of the past decade.

Sonia Johnson's experiences were especially wrenching to Mormon women because she came from such a strong Utah Mormon background and commitment. She was a practicing Mormon who held down three church positions, paid her full tithing, had completed her four-generation genealogical records, and regularly attended ward meetings. At the time of her public activities in favor of

the ERA, however, she was also a professionally trained woman living outside Utah and increasingly resentful of the strictures the Mormon hierarchy placed on its women. In particular, like many other
Mormon women of her background, she was deeply upset that the
Mormon church in the late 1970s was orchestrating, both directly
and through various front groups, a massive campaign to defeat the
Equal Rights Amendment. Johnson joined Mormons for ERA, which
actively publicized and criticized the church's anti-ERA activity with
imaginative tactics such as flying a plane over the church's semian-
nual conference with a banner proclaiming "Mother in Heaven Supports the ERA." Johnson herself first secured wide media attention
when she made an extremely articulate appearance at a United
States congressional investigation, vigorously challenging Utah Mormon Senator Orin Hatch. She became something of a celebrity, going on the lecture circuit to make her case.

Faced by such challenges, the Mormon church seriously miscal-
culated in handling Sonia Johnson. Not fully gauging the potential
media impact of this hitherto unknown Mormon woman, the church
in December 1979 tried and excommunicated her in proceedings
that, much like Anne Hutchinson's trial of 1637, were a travesty of
justice with no definite charges and no possibility of an effective defense. The national press was out in force and helped turn the trial
into a major media event that reflected very negatively on the Mormon church. Following her excommunication, Johnson increasingly
became a champion for women's rights outside the Mormon church
and had less direct contact with Mormons, except through the publication in 1981 of her powerful and revealing autobiography, *From
Housewife to Heretic*. In it she described an encounter with a Mormon leader, tellingly expressing her pain and that of other Mormon
women like her: "We had come hungering and thirsting for help, for
a reason to believe the leaders of our church were inspired, for a
reason not to become renegades. We had come asking for some
thoughtful answers. And he had given us a stone."[32]

Sonia Johnson's case created intense tensions within the Mormon church. Pro-ERA women became concerned whether they too
might be excommunicated, and many, like Sonia Johnson, were
sorely torn between their loyalties to their church and to women's
issues. Overall, in the church itself, the excommunication led to a

backlash against Mormon feminism. Something of a siege mentality developed. Church leaders such as Dallin Oaks, then president of Brigham Young University and later a member of the Quorum of the Twelve, declared after the excommunication that the controversy was an example of evil forces conspiring in the world at large against the church.[33] Despite a strong and continuing undercurrent of dissatisfaction among articulate Mormon women, the public front among Mormon women in Utah appears to have remained almost monolithic on this topic during the past decade.

Given this situation, are there any signs of possible positive changes in Mormon women's status in the future? The widespread interest in issues of the family and women's role in Utah today is a major factor suggesting that Mormon women's range of options may eventually be broadened. Even though the general tone of discussions tends to be muted by comparison with more militant statements of the larger society, many of the same concerns are raised, and conferences on women such as the ones held at Brigham Young University are well attended.[34] Some Mormon sociologists and family counselors warn of the dangers of the heavy Mormon emphasis on early marriage and too large families—factors that have contributed to a disturbingly high divorce rate among Mormons and to other family problems that at times approach in intensity those of the outer society.[35] Faced with a sizable number of young, single Mormon women, many of whom will not be able to find desirable husbands within the Mormon church, the church publishes books pointing out that there are also rewarding opportunities for women outside marrige and that remaining single should not be considered the end of the world.[36] Some bright young Mormon women have begun to point to research studies showing that married women who work at least part time outside the home generally have a better self-image and make more effective, rather than less effective, wives and mothers.[37] And articles discussing the Mormon concept of a Mother in Heaven and criticizing the exclusion of Mormon women from the priesthood appear in independent Mormon scholarly journals.[38]

Although such ideals are still outside the Mormon mainstream and are sharply criticized by some Mormon leaders, the church as a whole generally has skillfully crafted its policy statements to avoid totally cutting off any potentially fruitful options for its members. For example, official church pronouncements strongly criticize birth control yet allow it in cases when the woman's health or feelings make it desirable.[39] Similarly, another policy pronouncement sharply attacks abortion, while allowing it in exceptional cases such as rape.[40] Thus, church policy declarations that appear unequivocal to the casual reader usually are couched so that they are open to variant interpretations depending on individual circumstances and inclinations.

Partly as a result of such flexibility, the Mormon church has been remarkably successful in adapting to changes in the outside world without losing touch with its underlying goals. The insights and concerns of the larger society typically are filtered through a unique Mormon perspective. Birth control, for example, is practiced by many Mormons, and the Mormon birth rate during this century has followed the general rises and dips of American society as a whole, though always at a somewhat higher level.[41] Evidence from past policy development suggests that so long as Mormon women remain generally satisfied with a position that is essentially limited to the home, church policies toward their role are likely to remain restrictive; but as conditions in society change and as tensions develop within the Mormon home which clearly reflect the dysfunctional nature of certain church policies, those policies may well be gradually and significantly modified so that the organization may operate with maximum effectiveness.[42]

The responsibilities of leadership in a highly centralized organization such as the Mormon church are awesome. Effective new programs can be rapidly instituted within an entire organization, yet if the leadership makes fundamental errors in judgment, the negative effects can be similarly far-reaching. The current policy of correlation within the church holds particularly ambiguous potential, both for women and for Mormonism as a whole. If the policy is to work well, women, as well as other elements in the church, need to be actively and effectively involved in every issue that directly affects them. Otherwise, blunders and policy mistakes are almost inevitable. Even if the Mormon church continues to keep its women in a position of ultimate subordination to men, not to involve half the church in creating the policies that affect them is not only ethically questionable but organizationally dysfunctional as well. A decade after Sonia Johnson's much-publicized excommunication, Mormon women's profound dissatisfaction with their current constricted roles appears to have penetrated far below the intellectual leaders to rank-and-file women who help keep the basic operations of the church running. A quiet revolt may be brewing in the ranks that will force the church to act if it is to maintain its effectiveness as a functioning organization. [43]

As this book goes to press, the Mormon church has once again surprised both its supporters and its critics by making significant doctrinal changes in its treatment of women's status in the church. A front-page article in the *New York Times* of May 3, 1990, reports that in mid-April 1990 this rapidly growing religious group with 7.3 million members quietly changed key elements in its temple rituals that relate to women. Although Mormons are not supposed to discuss these rituals, which are considered sacred, reliable informants report that among the changes was the dropping of a vow in which women pledged obedience to their husbands (their husbands, by contrast, took an oath of obedience to God) and the dropping of a practice that required women to veil their faces at one point in the ceremony. Although these recent changes do not allow women to hold the Mormon priesthood, they clearly are an encouragement toward a greater degree of equality between men and women, both before God and in their family relationships. [44]

In conclusion, if organizational health is to be maintained, not simply for Mormon women but for the entire church, a balance must be maintained between order, on the one hand, and creativity, on the other. To establish an organizational straitjacket, to cut back too severely on the room for individual variation within the church, would be to threaten the possibility of the very universality to which Mormonism aspires. The need for continuing creativity and openness in dealing with the role of women within Mormonism is powerfully expressed by a woman who moved back to Utah after thirty-five years of living in Delaware. She stated: "I feel that what we're losing in the Church is diversity. There's such a push for uniformity and conformity that all the beautiful little nuances of differences are being swept aside. That's really what God enjoys. Otherwise he wouldn't make every leaf and snowflake different. You should have the freedom to have some time to be yourself, and to have people appreciate that you're different. You should appreciate this in your children and not try to push them all into a prescribed mold. . . . I think that in an authoritarian church this is one of the dangers. . . . We have to let some pilot projects develop in individual lives too. Until we do that, how are we going to let a woman make the individual contribution which is particularly her own?"[45] The role of women within Mormonism is surely one of the continuing challenges with which the church will have to grapple seriously in the years ahead.

CONCLUSION

12

A "PERMANENT REVOLUTION"?

Reflections on the Prospects for Radical Social Change

*T*HE EXPERIENCES of the Shakers, Oneida Perfectionists, and Mormons raise a host of complex questions. How different were these three groups from their larger society? To what extent did these communal experimenters intend to change women's roles and to what extent did they actually change women's roles? In what ways can these groups be said to have succeeded or failed in achieving their larger objectives, especially regarding the reorganizing of relations between the sexes? And why, ultimately, did each of these groups either give up its unusual sexual practices or gradually decline in size and impact?

Numerous previous studies have addressed these questions. Most of these analyses, however, have not concentrated closely enough on what the groups *themselves* were trying to do, but have instead used external analytical frameworks as the basis for judging the degree of consistency of these movements. The conclusion usually has been that the groups failed because they failed to live up to the critics' preconceived ideas of what they should have been doing. Whether or not the religious communitarians ever actually *intended* to achieve the goals the external analysts judged them against has often been ignored, especially when looking at their treatment of the role of women.[1]

Central to understanding the internal dynamic that impelled the Shakers, Oneidans, and Mormons to attempt to achieve radical social change was their millennial religious vision. Leaders of these movements truly believed that in some sense it was actually possible to bring into being an ideal earthly state, in their terms, "the king-dom of heaven on earth." In no instance was that ideal state seen as static, unchanging, or utopian. Rather the "perfection" that would accompany the millennium was seen by all three of these movements as a gradually unfolding process of change.[2]

The primary goal of that millennial development was to subor-dinate all aspects of life to the guidance of God, as understood by each group. Economic, political, social, and other concerns were all to be considered in the light of the larger religious vision of the movement. Even the role of women, one of the chief issues of this study, was to be treated as part of the broader concerns of the group, not as an independent variable. Put in social terms, these millenni-alists were convinced that their primary goal was to overcome the selfish individualism they felt was tearing their society apart and sub-stitute, instead, a new God-led society—which they saw as a sort of enlarged family. In that society, individual interests and development would be subordinate and complementary to the interests of the en-tire group, which in turn were seen as reflecting the will of God.

Different though the specific social *solutions* these three groups proposed may have been, their underlying *approaches* thus were strik-ingly similar. Those approaches were unpopular among many nine-teenth-century Americans influenced by a concern for individualism and self-development as their highest goal, and they also continue to be a source of ambivalence for many students of these movements today, especially for those feminists whose primary goal is to allow women to realize their own *individual* potential, to rise above the tra-ditional subordination of women's interests to men, their children, and their families.

Although these religious communitarians often appear to con-temporary social analysts to have been ahead of their time in their critique of inequities in women's position in America, their approach to changing such inequities differs sharply from those of many mod-ern analysts. Rather than highlighting conflict between the sexes as part of their efforts to improve women's position in society, these "utopian socialists," as they have been dubbed by their Marxist critics,[3] were very concerned to avoid direct conflict between the sexes by achieving cooperative communal solutions to perceived in-equities. Those solutions subordinated the interests of both men and women to the good of the larger community, which in turn was seen as representing the will of God.

Socially and intellectually, these efforts had roots in the Protestant Reformation, particularly its English and American Puritan expressions. The Shakers, Oneidans, and Mormons shared with their Puritan forebears a concern to restore the faith of early Christianity as they understood it, a stress on the priesthood of all believers, and a belief that the family was a microcosm of society, the model for the larger social order. The English Puritans had taken an essentially activist approach to the social turmoil of their day, rejecting monastic withdrawal from the world while demanding an almost monastic degree of commitment to the expression of religious ideals in daily life. The antebellum millennialists, by contrast, temporarily withdrew from the world in a seemingly monastic fashion while seeking within their communities to reunite religious and social life into a new, holistic synthesis.[4]

Both the Puritans and the religious communitarians struggled with the tensions between the desires of the individual and the demands of the group, seeking to go beyond an exclusive reliance on individual Bible interpretation to achieve a broader religious and social consensus. The diverse ways in which these groups articulated their ideal solutions to the status of women, and the social factors that contributed to those differing solutions, will be the primary focus of the remainder of this chapter.

I

The ways in which sex roles were restructured in the antebellum Shaker, Oneida Perfectionist, and Mormon communities may be used to illustrate the complex relationship of such movements to the larger society, as well as the powerful internal dynamic leading to change within each group. Perhaps the single issue that most clearly reflects the attitudes toward sex roles within these movements is their approach to religious authority—for religious authority ultimately underlay all other aspects of life within these groups.

The larger society to which these millennial movements responded was undergoing important religious changes during the antebellum period. With the elimination of state support for churches after the Revolutionary War, religious groups began to develop new, revivalistic techniques to attract members. Women were especially important in this effort. They constituted a majority of those attending revival meetings, and they were among the most fervent in seeking the conversion of their families and friends. Whereas the more traditional churches generally had not allowed women to preach or participate fully in worship, revivalists such as Charles Grandison Finney strongly encouraged innovations such as allowing women to pray in mixed public meetings. Although most revivalistic groups still formally held that women should be subordinate to men, they also provided new institutional means by which women could begin to participate more actively in the larger society. Moral reform groups, missionary organizations, Bible and tract societies, and a variety of other groups all depended heavily on women and indirectly encouraged them to become involved in the affairs of the society around them.[5]

The Shakers, Oneida Perfectionists, and Mormons all developed out of this broader revivalistic ferment, but they reacted in different ways to the increasing participation of women in religious life. The Shakers, most extreme of the revivalistic groups, both in their ecstatic worship services and in their insistence on celibacy, were also the most extreme in giving women positions of formal equality with men at all levels of their religious structure. Ann Lee, who founded the Shakers in America, was a woman, and women served as supreme head of the society at several later stages of its development. Not only was the group founded by a woman and led by women at different stages of its development, but it also believed that even God was dual in nature, composed of complementary and equal expressions of male and female elements.

The Oneida Perfectionists, influenced both by Finneyite revivalism and by the Shakers, retained much of the Shaker liberalism regarding the participation of women in religious life. Although John Humphrey Noyes was the patriarchal head and final authority at Oneida, he encouraged women to join actively in all aspects of the religious and social life of the community. Even though Noyes believed that men were ultimately superior to women, he was sympathetic to many of the concerns of antebellum feminists, and he sought within his own communities to develop cooperative approaches that would serve the interests of both men and women.

The Mormons, although they also made changes in women's religious status, were the most heavily male-dominated and the closest to conventional attitudes about women's role in religion. At the same time that all worthy adult male members of the Mormon church participated in its lay system of priesthood governance, women were excluded from any formal leadership in the system. Whereas the Shakers had encouraged women to take a leading role in religious government and John Humphrey Noyes had admitted that women could head a religious group under exceptional circumstances, the Mormon prophet-founder Joseph Smith flatly denied that women could ever be the legitimate head of any religious movement.[6] Woman's greatest role was in childbearing and child rearing, so that eventually a great patriarchal family could be established, linking the generations throughout time and all eternity.

These three divergent responses to revivalistic ferment suggest that although revivalism may have served as a catalyst that helped break down the old order and make possible the establishment of new patterns, revivalism by itself did not determine *which* new authority pattern of relations between the sexes would ultimately be adopted.

II

Economic life was another area that was undergoing rapid changes during the antebellum period, thereby placing special strains on relations between the sexes. The decades following the end of the Revolutionary War marked not only the beginning of rapid westward expansion but also the first stages of industrialization, with all its attendant challenges and problems. Men's and women's activities increasingly diverged, with men participating more and more in the larger market economy, while women were increasingly relegated to the home, precisely at the time that many of the home's strictly economic functions were being taken over by the larger society. With the changing economic demands on both men and women came a need for adjustment to new conditions.[7]

The communitarian economic concerns that expressed themselves in the Shaker, Oneida Perfectionist, and Mormon movements can be seen as part of an attempt to overcome the economic instabilities arising from unbridled competition in the developing market economy. A cohesive primary group was necessary to provide security in an uncertain world, but once again the three groups developed very different strategies for reorganizing male and female relationships within their new economic orders.

Somewhat paradoxically, the attitudes toward women and religious authority were different from the attitudes toward women in economic life in these three groups. The Shakers, most egalitarian in dealing with religious authority relations between the sexes, were the most conventional in the economic roles they assigned to men and women. Shaker women engaged in traditional women's work such as cooking, cleaning, and sewing, while Shaker men worked in the fields, shops, and other traditionally male locations. The Shakers' main quarrel was with the exploitative consequences of sexual intercourse and with the individualistic economic system, not with any particular division of work roles by sex.

In contrast to the Shakers, the Oneida Community was both in theory and in practice one of the most radical ventures ever attempted in America to reorganize relations between the sexes in economic life. Oneida's founder, John Humphrey Noyes, wanted to end all sexual distinctions in economic life that were not intrinsic—and there were very few that he considered intrinsic. He encouraged men and women to work together in vital and rewarding labor; he allowed some women to serve in positions of authority over men; and he let men or women do almost any kind of work they wished to do and could handle effectively. Noyes's main concern in the economic sphere appears to have been to overcome the instabilities and uncertainties of the outer society by creating a cohesive community home in which the interests of all could be met effectively.

If the highly traditional economic roles for women in the sexually egalitarian Shakers may appear surprising, the extremely varied and flexible economic roles for women in the patriarchal, male-dominated Utah Mormon society also demands explanation. Although it is true that the primary economic role for women in frontier Utah remained that of childbearer and child rearer—a vital function for a group attempting to settle and populate an arid and inhospitable new region—women also engaged in an unusually wide range of other activities. They ran farms and retail establishments, dominated the medical profession, participated in numerous economic and support activities through the Relief Society, and organized, published, and circulated a distinguished women's newspaper, the *Woman's Exponent.* Although no ideological rationale supported this extension of women's activities, the requirements of life in early Utah allowed, encouraged, and in some cases forced women to engage in many careers besides that of wife and mother.

What accounts for the divergence between the role of women in religious and economic life in these three groups? Although this complex question has no simple answers, these movements appear to have felt that a thoroughgoing reorganization of sex roles was less important in economic life than in religion. Thus, the concrete demands of the group rather than ideology per se appear to have played the most important part in causing changes in the economic relations between the sexes in these groups.

III

Sexual expression was yet another aspect of life that was changing for both men and women during the antebellum period. Sex outside of marriage had always been condemned, of course, but in the decades immediately preceding the Civil War, the earlier, relatively unrestrictive attitudes toward sexual expression *within* marriage were increasingly giving way to the thoroughgoing restrictiveness that has usually been labeled "Victorian." In contrast to earlier views that women were the sexually active "temptresses," the Victorian "cult of true womanhood" popularized a view of women as purer than men, free from sexual desires, and responsible for keeping in check the lascivious impulses of the naturally carnal male. While such attitudes may not have been fully reflected in the actual sexual practice of the time, demographic evidence, including the falling birth rate before the widespread availability of artificial means of contraception, suggests that these ideas about sexual self-control were indeed having an effect upon behavior. Many individuals appear to have seen the effort to impose control over sexual relations as part of a larger movement to restore order in a fragmented and fragmenting society.[8]

The Shakers, Oneida Perfectionists, and Mormons were deeply influenced by these new ideals of sexual self-control, and they in fact accentuated such concerns within their communities. Shaker celibacy, for instance, can be viewed as almost a parody of the restrictive literature of marital and sexual advice. The Shakers carried the implications of this literature to their extreme logical conclusion. If sex was basically a dangerous impulse and even in marriage should be engaged in infrequently, then why not go further and eliminate sexual intercourse altogether? By carefully separating the sexes and by allowing emotional release through ecstatic religious services, the Shakers were able to channel their energies toward achieving the needs of the group.

The Oneida Perfectionists, rather surprisingly, illustrate Victorian concerns for control and Victorian ambivalence toward sexuality even better than do the Shakers. Although outsiders typically fantasized about the "licentious" behavior that supposedly went on in this "free love" colony, where adult men and women frequently exchanged sexual partners, in reality complex marriage at Oneida was associated with control mechanisms that might appear even more restrictive in some respects than Shaker celibacy. Romantic liaisons were systematically broken up; group-criticism sessions dealt bluntly with any sexual behavior that did not conform to community norms; and birth control was accomplished by the highly restrictive and demanding practice of male continence or *coitus reservatus*. John Humphrey Noyes argued that his system simply required that self-control be exercised at one step further in the sexual process than did the Shakers; the Shakers did not allow sexual intercourse at all, while he allowed couples to come together but did not permit full sexual consummation, except when children were desired.[9] In the final analysis, Noyes's underlying goal was similar to that of the Victorians—he wanted to help his followers internalize new values of self-control rather than to depend on external social sanctions to direct their behavior.

Mormon sexual attitudes, like those at Oneida, are at least as complex and ambivalent as those of the outer society. On the one hand, Mormons not only encouraged sex for procreation, they in fact considered such relations as one of the chief ends and glories of life. On the other hand—and in contrast to the popular view of polygamy as licentious debauchery—the Mormons were even harsher in their condemnation of unauthorized sexual liaisons than was the larger society. Adultery was viewed as a heinous sin, second only to apostasy. Helping to build the Mormon kingdom by begetting and rearing righteous children in the families of the best men was the primary purpose of sexual intercourse, not the gratification of base animal instincts. Self-control was stressed constantly. Perhaps the restrictive aspects of polygamy, which coexisted with a fundamentally positive attitude toward sex and children, were partly a Mormon effort to demonstrate to themselves and to the world that their system was, in fact, a principled one, not the licentious "seraglio" that was portrayed by the non-Mormon world. Surely too, the redirection of sexual energies toward the realization of communal goals must have contributed significantly to the difficult enterprise of building the Mormon Zion in the American West.

Thus these three groups, whose practices appeared to be so different from those of the larger society, nevertheless shared with that society an extreme concern for controlling any potentially disruptive sexual expression. In each case, sex was a means to an end, not an end in itself, and hence pleasure was not the primary goal of sexual intercourse. Instead, the aim was to internalize values of sexual self-control so that individual impulses could be sublimated to the goals of the larger community, however those larger goals might be defined.

IV

Closely associated with Victorian ideals of sexuality and women's place was the Victorian idealization of the family and motherhood. One popular Victorian image was of a little white house in the countryside, surrounded by a white picket fence, and inside the house, father, mother, and several well-behaved children gathered together in the family circle, perhaps reading a good book or talking quietly. Although such ideals may not have accurately represented the way in which most Americans actually lived in an increasingly urban age, the literature of Victorian America nevertheless placed great emphasis on the nuclear family, on motherhood, and on woman's vital role in shaping a new generation that would in turn shape society. The family was seen as a bastion of security in an uncertain world, a retreat and refuge from the unbridled and unprincipled competition of the larger society.[10]

If these were the popular ideals, then how did groups like the Shakers, Oneida Perfectionists, and Mormons, which rejected or drastically modified the conventional nuclear family, justify their departure from the practices of the larger society? All three groups argued that they were not rejecting the family ideal but that instead they were raising that ideal to a higher level. An expanded family and a more broadly based communal loyalty would prove superior to the narrow nuclear family union. This argument was used even by the celibate Shakers, who called their basic communal units "families," referred to each other as "brother" and "sister," and addressed especially beloved adult members as "father" and "mother." Shaker communities were paternalistic (or maternalistic) oligarchies; decisions were made by the leaders, and average members were treated benevolently, if at times rather patronizingly, as though they were children.

John Humphrey Noyes, a Yale-trained academic, dealt even more skillfully and explicitly than the Shakers did with the problem of how ideal family relations were to be realized in his Oneida Community. Over and over again, Noyes described the community as an "enlarged family," and he vehemently rejected the claim that he was breaking the family apart. Rather, he declared, he was securing for all individuals in the community the benefits of the larger group. Whereas romantic love and marriages based on such love encouraged an individualism that undermined communal solidarity, at Oneida "each was married to all" in a complex marriage. Only the exclusive sexual, emotional, and economic attachments of the nuclear family were eliminated in favor of a more inclusive communal unity.

The Mormons were considerably closer to the family ideals and practices of the larger society than either the Shakers or the Oneida Perfectionists. In fact, Mormon literature of the polygamy period, whether for internal or external consumption, frequently sounds more Victorian than the writings of the Victorians. Perhaps reacting in part to the intensity of external attacks on their marriage prac-

tices, Mormons emphatically denied that they were breaking up the
family, demeaning motherhood, or failing to rear righteous and
healthy children. Rather, they argued, polygamy made it possible to
bring up more children in the families of the best men. Far from
criticizing the ideal of the family, Mormons saw family life and the
relationship between family and larger kinship networks as the ultimate basis for all progression, not only on earth but throughout all
eternity. To an almost unparalleled extent, the Mormon religion really was *about* the family; earthly and heavenly family ideals were
seen as identical.[11]

Thus the Shakers, Oneida Perfectionists, and Mormons all attempted to develop new family ideals that differed in certain significant respects from those of the larger society. The "family" to these
millennialists was far more than the basic biological unit; instead, it
represented the entire community and embraced the extended kinship ties between members of that group.

V

If such were the ideals of these groups, then how well did those ideals
work out in practice? To what extent were the alternative marital
and communal systems of these millennial groups related both to
their growth and to their decline?

Shaker celibacy served as the key defining feature of the group,
separating it from other revivalistic movements and calling forth an
intense level of commitment from its members. Like Catholic monasticism, celibacy in Shaker communities could prove a basis for
organizational strength, freeing believers from the divided loyalties
that inevitably result from family life so that they could devote their
full efforts to the service of the community and to God. During the
early, expansive, missionary phase of Shaker development, in particular, celibacy helped liberate intense proselytizing energies. Yet celibacy as practiced by the Shakers had obvious limitations. Whereas
Catholic monasticism could always draw on a pool of members from
a larger, noncelibate church, the Shaker organization was entirely
celibate and thus was totally dependent on converts from the outside
world. No consistent or reliable system of recruitment was ever de-

veloped by the group, and after the Civil War, as the organization went into an obvious decline, requirements for membership were loosened so much that in some cases the Shakers were reduced to advertising that they could provide members with "a secure home for life."[12] Although much of the early Shaker spirit still remained or was rechanneled into new activities, the group increasingly became more of a curiosity than a distinctive religious force during the years following the Civil War.

Oneida Community complex marriage, like Shaker celibacy, served important positive functions for the organization, but also possessed weaknesses that eventually undercut the system. Possibly even more than celibacy, complex marriage and its attendant practices required an intense level of commitment from community members and led to an almost unshakable loyalty. Yet by the same token, complex marriage was almost inherently self-limiting. Noyes originally had envisioned a network of "associated communities" which would spread throughout the country, but he found that continually inducting new members into the complex marriage system was exceedingly difficult. A system such as the one at Oneida could, he realized, only exist effectively on a limited scale under tight controls. As a result, as early as 1850 Noyes began to place his primary stress on doing a "small but safe business," and eventually he gave up his plans for further communal expansion. After a quarter of a century of successful small-scale communal living, even Oneida itself proved unable to sustain complex marriage. Faced with a decline in Noyes's leadership powers, the decay of old ideals, and a variety of complex social tensions, including those produced by Noyes's eugenics experiment, the Oneida Community decided to give up complex marriage and its other distinctive patterns of communal living by 1881.

Unlike Shaker celibacy or Oneida complex marriage, Mormon polygamy was a potentially viable way of organizing marriage and family relations in an ongoing community. In fact, throughout the world a majority of societies allow and practice polygamy in some form or other.[13] Yet in the monogamous American context, polygamy was similar to celibacy or complex marriage in that it demanded a high degree of commitment and was inherently self-limiting. For a firm monogamist to accept the idea that polygamy was divinely inspired required a great adjustment, but actually to practice polygamy was even more of a challenge. Even if all Mormons could have fully accepted such practices, external American opposition to polygamy would have created severe and continuing problems for the group. It is conceivable that if Utah had remained sufficiently isolated from American society for a longer period of time, polygamy might have survived as the ideal marital practice of the group. But if the Mormon church had not begun to give up the practice of polygamy in 1890, Mormonism could never have achieved any degree of acceptance in America. Instead, the group would have remained at best a deviant and despised subculture, rather than the world-embracing church it aspires to become.[14]

Thus in all three groups alternative marital beliefs and practices provided a source of initial organizational strength and a means of self-definition that was closely associated with the intense commitment of the earliest phase of development. In the long run, however, such unorthodox systems of relations between men and women hampered the continuing growth of each group, causing both internal tensions and external conflicts. Only the Mormons appear to have been able to make the successful transition from a persecuted subculture to a mainstream movement in America, and they were able to achieve that goal only by giving up polygamy and modifying other aspects of their beliefs and practices that were the source of major conflicts with the larger American society.

VI

In conclusion, do these unorthodox communal experiments provide new insights into the process of radical social change, especially regarding the status of women? Why, in each case, did these movements stop short of attempting as thoroughgoing a transformation as those advocated by some contemporary social critics?

The chief strength of each of these groups was also its chief weakness as far as radically revising relations between the sexes was concerned. The prophetic founders of these movements—and their followers who implemented and elaborated upon their original vision—had as their primary objective the reestablishment of a cohesive religious and social order in which the private interests of the individual would be subordinated to the larger interests of the group, which in turn were seen as reflecting the will of God. The prophet-founders were deeply disturbed by what they saw as the social disorder and rampant individualism around them, and they sought, like the leaders of other "revitalization movements" about which anthropologist Anthony F. C. Wallace has written, to create a harmonious new synthesis of religious and social truth.[15]

These groups also considered their efforts to change and improve conditions for women as ultimately subordinate to the larger goals of their movements. Reading between the lines of accounts of even the theoretically egalitarian Shakers, one realizes that even the articulate feminist-oriented liberal wing of that movement during the late nineteenth century, such as Frederick W. Evans, Anna White, and Leila S. Taylor, ultimately was making the case that improvements in women's status could best be achieved by individuals joining the Shakers and subordinating themselves to its discipline, rather than by seeking individual freedom and self-expression in the larger society.[16]

White and Taylor's eloquent 1904 interpretation of Ann Lee's motives is a case in point. They wrote:

> From the depths of woman's secret life, bearing the untold wrongs, the unwhispered shames of all womankind, of her to whom it was said and by whom it has been bitterly fulfilled, "Thy desire shall be to thy husband and he shall rule over thee," out of the dregs of society, knowing the pangs of ignorance, the toils and burdens, the pinching poverty of the downtrodden poor,—she conquered all by her mighty reliance on God, her soul uplift for herself and all womankind.[17]

A casual reading of this and other passages in the White and Taylor history suggests the dominance of a feminist message. In fact, over and over again throughout their book, this feminist message is subordinated to and integrated into the larger goal of achieving Shaker order. In their conclusion, White and Taylor declare, for instance, that individuals may be attracted to aspects of Shakerism, "but, unless baptized into the very life essence of the [Shaker] Gospel in all its phases of cooperation, practical communism, increasing revelation, a virgin life, peace and non-resistance, it will be but an attempt, a fruitless expenditure of time and talent."[18]

Similar subordination of concerns for women's status to the larger concerns of the group was even more evident in patriarchal movements such as those of the Oneida Perfectionists and Mormons. Noyes could eloquently criticize women's subordination to their husbands in monogamous marriage as "slavery," but his solution was an "enlarged family" in which both women and men subordinated their interests to those of the larger God-inspired community led by him. Joseph Smith and the Mormon leaders who followed him, with their attraction to Old Testament models of patriarchal polygamy, even more obviously subordinated women's interests to those they defined as central to the larger community. Even when Mormon women exhibited extraordinary independence and self-reliance, as in nineteenth-century Utah, that freedom was encouraged as part of the survival of the community rather than primarily to aid the advancement of individual women.

Jean E. Friedman's *Enclosed Garden,* which analyzes the relation of evangelical women and community in the South from 1830 to 1900, provides a suggestive point of comparison.[19] One of Friedman's primary arguments is that the limitation of feminist activism and self-assertion in the South during that period can be attributed, in large measure, to the fact that evangelical women in the South put their loyalty to family and kinship ties above their concerns for individual advancement and self-expression. Likewise, the unorthodox efforts of the Shakers, Oneidans, and Mormons to enlarge family and kinship ties within their communal orders inhibited their development of the more thoroughgoing feminist critiques of society that we have seen within the past two decades.

Does this mean that the Shakers, Oneidans, and Mormons are of little interest for those seeking to revitalize and improve relations between the sexes today? Perhaps we expect too much of these groups when we ask them to provide solutions to complex problems that we ourselves have not fully resolved. Historians are well aware that groups such as these operated in a different time and place than we do today. At least initially, their efforts may most fruitfully be evaluated within the context of their own time and problems rather than from the perspective of our society today.

Yet there is another sense in which these groups can be seen as having a transhistorical interest because they struggled with issues of perennial human concern. In reading through the myriad letters, diaries, and other accounts of these communal experimenters, I have been deeply impressed by the sincerity, dedication, and skill with which they attempted to establish a new and more satisfying way of life. Although the solutions these individuals developed to the religious and social chaos they perceived around them proved fleeting, this is hardly surprising. No social order is static or unchanging, especially when it demands the intense commitment and dedication that these experiments did. In an imperfect world, there are no permanent revolutions, only limited and transitory triumphs. But there is, I am convinced, continuing value in the pursuit of an impossible ideal.

NOTES

BIBLIOGRAPHY

INDEX

NOTES

ABBREVIATIONS

BYU Studies   *Brigham Young University Studies*

Dialogue   *Dialogue: A Journal of Mormon Thought*

JD   *Journal of Discourses*

JMH   *Journal of Mormon History*

MS, WRHS   Shaker Manuscripts in the Western Reserve Historical
               Society Library

UHQ   *Utah Historical Quarterly*

1. RELIGION, SEXUALITY, and WOMEN'S ROLES

    1. This chapter explores and elaborates upon some of the chief issues originally analyzed in Lawrence Foster, *Religion and Sexuality: Three American Communal
Experiments of the Nineteenth Century* (New York: Oxford Univ. Press, 1981), reprinted in paperbound edition, with identical pagination, as *Religion and Sexuality:
The Shakers, the Mormons, and the Oneida Community* (Urbana: Univ. of Illinois
Press, 1984). Throughout this book, I shall highlight and further develop some of
the key themes first raised in that earlier study. For a provocative alternative to the
perspective presented here, see Louis J. Kern, *An Ordered Love: Sex Roles and Sexuality in Victorian Utopias—the Shakers, the Mormons, and the Oneida Community*
(Chapel Hill: Univ. of North Carolina Press, 1981).

    2. For bibliographic entrées into the literature on these groups, see Arthur E.
Bestor, *Backwoods Utopias: The Sectarian and Owenite Phase of Communitarian Socialism in America, 1663–1829*, 2d enl. ed. (Philadelphia: Univ. of Pennsylvania Press,
1970), 287–310; T. D. Seymour Bassett's bibliography in Donald Drew Egbert and
Stow Persons, eds., *Socialism and American Life*, 2 vols. (Princeton: Princeton Univ.

Press, 1952) 2:91–140; Robert S. Fogarty, "Communal History in America," *Choice* 10 (June 1973): 578–90; Foster, *Religion and Sexuality,* 341–52; Philip N. Dare, *American Communes to 1860: A Bibliography* (New York: Garland, 1990); and Timothy Miller, *American Communes, 1860–1960: A Bibliography* (New York: Garland, 1990). Also useful are J. Gordon Melton's *The Encyclopedia of American Religions,* 3d ed. (Detroit: Gale, 1989); and *Biographical Dictionary of American Cult and Sect Leaders* (New York: Garland, 1986). For communal sex roles, the best entrée is Jon Wagner, "Sexuality and Gender Roles in Utopian Communities: A Critical Survey of Scholarly Work," *Communal Societies* 6 (1986): 172–88.

Among the overview analyses of these groups are Rosabeth Kanter, *Commitment and Community: Communes and Utopias in Sociological Perspective* (Cambridge, Mass.: Harvard Univ. Press, 1972); Dolores Hayden, *Seven American Utopias: The Architecture of Communitarian Socialism, 1790–1975* (Cambridge, Mass.: MIT Press, 1976); William M. Kephart, *Extraordinary Groups: An Examination of Unconventional Life-Styles,* 3d ed. (New York: St. Martin's, 1986); Raymond Lee Muncy, *Sex and Marriage in Utopian Communities: 19th-Century America* (Bloomington: Indiana Univ. Press, 1973); John M. Whitworth, *God's Blueprints: A Sociological Study of Three Utopian Sects* (London: Routledge & Kegan Paul, 1975); Robert H. Lauer and Jeanette Lauer, *The Spirit and the Flesh: Sex in Utopian Communities* (Metuchen, N.J.: Scarecrow, 1983); and Yaacov Oved, *Two Hundred Years of American Communes* (New Brunswick, N.J.: Transaction, 1988).

3. Perry Miller, *The New England Mind: From Colony to Province* (Boston: Beacon, 1961), Foreword.

4. The most useful analytical perspectives for the study of these groups are found in anthropological literature, including Anthony F. C. Wallace, "Revitalization Movements," *American Anthropologist* 58 (April 1956): 264–81; Kenelm Burridge, *New Heaven, New Earth: A Study of Millenarian Activities* (New York: Schocken, 1969); Victor W. Turner, *The Ritual Process: Structure and Anti-Structure* (Chicago: Aldine, 1969); I. C. Jarvie, *The Revolution in Anthropology* (Chicago: Regnery, 1969); and Michael Barkun, *Disaster and the Millennium* (New Haven: Yale Univ. Press, 1974). Women's roles in millenarian movements are discussed in I. M. Lewis, *Ecstatic Religion: An Anthropological Study of Spirit Possession and Shamanism* (Baltimore: Penguin, 1971). Weston La Barre, "Materials for a History of Studies of Crisis Cults: A Bibliographic Essay," *Current Anthropology* 12 (Feb. 1971): 3–41, provides a detailed bibliography and interpretation of many of the most important studies.

5. For treatments of the fluidity of American society during this period, see John Higham, *From Boundlessness to Consolidation: The Transformation of American Culture, 1848–1860* (Ann Arbor: William L. Clements Library, 1969); Rowland Berthoff, *An Unsettled People: Social Order and Disorder in American History* (New York: Harper & Row, 1971); Stanley M. Elkins, *Slavery: A Problem in American Institutional and Intellectual Life,* 3d. ed rev. (Chicago: Univ. of Chicago Press, 1976); Marvin Meyers, *The Jacksonian Persuasion: Politics and Belief* (Stanford: Stanford Univ. Press, 1960); Leonard Richards, *"Gentlemen of Property and Standing":' Anti-*

Abolitionist Mobs in Jacksonian America (New York: Oxford Univ. Press, 1970); Michael Feldberg, *The Turbulent Era: Riot and Disorder in Jacksonian America* (New York: Oxford Univ. Press, 1980); Ronald G. Walters, *American Reformers, 1815–1860* (New York: Hill & Wang, 1978); Alice Felt Tyler, *Freedom's Ferment: Phases of American Social History from the Colonial Period to the Outbreak of the Civil War* (New York: Harper & Row, 1962); David J. Rothman, *The Discovery of the Asylum: Social Order and Disorder in the New Republic* (Boston: Little, Brown, 1971); John S. Haller and Robin M. Haller, *The Physician and Sexuality in Victorian America* (Urbana: Univ. of Illinois Press, 1974); Stephen Nissenbaum, *Sex, Diet, and Debility in Jacksonian America: Sylvester Graham and Health Reform* (Westport, Conn.: Greenwood, 1980); Arthur E. Bestor, "Patent-Office Models of the Good Society: Some Relationships Between Social Reform and Westward Expansion," *American Historical Review* 43 (April 1953): 505–26; and John L. Thomas, "Romantic Reform in America, 1815–1860," *American Quarterly* 17 (Winter 1965): 656–81. On religious developments, see Nathan O. Hatch, *The Democratization of American Christianity* (New Haven: Yale Univ. Press, 1989).

6. The classic introduction to studies of this area is Whitney R. Cross, *The Burned-over District: The Social and Intellectual History of Enthusiastic Religion in Western New York, 1800–1850* (Ithaca, N.Y.: Cornell Univ. Press, 1950). A more recent comparative analysis is Michael Barkun, *Crucible of the Millennium: The Burned-over District of New York in the 1840s* (Syracuse, N.Y.: Syracuse Univ. Press, 1986). Paul E. Johnson's *A Shopkeeper's Millennium: Society and Revivals in Rochester, New York, 1815–1837* (New York: Hill & Wang, 1978), and Curtis D. Johnson, *Islands of Holiness: Rural Religion in Upstate New York, 1796–1860* (Ithaca, N.Y.: Cornell Univ. Press, 1989) provide provocative, and differing, interpretations of the role of religion in the Burned-over District. Also see P. Jeffrey Potash, *Vermont's Burned-over District: Patterns of Community Development and Religious Activity, 1761–1850* (New York: Carlson, 1991); David Ludlum, *Social Ferment in Vermont, 1791–1850* (New York: Columbia Univ. Press, 1939); and Slater Brown, *The Heyday of Spiritualism* (New York: Pocket Books, 1972). Curiously, Mary P. Ryan's fine *Cradle of the Middle Class: The Family in Oneida County, New York, 1790–1865* (Cambridge: Cambridge Univ. Press, 1981) almost completely omits any mention of the Oneida Community.

7. For additional perspectives on the Shakers, see Foster, *Religion and Sexuality*, 21–71. A fine introduction to the Shakers is Constance Rourke's essay "The Shakers" in Rourke, *The Roots of American Culture and Other Essays*, ed. Van Wyck Brooks (New York: Harcourt, Brace, 1942), 195–237. The rare *Testimonies of the Life, Character, Revelations, and Doctrines of Our Ever Blessed Mother Ann Lee and the Elders with Her* (Hancock, Mass.: J. Tallcott & J. Deming, Junrs., 1816) provides the most authoritative account of Ann Lee's experiences. For the most readable early Shaker historical and theological work, see Calvin Green and Seth Y. Wells, *A Summary View of the Millennial Church or United Society of Believers (Commonly Called Shakers)* (Albany, N.Y.: Packard & Van Benthuysen, 1823). A thorough and sympathetic Shaker history from a late nineteenth-century perspective is Anna White and Leila S. Taylor, *Shakerism: Its Meaning and Message* (Columbus, Ohio: Fred J. Heer, 1904).

The most important scholarly overview of the development of the northeastern Shaker societies in the eighteenth and nineteenth centuries is Priscilla J. Brewer, *Shaker Communities, Shaker Lives* (Hanover, N.H.: Univ. Press of New England, 1986). Also important are the classic studies by Edward Deming Andrews, especially his *The People Called Shakers: A Search for the Perfect Society,* new enl. ed. (New York: Dover, 1963). A comprehensive bibliography of printed sources by and about the Shakers is Mary L. Richmond, *Shaker Literature: A Bibliography,* 2 vols. (Hanover, N.H.: Univ. Press of New England, 1977). The most extensive Shaker manuscript collection is cataloged in Kermit J. Pike, *A Guide to Shaker Manuscripts in the Library of the Western Reserve Historical Society* (Cleveland: Western Reserve Historical Society, 1974).

8. For an introduction to Shaker contributions to American life and culture, see Rourke, "Shakers." More detailed analyses are found in Edward Deming Andrews's books *The People Called Shakers; The Community Industries of the Shakers* (Albany: State Univ. of New York Press, 1933); and *The Gift to Be Simple: Songs, Dances and Rituals of the American Shakers* (New York: Dover, 1962). Also see Edward Deming Andrews and Faith Andrews, *Visions of the Heavenly Sphere: A Study in Shaker Religious Art* (Charlottesville: Univ. Press of Virginia, 1969). Among the many other studies of Shaker material culture, see especially June Sprigg, *By Shaker Hands* (New York: Knopf, 1975), and Beverly Gordon, *Shaker Textile Arts* (Hanover, N.H.: Univ. Press of New England, 1980).

9. Although there was religious equality *between* the parallel men's and women's orders, there was an extremely hierarchical and unequal structure for both men and women *within* the orders. For an analysis of why Shaker women were not given equality with men in all areas of life, see Foster, *Religion and Sexuality,* 228–40. The most substantial scholarly analysis of the role of Shaker women is Marjorie Proctor-Smith, *Women in Shaker Community and Worship: A Feminist Analysis of the Uses of Religious Symbolism* (Lewiston, N.Y.: Mellen, 1985). Late nineteenth-century liberal Shaker approaches to celibacy and women's roles are analyzed in Sally L. Kitch, *Chaste Liberation: Celibacy and Female Cultural Status* (Urbana: Univ. of Illinois Press, 1989). For an analysis of the role of women in Shaker communities using quantitative data, see D'Ann Campbell, "Women's Life in Utopia: The Shaker Experiment in Sexual Equality Reappraised, 1810–1860," *New England Quarterly* 51 (Mar. 1978): 23–38. The best brief critique of Shaker egalitarianism toward women is Jane F. Crossthwaite, " 'A White and Seamless Robe': Celibacy and Equality in Shaker Art and Theology," *Colby Library Quarterly* 25 (Sept. 1989): 188–98.

10. Richard Pelham's pamphlet was printed in Boston by Rand, Avery, in 1874.

11. On the strengths and weaknesses of the Shaker celibate system, see Foster, *Religion and Sexuality,* 228–45.

12. For perspectives on Shaker membership, including quantitative analyses of the Sodus Bay Community and the New Lebanon Second Family, see Foster, *Religion and Sexuality,* 48–58. Edward Deming Andrews's impressionistic estimate in *People Called Shakers,* 224, that Shaker membership peaked at some six thousand

individuals before the Civil War is undoubtedly in error. Perhaps it is based on an extrapolation from the United States census data on the maximum number of individuals who could be *accommodated* in Shaker meetinghouses (which were not always filled to capacity). The Shakers' own highest membership estimate of 4,100 in about 1830 is found in the New Lebanon Shaker manuscript "Introduction to Records of Sacred Communications," Western Reserve Historical Society, ca. 1843. More recent demographic analyses based on Shaker and on United States census data suggest that Shaker membership never reached four thousand individuals at any time after 1840. The 1840 census identified 3,608 Shakers, exclusive of the few black members whose numbers could not be identified; 3,842 Shakers in 1850; and 3,502 in 1860. Prior to 1840, the United States census reported only the names of heads of households and thus does not provide sufficient evidence to determine the full membership of the group.

On this issue, see William Sims Bainbridge's articles "Shaker Demographics, 1840–1900: An Example of the Use of U.S. Census Enumeration Schedules," *Journal for the Scientific Study of Religion* 21 (1984): 352–65, and "The Decline of the Shakers: Evidence from the United States Census," *Communal Societies* 4 (1984): 19–34; Priscilla J. Brewer's articles "The Demographic Features of the Shaker Decline, 1787–1900," *Journal of Interdisciplinary History* 15 (1984): 31–52, and "'Numbers Are Not the Thing for Us to Glory In': Demographic Perspectives on the Decline of the Shakers," *Communal Societies* 7 (1987): 25–35; Brewer, *Shaker Communities*; and Campbell, "Women's Life in Utopia." For information on the predominantly black Shaker out-family in Philadelphia, see Jean McMahon Humez, ed., *Gifts of Power: The Writings of Rebecca Jackson, Black Visionary, Shaker Eldress* (Amherst: Univ. of Massachusetts Press, 1981), and Richard E. Williams, *Called and Chosen: The Story of Mother Rebecca Jackson and the Philadelphia Shakers* (Metuchen, N.J.: Scarecrow, 1981). An analysis of Shaker appeal to the Millerites is found in chapter 4 of this book.

13. Charles Nordhoff, *The Communistic Societies of the United States: From Personal Visit and Observation* (New York: Harper & Bros., 1875), 271. Another classic nineteenth-century study that complements Nordhoff's account is John Humphrey Noyes, *History of American Socialisms* (Philadelphia: Lippincott, 1870).

14. For additional perspectives on the Oneida Community, see Foster, *Religion and Sexuality*, 72–122. Among the secondary accounts of Oneida, the most important remains the biography by Robert Allerton Parker, *A Yankee Saint: John Humphrey Noyes and the Oneida Community* (New York: G. P. Putnam's Sons, 1935). The only book-length analysis of John Humphrey Noyes by a psychoanalytically trained historian is Robert David Thomas, *The Man Who Would Be Perfect: John Humphrey Noyes and the Utopian Impulse* (Philadelphia: Univ. of Pennsylvania Press, 1977). An annotated bibliography of almost all printed materials put out by the Oneida Perfectionists is Lester G. Wells, *The Oneida Community Collection in the Syracuse University Library* (Syracuse, N.Y.: Syracuse University Library, 1961). Two rich collections of primary documents edited by George Wallingford Noyes are *Religious Experience of John Humphrey Noyes* (New York: Macmillan, 1923) and *John Humphrey Noyes: The Putney Community* (Oneida, N.Y.: By the Author, 1931).

The most important primary source on John Humphrey Noyes and his various communal efforts is the periodicals that he and his associates published between 1834 and 1879. These periodicals went by many different titles, including *The Circular* (Brooklyn and Oneida, N.Y., 1851–64). Maren Lockwood Carden, *Oneida: Utopian Community to Modern Corporation* (Baltimore: Johns Hopkins Univ. Press, 1969), provides a sociological analysis that also deals, somewhat less effectively, with events after the breakup of the community. Robert S. Fogarty's thesis on the sources of Oneida membership is presented in his article, "Oneida: A Utopian Search for Religious Security," *Labor History* 14 (Spring 1973): 207–27. By far the most detailed membership information is presented in John B. Teeple, *The Oneida Family: Genealogy of a 19th Century Perfectionist Commune* (Oneida, N.Y: Oneida Community Historical Committee, 1984)

15. A model analysis of the end of the community is provided in Constance Noyes Robertson, *Oneida Community: The Breakup, 1876–1881* (Syracuse, N.Y.: Syracuse Univ. Press, 1972). Other analyses bearing on the breakup are found in Parker, *Yankee Saint,* 284–304; Carden, *Oneida,* 59–111; and Robert S. Fogarty, "The Oneida Community, 1848–1880: A Study in Conservative Christian Utopianism" (Ph.D. diss., Univ. of Denver, 1968). Analyses of the breakup that make use of the theoretical perspectives of Max Weber are presented in Spencer C. Olin, Jr., "The Oneida Community and the Instability of Charismatic Authority," *Journal of American History* 67 (Sept. 1980): 285–300; and in Ira L. Mandelker, *Religion, Society, and Utopia in Nineteenth-Century America* (Amherst: Univ. of Massachusetts Press, 1984).

16. Allan Estlake [Abel Easton], *The Oneida Community* (London: George Redway, 1900), 56.

17. For Oneida sources on mutual criticism, see *First Annual Report of the Oneida Association* (Oneida Reserve, N.Y.: Leonard, 1849), 10–11; *Mutual Criticism* (Oneida, N.Y.: Office of the *American Socialist,* 1876); and the column "Criticism," which ran in the community newspapers, beginning with the *Spiritual Magazine,* Dec. 22, 1849. Valuable secondary accounts of criticism are found in Parker, *Yankee Saint,* 215–26; Carden, *Oneida,* 71–77; and Foster, *Religion and Sexuality,* 98–100. Ibid., 93–98, provides a detailed analysis of male continence and its function in the Oneida Community. Early Oneida sources relating to male continence include the "Bible Argument Defining Relation of the Sexes in the Kingdom of Heaven," in *First Annual Report of the Oneida Association,* 27–35, presented in final form in *Bible Communism: A Compilation of the Annual Reports and Other Publications of the Oneida Association and Its Branches* (Brooklyn, N.Y.: Office of the *Circular,* 1853), 40–53. For later accounts, see John Humphrey Noyes, *Male Continence* (Oneida, N.Y.: Office of *Oneida Circular,* 1872); John Humphrey Noyes, *Dixon and His Copyists . . .* (Wallingford, Conn.: Oneida Community, 1872); and Theodore R. Noyes, "Report on Nervous Diseases in the Oneida Community," in John Humphrey Noyes, *Essay on Scientific Propagation* (Oneida, N.Y: Oneida Community, 1872), 25–32. Carden, *Oneida,* 51, presents the conclusion about the number of unplanned births, using figures from Hilda Herrick Noyes and George Wallingford Noyes, "The Oneida

Community Experiment in Stirpiculture," Scientific Papers of the Second International Congress of Eugenics, 1921, in *Eugenics, Genetics, and the Family* (Baltimore: William & Wilkins, 1923). The physiological mechanisms by which male continence was possible have been confirmed in Alfred C. Kinsey, Wardell Pomeroy, and Clyde Martin, *Sexual Behavior in the American Male* (Philadelphia: Saunders, 1948), 158–61.

18. The first analysis to make use of Noyes's own published assessment of antebellum feminism is Lawrence Foster, "Free Love and Feminism: John Humphrey Noyes and the Oneida Community," *Journal of the Early Republic* 1 (Summer 1981): 165–83. Other feminist analyses of John Humphreys Noyes and Oneida include Marlyn Hartzell Dalsimer, "Women and Family in the Oneida Community, 1837–1881" (Ph.D. diss., New York Univ., 1975); Louis J. Kern, "Ideology and Reality: Sexuality and Women's Status in the Oneida Community," *Radical History Review* 20 (Spring/Summer 1979): 181–205; Kern, *An Ordered Love*, 207–79; Joseph Kirschner, "Women and the Communal Experience: The Oneida Community, 1849–1877," paper presented in 1979 and read through the courtesy of the author; and Ellen Wayland-Smith, "The Status and Self-Perception of Women in the Oneida Community," *Communal Societies* 8 (1988): 18–53.

Revealing primary information on women's reactions is found in the Anita Newcomb McGee Papers in the Kinsey Institute; Jane Kinsley Rich and Nelson M. Blake, eds., *A Lasting Spring: Jessie Catherine Kinsley, Daughter of the Oneida Community* (Syracuse, N.Y.: Syracuse Univ. Press, 1983); Corinna Ackley Noyes, *The Days of My Youth* (Kenwood, N.Y.: The Mansion, 1960); Harriet M. Worden, *Old Mansion House Memories* (Oneida, N.Y.: N.p., 1950); and Constance Noyes Robertson, ed., *Oneida Community: An Autobiography, 1851–1876* (New York: Syracuse Univ. Press, 1970).

19. Foster, *Religion and Sexuality*, 120–21, considers some of these points at greater length.

20. For additional perspectives on the nineteenth-century Mormons, see Foster, *Religion and Sexuality*, 123–225. The classic book-length introduction to Mormonism by a non-Mormon is Thomas F. O'Dea, *The Mormons* (Chicago: Univ. of Chicago Press, 1957). Leonard J. Arrington and Davis Bitton, *The Mormon Experience: A History of the Latter-day Saints* (New York: Knopf, 1979), presents a balanced and insightful analysis of key themes in Mormon history. A thorough chronological narrative of Mormon development, with detailed bibliography of major scholarly studies, is James B. Allen and Glen M. Leonard, *The Story of the Latter-Day Saints* (Salt Lake City: Deseret, 1976). An invaluable aid to the location of early Mormon and Mormon-related imprints is Chad Flake, ed., *A Mormon Bibliography, 1830–1930: Books, Pamphlets, Periodicals, and Broadsides Relating to the First Century of Mormonism* (Salt Lake City: Univ. of Utah Press, 1978). A similarly thorough and indispensable source for Mormon manuscripts is Davis Bitton, *Guide to Mormon Diaries and Autobiographies* (Provo: Brigham Young Univ. Press, 1977).

Recent interpretive studies that relate Mormonism to American culture and to other new religious movements are Mark P. Leone, *Roots of Modern Mormon-*

ism (Cambridge, Mass.: Harvard Univ. Press, 1979); Klaus J. Hansen, *Mormonism and the American Experience* (Chicago: Univ. of Chicago Press, 1981); and Jan Shipps, *Mormonism: The Story of a New Religious Tradition* (Urbana: Univ. of Illinois Press, 1985). Many classic essays are reprinted in Marvin S. Hill and James B. Allen, eds., *Mormonism and American Culture* (New York: Harper & Row, 1972). On Joseph Smith, Fawn M. Brodie's pathbreaking biography, *No Man Knows My History: The Life of Joseph Smith, the Mormon Prophet,* 2d ed. rev. (New York: Knopf, 1971) has been qualified but not superseded by Donna Hill, *Joseph Smith: The First Mormon* (Garden City, N.Y.: Doubleday, 1977).

Extraordinarily valuable for understanding Joseph Smith are Dean C. Jessee, ed., *The Personal Writings of Joseph Smith* (Salt Lake City: Deseret, 1984); Scott H. Faulring, ed., *An American Prophet's Record: The Diaries and Journals of Joseph Smith* (Salt Lake City: Signature, 1989); and Andrew F. Ehat and Lyndon W. Cook, eds., *The Words of Joseph Smith* (Provo: Religious Studies Center, Brigham Young Univ., 1980). These scholarly compilations complement and supersede much of Joseph Smith, Jr., *History of the Church of Jesus Christ of Latter-day Saints: Period I,* ed. Brigham H. Roberts, 6 vols., 2d. ed. rev. (Salt Lake City: Deseret, 1948).

21. Classic introductions to the issues raised by Nauvoo Mormonism are found in Robert B. Flanders, *Nauvoo: Kingdom on the Mississippi* (Urbana: Univ. of Illinois Press, 1965), and in Klaus J. Hansen, *Quest for Empire: The Political Kingdom of God and the Council of Fifty in Mormon History* (East Lansing: Michigan State Univ. Press, 1967). Attitudes toward the Nauvoo experience by Mormons, non-Mormons, and members of the Reorganized Church of Jesus Christ of Latter Day Saints are ably set forth in essays by Glen M. Leonard, Richard P. Howard, John E. Hallwas, and Ronald K. Esplin in *JMH* 16 (1990): 25–86.

22. On Mormonism in Utah during the nineteenth century, the starting point is Leonard J. Arrington, *Great Basin Kingdom: An Economic History of the Latter-day Saints, 1830–1900* (Cambridge, Mass.: Harvard Univ. Press, 1958). The first scholarly biography of Brigham Young fully utilizing available primary and secondary sources is Leonard J. Arrington, *Brigham Young: American Moses* (New York: Knopf, 1985). A briefer biography that sets Brigham Young into his nineteenth-century context is Newell G. Bringhurst, *Brigham Young and the Expanding American Frontier* (Boston: Little, Brown, 1986). Two conflicting earlier approaches to Brigham Young are provided in Morris Robert Werner, *Brigham Young* (New York: Harcourt, Brace, 1925), and Susa Young Gates and Leah D. Widtsoe, *The Life Story of Brigham Young* (New York: Macmillan, 1930).

The most thorough nineteenth-century Mormon defense of polygamy is found in *The Seer,* a periodical edited and published by Orson Pratt in Washington, D.C., and Liverpool, England, between 1853 and 1854. For the crusade against Mormon polygamy, the best book-length treatment is Gustive O. Larson, *The "Americanization" of Utah for Statehood* (San Marino, Calif.: Huntington Library, 1971). A brilliant analysis of post-1890 polygamy is found in D. Michael Quinn, "LDS Church Authority and New Plural Marriages, 1890–1904," *Dialogue:* 18

(Spring 1985): 9–105. Jan Shipps, "From Satyr to Saint: American Attitudes Toward the Mormons, 1860–1960" (paper presented at the 1973 annual meeting of the Organization of American Historians, Chicago), analyzes the dramatic improvement in American attitudes toward the Mormons during the twentieth century.

23. The first non-Mormon analysis of the origin of Mormon polygamy that is based on full access to the holdings on polygamy in the Archives of the Historical Department of the Church of Jesus Christ of Latter-day Saints in Salt Lake City, Utah, is presented in Foster, *Religion and Sexuality*, 123–80. Danel W. Bachman, "A Study of the Mormon Practice of Plural Marriage Before the Death of Joseph Smith" (M.A. thesis, Purdue Univ., 1975), provides a detailed treatment of the early development of polygamy from a Mormon perspective. Charles A. Shook, *The True Origin of Mormon Polygamy* (Cincinnati: Standard, 1914), presents documentary evidence and analysis that conclusively establishes Joseph Smith's responsibility for the introduction of Mormon polygamy. An ambitious but factually and conceptually flawed attempt to present the development of Mormon polygamy from its inception to the present is found in Richard S. Van Wagoner, *Mormon Polygamy: A History* (Salt Lake City: Signature, 1986).

A recent biography that for the first time convincingly analyzes the complex personal dynamics between Joseph Smith and his first wife, Emma, especially over polygamy, is Linda King Newell and Valeen Tippetts Avery, *Mormon Enigma: Emma Hale Smith—Prophet's Wife, "Elect Lady," Polygamy's Foe* (Garden City, N.Y.: Doubleday, 1984). Linda King Newell, "Emma Hale Smith and the Polygamy Question," *John Whitmer Historical Association Journal* 4 (1984): 3–15, highlights some of the chief conclusions of that analysis. Also suggestive is Lawrence Foster, "A Little-Known Defense of Polygamy from the Mormon Press in 1842," *Dialogue* 9 (Winter 1974): 21–34. Scholarly studies of Mormon polygamy are assessed in Davis Bitton, "Mormon Polygamy: A Review Article," *JMH* 4 (1977): 101–18.

24. On polygamy in Utah, a starting point is Stanley S. Ivins, "Notes on Mormon Polygamy," *Western Humanities Review* 10 (Summer 1956): 229–39. Ivins's interpretation is elaborated and qualified in James E. Smith and Philip R. Kunz, "Polygyny and Fertility in Nineteenth-Century America," *Population Studies* 30 (1976): 465–80. Going beyond either the Ivins or the Smith and Kunz articles is the path-breaking work summarized in Lowell "Ben" Bennion, "The Incidence of Mormon Polygamy in 1880: 'Dixie' Versus Davis Stake," *JMH* 11 (1984): 27–42. Kimball Young, *Isn't One Wife Enough? The Story of Mormon Polygamy* (New York: Holt, 1954), is a useful anecdotal account of Utah polygamy practice.

The most comprehensive assessment of recent scholarship on polygamy is Jessie L. Embry, *Mormon Polygamous Families: Life in the Principle* (Salt Lake City: Univ. of Utah Press, 1987). An exceptionally valuable source on all aspects of Mormon kinship is D. Michael Quinn, "Organizational Development and Social Origins of the Mormon Hierarchy, 1832–1932: A Prosopographical Study" (M.A. thesis, Univ. of Utah, 1973).

Annie Clark Tanner, *A Mormon Mother: An Autobiography* (Salt Lake City: Published by the Tanner Trust Fund, Univ. of Utah Library, 1983), and Juliaetta Bateman Jensen, *Little Gold Pieces: The Story of My Mormon Mother's Life* (Salt Lake City: Stanway, 1948), provide frank and revealing accounts of life under polygamy. Useful topical and biographical essays are presented in Claudia Bushman, ed., *Mormon Sisters: Women in Early Utah* (Cambridge, Mass.: Emmeline, 1976), and in Vicky Burgess-Olson, ed., *Sister Saints* (Provo: Brigham Young Univ. Press, 1978). An invaluable source for women's perceptions is the *Woman's Exponent*, a periodical by and for Mormon women published between 1872 and 1914. Lawrence Foster, "Polygamy and the Frontier: Mormon Women in Early Utah," *UHQ* 50 (Summer 1982): 268–89, provides an overview of Mormon women's experiences under polygamy. Perceptive analyses of the dynamics of life in polygamous families in Nauvoo and in Utah are found in Stanley B. Kimball, *Heber C. Kimball: Mormon Patriarch and Pioneer* (Urbana: Univ. of Illinois Press, 1981), and James B. Allen, *Trials of Discipleship: The Story of William Clayton, a Mormon* (Urbana: Univ. of Illinois Press, 1987). On the travails of the Kimball family, also see Lawrence Foster, " 'Reluctant Polygamists': The Strains and Challenges of the Transition to Polygamy in a Prominent Mormon Family," in Carl Guarneri and David Alvarez, eds., *Religion and Society in the American West: Historical Essays* (Lanham, Md.: Univ. Press of America, 1987), 131–52.

25. For an analysis of the changing role of Mormon women during the past century, see Lawrence Foster, "From Frontier Activism to Neo-Victorian Domesticity: Mormon Women in the Nineteenth and Twentieth Centuries," *JMH* 6 (1979): 3–21. Marilyn Warenski, *Patriarchs and Politics: The Plight of the Mormon Woman* (New York: McGraw-Hill, 1980); Sonia Johnson, *From Housewife to Heretic* (Garden City, N.Y.: Doubleday, 1981); and Robert Gottlieb and Peter Wiley, *America's Saints: The Rise of Mormon Power* (New York: Harcourt Brace Jovanovich, 1986), provide critical assessments of the current status of Mormon women. A more positive perspective is found in Mary Lythgoe Bradford, ed., *Mormon Women Speak: A Collection of Essays* (Salt Lake City: Olympus, 1982). Maureen Ursenbach Beecher and Lavina Fielding Anderson, eds., *Sisters in Spirit: Mormon Women in Historical and Cultural Perspective* (Urbana: Univ. of Illinois Press, 1987), presents theologically oriented essays on Mormon women and their roles. For a review of the range of materials available on Mormon women, see David J. Whittaker and Carol C. Madsen, "History's Sequel: A Source Essay on Women in Mormon History," *JMH* 6 (1979): 123–45; and Lyn Scott and Maureen Ursenbach Beecher, "Mormon Women: A Bibliography in Process, 1977–1985," *JMH* 12 (1985): 113–27.

2. CELIBACY and FEMINISM

1. For a more detailed discussion of many of the issues raised in this chapter, see Foster, *Religion and Sexuality*, 21–71, 226–47.

2. Andrews, *People Called Shakers*, 224, popularized the incorrect idea that Shaker membership peaked at some six thousand before the Civil War. For a discussion of the recent scholarship on this issue, see chap. 1, n. 9.

3. Henri Desroche, *The American Shakers: From Neo-Christianity to Pre-Socialism*, trans. and ed. John K. Savacool (Amherst: Univ. of Massachusetts Press, 1971), 293–96, notes that Robert Owen's *New View of Society: Tracts Relative to This Subject* (1818) includes a lengthy favorable statement about the Shakers and that Friedrich Engels, in February 1845, argued that the Shakers showed that communism could be practiced successfully. John Humphrey Noyes, founder of the Oneida Community, described the success of the Shakers as "the 'specie basis' that has upheld all the paper theories, and counteracted the failures, of the French and English schools." Noyes, *American Socialisms*, 670.

4. Rourke, "Shakers," 198.

5. Among the treatments that emphasize Shaker egalitarianism toward women, see Andrews, *People Called Shakers*; Desroche, *American Shakers*, which develops the term *ascetic feminism* to describe the Shaker approach to women; Campbell, "Women's Life in Utopia"; Barbara Brown Zikmund, "The Feminist Thrust of Sectarian Christianity," in Rosemary Radford Ruether and Eleanor McLaughlin, eds., *Women of Spirit: Female Leadership in the Jewish and Christian Traditions* (New York: Simon & Schuster, 1979), 206–24; Mary Farrell Bednarowski, "Outside the Mainstream: Women's Religion and Women Religious Leaders in Nineteenth-Century America," *Journal of the American Academy of Religion* 48 (1980): 207–31; Foster, *Religion and Sexuality*, 21–71, 226–47; Humez, ed., *Gifts of Power*; Rosemary Radford Ruether, "Women in Utopian Movements," in Rosemary Radford Ruether and Rosemary Keller, eds., *Women and Religion in America: The Nineteenth Century* (New York: Harper & Row, 1981), 46–53; Jeanette C. Lauer and Robert H. Lauer, "Sex Roles in Nineteenth-Century American Communal Societies," *Communal Societies* 3 (1983): 16–28; Proctor-Smith, *Women in Shaker Community*; and Crossthwaite, "'A White and Seamless Robe.'" For a thought-provoking but incomplete analysis of post-Civil War liberal Shaker attitudes, see Kitch, *Chaste Liberation*. Although Brewer's *Shaker Communities*, does not focus specifically on Shaker women, it provides the best overall understanding of Shaker life in the eighteenth and nineteenth centuries.

6. Ruether, "Women in Utopian Movements," 48. Among the most useful Shaker publications emphasizing equality for women are Benjamin Seth Youngs, *The Testimony of Christ's Second Appearing . . .* (Lebanon, Ohio: John McClean, 1808); Green and Wells, *Millennial Church*; *Testimonies of Ann Lee*; Frederick W. Evans, *Autobiography of a Shaker, and Revelation of the Apocalypse* (Mt. Lebanon, N.Y.: F. W. Evans, 1869); and White and Taylor, *Shakerism*.

7. See Andrews, *People Called Shakers*; Proctor-Smith, *Women in Shaker Community*; and Brewer, *Shaker Communities*. For the most substantial critique of the Shakers as a feminist prototype, see Kern, *An Ordered Love*, 76–124.

8. Andrews, *Community Industries of the Shakers*. For other accounts of Shaker material culture, see Edward Deming and Faith Andrews, *Work and Worship: The Economic Order of the Shakers* (Greenwich, Conn.: New York Graphic Society, 1974); Gordon, *Shaker Textile Arts*; Hayden, *Seven American Utopias*; William Lassiter, *Shaker Architecture* (New York: Bonanza, 1966); Flo Morse, *The Shakers and the World's People* (New York: Dodd, Mead, 1980); and Sprigg, *By Shaker Hands*.

9. This analysis is limited largely to the period before the Civil War, when Shaker vitality and originality were greatest, and draws more on northeastern than on midwestern Shaker sources. On the role of celibacy, also see Crossthwaite, " 'A White and Seamless Robe,' " and Kitch, *Chaste Liberation.*

10. This emphasis is overwhelming in the Shaker sources discussed in n. 6, above.

11. White and Taylor, *Shakerism,* 246.

12. For overviews of the complex role of celibacy in Christian history, see Henry Charles Lea, *The History of Sacerdotal Celibacy in the Christian Church* (New York: Russell & Russell, 1957); Peter Brown, *The Body and Society: Men, Women, and Sexual Renunciation in Early Christianity* (New York: Columbia Univ. Press, 1988); and Elaine Pagels, *Adam and Eve and the Serpent* (New York: Random House, 1988).

13. For some treatments of women and Christian monasticism, see R. W. Southern, *Western Society and the Church in the Middle Ages* (Harmondsworth: Penguin, 1970). 309–31; Eileen Edna Power, *Medieval Women,* ed. Michael Postan (Cambridge: Cambridge Univ. Press, 1975), chap. 5; Lina Eckenstein, *Women Under Monasticism: Chapters on Saint Lore and Convent Life Between A.D. 500 and A.D. 1500* (Cambridge: Cambridge Univ. Press, 1986); Shulamith Shahar, *The Fourth Estate: A History of Women in the Middle Ages* (London: Methuen, 1983), chaps. 3 and 8; and M. Bateson, "Origins and Early History of Double Monasteries," *Transactions of the Royal Historical Society* 13 (1899): 137–98. On the role of Mary in Roman Catholicism, one of many possible starting points is Marina Warner, *Alone of All Her Sex: The Myth and Cult of the Virgin Mary* (New York: Pocket Books, 1976).

14. See Kenneth Ronald Davis, *Anabaptism and Asceticism: A Study in Intellectual Origins* (Scottdale, Pa.: Herald, 1974). For male-dominated Germanic communal groups that emigrated to the United States, see Nordhoff, *Communistic Societies.* On Rappite celibacy and its origins, see Karl J. R. Arndt, *George Rapp's Harmony Society, 1785–1847,* rev. ed. (Rutherford, N.J.: Fairleigh Dickinson Univ. Press, 1972), 416–48. On Amana, see Jonathan G. Andelson, "The Gift to be Single: Celibacy and Religious Enthusiasm in the Community of True Inspiration," *Communal Societies* 5 (1985): 1–32. Jon Wagner, ed., *Sex Roles in Contemporary American Communes* (Bloomington: Indiana Univ. Press, 1982), refutes the notion that communitarian experiments in America have necessarily been egalitarian in relations between the sexes.

15. The only detailed scholarly study of this earliest phase of Shaker development that can be held to the highest scholarly standards throughout is Clarke Garrett's *Spirit Possession and Popular Religion: From the Camisards to the Shakers* (Baltimore: Johns Hopkins Univ. Press, 1987), esp. 140–241.

16. The earliest published Shaker accounts that deal with this period in detail are found in *Testimonies of Ann Lee.*

17. Ibid., 45.

18. For scholarly discussions of this period, see Garrett, *Spirit Possession;*

Stephen A. Marini, *Radical Sects of Revolutionary New England* (Cambridge, Mass.: Harvard Univ. Press, 1982); and Edward R. Horgan, *The Shaker Holy Land: A Community Portrait* (Harvard, Mass.: Harvard Common Press, 1982).

19. See Garrett, *Spirit Possession.*

20. Foster, *Religion and Sexuality,* 28–30, discusses some key elements in early Shaker belief and practice.

21. *Testimony of Christ's Second Appearing,* 31.

22. Many examples of Lee's ecstatic utterances are reported in *Testimonies of Ann Lee,* 204–35.

23. Ibid., 329.

24. Recollections of Thankful Goodrich, in Alonzo Hollister, ed., "Book of Immortality" MS, WRHS, 78–79.

25. Proctor-Smith, *Women in Shaker Community,* 105.

26. Personal letter from Clarke Garrett, dated Feb. 1, 1988.

27. John F. C. Harrison, *The Second Coming: Popular Millenarianism, 1780–1850* (New Brunswick, N.J.: Rutgers Univ. Press, 1979), 1–54.

28. Valentine Rathbun, *An Account of the Matter, Form, and Manner of a New and Strange Religion . . .* (Providence, R.I.: Bennett Wheeler, 1781). Rathbun dated his account Dec. 5, 1780.

29. Letter from Clarke Garrett, Feb. 1, 1988.

30. Amos Taylor, *A Narrative of the Strange Principles, Conduct, and Character of the People Known by the Name of Shakers* (Worcester, Mass.: The Author, 1782).

31. Reported in Garrett, *Spirit Possession,* 189–90.

32. Joseph Meacham, *A Concise Statement of the Principles of the Only True Church . . .* (Bennington, Vt.: Haswell & Russell, 1790). For the discussion of manuscript accounts by Meacham, see Brewer, *Shaker Communities,* 25.

33. Thomas Brown, who left the Shakers, provided one of the most valuable early analyses of Shaker belief and practice in *An Account of the People Called Shakers: Their Faith, Doctrines, and Practice* (Troy, N.Y.: Parker & Bliss, 1812).

34. Most scholarship has not appreciated the subtlety of the Christology in the *Testimony of Christ's Second Appearing* and the degree to which opposing conceptions of Ann Lee's role continue to be represented in the earliest Shaker publications. Especially revealing in this regard is *Testimonies of Ann Lee.*

35. This succinct statement is found in the version of the Joseph Meacham manuscript edited by Theodore E. Johnson and published in the *Shaker Quarterly* 10 (Spring 1969); 26. A longer and more elaborate statement is found in *Testimonies of Ann Lee,* 21.

36. The earliest Shaker theological treatises such as the *Testimony of Christ's Second Appearing* include the characteristic Protestant attack on Roman Catholic corruption during the thousand years after Constantine's conversion, criticize medieval monasticism for becoming part of the corrupt established church, and link themselves in spirit with the heretics presecuted by the Roman church.

37. Quotations in this and the following two paragraphs that are not otherwise identified are from Calvin Green, "Biographic Memoir of the Life, Character & Important Events in the Ministration of Mother Lucy Wright" (New Lebanon, N.Y., 1870; MS, WRHS). Also see "Collection of the Writings of Father Joseph Meacham Respecting Church Order and Government" (New Lebanon, N.Y., 1791–96; MS, WRHS), and White and Taylor, *Shakerism*, 63–112.

38. Proctor-Smith, *Women in Shaker Community*, 47.

39. See the summary in Green and Wells, *Millennial Church*, 58–67.

40. T. D. Seymour Bassett in Egbert and Persons, eds., *Socialism and American Life*, 2:391.

41. Andrews, *Community Industries of the Shakers*, 37.

42. Proctor-Smith, *Women in Shaker Community*, 62.

43. Nordhoff, *Communistic Societies*, 166.

44. Andrews, *People Called Shakers*, 143–44.

45. Ibid., 70–93.

46. Richard McNemar, *The Kentucky Revival . . .* (Cincinnati: John W. Browne, 1807); *Testimony of Christ's Second Appearing* (1808); *Millennial Praises . . .* (Hancock, Mass: J. Tallcott, 1812); *Testimonies of Ann Lee* (1816); John Dunlavy, *The Manifesto, or, A Declaration of the Doctrine and Practice of the Church of Christ* (Pleasant Hill, Ky.: P. Betrand, 1818); and Green and Wells, *Millennial Church* (1823).

47. Although Shaker concerns with celibacy are voiced throughout the *Millennial Church*, this summary is based on pages 129–43, entitled "The Cause, Nature, and Effects of Man's Loss from God."

48. Ibid., 132–33.

49. See Linda Gordon, *Woman's Body, Woman's Right: A Social History of Birth Control in America* (New York: Penguin, 1977); and James C. Mohr, *Abortion in America: The Origins and Evolution of National Policy* (New York: Oxford Univ. Press, 1978).

50. The Shakers frequently were frustrated by the inability of most outsiders to understand—much less agree with—their celibate commitment. See, for instance, *Testimony of Christ's Second Appearing* (1810), 618.

51. Lewis, *Ecstatic Religion*, and Suzanne Youngerman, "'Shaking Is No Foolish Play': An Anthropological Perspective on the American Shakers—Person, Time, Space, and Dance Ritual" (Ph.D. diss., Columbia Univ., 1983).

52. Proctor-Smith, *Women in Shaker Community*, 205–7.

53. Ibid., 162–63.

54. It would be interesting to try to determine whether Joseph Meacham or Lucy Wright played a predominant role in pushing for the establishment of equal men's and women's orders in the Shakers. Available evidence on this point is inconclusive, but it may be significant that the chief account of the creation of the separate and equal orders for both sexes comes from a biographical sketch of Lucy Wright rather than of Joseph Meacham.

3. SHAKER SPIRITUALISM and SALEM WITCHCRAFT

1. An earlier version of this chapter was published in *Communal Societies* 5 (1985): 176–93.

2. White and Taylor, *Shakerism*, 223

3. For key treatments of the Shaker spiritual manifestations that began in 1837, see Andrews, *People Called Shakers*, 152–76; Brewer, *Shaker Communities*, 115–35; Foster, *Religion and Sexuality*, 62–71; Proctor-Smith, *Women in Shaker Community*, 174–219; Eric Rohman, "Words of Comfort, Gifts of Love: Spirit Manifestations Among the Shakers, 1837–1845" (B.A. thesis, Antioch College, 1971); White and Taylor, *Shakerism*, 219–52; Henry Clay Blinn, *The Manifestation of Spiritualism Among the Shakers, 1837–1847* (East Canterbury, N.H.: N.p., 1899); David Lamson, *Two Years' Experience Among the Shakers* (West Boylston, Mass.: The Author, 1848); Hervey Elkins, *Fifteen Years in the Senior Order of Shakers* (Hanover, N.H.: Dartmouth Press, 1853); and the extensive manuscript collections in the Library of the Western Reserve Historical Society, Cleveland, Ohio, and the Library of Congress, Washington, D.C.

On the larger Spiritualist movement after 1848, see Cross, *Burned-over District*, 341–52; Brown, *Heyday of Spiritualism*; Geoffrey K. Nelson, *Spiritualism and Society* (London: Routledge & Kegan Paul, 1969); J. Stillson Judah, *The History and Philosophy of the Metaphysical Movements in America* (Philadelphia: Westminster, 1967), esp. 22–49; and Howard Kerr and Charles L. Crow, eds., *The Occult in America: New Historical Perspectives* (Urbana: Univ. of Illinois Press, 1983).

4. Rohman's "Words of Comfort" provides valuable insights into this difficult and tumultuous period, as does Whitworth, *God's Blueprints*.

5. Miller, *New England Mind: From Colony to Province*, 191.

6. The spiritual manifestations have tended to be treated as the work of quaint eccentrics by those interested primarily in Shaker material culture. For examples of the fraud argument, see John Patterson MacLean, "Spiritualism Among the Shakers of Union Village, Ohio," in his *Shakers of Ohio: Fugitive Papers Concerning the Shakers of Ohio, with Unpublished Manuscripts* (Columbus, Ohio: F. J. Heer, 1907), 388–415; and Marguerite Fellows Melcher, *The Shaker Adventure* (Princeton: Princeton Univ. Press, 1941), 248–50. The argument for Shaker psychopathology was frequently put forward by anti-Shaker writers before the Civil War.

7. Studies of the Salem witchcraft trials that have influenced this analysis include Kai T. Erikson, *Wayward Puritans: A Study in the Sociology of Deviance* (New York: Wiley, 1966), 137–59; John Demos, "Underlying Themes in the Witchcraft of Seventeenth-Century New England," *American Historical Review* 75 (1970): 1311–26; Chadwick Hansen, *Witchcraft at Salem* (New York: New American Library, 1969); and Paul Boyer and Stephen Nissenbaum, *Salem Possessed: The Social Origins of Witchcraft* (Cambridge, Mass.: Harvard Univ. Press, 1974). On the broader context of New England witchcraft, see Frederick C. Drake, "Witchcraft in the American Colonies, 1647–62," *American Quarterly* 20 (Winter 1968): 694–725; John Demos, *Entertaining Satan: Witchcraft and the Culture of Early New England* (New

York: Oxford Univ. Press, 1982); Richard Weisman, *Witchcraft, Magic, and Religion in 17th-Century Massachusetts* (Amherst: Univ. of Massachusetts Press, 1984); and Carol F. Karlsen, *The Devil in the Shape of a Woman: Witchcraft in Colonial New England* (New York: Norton, 1987).

8. Among the most valuable Shaker manuscripts in the Library of the Western Reserve Historical Society, cataloged by Kermit J. Pike, are New Lebanon "Introduction to Records of Sacred Communications," an overview of the spiritualist period from the perspective of the leadership at New Lebanon; Alonzo Hollister, "Shakers and Spiritualism" (New Lebanon, n.d.), as well as numerous other collections of spiritual experiences recorded by his hand; and "A Record of Heavenly Gifts, Messages and Communications" (Watervliet, 1839–41), a collection of revelations making clear the various social problems and tensions associated with the spiritualist phenomena at Watervliet. For published Shaker accounts, see Evans, *Autobiography*; Giles B. Avery, *Autobiography* (East Canterbury, N.H.: N.p., 1891); Blinn, *Spiritualism*; and White and Taylor, *Shakerism*. Indispensable accounts by those who left the Shakers are given in Lamson, *Among the Shakers*; and Elkins, *Senior Order of Shakers*.

For a summary of the declension that immediately preceded the 1837 revival, see the New Lebanon "Introduction to Records of Sacred Communications," 11–13. "Remarks on the Necessity of Reforming the Morals and Improving the Religious Condition of Our Children" (New Lebanon, 1830; MS, WRHS), written in the same hand as the "Introduction," gives a detailed account of the problems the Shakers were having in keeping children who reached puberty in the society.

9. The rare *Testimonies of Ann Lee* provides many examples of Ann Lee's positive trance experiences, suggesting how sexual desires could be sublimated in ecstatic religious phenomena. Calvin Green, an important early Shaker leader, also discussed the Shaker worship activities as a form of conscious sublimation and redirection of sexual energy. Calvin Green, "Autobiography" (Mt. Lebanon, 1861; MS, WRHS), 30.

10. For an analysis of the interconnections between the Shaker and Millerite movements in the 1840s, see chap. 4.

11. The New Lebanon "Introduction to Records of Sacred Communications," 41–44, summarizes the wide range of phenomena involved, as does Elkins, *Senior Order of Shakers*, 35. For anthropological perspectives on similar phenomena, see chap. 1, n. 4, above, and Erica Bourguignon, ed., *Religion, Altered States of Consciousness, and Social Change* (Columbus: Ohio State Univ. Press, 1973); William Sargant, *Battle for the Mind: A Physiology of Conversion and Brainwashing* (Garden City, N.Y.: Doubleday, 1957); Norman R. Cohn, *The Pursuit of the Millennium: Revolutionary Millenarians and Mystical Anarchists of the Middle Ages*, rev. enl. ed. (New York: Oxford Univ. Press, 1970); and Sylvia L. Thrupp, ed., *Millennial Dreams in Action: Studies in Revolutionary Religious Movements* (New York: Schocken, 1970).

12. Rohman, "Words of Comfort," suggests the typology used here.

13. Blinn, *Spiritualism*, 24.

14. Rohman, "Words of Comfort," 9–11.

15. "Messages of Mother Ann to the Church at New Lebanon, April 22, 1838, Through Philemon Stuart [sic], Sabbath, P.M." (New Lebanon, 1838; MS, WRHS) is a detailed account of this episode, which appears to have more of a sermonic than an involuntary character.

16. For evidence that the Shaker spiritual revelations were not seen by the leadership as cynical manipulation, but rather as part of normal hierarchical control in the Shaker communities, see Avery, *Autobiography*, 12, and Robert F. W. Meader, "The Vision of Brother Philemon," *Shaker Quarterly* 10 (Spring 1970): 8–17.

17. John Patterson Maclean, *A Sketch of the Life and Labors of Richard McNemar* (Franklin, Ohio: Printed for the author by the *Franklin Chronicle*, 1905), suggests that some collusion between the medium and Freegift Wells may well have been present. Any conscious collusion appears unlikely, however, based on Freegift Wells's later disillusioned statements about spiritualist phenomena in his "Testimonies, Predictions, and Remarks" (Watervliet, N.Y., n.d.; MS, WRHS), 19. Also see the McNemar papers at the Library of Congress.

18. That the Shakers shared much of the cultural baggage of their contemporaries is suggested by the fact that the figures from whom the Shakers received revelations were strikingly similar to the heroes and heroines of the school textbooks of the period, as described in Ruth Miller Elson, *Guardians of Tradition: American Schoolbooks of the Nineteenth Century* (Lincoln: Univ. of Nebraska Press, 1964).

19. Andrews, *People Called Shakers*, 267. For purposes of comparison, see the Shaker Laws of 1821 in *Shaker Quarterly* 7 (Summer 1967): 35–58, and the Laws of 1860 in *Shaker Quarterly* 11 (Winter 1971): 139–65.

20. For quantitative analyses of changing patterns of Shaker membership retention during this period, see Foster, *Religion and Sexuality*, 54–58; Bainbridge, "Decline of the Shakers"; and Brewer, "Demographic Features of Shaker Decline."

21. For some of the social tensions that were affecting the Massachusetts Puritans and Salem Village in the 1690s, see n. 7, above.

22. Drake, "Witchcraft in the American Colonies." On English witchcraft, see A. D. J. MacFarlane, *Witchcraft in Tudor and Stuart England: A Regional and Comparative Study* (London: Routledge & Kegan Paul, 1970), and Keith Thomas, *Religion and the Decline of Magic: Studies in Popular Belief in Sixteenth and Seventeenth Century England* (New York: Charles Scribner's Sons, 1971). For an overview analysis of European witchcraft persecution, see Brian P. Levack, *The Witch-Hunt in Early Modern Europe* (London: Longman, 1989).

23. Marc Mappen, ed., *Witches and Historians: Interpretations of Salem* (Huntington, N.Y.: Krieger, 1980), presents excerpts from most of the major social and psychological interpretations of the Salem witchcraft phenomena. Also see n. 7, above.

24. Miller, *New England Mind: From Colony to Province*, 191–208, and Foster, *Religion and Sexuality*, 70–71.

25. An overview of medical approaches to such phenomena is Ilza Veith, *Hysteria: The History of a Disease* (Chicago: Univ. of Chicago Press, 1965). For

Freud's analysis, see his *Selected Papers on Hysteria and other Psychoneuroses*, trans. A. A. Brill (New York: Journal of Nervous and Mental Diseases, 1912). Other studies stressing the negative aspects of these phenomena include George Rosen, *Madness and Society: Chapters in the Historical Sociology of Mental Illness* (Chicago: Univ. of Chicago Press, 1968); and Carroll Smith-Rosenberg, "The Hysterical Woman: Sex Roles and Role Conflict in 19th-Century America," *Social Research* 39 (Winter 1972): 652–78.

26. Also see William Sargant, *The Mind Possessed: A Physiology of Possession, Mysticism, and Faith Healing* (New York: Penguin, 1975). Essentially positive, yet sensitive to the ambiguity of altered states of consciousness, are William James, *The Varieties of Religious Experience* (1902; reprint New York: New American Library, 1958); and John White, ed., *The Highest State of Consciousness* (Garden City, N.Y.: Doubleday, 1972). J. A. Hadfield, *Dreams and Nightmares* (Baltimore: Penguin, 1954), points out the role that unconscious processes through dreams can play in psychic integration.

27. Marion L. Starkey, *The Devil in Massachusetts* (London: Robert Hale, 1952), 10.

28. The Shaker elder Frederick W. Evans argued in his 1881 pamphlet *New England Witchcraft and Spiritualism* (N.p.) that if nineteenth-century spiritualists had lived in seventeenth-century Massachusetts, they might well have been prosecuted as witches. Boyer and Nissenbaum, *Salem Possessed*, 27–30, compare the phenomena that precipitated the Salem witchcraft trials and the phenomena at Northhampton, Massachusetts, in 1734, that served as a precursor to the first Great Awakening.

29. Lewis, *Ecstatic Religion*, esp. 66–205. For other anthropological analyses, see n. 11, above.

30. Demos, "Witchcraft of Seventeenth-Century New England"; Boyer and Nissenbaum, *Salem Possessed*.

31. Using the manuscript records at the Library of Congress in Washington, D.C., and at the Western Reserve Historical Society in Cleveland, Ohio, in conjunction with census data and other materials, one could reconstruct the conflict at Union Village in much the same detail that Boyer and Nissenbaum reconstructed the conflict at Salem.

32. Avery, *Autobiography*, 15.

33. Blinn, *Spiritualism*, 38–39.

34. Walter F. Prince, "The Shakers and Psychical Research: A Notable Example of Cooperation," *Journal of the American Society for Psychical Research* 12 (1918): 63.

4. HAD PROPHECY FAILED?

1. This chapter is a revision of an article that was first published in Ronald L. Numbers and Jonathan M. Butler, eds., *The Disappointed: Millerism and Millenarianism in the Nineteenth Century* (Bloomington: Indiana Univ. Press, 1987), 173–88.

On the Shakers and the great revivals, see Stow Persons, "Christian Communitarianism in America," in Egbert and Persons, eds., *Socialism and American Life.* For scholarly studies of Shaker membership, see chap. 1, n. 11.

2. *Day-Star* 5 (Feb. 18, 1845): 3. For bibliographical details on the *Western Midnight Cry* and the *Day-Star,* see Richmond, *Shaker Literature,* 1:69.

3. *Day-Star* 10 (May 9, 1846): 44.

4. Richmond, *Shaker Literature,* 1:69.

5. Ibid., 69.

6. A detailed summary of the proceedings at Enfield was provided in the *Day-Star* on Aug. 25, 1846, and in subsequent issues.

7. MacLean, *Richard McNemar,* 61n.

8. *Day-Star* 11 (Aug. 8, 1846): 18.

9. *The Manifesto* 21 (Nov. 1891): 250–51, prints Jacobs's letter to Elder Hervey L. Eads and Elder Henry C. Blinn's favorable comment.

10. John Patterson MacLean, *A Bibliography of Shaker Literature* (Columbus, Ohio: F. J. Heer, 1905), 6.

11. Rourke, "Shakers."

12. Stephen A. Marini, *Radical Sects of Revolutionary New England* (Cambridge, Mass.: Harvard Univ. Press, 1982).

13. Cross, *Burned-over District,* 32.

14. Green and Wells, *Millennial Church,* 132–33.

15. See *Testimony of Christ's Second Appearing,* and Green and Wells, *Millennial Church.* Rourke, "Shakers," provides a revealing secondary analysis of Shaker theology, one heavily influenced by White and Taylor, *Shakerism.* Normative Shaker christological beliefs of the early nineteenth century are succinctly presented in the following affirmation: "Christ first appeared in Jesus of Nazareth, by which he was constituted the head of the new spiritual creation of God. . . . [The human tabernacle of Ann Lee] was a chosen vessel, occupied as an instrument, by the spirit of Christ, the Lord from Heaven, in which the second appearance of that Divine spirit was ushered into the world." Green and Wells, *Millennial Church,* 216, 219.

16. See Persons, "Christian Communitarianism," and Cross, *Burned-over District.*

17. "Introduction to Records of Sacred Communications," 10.

18. Brown, *People Called Shakers,* 343.

19. "Introduction to Records of Sacred Communications," 10.

20. William Hepworth Dixon, *New America,* 6th ed., 2 vols. (London: Hurst & Blackett, 1867), 2:86.

21. Noyes, *American Socialisms,* 670.

22. "Introduction to Records of Sacred Communications."

23. Possibly the most disruptive episode was the expulsion in 1839 of the venerable Richard McNemar from the Union Village, Ohio, community he had helped found.

24. For a summary of reactions, see Cross, *Burned-over District*, 307–21, and David T. Arthur, "Millerism," in Edwin S. Gaustad, ed., *The Rise of Adventism: Religion and Society in Mid-Nineteenth-Century America* (New York: Harper & Row, 1974), 154–72.

25. Jacobs prints extracts from a letter of John Dunlavy to Barton W. Stone in 1805 during the Kentucky Revival, *Day-Star* 11 (June 13, 1846): 6–9.

26. Ibid., 10 (May 23, 1846): 56.

27. See O. L. Crosier's "Visit to the Shakers," printed in its entirety, ibid. 11 (Aug. 8, 1846): 18–19.

28. Ibid. 10 (May 9, 1846): 44.

29. Letter of April 24, 1846, from Henry B. Bear, ibid. Bear's pamphlet, *Henry B. Bear's Advent Experience* (Whitewater, Ohio, n.d.), is one of the finest summations of the emotional and intellectual processes through which a thoughtful Millerite went during the 1840s. The text of the pamphlet is reprinted in its entirety in Numbers and Butler, eds., *The Disappointed*, 217–26.

30. *Day-Star* 10 (May 23, 1846): 51.

31. Ibid. 11 (June 13, 1846): 9.

32. Ibid., 5.

33. Numerous discussions by Enoch Jacobs show that Shaker theology was sometimes difficult to justify to Millerites but that Jacobs continually stressed the importance of considering the whole achievement of the Shakers rather than individual bits of theology in isolation.

34. For example, see the letter from Sister E. S. Willard approving of celibacy prior to Christ's second advent, ibid. 10 (May 9, 1846): 42.

35. Ibid.

36. Ibid. 11 (June 13, 1846): 12.

37. See the analysis in Foster, *Religion and Sexuality*, 54–58. Approximately 20 percent of converts either remained in the Second Family or transferred to another Shaker group.

38. Ibid., 56.

39. Ibid., 56–58.

40. MacLean, *Bibliography of Shaker Literature*, 19–20. MacLean's misspelling of the name of Enoch Jacobs' wife as Electra, rather than Electa, has been corrected here.

41. *Day-Star* 11 (Aug. 8, 1846): 18.

42. Ibid. 11 (Nov. 7, 1846): 36.

43. Blinn, *Spiritualism*, 49.

44. Andrews, *People Called Shakers*, 160–61.

45. White and Taylor, *Shakerism*, 235.

46. For a provocative analysis of the transformation of the Adventist movement after the Great Disappointment, see Jonathan M. Butler, "Adventism and the

American Experience," in Gaustad, ed., *Rise of Adventism*, 173-206; and Gary Land, ed., *Adventism in America: A History* (Grand Rapids, Mich.: Eerdmans, 1986).

5. THE PSYCHOLOGY of FREE LOVE

1. This chapter was originally published under the title "The Psychology of Free Love in the Oneida Community," *Australasian Journal of American Studies* 5 (Dec. 1986): 14-26.

2. For bibliographic treatments of communitarian socialism in America, see chap. 1, n. 2, above. Major works on the Oneida Community itself are cited chap. 1, n. 13.

3. The characterization of Noyes as a "Yankee Saint" is found in Parker, *Yankee Saint*. For the comment that Noyes has been treated as a "Vermont Casanova," see Thomas, *Man Who Would Be Perfect*. The comparison of Noyes and Hitler appears in Erik Achorn, "Mary Cragin: Perfectionist Saint," *New England Quarterly* 28 (1955): 490-518.

4. Among the noteworthy treatments of Noyes's psychology that make use of manuscript sources that have recently been made available at the Syracuse University Library are Michael Barkun, " 'The Wind Sweeping Over the Country': John Humphrey Noyes and the Rise of Millerism," in Numbers and Butler, eds., *The Disappointed*, 153-72; and Michael Barkun, "The Visionary Experiences of John Humphrey Noyes," *Psychohistory Review* 16 (Spring 1988): 313-34.

5. Noyes used his broad-ranging mind to analyze and skillfully explain the limitations of virtually all the social, intellectual, and religious theories influential in nineteenth-century America. For example, his analysis of the social rationalizations underlying the sexual theories of the Swedish scientist and mystic Emanuel Swedenborg is a devastating tour de force that few modern analysts could surpass. See "Swedenborg on Pellicacy and Concubinage," *Perfectionist and Theocratic Watchman* 5 (Jan. 31, 1846): 90. Had Noyes known of Sigmund Freud, he could have provided a similarly trenchant analysis, using Noyesian sexual perspectives, of how Freud's personal experiences influenced his sexual rationalizations and theories. It makes no more sense to reduce Noyes's experiences to Freudian categories than it would to reduce Freud's experiences to Noyesian categories.

6. Burridge, *New Heaven, New Earth*, 162.

7. James, *Varieties of Religious Experience*, 36-37.

8. On Noyes's early life, see Parker, *Yankee Saint*; Thomas, *Man Who Would Be Perfect*; and G. W. Noyes, ed., *Religious Experience*.

9. See John Humphrey Noyes, *Confessions of John H. Noyes, Part I: Confession of Religious Experience, Including a History of Modern Perfectionism* (Oneida Reserve, N.Y.: Leonard, 1849); G. W. Noyes, ed., *Religious Experience*; and Foster, *Religion and Sexuality*, 75-79.

10. "A Word of Warning," *Perfectionist and Theocratic Watchman* 5 (July 12, 1845): 34.

11. Among other things, Noyes declared in a letter, printed without his permission in the antiestablishment newspaper *The Battle Axe and Weapons of War*, "In a holy community, there is no more reason why sexual intercourse should be restricted by law, than why eating and drinking should be—and there is as little occasion for shame in the one case as in the other."

12. In 1838 Noyes married Harriet Holton, in part influenced by the social and financial resources she could devote to his cause. "Financial Romance: How the O.C. Got Its Capital," *Circular* 2, n.s. (Jan. 8, 1866): 366.

13. In addition to their primary community at Oneida, Noyes's perfectionist followers also maintained a smaller sister community at Wallingford, Connecticut, as well as short-lived groups at Brooklyn, New York; Newark, New Jersey; Putney, Vermont; and Cambridge, Vermont, among other locations. Carden, *Oneida*, 40–41.

14. *First Annual Report of the Oneida Association*, 11–12. Also see Noyes's *Confessions*; his *The Berean: A Manual for the Help of Those Who Seek the Faith of the Primitive Church* (Putney, Vt.: Office of the *Spiritual Magazine*, 1847); and G. W. Noyes, ed., *Religious Experience*. Strange though Noyes's beliefs might sound, they always represented an attempt to stake out a middle ground between the theological extremes of his day.

15. Foster, *Religion and Sexuality*, 90–93.

16. Robert Dale Owen had earlier drawn a distinction in his pamphlet *Moral Physiology* between sexual intercourse for "amative" and "propagative" purposes. Whereas Owen had favored *coitus interruptus* as the method for avoiding procreation, however, Noyes, with his characteristically Victorian opposition to wasting the male seed, came to favor *coitus reservatus*. For a lively scholarly analysis of Victorian concerns about loss of male semen, see Graham J. Barker-Benfield, "The Spermatic Economy: A Nineteenth-Century View of Sexuality," *Feminist Studies* 1 (1972): 45–74. For the key primary Oneida sources on male continence, see chap. 1, n. 16.

17. Noyes, "Bible Argument Defining the Relations of the Sexes in the Kingdom of Heaven," in *First Annual Report of the Oneida Association*, 32. Noyes appears to have developed his theory and practice of male continence without reference to similar practices in Tantric and other non-Western religious movements.

18. John Humphrey Noyes, *Male Continence*, 7, 9.

19. Ibid., 8.

20. Carden, *Oneida*, 51, finds evidence that thirty-one births occurred at Oneida between 1848 and 1868, but some of these births were planned. The R. L. Dickinson Papers at the Kinsey Institute indicate that only twelve unplanned births occurred during that period. Whatever the true number, the figure for accidental births was remarkably low.

21. For a summary of the major printed sources on Oneida, see Wells, *Oneida Community Collection*.

22. Theodore R. Noyes, M.D., "Report on Nervous Diseases in the Oneida Community," as printed in John Humphrey Noyes, *Essay on Scientific Propagation* (Oneida, N.Y.: Oneida Community, 1872), 25–32. Also see Ely van de Warker, "Gynecological Study of the Oneida Community," *American Journal of Obstetrics and Diseases of Women and Children* 17 (Aug. 1884): 755–810. Note that the contemporary analysis of male sexual behavior by Alfred Kinsey and his associates argues that men practicing *coitus reservatus* can indeed achieve orgasm without ejaculation and describes how this can occur. Kinsey et al., *Sexual Behavior in the Human Male*, 158–61.

23. Noyes, *Male Continence*, 20.

24. Pierrepont B. Noyes, *My Father's House: An Oneida Boyhood* (New York: Farrar & Reinhart, 1937), 131; Estlake, *Oneida Community*, 26.

25. Celibacy was a theoretical alternative to complex marriage and was practiced by some of the men. See P. B. Noyes, *My Father's House*, 150 and passim.

26. Noyes, *Male Continence*, 20.

27. Norman Himes, *Medical History of Contraception* (1936; reprint New York: Schocken, 1970), 271.

28. Havelock Ellis, *Studies in the Psychology of Sex* (Philadelphia: F. A. Davis, 1911), 553.

29. See Barker-Benfield, "Spermatic Economy," as well as other essays collected in Thomas L. Altherr, ed., *Procreation or Pleasure: Sexual Attitudes in American History* (Malabar, Fla.: Krieger, 1983).

30. Noyes, *Male Continence*, 21.

31. For key primary and secondary references to mutual criticism, see chap. 1, n. 16.

32. Foster, *Religion and Sexuality*, 100–116. During one six-month period between March and August 1852, internal and external pressures were so great that the group temporarily gave up the sexual aspects of the practice of complex marriage.

33. *Handbook of the Oneida Community, Containing a Brief Sketch of Its Present Condition, Internal Economy and Leading Principles*, no. 2 (Oneida, N.Y.: Oneida Community, 1871), 56.

34. Foster, *Religion and Sexuality*, 116–18.

35. Carden, *Oneida*, 30.

36. Foster, *Religion and Sexuality*, 85–86, 105–6.

37. Thomas uses modern ego psychology to develop the first convincing book-length psychological analysis of Noyes's motivation.

38. Carden, *Oneida*, 107.

39. Fogarty, "Oneida Community."

40. Carden, *Oneida*, 77.

41. It is difficult to see how simple social characteristics such as the geographical, occupational, or economic status of community members could fully account

for the attraction of individuals to the group. *Bible Communism*, 22, accurately states that "the main body of those have joined the Association at Oneida, are sober, substantial men and women of good previous character and position in society." Problems with the status anxiety and frustration-aggression models in explaining reform in general and Noyes's efforts in particular are discussed in Robert David Thomas, Jr., "The Development of a Utopian Mind: A Psychoanalytic Study of John Humphrey Noyes, 1828–1869" (Ph.D. diss., State Univ. of New York at Stony Brook, 1973), 1–10.

42. *Handbook of the Oneida Community, 1875* (Oneida, N.Y.: Office of the *Oneida Circular*, 1875), 15.

43. Fogarty, "Oneida Community"; and Persons, "Christian Communitarianism."

44. Foster, *Religion and Sexuality*, 110.

45. Ibid., 116–18.

46. P. B. Noyes, *My Father's House*, 138.

6. FREE LOVE and FEMINISM

1. An earlier version of this chapter was published in *Journal of the Early Republic* 1 (Summer 1981): 165–83. Among the treatments suggesting that Noyes may have been ahead of his time, see Parker, *Yankee Saint*; Victor F. Calverton, "Oneida: The Love Colony," in his *Where Angels Dared to Tread: Socialist and Communist Utopian Colonies in the United States* (New York: Bobbs-Merrill, 1941), 245–87; Mulford Q. Sibley, "Oneida's Challenge to American Culture," in Joseph J. Kwiat and Mary C. Turpie, eds., *Studies in American Culture* (Minneapolis: Univ. of Minnesota Press, 1959), 41–62; and Richard A. Hoehn, "The Kingdom Goes Joint Stock: Learning from Oneida 100 Years Later," *Christian Century*, Jan. 28, 1981, pp. 77–80.

2. For some analyses of Oneida from contemporary feminist perspectives, see chap. 1, n. 18. Many feminist critiques of the Oneida Community assume that unless Oneida gave its women full self-determination (which it did not give its men either), then it must be viewed as having failed in reorganizing relations between the sexes. Such an argument does not take seriously the underlying concerns of communitarian groups such as Oneida which were opposed to the disruptive individualism of their day and sought instead to establish a new basis of authority growing out of a mutual religious and communal commitment by both men and women. Other critical accounts have ranged from that of Achorn, "Mary Cragin," which compared Noyes to Hitler, to Ernest R. Sandeen, "John Humphrey Noyes as the New Adam," *Church History* 40 (Mar. 1971): 82–90, which suggests that Noyes suffered from serious emotional disturbances.

3. For the basic theological statement by Noyes on the superiority of the male to the female principles, see articles in his *Berean*, particularly "Condensation

of Life," 487–93. Since "spirituality" was the basis for authority at Oneida, Noyes reversed the popular Victorian notion and argued that men were more "spiritual" than women. "Women's Character," *Circular* 3 (Jan. 14, 1854): 72.

4. *First Annual Report of the Oneida Association*, 41. For the basic rationale underlying the institution of the Bloomer-style outfit, see ibid., 8–10, 40–41. Similar outfits were instituted for various reasons in several other antebellum groups, including the Strangite Mormons and the Brigham Young Mormons.

5. The original idea behind the eugenics experiment is described ibid., 33–34, and elaborated in Noyes's *Scientific Propagation*. Noyes argues, for example, that man's natural superiority over women is suggested by the fact that a great man can sire children by any number of women at the same time, while a woman can bear only one child at a time. Ibid., 18.

6. Somewhat ironically, writers analyzing the Oneida Community from feminist perspectives almost never have dealt explicitly with Noyes's *own* critique of antebellum feminism and the women's rights movement.

7. Cross, *Burned-over District*, 333. Robert David Thomas's fine social-psychological study *The Man Who Would be Perfect* describes with great sophistication how Noyes managed successfully to fuse the conflicting elements of his time into a new synthesis.

8. G. W. Noyes, ed., *Religious Experience*, 306. This was an unpublished portion of Noyes's famous letter that was excerpted in *The Battle-Axe and Weapons of War*. On the social and religious disorder of western Vermont, see Ludlum, *Social Ferment in Vermont*. On Noyes's family background and how it influenced the development of his sense of mission, see Thomas, *Man Who Would Be Perfect*.

9. The most succinct summary of this position is found in Noyes's "Bible Argument" in the *First Annual Report of the Oneida Association*, 27–28.

10. For a few of the numerous articles developing this position, see "Practical Communism," *Circular* 2 (June 13, 1852): 121; "Industrial Marriage," *Circular* 3 (Mar. 18, 1854): 179; "Working Schools," *Circular* 3 (Mar. 23, 1854): 186; "Our Home," *Circular* 3 (Oct. 21, 1854): 550; and "The Moral Advantages of Combination," *Circular* 3 (Mar. 16, 1854): 176.

11. "Bible Argument," 27–28.

12. Ibid., 25.

13. *Slavery and Marriage, A Dialogue: Conversation Between Judge North, Major South, and Mr. Free Church* (Oneida, N.Y.: Oneida Community, 1850); "The Family and Its Foil," *Circular* 3 (Nov. 16, 1854): 594; and *Bible Communism*, 79–80.

14. See "Becoming as Little Children," *Spiritual Magazine* 2 (Dec. 22, 1849): 339; "The Social Principle Primary," *Free Church Circular* 3 (Sept. 23, 1850): 249–50; "Egotism for Two," *Circular* 3 (Apr. 11, 1854): 219–20; and "The Family and Its Foil," *Circular* 3 (Nov. 16, 1854): 594.

15. See "Bible Argument"; *Bible Communism*; *Handbook of the Oneida Community*, . . . (Wallingford, Conn.: Office of the *Circular*, 1867), 64; *Handbook of the Oneida Community* (1871), 56.

16. "The Battle-Axe Letter," *Witness* 1 (Jan. 23, 1839): 50; "Introduction," *Spiritual Moralist* 1 (June 13, 1842): 1.

17. For the best overview of the development of these new methods of social control, see G. W. Noyes, ed., *John Humphrey Noyes*; Parker, *Yankee Saint*; Carden, *Oneida*; and Foster, *Religion and Sexuality*.

18. Parker, *Yankee Saint*; Carden, *Oneida*; Kern, *An Ordered Love*; and Foster, *Religion and Sexuality*, discuss the ways in which sex roles and daily activities were modified at Oneida. Even Dalsimer's critical account "Women and the Family in the Oneida Community," 242–77, shows that significant modifications were made in women's work at Oneida. Although a tendency eventually developed for individuals to return to more sex-stereotyped occupational roles, there were almost no formal institutional blocks to individuals pursuing any activities in which they were genuinely interested.

19. The overriding concern that Noyes had with his own personal authority and control is stressed in *Spiritual Magazine* 2 (July 11, 1842): 57–59; and by G. W. Noyes, ed., *John Humphrey Noyes*, 25–33. Also see Thomas's observations in his *Man Who Would Be Perfect*; and Richard DeMaria, *Communal Love at Oneida: A Perfectionist Vision of Authority, Property, and Sexual Order* (New York: Mellen, 1978).

20. A concern for the spirit not the letter of the law, faith not works, underlay Noyes's conversion to perfectionism in 1834 and his entire subsequent career. *Circular* 2 (Mar. 7, 1852): 66.

21. "Woman's Slavery to Children," *Spiritual Magazine* 1 (Sept. 15, 1846): 109–10.

22. Noyes's chief hero was St. Paul, but Noyes always followed the *spirit* of Paul's concerns rather than narrowly adopting particular *practices* that Paul had advocated in response to a particular time and place. In general, Noyes tended to interpret away Paul's more restrictive statements about women and emphasize instead his underlying flexibility of approach—that in Christ there was neither Jew nor gentile, slave nor free, man nor woman. For instance, see "Marriage Nailed to the Cross," *Witness* 2 (Dec. 10, 1841): 76–77.

23. The best secondary accounts of the system of ascending and descending fellowship are found in Parker, *Yankee Saint*; Carden, *Oneida*; and DeMaria, *Communal Love at Oneida*. Noyes himself usually discussed this informal system obliquely, even while recognizing that it underlay the entire structure of community government. For instance, see *Mutual Criticism*; "Socialism in Two Directions," *Circular* 3 (Apr. 29, 1854): 250; "Home Talk #24," *Circular* 3 (Sept. 19, 1854): 496; and Alfred Barron and George Noyes Miller, eds., *Home-talks by John Humphrey Noyes* (Oneida, N.Y.: Oneida Community, 1875).

24. See Kirk Jeffrey, "The Family as a Utopian Retreat from the City: The Nineteenth Century Contribution," in Sallie TeSelle, ed., *The Family, Communes, and Utopian Societies* (New York: Harper & Row, 1972), 21–41. For a classic statement suggesting that that Victorian women were retreating from reality, see Barbara Welter, "The Cult of True Womanhood, 1820–1860," *American Quarterly* 18 (Summer 1966), 151–74.

25. Noyes did not accept the idea that his communities were utopian in the sense of engaging in impractical withdrawal from the larger society; in fact, he criticized other groups for many of the utopian characteristics that have commonly been imputed to his own efforts.

26. This viewpoint is most clearly articulated in Noyes's *American Socialisms*, 26, where he argues that the two great efforts at social reconstruction in the antebellum period came, on the one hand, from the religious revivalists, whose great idea was "the regeneration of the soul," and, on the other hand, from the secular associationists, whose great complementary idea was "the regeneration of society, which is the soul's environment."

27. Robert Fogarty's "Oneida" was an early study that recognized the extraordinary importance that the press had for Noyes. Also see "Association," *Spiritual Magazine* 1 (Mar. 15, 1846): 6; and "Brooklyn and Oneida," *Circular* 1 (Nov. 23, 1851): 6.

28. Although Noyes was sympathetic toward many of the concerns of activist women of his time, he typically did not devote much space in his newspapers to the feminist movement as such. When he did mention the antebellum women's movement directly, it was usually as an informational item with appended comments. One noteworthy exception to this pattern was the entire issue of the *Free Church Circular* for Dec. 2, 1850, which was devoted to women's rights. For the idea that married women's status was similar to that of slave, see *Slavery and Marriage; Bible Communism*, 123–28; and "Women and Slaves," *Circular* 3 (Dec. 17, 1853): 23. The important linkage between Noyes and Garrison is analyzed in John L. Thomas, *William Lloyd Garrison* (Boston: Little, Brown, 1963), 228–32. For the broader context of Noyes's attitudes toward women, see the *Spiritual Moralist* for June 13 and June 25, 1842.

29. This line of argument is repeated on numerous occasions. A classic statement is that of Susan C. Hamilton, English-born convert to Noyes's perfectionism, in "Communism, Woman's Best Friend," *Circular* 3 (Mar. 18, 1854): 180.

30. "Woman-Suppression," *Circular* 3 (May 27, 1854): 298. This optimistic tone is also characteristic of many of Noyes's other statements on this topic. Noyes's chief reservations about antebellum feminists related to means, not ends. He was also disturbed by feminists such as the Grimké sisters who attacked St. Paul, his personal hero and model. See "Semi-Infidelity Among Reformers," *Perfectionist* 3 (June 1, 1843): 30.

31. For a suggestion of the striking similarities between Noyes's approach and that of conservatives such as Catharine Beecher, see Kathryn Kish Sklar, *Catharine Beecher: A Study in American Domesticity* (New Haven: Yale Univ. Press, 1973), esp. 151–67.

32. "The Liberty of Union," *Circular* 1 (Jan. 4, 1852): 86.

33. Garry Wills, "Feminists and Other Useful Fanatics: The Politics of Crazy Jane," *Harper's*, June 1976, pp. 35–42.

34. Wayland-Smith, "Women in the Oneida Community," 18–53.

35. Carol Gilligan, *In a Different Voice: Psychological Theory and Women's Development* (Cambridge, Mass.: Harvard Univ. Press, 1982).

36. Ibid., 70.

37. Wayland-Smith, "Women in the Oneida Community," 26.

38. Ibid., 26.

39. Although Wayland-Smith's argument serves as a useful corrective to the recent feminist analyses that portray Oneida as oppressive for women, her analysis may miss the fact that Noyes's dominant effort was to maintain a *balance* between the polarities of existence, including those conventionally attributed to either "masculine" or "feminine" characteristics. Thus, Richard DeMaria may ultimately be most accurate in characterizing the goal at Oneida as the achievement of androgyny. See *Communal Love at Oneida,* 96–103.

40. Note that Marxian socialists emphasized that changing the overall economic system was a necessary precursor to "liberating" women. Noyes, similarly, emphasized that reestablishing common religious value premises must come before a true reconciliation of the sexes would be possible.

41. "Liberty to Change," *Circular* 3 (Aug. 8, 1854): 422. For the scholarly argument that Noyes was basically a "conservative," see esp. Fogarty, "Oneida Community."

7. THE RISE and FALL of UTOPIA

1. This chapter is a revision of an article published in *Communal Societies* 8 (1988): 1–17. For the March 1852 announcement, see "The Past, Present, and Future," *Circular* 1 (Mar. 7, 1852): 66. The August 1852 statement appears in *Circular* 1 (Aug. 29, 1852): 170.

2. *O.C. Journal,* Aug. 28, 1879, and *American Socialist,* Sept. 4, 1879, as quoted in Robertson, *Oneida Community: The Breakup,* 160, 161.

3. Noyes, *American Socialisms,* esp. 646–57; Kanter, *Commitment and Community;* and Jon Wagner, "Success in Intentional Communities: The Problem of Evaluation," *Communal Societies* 5 (1985): 89–100.

4. For a summary of this early phase of Noyes's life, see Foster, *Religion and Sexuality,* 72–82.

5. Ibid., 82–102. Noyes's "Bible Argument" initially appeared in the *First Annual Report of the Oneida Association,* was elaborated in final form in *Bible Communism,* and was presented in abridged form in Noyes, *American Socialisms,* 623–37. The membership information is derived from the first three annual reports of the Oneida Association.

6. "Bible Argument," 27–28.

7. As quoted in Robertson, *Oneida Community: The Breakup,* 10. For discussions of the crucial role played by the press at Oneida, see chap. 6, above; and Fogarty, "Oneida."

8. G. W. Noyes, ed., *John Humphrey Noyes.*

9. For an overview of these practices, see chap. 5, above.

10. *Circular* 3 (Jan. 17, 1854): 75.

11. Fogarty, "Oneida Community," 162.

12. Parker, *Yankee Saint*, 187–89.

13. As early as 1850, the Oneida Community publicly stated that it was not actively seeking new members. "Plans and Prospects," *Free Church Circular* 3 (Oct. 21, 1850): 281.

14. "A Complaint Answered," *Free Church Circular* 3 (Oct. 3, 1850): 270.

15. "The Past, Present, and Future," *Circular* 1 (Mar. 7, 1852): 66. In preparing this chapter, I have not been able to use surviving manuscript sources that could make possible a full reconstruction of the specific tensions associated with the 1852 crisis. However, Professor Milton H. Jannone, who has had the opportunity to work intensively with those manuscript sources, very kindly shared with me thirty pages of quotations on the crisis that he made from manuscript and printed Oneida materials. Jannone's impressive compilation shows that one important local source of hostility toward Oneida during the early 1850s came from the Hubbard family, whose daughter Tryphena Hubbard had joined Oneida on August 29, 1848, the same day that she "married" Henry Seymour.

That "marriage" and Tryphena's relationship with the community proved tumultuous and unhappy. The Hubbards eventually initiated legal suits against the community for the physical abuse and the seduction of their daughter. The situation became so serious that the community considered dissolving itself rather than go through a lengthy public trial, and at one point in 1852 more than half of the community members had temporarily left Oneida. Eventually, however, the suits were dropped after the community got influential local leaders to intercede on its behalf and agreed to pay the Hubbard family three hundred dollars. Milton H. Jannone, "The Dispersion from Oneida in 1852" (MS compilation conveyed to me on Jan. 18, 1991). The opening of most of the surviving Oneida manuscripts held in the Syracuse University Library to researchers in February 1991 should make possible a detailed reconstruction of the problems that contributed to the 1852 crisis. Those problems may well have been every bit as complex as the ones that led to the eventual breakup of the community in 1879–81.

16. See "The Second Course," *Circular* 1 (Apr. 4, 1852): 82; "Past Enjoyments," Ibid., 83; "Hints to the Peaceable," *Circular* 1 (May 2, 1852): 98; and "Things Proved," *Circular* 1 (May 23, 1852): 110.

17. Estlake, *Oneida Community*, 40–41. Emphasis added.

18. "The Second Course," *Circular* 1 (Apr. 4, 1854): 82.

19. It is significant that many of these articles coupled the terms "disease and death." For Noyes's basic statement on the topic, see "Abolition of Death" in *Berean*, 476–86.

20. *Circular* 1 (Feb. 1, 1852): 51.

21. "The Rival of Christ," *Circular* 1 (Apr. 4, 1852): 82; "A Bible Contest," *Circular* 1 (Apr. 11, 1852): 87. These articles were written by Noyes's sister Harriet.

22. *Bible Communism*, [4].

23. "The Message," *Circular* 1 (Aug. 1, 1852): 150.

24. *Circular* 1 (Aug. 1, 1852): 150

25. *Circular* 1 (Aug. 29, 1852): 170. The capitalization of the original has been eliminated in this quotation from the "Theocratic Platform."

26. *Circular* 3 (Apr. 15, 1854): 226.

27. Most of the studies that deal with the breakup of the Oneida Community tend toward a monocausal approach. Fogarty, "Oneida Community," stresses the disruptive role of the stirpiculture or eugenics experiment; Carden, *Oneida*, highlights sexual conflicts over the question of which men should initiate virgins into sexual experience; Parker, *Yankee Saint*, places considerable stress on external factors; Olin, "Instability of Charismatic Authority," employs Weberian theories of leadership. Each of these studies provides useful perspectives for the analysis that follows, but the only comprehensive, multicausal study of the breakup with full documentation is Robertson's *Oneida Community: The Breakup*.

28. For a brief treatment of the stirpiculture experiment, see Foster, *Religion and Sexuality*, 118–20.

29. Robertson, *Oneida Community: The Breakup*, 160.

30. *Puck*, Feb. 26, 1879, reprinted in Parker, *Yankee Saint*, 280.

31. On the changes following the end of the communal phase at Oneida, see Pierrepont B. Noyes, *A Godly Heritage* (New York: Rinehart, 1958), and Carden, *Oneida*.

32. Foster, *Religion and Sexuality*, 120–22.

33. Arthur Hugh Clough, "Say Not the Struggle Naught Availeth," quoted in Louis Untermeyer, *A Treasury of Great Poems: English and American*, rev. and enl. ed. (New York: Simon and Schuster, 1955), 887.

8. BETWEEN TWO WORLDS

1. For a fuller treatment of many of the topics discussed here, see Foster, *Religion and Sexuality*, 123–80. A complementary Mormon perspective is found in Bachman, "Plural Marriage." For sources describing the Louisa Beaman marriage, see Andrew Jensen's *Historical Record* 5 (May 1887): 232; and the composite account in Brodie, *No Man Knows My History*, 465.

2. For the earliest detailed apostate critique of Joseph Smith's polygamy, see John C. Bennett, *The History of the Saints; or, An Exposé of Joe Smith and Mormonism* (Boston: Leland & Whiting, 1842). Orson Pratt's periodical *The Seer* contains the most detailed early defense of Mormon polygamy. For some other key accounts, see notes 5–8 in this chapter.

3. Newell and Avery, *Mormon Enigma*. The portions of this essay dealing with Emma Hale Smith draw heavily on this path-breaking and, in my view, definitive, biography.

4. See the anthropological analysis in Turner's *Ritual Process*. A revealing discussion of how Turner's approach helps understand contemporary "cult" groups is presented in J. Gordon Melton and Robert L. Moore, *The Cult Experience: Responding to the New Religious Pluralism* (New York: Pilgrim, 1982), 47–69.

In attempting to convey the full complexity of early Mormon polygamous development, this analysis deliberately avoids any rigorously theoretical analysis. Any highly articulated analysis would omit consideration of data not directly related to the formal concepts within which the analysis was made. Theoretical perspectives are used here to suggest ways of better understanding the phenomena rather than to restrict the range of interpretations possible.

5. Shook, *Mormon Polygamy*, reproduces and skillfully analyzes most of the early evidence—including statements by almost every early leader of the Reorganized Church of Jesus Christ of Latter Day Saints (RLDS)—that links Joseph Smith beyond any reasonable doubt to the intellectual genesis and the practice of polygamy. With the passage of time and vigorous efforts by Joseph Smith III and others, the RLDS church eventually began to deny Joseph Smith's responsibility for polygamy. Only recently has this position begun to change significantly. See esp. Richard P. Howard, "The Changing RLDS Response to Mormon Polygamy: A Preliminary Analysis," *John Whitmer Historical Association Journal* 3 (1983): 14–29, and Imogene Goodyear, "Joseph Smith and Polygamy: An Alternative View," *John Whitmer Historical Association Journal* 4 (1984): 16–21.

For LDS evidence that Joseph Smith was responsible for introducing polygamy, see Joseph F. Smith, Jr. [Joseph Fielding Smith], *Blood Atonement and the Origin of Plural Marriage: A Discussion* (Salt Lake City: Deseret News, 1905); Andrew Jenson, "Plural Marriage," *Historical Record* 5 (May 1887): 219–34; and Bachman, "Plural Marriage."

6. Among the critiques that must be considered seriously in making a historical reconstruction of the early development of polygamy, see Bennett, *History of the Saints*; Oliver H. Olney, *The Absurdities of Mormonism Portrayed* (Hancock County, Ill: N.p., 1843); *The Nauvoo Expositor*, June 7, 1844; John Hyde, Jr., *Mormonism: Its Leaders and Designs* (New York: W. P. Fetridge, 1857): T. B. H. Stenhouse, *The Rocky Mountain Saints: A Full and Complete History of the Mormons* (New York: D. Appleton, 1873); John D. Lee, *Mormonism Unveiled; or, The Life and Confessions of the Late Mormon Bishop, John D. Lee*, ed. W. W. Bishop (St. Louis: Bryan, Brand, 1877); and Wilhelm Wyl, *Joseph Smith, the Prophet, His Family and Friends: A Study Based on Facts and Documents* (Salt Lake City: Tribune, 1886).

Such accounts based on firsthand documentation should not be confused with the vast body of nineteenth-century anti-Mormon treatments that are semi-novelistic in character and usually historically valueless for understanding the early development of polygamy. For this latter genre, see Leonard J. Arrington and Jon Haupt, "Intolerable Zion: The Image of Mormonism in Nineteenth Century American Literature," *Western Humanities Review* 22 (Summer 1968): 243–60, and Charles A. Cannon, "The Awesome Power of Sex: The Polemical Campaign Against Mormon Polygamy," *Pacific Historical Review* 43 (Feb. 1974): 61–82.

7. For an introduction to the complex process by which Joseph Smith received and interpreted revelation, see LDS Doctrine and Covenants, esp. sections 6 through 10; Joseph Smith, Jr., *History of the Church*, 5: xxxiv–xlvi; Eduard Meyer, *The Origin and History of the Mormons*, trans. Heinz F. Rahde and Eugene Seaich (Salt Lake City: Univ. of Utah Press, 1961), 30–38; Richard P. Howard, *Restoration Scriptures: A Study of Their Textual Development* (Independence, Mo.: Herald, 1969); Brigham H. Roberts, *Studies of the Book of Mormon*, ed. Brigham D. Madsen (Urbana: Univ. of Illinois Press, 1985); Jessee, ed., *Personal Writings of Joseph Smith*; Faulring, ed., *American Prophet's Record*; Ehat and Cook, eds., *Words of Joseph Smith*; Andrew F. Ehat, "Joseph Smith's Introduction of Temple Ordinances and the 1844 Mormon Succession Question" (M.A. thesis, Brigham Young Univ., 1982); and Lawrence Foster, "First Visions: Personal Reflections on Joseph Smith's Religious Experience," *Sunstone* 8 (Sept.–Oct. 1983): 39–43.

8. For some psychological reductionist approaches, see Isaac Woodbridge Riley, *The Founder of Mormonism: A Psychological Study of Joseph Smith, Jr.* (New York: Dodd, Mead, 1902); Brodie, *No Man Knows My History*, 418–21; and Kern, *An Ordered Love*, 137–43. Marvin Hill, "Secular or Sectarian History? A Critique of *No Man Knows My History*," *Church History* 33 (Mar. 1974): 78–96, criticizes Brodie's tendencies toward psychological reductionism. For an analysis by a Mormon psychiatrist, see C. Jess Groesbeck, "The Smiths and Their Dreams and Visions: A Psycho-Historical Study of the First Mormon Family," *Sunstone* 12 (Mar. 1988): 22–29.

9. If evidence be needed that Joseph Smith had a strong sex drive, starting points are Brodie, *No Man Knows My History*, and Newell and Avery, *Mormon Enigma*.

10. Foster, *Religion and Sexuality*, 128–39; Bachman, "Plural Marriage," 1–103; Marvin Hill, "The Shaping of the Mormon Mind in New England and New York," *BYU Studies* 9 (Spring 1969): 351–72, and *Quest for Refuge: The Mormon Flight from American Pluralism* (Salt Lake City: Signature, 1989); Mario S. De Pillis, "The Quest for Religious Authority and the Rise of Mormonism," *Dialogue* 1 (Fall 1966): 68–88, and "Social Sources of Mormonism," *Church History* 37 (Mar. 1968): 50–79. On early Mormon biblical "literalism" see Gordon Irving, "The Mormons and the Bible in the 1830s," *BYU Studies* 15 (Summer 1973): 473–88; and Sterling M. McMurrin, *The Theological Foundations of the Mormon Religion* (Salt Lake City: Univ. of Utah Press, 1965).

11. Foster, *Religion and Sexuality*, 134–39; Hansen, *Quest for Empire*. Benjamin F. Johnson, *My Life in Review* (Independence, Mo.: Zion's Printing and Publishing Company, 1947), 388, mentions his extensive kinship ties.

12. The best treatment of Mormon Nauvoo as a Jacksonian boom town is Flanders, *Nauvoo*. Also see Annette P. Hampshire, *Mormonism in Conflict: The Nauvoo Years* (New York: Mellen, 1985); Stanley B. Kimball, ed., "The Mormons in

Early Illinois," *Dialogue* 5 (Spring 1970): 7–79; Richard D. Poll, "Nauvoo and the New Mormon History: A Bibliographic Survey," *JMH* 5 (1978): 105–23; and articles in *JMH* 16 (1990): 25–86.

13. O'Dea, *The Mormons*, 53–54. T. Edgar Lyon informed me, in a letter dated May 18, 1978, of his research showing that the population of Nauvoo was second to that of Chicago in 1845.

14. For instance, see William Mulder and A. Russell Mortensen, eds., *Among the Mormons: Historic Accounts by Contemporary Observers* (New York: Knopf, 1968), 115–17.

15. This informal estimate of the number of deaths in Nauvoo was made by Kenneth W. Godfrey, "Some Thoughts Regarding an Unwritten History of Nauvoo" (paper presented at the annual meeting of the Mormon History Association, Nauvoo, Ill., Apr. 1974), 2n.

16. Letter of Parley P. Pratt to Mary Ann Frost Pratt, dated July 6, 1840, Parley P. Pratt Papers, LDS Archives, box 1, folder 6.

17. Letter of Eunice B. Shurtliff, dated Dec. 24, 1842, as recorded in Luman Andros Shurtliff, Biographical Sketch, a typescript copied from the original by the Federal Writers Project of Ogden, Utah. Copy in the Huntington Library, San Marino, Calif., 58–59.

18. S. George Ellsworth, ed., *Dear Ellen: Two Mormon Women and Their Letters* (Salt Lake City: Univ. of Utah Library, 1974), 42.

19. The Mormon leader John D. Lee, writing after he had apostatized, noted, for example, that when the doctrine of "sealing" began to be introduced in the early 1840s, Saints were told "that they were married to each other only by their own covenants [until they were sealed under the "new and everlasting covenant"], and that if their marriage relations had not been productive of blessings and peace, and they felt it oppressive to remain together, they were at liberty to make their own choice, as much as if they had not been married." Lee, *Mormonism Unveiled*, 146. This statement is corroborated by the statement of Lucy A. Young, wife of Brigham Young's brother Phineas, who wrote: "With a sad heart I found all the married people at liberty to choose new companions if they so desired." Lucy A. Young to Joseph III, May 22, no year, RLDS Library-Archives, cited in Newell and Avery, *Mormon Enigma*, 172.

Significantly, the only publication advocating polygamy that was put out under official Mormon auspices prior to Joseph Smith's death combined a "biblical" justification for easy divorce for dissatisfied wives with a "biblical" argument for male polygamy. Udney Hay Jacob, *An Extract, from a Manuscript Entitled The Peace Maker, or the Doctrines of the Millennium* . . . (Nauvoo, Ill.: J. Smith, Printer, 1842). See Foster, "A Little-Known Defense of Polygamy."

For evidence that much divorce or desertion and remarriage occurred both during the last years in Nauvoo and during the period at Winter Quarters in 1846–47, see Bachman, "Plural Marriage," 124–36; Richard E. Bennett, *Mormons at the Missouri, 1846–1852: "And Should We Die . . ."* (Norman: Univ. of Oklahoma Press, 1987); and Maureen Ursenbach Beecher, "Women at Winter Quarters," *Sun-*

stone 8 (July–Aug. 1983): 26–39. An extreme example of the extent of such marital shifting is furnished by Heber C. Kimball, who had forty wives, most of them taken in Nauvoo, ten of whom left him, while six others remain unaccounted for in Utah. Stanley B. Kimball, *Heber C. Kimball*; and Foster, " 'Reluctant Polygamists.' "

20. Foster, *Religion and Sexuality*, 143–46. Five revelations—and four other statements now accepted as revelation by the Utah branch of the Mormon church—were given between January 19, 1841, and July 12, 1843. Printed today as sections 124 through 132 of the LDS Doctrine and Covenants, these revelations provided the doctrinal basis for a new worldview that made possible the introduction of plural marriage.

21. O'Dea, *The Mormons*, 61.

22. Bennett, *History of the Saints*. Bennett's statements, as recorded in the affidavits of women whom he allegedly seduced under the pretext of the developing polyamous beliefs, are very similar to those reported in some later Utah testimonies and affidavits. Foster, *Religion and Sexuality*, 316, n. 147.

23. Foster, *Religion and Sexuality*, 169–74.

24. *Journal of Discourses*, 26 vols. (Liverpool, Eng.: F. D. Richards and others, 1854–86), 3:266; speech of July 14, 1855.

25. Orson F. Whitney, *Life of Heber C. Kimball* (Salt Lake City: Kimball Family, 1888), 336.

26. Johnson, *My Life in Review*, 94.

27. Jenson, "Plural Marriage," 233–34; Brodie, *No Man Knows My History*, 335–36, 457–88; Stanley S. Ivins's Miscellaneous Folder in his collection at the Utah State Historical Society, reprinted in Jerald Tanner and Sandra Tanner, *Joseph Smith and Polygamy* (Salt Lake City: Modern Microfilm, n.d.), 41–47. Bachman, "Plural Marriage," provides the most comprehensive Mormon listing and assessment of the affidavits concerning Joseph Smith's plural marriages, while Newell and Avery, *Mormon Enigma*, presents the most convincing narrative analysis of Smith's major polygamous relationships. Also see Stanley B. Kimball, *Heber C. Kimball*; Allen, *Trials of Discipleship*; and Kahlile Mehr, "Women's Response to Plural Marriage," *Dialogue* 18 (Fall 1985): 84–97.

28. The chief source used here for Lucy Walker's experience is a typescript copy of her account made by the Federal Writers' Project in 1940. Also useful is the testimony in the *Complainant's Abstract* of the Temple Lot Case (Lamoni, Iowa: Herald, 1893).

  Some of Joseph Smith's other plural wives for whom extensive documentation exists include Eliza R. Snow, Mary Elizabeth Rollins Lightner, Sarah Ann Whitney, Emily and Eliza Partridge, Helen Mar Kimball, and Melissa Lott. See Bachman, "Plural Marriage," 144–56.

29. Because Lucy Walker's accounts were written many years after the events she describes, her lack of clarity in giving dates is understandable. According to Joseph F. Smith, Jr., *Blood Atonement and the Origin of Plural Marriage*, 55, William Clayton's Private Journal for May 1, 1843, states: "At the Temple. At 10 married

Joseph to Lucy Walker." For an unauthorized typescript version of Clayton's journal published by Jerald and Sandra Tanner, see *Clayton's Secret Writings Uncovered: Extracts from the Diaries of Joseph Smith's Secretary, William Clayton* (Salt Lake City: Modern Microfilm, 1982).

30. Handwritten statement in the form of a letter, without salutation but presumably to her children, dated March 30, 1881, and signed by Helen Mar Kimball Smith Whitney, in LDS Archives, Helen Mar Kimball Whitney Papers. Reproduced here with original capitalization and spelling.

31. Typescript analysis of various characteristics of Joseph Smith's plural wives, as indicated in the Vesta P. Crawford Papers, University of Utah Special Collections. For a more systematic assessment, see Bachman, "Plural Marriage," 104–43.

32. Compare this type of experience to conventional rites of passage as described in Arnold Van Gennep, *The Rites of Passages*, trans. Monika B. Vizedom and Gabrielle L. Caffee (Chicago: Univ. of Chicago Press, 1960), and Turner, *Ritual Process*.

33. Vilate Kimball, Letter dated June 24, 1843, to Heber C. Kimball, in Winslow Whitney Smith Papers, box 5, folder 2, LDS Archives. The letter also was printed in part in Helen Mar Kimball Whitney, "Scenes and Incidents at Nauvoo," *Woman's Exponent* 11 (Sept. 15, 1882): 58.

34. See Quinn, "Mormon Hierarchy," 246–91.

35. *Historical Record* 6 (May 1887): 237.

36. See Foster, *Religion and Sexuality*, 156.

37. Typical of such statements in the Temple Lot Case (complete transcript), 96–97, 99, Mellissa Willes denied that she had any children by Joseph Smith, but she refused to say anything about other children that he may have had because "I told you that I couldn't swear to any body else's children but my own."

38. Even Joseph Smith's acknowledged plural wives went by the names of the men whom they remarried, or, as in the atypical case of Eliza R. Snow, who was remarried to Brigham Young but had no children by him, retained their maiden names. Children born to wives of Joseph Smith who had been sealed to him for eternity bore the names of their natural fathers even though Mormon theology taught that the children would belong to Joseph Smith's family after they died. Thus it may be assumed that if Smith had children by any of his plural wives, they would have borne the surnames of the families that reared them.

39. Conversation with James L. Kimball, Jr., regarding cases of children who appear in early Utah census records but not in those from Nauvoo. Such discrepancies could be owing to errors by the census takers, various forms of "adoption" by Mormons, or factors connected with the early development of polygamy.

40. Mary E. Rollins Lightner, Remarks at Brigham Young University, Apr. 14, 1905, typescript in Brigham Young University Archives, 5.

41. Handwritten statement by Lucy Meserve Smith, dated May 18, 1892, in the George A. Smith Papers, University of Utah Special Collections.

42. Josephine R. Fisher, affidavit, Feb. 24, 1915, LDS Archives.

43. This popular story is examined and critiqued in Maureen Ursenbach Beecher, Linda King Newell, and Valeen Tippetts Avery, "Emma, Eliza, and the Stairs," *BYU Studies* 22 (Winter 1982): 87–96.

44. This statement is fully compatible with other Mormon and apostate accounts.

45. Personal conversation with T. Edgar Lyon, July 19, 1974. Also see T. Edgar Lyon, "The Development of Church Organization and Doctrine, 1839–1846" (Mimeo, LDS institute of Religion talk, March 1, 1968), 9.

46. This letter, dated June 23, 1846, was sent by Brigham Young to his plural wife "Mrs. Hariot [sic] Cook." On the corner of the letter, its destination is indicated as "Snow House." Reproduced in full in Fawn M. Brodie, "A Letter from the Camp of Israel, 1846," *Princeton University Library Chronicle* 33 (Autumn 1971): 67–70.

47. Sarah Melissa Granger affidavit in Jenson, *Historical Record*, 6:232.

48. For early published accounts of these cases, see Bennett, *History of the Saints*, 226–52.

49. Ibid., 236–40. The discussion of the Brotherton case that follows is based on this affidavit.

50. *Utah Genealogical and Historical Magazine* 27 (1936): 108–9.

51. Joseph Lee Robinson, Journal, typescript in Brigham Young University Library Special Collections, 22.

52. Bennett, *History of the Saints*, 243–45; Joseph Smith, Jr., *History of the Church*, 5:136.

53. Bennett, *History of the Saints*, 226–32. For Sarah Pratt's side of this case, see Richard S. Van Wagoner, "Sarah M. Pratt: The Shaping of An Apostate, *Dialogue* 19 (Summer 1986): 69–99.

54. Brodie, *No Man Knows My History*, 304; Richard S. Van Wagoner, "Mormon Polyandry in Nauvoo," *Dialogue* 18 (Fall 1985): 67–83; Van Wagoner, *Mormon Polygamy*, 37–46; and Bachman, "Plural Marriage," 124–36. For my analysis, see *Religion and Sexuality*, 163–66. In a paper presented at the Sunstone Theological Symposium, Aug. 22, 1986, entitled "Pseudo-Polyandry: Explaining Mormon Polygyny's Paradoxical Companion," Andrew F. Ehat criticizes the use of the term *polyandry* to refer to the marital practices in Nauvoo, but he fails to mention my analysis of the "proxy husband" argument as a possible way of explaining these puzzling relationships.

55. Whitney, *Heber C. Kimball*, 333–35.

56. Foster, *Religion and Sexuality*, 161–62.

57. Ibid., 312–13, n. 132, cites the Brigham Young letter.

58. Letter dated Jan. 25, 1892, in Papers of George A. Smith Family, University of Utah Library Special Collections, cited in Bachman, "Plural Marriage," 135.

59. *The Wasp,* Aug. 27, 1842; John McIlwrick, Elizabeth Brotherton, Mary McIlwrick, affidavit, Aug. 27, 1842, in *Affidavits and Certificates Disproving the Statements and Affidavits Contained in John C. Bennett's Letters* (Nauvoo, Ill.: N.p., Aug. 31, 1842), cited in Bachman, "Plural Marriage," 246–48.

60. Stephen Markham affidavit, Aug. 29, 1842, in *Affidavits and Certificates,* quoted in Bachman, "Plural Marriage," 240. Also see Shook, *Mormon Polygamy,* 64–71.

61. Stephen and Zeruiah Goddard affidavit, Aug. 31, 1842, in *Affidavits and Certificates,* quoted in Bachman, "Plural Marriage," 235.

62. Van Wagoner, "Sarah M. Pratt," 79.

63. Joseph Smith, Jr., *History of the Church,* 5:286.

64. Helen Mar Kimball Whitney, *Plural Marriage as Taught by the Prophet Joseph Smith . . .* (Salt Lake City: Juvenile Instructor Office, 1882), 15. Also see the discussion of this issue in Foster, *Religion and Sexuality,* 317–18, n. 159.

65. This study, especially in its full manuscript version, is a true breakthrough for understanding the relationship between Joseph and Emma. With the authors' permission, the following discussion of Emma's reactions draws heavily on *Mormon Enigma,* esp. 64–67, 95–118, 130–56, 170–82, and 296–303, compressing many of the key points of this truly extraordinary analysis. The longer manuscript version of this study is available in the libraries of the University of Utah, Brigham Young University, Utah State University, and the Reorganized Church of Jesus Christ of Latter Day Saints, Independence, Mo. Newell and Avery's work supersedes all previous studies of Emma Hale Smith.

66. Newell and Avery, *Mormon Enigma,* xi.

67. Hiel Lewis, "The Mormon History," *Amboy Journal,* Aug. 6, 1879, cited in Newell and Avery, *Mormon Enigma,* 64.

68. Brodie, *No Man Knows My History,* 119; Hill, *Joseph Smith,* 146.

69. Cowdery Letterbook, esp. the letters for Feb. 24, 1838, and Jan. 21, 1838, copies in the Huntington Library, San Marino, California. Also see Benjamin F. Johnson, Letter to George Gibbs, one of several typescripts with alternative pagination in LDS Church Archives; and the July 1872 letter of William E. McClellan to Joseph Smith III, the original of which is in the RLDS Archives in Independence, Mo.

70. Statement of Mrs. Warner Alexander, LDS Archives, cited in Newell and Avery, *Mormon Enigma,* 65.

71. Brodie, *No Man Knows My History,* 252–53, 301–2, and 459–62.

72. A revelation dated July 17, 1831, that Joseph Smith allegedly gave to seven elders near the boundary, west of Jackson County, Missouri, mentions the possibility of Mormon leaders marrying Indian women. That revelation, in the handwriting of W. W. Phelps in the 1850s and 1860s, goes on to mention that Phelps, who recorded the revelation, asked Joseph Smith privately about three years after it was given "how 'we,' that were mentioned in the revelation could take wives

of the natives as we were all married men. He replied instantly 'In the same manner that Abraham took Hagar and Keturah; that Jacob took Rachel, Bilhah, and Zilpah; by revelation—the saints of the Lord are always directed by revelation." For a full discussion of this document, see Foster, *Religion and Sexuality,* 134–35.

73. Joseph Smith, Jr., *Doctrine and Covenants of the Church of Jesus Christ of Latter-Day Saints . . .* (Kirtland, Ohio: F. G. Williams, 1835), 251.

74. George A. Smith, discourse of Aug. 13, 1871, *JD*, 14:213, cited in Bachman, "Plural Marriage," 176.

75. Joseph Lee Robinson, Journal, 24–27; Foster, *Religion and Sexuality* (1984 ed.), 305, n. 75; Newell and Avery, *Mormon Enigma*, 95–96.

76. Newell and Avery, *Mormon Enigma*, 98.

77. *Deseret Evening News*, Oct. 18, 1879. Italics in original.

78. Orson Pratt, discourse of Oct. 7, 1869, *JD*, 13:194.

79. Newell and Avery, *Mormon Enigma*, 114.

80. See the brilliant analysis, ibid., 106–18, based primarily on the minutes of the Nauvoo Female Relief Society, LDS Archives.

81. Ibid., 134–37; Beecher, Newell, and Avery, "Emma, Eliza, and the Stairs."

82. Emily D. P. Young, "Autobiography of Emily D. P. Young," *Woman's Exponent* 14:37–38; Emily D. P. Young, "Incidents of the Early Life of Emily Dow Partridge." December 1876, Salt Lake City, typescript in University of Utah Archives; Newell and Avery, *Mormon Enigma*, 137–39.

83. Ibid., 139–42.

84. Ibid., 142.

85. Ibid., 143.

86. *Historical Record*, 6:240.

87. Emily Dow Partridge Smith Young, "Testimony That Cannot Be Refuted," *Woman's Exponent*, 12:164–65.

88. Emily D. P. Young, "Early Life of Emily Dow Partridge," 5.

89. Newell and Avery, *Mormon Enigma*, 147. Other plural wives included Eliza R. Snow, Alvira Coles, Sarah Cleveland, and Sarah Ann Whitney.

90. William Clayton's statement of Feb. 16, 1874, is printed in Jensen, *Historical Record*, 6:224–26, and is most readily available in Brigham H. Roberts, *A Comprehensive History of the Church of Jesus Christ of Latter-day Saints: Century I*, 6 vols. (Provo: Brigham Young Univ. Press, 1965), 2:106–7. That statement is corroborated in a Clayton diary entry for that date, quoted in Lyndon W. Cook, *The Revelations of the Prophet Joseph Smith* (Provo: Seventy's Mission Bookstore, 1981), 294. Joseph Smith, Jr., *History of the Church*, 5:509, is the most readily accessible source for the Smith diary reference to spending most of the following day talking with Emma.

For the most detailed assessment of the evidence relating to the dictation and recording of the revelation, including a photocopy of part of the first part of the manuscript version of the revelation in Joseph Kingsbury's hand, see Bachman, "Plural Marriage," 204–16. The other manuscript version of the revelation held in the LDS Archives is in the handwriting of Willard D. Richards. I have carefully examined photocopies of both of these manuscript versions of the revelation in the LDS Archives, and they appear identical in wording to the text of the version as published in the LDS Doctrine and Covenants, Section 132.

91. For evidence of the possible Kirtland origins of much of the revelation, see Danel W. Bachman, "New Light on an Old Hypothesis: The Ohio Origins of the Revelation on Eternal Marriage," *JMH* 5 (1978): 19–32; and Bachman, "Plural Marriage," 47–103.

92. Newell and Avery, *Mormon Enigma*, 153.

93. For example, see the statement of Joseph Lee Robinson in his periodical *The Return* 3 (Feb. 1891): 29.

94. Diary of Joseph Smith for July 15, 1843, cited in Newell and Avery, *Mormon Enigma*, 154.

95. The evidence about how the original revelation may have been destroyed is analyzed, ibid., 153–55.

96. Diary of William Clayton, Aug. 16, 1843.

97. *Mormon Enigma*, 158.

98. Ibid. Also see Ehat, "Joseph Smith's Introduction of Temple Ordinances," 94–96; and David John Buerger, "The Fullness of the Priesthood: The Second Anointing in Latter-day Saint Theology and Practice," *Dialogue* 16 (Spring 1983): 10–44.

99. Newell and Avery, *Mormon Enigma*, 161. Also see D. Michael Quinn, "Latter-day Saint Prayer Circles," *BYU Studies* 19 (Fall 1978): 79–105.

100. Affidavit of Bathsheba W. Smith, Nov. 19, 1903, LDS Archives, cited in Newell and Avery, *Mormon Enigma*, 172.

101. Eudocia Baldwin Marsh, "When the Mormons Dwelt Among Us," *The Bellman*, Apr. 1, 1916, p. 375.

102. Newell and Avery, *Mormon Enigma*, 174–75.

103. Ibid., 175.

104. Ibid., 178.

105. Joseph Smith III, *Joseph Smith III and the Restoration*, ed. Mary Audentia Smith Anderson (Independence, Mo.: Herald, 1952), 74–75.

106. Newell and Avery, *Mormon Enigma*, 179–80.

107. *Nauvoo Expositor*, June 7, 1844. On the martyrdom, see Dallin H. Oaks and Marvin S. Hill, *Carthage Conspiracy: The Trial of the Accused Assassins of Joseph Smith* (Urbana: Univ. of Illinois Press, 1975); and Dean C. Jessee, "Return to Carthage: Writing the History of Joseph Smith's Martyrdom," *JMH* 8 (1981): 3–20.

108. James, *Varieties of Religious Experience*, 24.

109. Ibid., 33

110. Ibid., 37.

111. I am grateful to Dr. Groesbeck for sharing with me some of his unpublished papers on this topic.

112. For discussions of David Hyrum Smith's case, see Valeen Tippetts Avery, "Insanity and the Sweet Singer: A Biography of David Hyrum Smith, 1844–1904" (Ph.D. diss., Northern Arizona Univ., 1984); Valeen Tippetts Avery, "Irreconcilable Differences: David H. Smith's Relationship with the Muse of Mormon History," *JMH* 15 (1989): 3–14; and Newell and Avery, *Mormon Enigma*, 288–95. Of the six other male descendants diagnosed as having mental disorders, one committed suicide at about age forty-five after showing signs of manic-depression; and another, who had been diagnosed as schizophrenic (dementia paradoxia), also committed suicide. Documents in my possession from a living associate of the Smith family. Name withheld by request.

113. Harold I. Kaplan and Benjamin J. Sadock, *Comprehensive Textbook of Psychiatry/IV*, 4th ed. (Baltimore: Williams & Wilkins, 1985), 761.

114. For a discussion of this period of Joseph Smith's life, see the treatments in Joseph Smith, Jr., *History of the Church*, vols. 4 and 5; Roberts, *Comprehensive History*, vol. 2; Brodie, *No Man Knows My History*; Hill, *Joseph Smith*; Flanders, *Nauvoo*; Hansen, *Quest for Empire*; Newell and Avery, *Mormon Enigma*; Foster, *Religion and Sexuality*; and Bachman, "Plural Marriage."

115. Bachman, "Plural Marriage," 179, based on Helen Mar Whitney, "Scenes in Nauvoo," *Woman's Exponent* 10 (Aug. 15, 1881): 42.

116. Although this was the emphasis in the original edition of *No Man Knows My History*, Brodie's "Supplement" to the second, revised and enlarged edition in 1971, 405–25, increasingly emphasizes theories of psychological disorder in trying to explain the Mormon prophet's behavior.

117. The close connection between mania and depression is one reason that the syndrome is classed as a "bipolar disorder" in the psychiatric literature.

118. Mary Rollins Lightner, Remarks at Brigham Young University, April 14, 1905, 5.

119. *Millennial Star* 5 (Nov. 1844): 93. See the letter of George A. Smith to Joseph Smith III, dated Oct. 9, 1969, as reproduced in Raymond T. Bailey, "Emma Hale: Wife of the Prophet Joseph Smith" (M.A. thesis, Brigham Young University, 1952), 84.

120. James, *Varieties of Religious Experience*, 37.

121. The documentary sources relevant to this argument are John Humphrey Noyes's *Confessions*; and G. W. Noyes, ed., *Religious Experience* and *John Humphrey Noyes*. For scholarly analyses bearing on this point, see esp. Barkun, "John Humphrey Noyes and the Rise of Millerism," and "Visionary Experiences of John Humphrey Noyes"; and Thomas, *Man Who Would Be Perfect*. For the most authoritative primary evidence of Ann Lee's extraordinary mood swings, see *Testimonies of Mother Ann Lee*. A scholarly analysis with bearing on this topic is Garrett, *Spirit Possession*.

122. Robert S. Paul, *The Lord Protector: Religion and Politics in the Life of Oliver Cromwell* (Grand Rapids, Mich.: Eerdmans, 1964), convincingly argues that Cromwell displayed definite manic-depressive tendencies.

123. For the best discussion of how Emma dealt with the polygamy issue during her last years of life, see Newell and Avery, *Mormon Enigma*, esp. 296–303. The remainder of this essay draws heavily on their analysis.

124. For the printed statement, see "Last Testimony of Sister Emma," *Saints' Herald* 36 (Oct. 1, 1879): 289–90. Evaluations of that statement are provided in Foster, *Religion and Sexuality*, 307, n. 86; and in Newell and Avery, *Mormon Enigma*, pp. 300–302. On Joseph Smith III's attitudes, see Roger D. Launius, "Methods and Motives: Joseph Smith III's Opposition to Polygamy, 1860–90," *Dialogue* (Winter 1987): 105–20.

125. Newell and Avery, *Mormon Enigma*, 301–2.

126. Lorenzo Snow to Francis M. Lyman, Aug. 10, 1901, "Correspondence to the First Presidency, Jan. 1901–May 1902," Vol. 36, LDS Archives, cited in Newell and Avery, *Mormon Enigma*, 303.

9. JAMES J. STRANG

1. An earlier version of this chapter was published in *Church History* 50 (Summer 1981): 182–192. For a discussion of polygamy practice, or allegations of polygamy practice, among the followers of William Smith, Sidney Rigdon, and James J. Strang, see Lawrence Foster, "Between Two Worlds: The Origins of Shaker Celibacy, Oneida Community Complex Marriage, and Mormon Polygamy" (Ph.D. diss., Univ. of Chicago, 1976), 301–7, 310–14, 340–56; and Foster, *Religion and Sexuality*, 186–95. On polygamy as practiced by Alphaeus Cutler and his followers, see Danny L. Jorgensen, "Antecedents of the Cutlerite Schism of 1853" (paper presented at the annual meeting of the Mormon History Association, June 1990). For Lyman Wight's colony, see Davis Bitton, "Mormons in Texas, The Ill-Fated Lyman Wight Colony," *Arizona and the West* 2 (Spring 1969): 5–26.

2. Klaus J. Hansen, "James J. Strang and the Amateur Historian," *Dialogue* 6 (Spring 1971): 76.

3. Among the sources consulted for this chapter are Milo M. Quaife, *The Kingdom of Saint James: A Narrative of the Mormons* (New Haven: Yale Univ. Press, 1930); Roger Van Noord, *King of Beaver Island: The Life and Assassination of James Jesse Strang* (Urbana: Univ. of Illinois Press, 1988); John Quist, "Polygamy Among James Strang and His Followers," *John Whitmer Historical Association Journal* 9 (1989): 31–48; Milo M. Quaife, "Polygamy at Beaver Island," *Michigan History Magazine* 5 (1921): 333–55; Klaus J. Hansen, "The Making of King Strang: A Reexamination," *Michigan History* 46 (Sept. 1962): 201–19; Dale L. Morgan, "A Bibliography of the Church of Jesus Christ of Latter Day Saints [Strangite]," *Western Humanities Review* 5 (Winter 1950–51): 42–114; and the James J. Strang Papers in the Coe Collection of the Beinecke Library at Yale University, including Dale L. Morgan's "Summary Description of the Strang Manuscripts."

For Strang's writings, see esp. Mark A. Strang, ed., *The Diary of James J. Strang: Deciphered, Transcribed, Introduced and Annotated* (East Lansing: Michigan State Univ. Press, 1961); the Strangite newspapers, the *Voree Herald* and the *Northern Islander*; James J. Strang, *The Diamond: Being the Law of Prophetic Succession, and a Defense of the Calling of James J. Strang as Successor to Joseph Smith* (Voree, Wis.: Gospel Herald, 1848); idem, *The Prophetic Controversy: A Letter from James J. Strang to Mrs. Corey* (Saint James, Mich.: Cooper & Chidester, 1856); and Wingfield Watson, ed., *The Revelations of James J. Strang* (Boyne, Mich., 1885). Also essential is Strang's eloquent *Book of the Law of the Lord* (Saint James, Mich.: Royal Press, 1856).

Van Noord, *King of Beaver Island*, 245, argues that despite Strangite claims of more than two thousand inhabitants of Beaver Island, a more realistic estimate of the population would be somewhat more than five hundred individuals by the mid-1850s.

4. Quaife, *Kingdom of Saint James*, 138.

5. Mark A. Strang, ed., *Diary of James J. Strang*, 9, 17, 19, 22.

6. Ibid., 32. It is interesting that at the time of the South Carolina nullification crisis of 1832, Joseph Smith also had a similar visionary sense that a major civil conflict was impending. Both Strang and Smith were extraordinarily sensitive to the chief currents of their time and interpreted them as having cosmic importance.

7. In his Calendar of the Strang Papers, 24–28, Dale L. Morgan notes a number of factors that suggest a forgery, including the fact that the letter is hand-printed; the signature of the letter, written by the same hand as the text, bears not the slightest resemblance to Joseph Smith's distinctive signature; and the content of the letter itself is extremely uncharacteristic of Joseph Smith's writing style but is strikingly similar to a beautiful passage in Strang's own diary for March 20, 1833. I have carefully examined the original "letter of appointment" and fully concur with Morgan's judgments.

8. Morgan, "Summary Description of the Strang Manuscripts," 17.

9. For a more detailed evaluation of Strang's motivation and career, see Foster, "Between Two Worlds," 340–56.

10. Quaife, *Kingdom of Saint James*, 98, quoting the *Voree Herald*, Aug. 12, 1847.

11. The fullest discussion of polygamy as practiced by Strang and his supporters is Quist, "Polygamy Among James Strang." Also see Quaife's *Kingdom of Saint James*, 96–115, and "Polygamy at Beaver Island."

12. Quist, "Polygamy Among James Strang," questions whether Joseph Smith's commitment to polygamy influenced Strang. As I suggested in "Between Two Worlds," 345–47, John C. Bennett may have provided the link between Smith and Strang.

13. One of the most detailed presentations of Strang's social argument for polygamy is found in his article in the *Northern Islander*, March 2, 1854, the source

for the quotations that follow. The article defends the pro-polygamy arguments of Orson Pratt's Mormon periodical *The Seer*. An extended footnote to the 1856 edition of the *Book of the Law of the Lord*, 318–28, presents a similar social argument for polygamy and also draws on Old Testament sources. The original, unamplified edition of the *Book of the Law of the Lord* (St. James, Mich., [1851]), however, contains no statements directly supporting polygamy.

14. For the practical operation of Strang's polygamy system on Beaver Island, see Quaife, *Kingdom of Saint James*, 106–10; Van Noord, *King of Beaver Island*, 81–83, 107–9, 167–68, 223–26; and Quist, "Polygamy Among James Strang."

15. Quaife, *Kingdom of Saint James*, 107–8; statement of Strang's last surviving wife, Mrs. Sara A. Wing, interviewed by Quaife in the summer of 1920.

16. Ibid., 101, quoting Strang's statement in the *Northern Islander*, Oct. 11, 1855.

17. Myraetta A. Losee to James J. Strang, May 5, 1846, Strang Papers.

18. Calendar of the Strang Papers, introduction to a letter of Louisa S[anger] to James J. Strang, dated July 15, [1846].

19. Louisa S[anger] to James J. Strang, ca. Nov. 1846, Strang Papers.

20. Louisa S[anger] to James J. Strang, Aug. 19, [1849].

21. Burridge, *New Heaven, New Earth*, 162. Burridge's essay "The Prophet," ibid., 153–63, is a incisive introduction to the study of such figures.

22. Extremely suggestive for such a line of argument are Hans Kung, *Infallible?: An Inquiry* (Garden City, N.Y.: Doubleday, 1972); Abraham Joshua Heschel, *The Prophets*, 2 vols. (New York: Harper & Row, 1969); Wallace, "Revitalization Movements"; and Lewis, *Ecstatic Religion*.

23. John C. Bennett played a brief but highly disruptive role under James J. Strang, as he had earlier under Joseph Smith. When Strang began to provide a significant challenge to Brigham Young in 1846, Bennett joined Strang's organization and rose rapidly to second in command, only to fall from favor and be expelled in 1847 because of his opportunism and brazen immorality. Foster, "Between Two Worlds," 345–47.

10. POLYGAMY and the FRONTIER

1. A previous version of this chapter was published in the *Utah Historical Quarterly* 50 (Summer 1982): 268–89. Kimball Young's *Isn't One Wife Enough?* is a classic study focusing on Utah polygamy. Jessie L. Embry's *Mormon Polygamous Families* qualifies and largely supersedes much of Young's earlier path-breaking work. Also see Van Wagoner, *Mormon Polygamy*; and Richard D. Poll et al., eds., *Utah's History* (Provo: Brigham Young Univ. Press, 1978).

2. Among the historically important treatments of Mormon polygamy by apostates, see chap. 8, n. 6; and Fanny Stenhouse, *"Tell It All": The Story of a Life's Experience in Mormonism* (Hartford, Conn.: A. D. Worthington, 1875). Seminovel-

istic attacks on Mormon polygamy are surveyed in Arrington and Haupt, "Intolerable Zion." Mormon defenses of polygamy are presented in Orson Pratt, *The Seer* (Washington, D.C., and Liverpool: S. W. Richards, 1853–54); Helen Mar Kimball Whitney, *Why We Practice Plural Marriage* (Salt Lake City: Juvenile Instructor Office, 1884); and periodical publications such as the *Journal of Discourses,* the *Deseret News,* and the *Woman's Exponent.* Bitton, "Mormon Polygamy," and Scott and Beecher, "Mormon Women," provide bibliographic analyses of recent scholarship on polygamy.

3. See Bitton, *Guide to Mormon Diaries and Autobiographies;* Stanley Snow Ivins's notebooks and transcripts in the Utah State Historical Society Library, Salt Lake City; the Kimball Young Papers in the Huntington Library, San Marino, Calif.; Flake, *Mormon Bibliography;* and Mehr, "Plural Marriage."

4. Interview of Mrs. Hubert Bancroft with Mrs. F. D. Richards, "The Inner Facts of Social Life in Utah," 11, Hubert Howe Bancroft Collection of Mormon Manuscripts, Bancroft Library, Univ. of California at Berkeley. Unless otherwise indicated, most of the evidence about Jane and Franklin Richards comes from this source and from "Reminiscences of Mrs. Franklin D. Richards" and "Narrative of Franklin Dewey Richards," both manuscripts in the Bancroft Collection. Also see Andrew Jenson, *Latter-day Saint Biographical Encyclopedia,* 4 vols. (Salt Lake City: Andrew Jenson History Co., 1901–36), 2:115–21; Quinn, "Mormon Hierarchy," 271; and Connie Duncan Cannon, "Jane Snyder Richards: The Blue-White Diamond," in Vicky Burgess-Olson, ed., *Sister Saints* (Provo: Brigham Young Univ. Press, 1978), 173–98.

5. Cannon, "Jane Snyder Richards," 175–77.

6. In levirate marriage as described in Deuteronomy 25:5–10, it was the duty of the brother of a man who died without leaving any male heir to take the dead man's wife as his own and sire children by her to perpetuate the dead brother's name and family line. In the Mormon system, as practiced in this instance, women who had been sealed to Willard Richards for "time and eternity" were remarried following his death "for time only" to Franklin D. Richards. Children born to that union were considered to belong to the Willard Richards family in the afterlife, according to Mormon marital theory.

7. "Social Life in Utah," 18.

8. Annie Clark Tanner, *Mormon Mother,* 116, 1. Also see Whitney, *Why We Practice Plural Marriage,* 23–24; James E. Hulett, Jr., "The Sociological and Social Psychological Aspects of the Mormon Polygamous Family" (Ph.D. diss., Univ. of Wisconsin, 1939); Vicky Burgess-Olson, "Family Structure and Dynamics in Early Utah Mormon Families, 1847–1885" (Ph.D. diss., Northwestern Univ., 1975), 69–82; and Embry, *Mormon Polygamous Families,* 41–52.

9. "Social Life in Utah," 6.

10. Ivins, "Notes on Mormon Polygamy." Ivins's interpretation is elaborated and qualified in Smith and Kunz, "Polygyny and Fertility." United States census figures for Utah Territory before 1890 show an approximately equal balance between

men and women, always with a slightly higher number of men. For more recent demographic assessments, see Bennion, "Incidence of Mormon Polygamy"; D. Gene Pace, "Wives of Nineteenth-Century Mormon Bishops: A Quantitative Analysis," *Journal of the West* 21 (Apr. 1982): 49–57; Embry, *Mormon Polygamous Families*, 29–40; and Larry M. Logue, *A Sermon in the Desert: Belief and Behavior in Early St. George, Utah* (Urbana: Univ. of Illinois Press, 1988), 129–49.

11. Arrington, *Great Basin Kingdom*, 38. Also see Dean L. May, "The Making of Saints: The Mormon Town as a Setting for the Study of Cultural Change," *UHQ* 45 (1977): 75–92.

12. Young, *Isn't One Wife Enough?* 56–57. Embry, *Mormon Polygamous Families*, also emphasizes the harmonious relationships in many plural marriages. Other recent studies such as Van Wagoner's *Mormon Polygamy*, however, increasingly are stressing the tensions that often existed behind the public appearance of harmony in prominent polygamous families.

13. Both Kimball Young and James E. Hulett, Jr., emphasize the extraordinary range of personal reactions possible to polygamy. For additional evidence, see Quinn, "Mormon Hierarchy," 177–245.

14. Whitney, *Why We Practice Plural Marriage*, 53. Of course, children were stars in the crown of the monogamous mother as well. Although plural families of three or more wives appear to have had fewer children per wife than monogamous wives did on the average, the objective was not producing the largest number of children per wife but rather the largest total number of children in the families of the best men, where, presumably, they would be reared under the most advantageous circumstances. See Ivins, "Notes on Mormon Polygamy," 236–37; Quinn, "Mormon Hierarchy," 246–91; Burgess-Olson, "Early Utah Mormon Families," 100–104; Smith and Kunz, "Polygyny and Fertility," 471; and Embry, *Mormon Polygamous Families*, 151–74.

15. Gail Farr Casterline, " 'In the Toils' or 'Onward for Zion': Images of the Mormon Woman, 1852–1890" (M.A. thesis, Utah State Univ., 1974), 71.

16. Mrs. S. A. Cooks, "Theatrical and Social Affairs in Utah" (Salt Lake City, 1884), 5–6, in Bancroft Collection.

17. For female support networks, see Carroll Smith Rosenberg, "The Female World of Love and Ritual: Relations Between Women in Nineteenth Century America," *Signs: Journal of Women in Culture and Society* 1 (Autumn 1975): 1–29. A Mormon analysis from a similar perspective is Maureen Ursenbach Beecher, "Sisters, Sisters Wives, and Sisters in the Faith: Support Systems Among Nineteenth Century Mormon Women" (paper presented at the Conference on the History of Women, Saint Paul, Minn., Oct. 22, 1977). Also see Burgess-Olson, "Early Utah Mormon Families," 87–90; and Embry, *Mormon Polygamous Families*, 137–49. Ivins, "Notes on Mormon Polygamy," 234, observes that of a sample of 1,642 polygamists, 10 percent married one or more pairs of sisters. In Embry's sample, 25 percent of the families included wives who were sisters. *Mormon Polygamous Families*, 141.

18. Casterline, " 'In the Toils,' " 71.

19. "Social Life in Utah," 13–14.

20. Mrs. Joseph Horne, "Migration and Settlement of the Latter Day Saints" (Salt Lake City, 1884), 34–35, in Bancroft Collection. Mary Isabella Horne was Relief Society president of the Salt Lake Stake and a prominent woman in her own right.

21. Letter of Mrs. Mary J. Tanner, Provo, Utah, 1880, 5–6, in Bancroft Collection. Casterline, " 'In the Toils,' " 103, discusses the argument of Mormon women that polygamy freed them from masculine demands and allowed for a healthy continence. It also made possible continence during pregnancy and lactation, as recommended by nineteenth-century medical theory, and therefore was seen as making for healthier, better-spaced babies.

22. San Francisco Examiner, Nov. 8, 1896, as quoted in Cannon, "Awesome Power of Sex," 76n. For accounts of this remarkable woman, see Jean Bickmore White, "Dr. Martha Hughes Cannon: Doctor, Wife, Legislator, Exile," in Burgess-Olson, ed., Sister Saints, 383–97, and Barbara Hayward, "Teaching the Slavish Virtues: The Public Life of Martha Hughes Cannon," Century 2: A Brigham Young University Student Journal 2 (1978): 1–15.

23. Burgess-Olson, "Early Utah Mormon Families," 135; Casterline, " 'In the Toils,' " 77; and Keith Calvin Terry, "The Contribution of Medical Women During the First Fifty Years in Utah" (M.A. thesis, Brigham Young Univ., 1964).

24. See Jill Mulvay Derr, "Woman's Place in Brigham Young's World," BYU Studies 18 (Spring 1978): 377–95; Shauna Adix, "Education for Women: The Utah Legacy," Boston University Journal of Education 159 (Aug. 1977): 38–49; Karen Neff Preece, "Attitudes Towards Women's Rights and Roles in Utah Territory, 1847–1887" (M.A. thesis, Univ. of Utah, 1982); and Maureen Ursenbach Beecher, Carol Cornwall Madsen, and Jill Mulvay Derr, "The Latter-day Saints and Women's Rights, 1870–1920: A Brief Survey," Task Papers in LDS History, no. 29 (Salt Lake City: Historical Department, Church of Jesus Christ of Latter-day Saints, 1979).

Although Wyoming in 1869 was the first territory to pass a bill granting woman suffrage, women in Utah actually went to the polls in 1870 under a similar bill passed that year and cast their votes before women in Wyoming did. Articles on this topic include Thomas G. Alexander, "An Experiment in Progressive Legislation: The Granting of Woman Suffrage in Utah in 1870," UHQ 38 (Winter 1970): 20–30; Beverly Beeton, "Woman Suffrage in Territorial Utah," UHQ 46 (Spring 1978): 100–120; Jean Bickmore White, "Woman's Place Is the Constitution: The Struggle for Equal Rights in Utah in 1895," UHQ 42 (Fall 1974): 344–69; and T. A. Larson, "Woman Suffrage in Western America," UHQ 38 (1970): 7–19. The campaign by Mormon women in support of polygamy is discussed in Casterline, " 'In the Toils,' " 94–100.

25. General Board of the Relief Society, History of the Relief Society, 1842–1966 (Salt Lake City: General Board of the Relief Society, 1966), 18. Also see Leonard J. Arrington, "The Economic Role of Pioneer Mormon Women," Western Humanities Review 9 (Spring 1955): 145–64; and Maureen Ursenbach Beecher, "Women's Work on the Mormon Frontier," UHQ (Summer 1981): 276–90.

26. Casterline, " 'In the Toils,' " 83–94; Sherilyn Cox Bennion, "The Woman's Exponent: Forty-two Years of Speaking for Women," *UHQ* 44 (1976): 222–39; Carol Cornwall Madsen, " 'Remember the Women of Zion': A Study of the Editorial Content of the *Woman's Exponent*, A Mormon Woman's Journal" (M.A. thesis, Univ. of Utah, 1977); and Sherilyn Cox Bennion, "Enterprising Ladies: Utah's Nineteenth-Century Women Editors," *UHQ* 49 (Summer 1981): 291–304.

27. Casterline, " 'In the Toils,' " 80–81.

28. Hulett, "Mormon Polygamous Family," 308–403; Young, *Isn't One Wife Enough?* 191–225; Burgess-Olson, "Early Utah Mormon Families," 117–19; and Embry, *Mormon Polygamous Families*, 121–36.

29. "Reminiscences of Mrs. F. D. Richards," 47.

30. See especially John W. Gunnison, *The Mormons, or, Latter-day Saints in the Valley of the Great Salt Lake* (Philadelphia: Lippincott, Grambo, 1852), and Richard F. Burton, *City of the Saints, and Across the Rocky Mountains to California* (1861; rpt. New York: Knopf, 1963), with an introduction by Fawn M. Brodie.

31. "Social Life in Utah," 1, and "Reminiscences of Mrs. F. R. Richards," 55.

32. The law is printed in *Acts, Resolutions and Memorials, Passed at the Several Annual Sessions of the Legislative Assembly of the Territory of Utah* (Great Salt Lake City, 1855), 162–64.

33. Brigham Young's statements appear in Historian's Office Journal, 1858–59 Book, (Dec. 15, 1858): 11, and (Dec. 17, 1858): 15, Archives Division, Historical Department, Church of Jesus Christ of Latter-day Saints, Salt Lake City.

34. See *JD* 4: 55–56, and Brigham Young's Office Journal, 1858–63 (Oct. 8, 1861): 300, LDS Archives. A summary of Brigham Young's speech of Oct. 8, 1861, is found in the entry for that date in James Beck's Notebook I, 1859–65, LDS Archives. The original speech, recorded stenographically by G. D. Watt, is in LDS Archives and has been reproduced in an unauthorized transcription in Dennis R. Short, *For WoMen Only: The Lord's Law of Obedience* (Salt Lake City: Dennis R. Short, 1977), 85–90.

35. For a discussion of the pamphlet, its argument, and its significance, see Foster, "A Little-Known Defense of Polygamy."

36. The existence and whereabouts of the divorce records, which have now been microfilmed, are reported in Eugene E. Campbell and Bruce L. Campbell, "Divorce Among Mormon Polygamists: Extent and Explanations," *UHQ* 24 (1978): 4–23. Ibid., 6, bases its figures on Quinn "Mormon Hierarchy," 248–91. Quinn, 154–56, provides information on some of Brigham Young's wives who were not publicly acknowledged and bore him no children. Also see Jeffrey Ogden Johnson, "Determining and Defining 'Wife': The Brigham Young Households," *Dialogue* 20 (Fall 1987): 57–70.

37. Hulett, "Mormon Polygamous Family," 11, 406; Burgess-Olson, "Early Utah Mormon Families," 59–68; and Embry, *Mormon Polygamous Families*, 73–87. Housing patterns of leaders ran the gamut from Brigham Young, second president of the church, who set up most of his wives and children in two large houses, to

John Taylor, third president of the church, who eventually established all his wives in separate houses. For Brigham Young's remarkable household, see Clarissa Young Spencer and Mabel Harmer, *Brigham Young at Home* (Salt Lake City: Deseret News, 1947), esp. 15–80.

38. For bibliographic introductions to the extensive literature on the political campaign against Mormon polygamy, see Allen and Leonard, *Story of the Latter-day Saints*, 681–87, and Bitton "Mormon Polygamy," 106–11. The best book-length treatment of the crusade against polygamy is Larson, *"Americanization" of Utah for Statehood*. A fine scholarly analysis of the complex struggle for statehood is Edward Leo Lyman, *Political Deliverance: The Mormon Quest for Utah Statehood* (Urbana: Univ. of Illinois Press, 1986).

For reactions during the immediate aftermath of the manifesto of 1890, see Kenneth Cannon II, "Beyond the Manifesto: Polygamous Cohabitation Among LDS General Authorities After 1890," *UHQ* 46 (Winter 1978): 24–36; Jan Shipps, "The Principle Revoked: A Closer Look at the Demise of Plural Marriage," *JMH* 11 (1984): 65–78; Quinn, "LDS Church Authority and New Plural Marriages," 9–105; and Martha S. Bradley, "Changed Faces: The Official LDS Position on Polygamy, 1890–1990," *Sunstone* 14 (Feb. 1990): 26–33. Also see Thomas G. Alexander, *Mormonism in Transition: A History of the Latter-day Saints, 1890–1930* (Urbana: Univ. of Illinois Press, 1986); and Foster, "From Frontier Activism to Neo-Victorian Domesticity," 3–21, which has been revised as chapter 11 of this book. For current Mormon polygamy, see Verlan M. LeBaron, *The LeBaron Story* (Lubbock, Tex.: Keels, 1981); Dorothy Allred Solomon, *In My Father's House: An Autobiography* (New York: Franklin Watts, 1984); and Mellissa Merrill (pseud.), *Polygamist's Wife* (Salt Lake City: Olympus, 1975).

39. Beecher, "Women's Work on the Mormon Frontier."

40. Remi Clignet, *Many Wives, Many Powers: Authority and Power in Polygynous Families* (Evanston, Ill.: Northwestern Univ. Press, 1970). Embry, *Mormon Polygamous Families*, 3–16, provides some initial comparisons.

41. Miller, *New England Mind: From Colony to Province*, Foreword.

11. FROM ACTIVISM to DOMESTICITY

1. This chapter is a revision of an article published in *JMH* 6 (1979): 3–21.
5. For a complementary analysis, see Vella Neil Evans, "Mormon Women and the Right to Wage Work," *Dialogue* 23 (Winter 1990): 45–61. On the image and reality of Mormon women's lives, see Leonard J. Arrington's "Blessed Damozels: Women in Mormon History," *Dialogue* 6 (Summer 1971): 21–31, "Persons for All Seasons: Women in Mormon History," *BYU Studies* 20 (Fall 1979): 39–58, and "Pioneer Mormon Women"; Arrington and Haupt, "Intolerable Zion"; Cannon, "Awesome Power of Sex"; and Casterline, " 'In the Toils.' "

For treatments of twentieth-century Mormon women, see Claudia Bushman, ed., *Mormon Sisters*; Bradford, ed., *Mormon Women Speak*; essays in *Dialogue*,

Sunstone, and *Exponent II*; overview analyses in Allen and Leonard, *Story of the Latter-day Saints*, and Arrington and Bitton, *Mormon Experience*; Warenski's *Patriarchs and Politics*; Johnson's *From Housewife to Heretic*; and Gottlieb and Wiley's *America's Saints*. For bibliographic starting points, see Madsen and Whittaker, "History's Sequel," and Scott and Beecher, "Mormon Women."

2. For accounts suggesting some of the main themes of this early period, see O'Dea, *The Mormons*; Arrington, *Great Basin Kingdom*; and the sources in chap. 8, n. 10.

3. Foster, *Religion and Sexuality*, 125–180; Bachman, "Plural Marriage"; and Newell and Avery, *Mormon Enigma*.

4. Johnson, *My Life in Review*, 94. For another early form of kinship linkage, see Gordon Irving, "The Law of Adoption: One Phase of the Mormon Concept of Salvation, 1830–1900," *BYU Studies* 14 (Spring 1974): 291–314.

5. For a discussion of this theology and its implications, see O'Dea, *The Mormons*, 53–63, and chap. 8, above.

6. A fine study of the earliest Mormon attitudes toward women, on which this paragraph is based, is Ileen Ann Waspe, "The Status of Women in the Philosophy of Mormonism from 1830 to 1845" (M.A. thesis, Utah State Univ., 1942). For a comparison with the Utah period, see Karen Preece Neff, "Attitudes Toward Women's Rights and Roles in Utah Territory, 1847–1887" (M.A. thesis, Utah State Univ., 1982).

7. Waspe, "Status of Women," 195–216.

8. Welter's classic analysis, "Cult of True Womanhood," has been qualified and challenged by Daniel Scott Smith, "Family Limitation, Sexual Control, and Domestic Feminism in Victorian America," in Mary W. Hartman and Lois Banner, eds., *Clio's Consciousness Raised: New Perspectives on the History of Women* (New York: Harper & Row, 1974), 119–36; Sklar, *Catharine Beecher*; and Frances B. Cogan, *All-American Girl: The Ideal of Real Womanhood in Mid-Nineteenth-Century America* (Athens: Univ. of Georgia Press, 1989).

9. For an analysis of Brigham Young's attitudes toward women, see Derr, "Woman's Place in Brigham Young's World."

10. Arrington's "Pioneer Mormon Women" suggests that Mormon women exhibited an almost unique degree of versatility during the pioneer period, but Beecher's "Women's Work on the Mormon Frontier" finds no significant differences between the economic roles and versatility of women in Mormon and non-Mormon areas of the American West.

11. White, "Martha Hughes Cannon"; and Hayward, "Martha Hughes Cannon." On Utah women's activities outside the home, see Sherilyn Cox Bennion, "Enterprising Ladies"; Christine Croft Waters, "Pioneering Women Physicians, 1847–1890," in John Sillitoe, ed., *From Cottage to Market: The Professionalization of Women's Sphere* (Salt Lake City: Utah Women's History Association, 1983), 47–61; and Jill Mulvay Derr, "Zion's Schoolmarms," in Claudia Bushman, ed., *Mormon Sisters*, 67–87.

12. Helen Mar Kimball Whitney, *Why We Practice Plural Marriage*; and Casterline, " 'In the Toils,' " 94–100.

13. On women's reactions to the late nineteenth-century antipolygamy persecutions, see Tanner, *A Mormon Mother*; Jensen, *Little Gold Pieces*; Kimberly Jensen James, " 'Between Two Fires': Women on the 'Underground' of Mormon Polygamy," *JMH* 8 (1981): 49–62; and Dorothy Geneve Young Willey, "Childhood Experiences in Mormon Polygamous Families at the Turn of the Century" (M.A. thesis, Utah State Univ., 1983). For polygamy and feminism, see Casterline, " 'In the Toils,' " and Joan Iverson, "Feminist Implications of Mormon Polygamy," *Feminist Studies* 10 (Fall 1984): 505–22.

14. General Board of the Relief Society, *A Centenary of the Relief Society, 1842–1942* (Salt Lake City: General Board of the Relief Society, 1942); and Arrington, "Pioneer Mormon Women." On Eliza R. Snow and her role, consult the many articles by Maureen Ursenbach Beecher, including "The Eliza Enigma: The Life and Legend of Eliza R. Snow," *Dialogue* 11 (Spring 1978): 30–43; and Jill Mulvay Derr, "Eliza R. Snow and the Woman Question," *BYU Studies* 16 (Winter 1976): 250–64. For the leadership role of women, see Maureen Ursenbach Beecher, " 'Leading Sisters': A Female Hierarchy in Nineteenth Century Mormon Society," *JMH* 9 (1982): 26–39.

15. Casterline, " 'In the Toils,' " 83–94; Sherilyn Cox Bennion, "*Woman's Exponent;*" Madsen, " 'Remember the Women of Zion' "; and Carol C. Madsen, "A Bluestocking in Zion: The Literary Life of Emmeline B. Wells," *Dialogue* 16 (Spring 1983): 125–40.

16. Among the articles on this topic, see those cited in chap. 10, n. 25.

17. See coverage in *Woman's Exponent*, and *"Mormon" Women's Protest: An Appeal for Freedom and Equal Rights* ([Salt Lake City:] Deseret News, [1886]).

18. For treatments of the gap between ideal and reality in women's lives, see Carroll Smith Rosenberg, "Hysterical Woman"; Haller and Haller, *Physician and Sexuality in Victorian America*; Anne Firor Scott, *The Southern Lady: From Pedestal to Politics, 1830–1930* (Chicago: Univ. of Chicago Press, 1970); and Patricia Branca, "Image and Reality: The Myth of the Idle Victorian Woman," In Hartman and Banner, eds., *Clio's Consciousness Raised*, 179–91.

19. On the convergence between Mormon and non-Mormon patterns of women's work outside the home, see Howard M. Bahr, "The Declining Distinctiveness of Utah's Working Women," *BYU Studies* 19 (Summer 1979): 525–43. An insensitive criticism of women's work outside the home was printed in the Social Relations Lesson No. 7 for April 1978 in *Relief Society Courses of Study, 1977–78* (Salt Lake City: Church of Jesus Christ of Latter-day Saints, 1977). Lavina Fielding Anderson, "A Voice from the Past: The Benson Instructions for Parents," *Dialogue* 21 (Winter 1988): 103–13, discusses the Benson statement. Rodney Turner, *Woman and the Priesthood* (Salt Lake City: Deseret, 1972), displays highly restrictive attitudes.

20. Edward A. Geary, "The Genteel Tradition in Mormondom: A Speculative Inquiry" (unpublished paper secured through the courtesy of the author). This

paragraph is based on Geary's paper. On frontier attempts to replicate Victorian standards, see Julie Roy Jeffrey, *Frontier Women: The Trans-Mississippi West, 1840–1880* (New York: Hill & Wang, 1979).

21. Women frequently exercise greater power during socially and religiously transitional periods. Lewis, *Ecstatic Religion.*

22. On Mormon acculturation, see Larsen, *"Americanization" of Utah for Statehood;* Allen and Leonard, *Story of the Latter-day Saints;* Leone, *Roots of Modern Mormonism;* Alexander, *Mormonism in Transition;* Gottlieb and Wiley, *America's Saints;* Gordon Shepherd and Gary Shepherd, *A Kingdom Transformed: Themes in the Development of Mormonism* (Salt Lake City: Univ. of Utah Press, 1984); and O'Dea, *The Mormons,* 222–57.

23. For some of the paradoxes of American ethnic history, see Stephen Steinberg, *The Ethnic Myth: Race, Ethnicity, and Class in America* (New York: Atheneum, 1981). For Mormon changes, see Harold T. Christensen and Kenneth L. Cannon, "The Fundamentalist Emphasis at Brigham Young University: 1935–1973," *Journal for the Scientific Study of Religion* 17 (1978): 53–57. On recent theological acculturation, see O. Kendall White, Jr., *Mormon Neo-Orthodoxy: A Crisis Theology* (Salt Lake City: Signature, 1987).

24. For the best analysis of women's changing status in the Mormon church since World War II, see Gottlieb and Wiley, *America's Saints,* 187–213.

25. Karn J. Winkle, "Brigham Young University Challenges Part of the Bias Law," *Chronicle of Higher Education,* Oct. 28, 1975; John Walsh, "Brigham Young University: Challenging the Federal Patron," *Science* 191 (Jan. 16, 1976): 160–63; and Elouise Bell, "The Implications of Feminism for BYU," *BYU Studies* 16 (Summer 1976): 527–40.

26. The statement of the First Presidency against the ERA was printed in the *"Church News"* section of the *Deseret News* on Oct. 30, 1976, as well as in the *Ensign* 6 (Dec. 1976): 79. Boyd K. Packer, "The Equal Rights Amendment," *Ensign* 7 (Mar. 1977): 6–9, makes similar points. Also revealing is Lisa Cronin Wohl, "A Mormon Connection? The Defeat of the ERA in Nevada," *Ms.,* July 1977, 68–85.

27. Dixie Snow Huefner, "Church and Politics at the Utah IWY Conference," *Dialogue* 11 (Spring 1978): 58–75.

28. On more recent Mormon attitudes toward the ERA and women's rights, consult Warenski, *Patriarchs and Politics,* "Epilogue" in the 1980 edition, 278–306; Johnson, *From Housewife to Heretic;* Mary L. Bradford, "The Odyssey of Sonia Johnson," *Dialogue* 14 (Summer 1981): 14–26; Linda Sillitoe, "Church Politics and Sonia Johnson: The Central Conundrum," *Sunstone,* Jan.–Feb. 1980; and Gottlieb and Wiley, *America's Saints,* 187–213.

29. Writers such as Warenski have commented repeatedly on the lack of positive response of grass-roots Mormon women to feminist activism.

30. For Mormon racial policies, see Lester E. Bush and Armand L. Mauss, eds., *Neither White nor Black: Mormon Scholars Confront the Race Issue in a Universal Church* (Midvale, Utah: Signature, 1984); Lester Bush, "Mormonism's Negro Doc-

trine: An Historical Overview," *Dialogue* 18 (Spring 1973): 11–68; Newell G. Bring-hurst, *Saints, Slaves, and Blacks: The Changing Place of Black People Within Mormonism* (Westport, Conn.: Greenwood, 1981); Gottlieb and Wiley, *America's Saints*, 157–86; Mark L. Grover, "Religious Accommodation in the Land of Racial Democracy: Mormon Priesthood and Black Brazilians," *Dialogue* 17 (Autumn 1984): 23–34.

31. Quoted in Warenski, *Patriarchs and Politics*, 287.

32. Johnson, *From Housewife to Heretic*, 104.

33. Gottlieb and Wiley, *America's Saints*, 208.

34. Linda P. Wilcox, "Crying Change in a Permanent World: Contemporary Mormon Women on Motherhood," *Dialogue* 18 (Summer 1985): 116–27; and Francine R. Bennion, "Mormon Women and the Struggle for Definition: What Is the Church?" *Sunstone* 6 (Nov.–Dec. 1981): 17–20. More conventional perspectives are presented in Maren M. Mouritsen, ed., *Woman to Woman: Selected Talks from the BYU Women's Conferences* (Salt Lake City: Deseret, 1986).

35. Phillip R. Kunz, ed., *The Mormon Family* (Provo: Brigham Young Univ. Press, 1977); Howard M. Bahr, "Religious Contrasts in Family Role Definitions and Performance: Utah Mormons, Catholics, Protestants, and Others," *Journal for the Scientific Study of Religion* 20 (1981): 251–60; Howard M. Bahr, S. J. Condie, and K. L. Goodman, *Life in Large Families: Views of Mormon Women* (Washington, D.C.: Univ. Press of America, 1982); Tim B. Heaton, "Four Characteristics of the Mormon Family: Contemporary Research on Chastity, Conjugality, Children, and Chauvinism," *Dialogue* 20 (Summer 1987): 101–14; and Harry P. Bluhm, David C. Spendlove, and Dee Wayne West, "Depression in Mormon Women," *Dialogue* 19 (Summer 1986): 150–55.

36. Examples of the books that the Deseret Book Company has directed at the woman who is temporarily or permanently without a husband are Wayne J. Anderson, *Alone But Not Lonely: Thoughts for the Single, Widowed, or Divorced Woman* (Salt Lake City: Deseret, 1973); and Carol L. Clark and Blythe Darlyn Thatcher, eds., *A Singular Life: Perspectives on Being Single by Sixteen Latter-day Saint Women* (Salt Lake City: Deseret, 1987). For a scholarly analysis, see Lavina Fielding Anderson, "Ministering Angels: Single Women in Mormon Society," *Dialogue* 16 (Autumn 1983): 59–72.

37. Francine Bennion, "LDS Working Mothers," *Sunstone* 2 (Spring 1977): 6–15.

38. See Beecher and Anderson, eds., *Sisters in Spirit*; articles on "Women and Priesthood" in the autumn 1984 issue of *Dialogue*; and Linda King Newell, "The Historical Relationship of Mormon Women and Priesthood," *Dialogue* 18 (Fall 1985): 21–32.

39. The First Presidency statement on birth control, dated April 14, 1969, is quoted in its entirety in David H. Coombs, "The LDS Church: Birth Control and Family Planning" (research paper presented to the Educational Psychology Department at Brigham Young University in partial fulfillment of the Degree of Doctor of

Education, Aug. 1974). Also see Lester E. Bush, Jr., "Birth Control Among the Mormons: Introduction to an Insistent Question," *Dialogue* 10 (Autumn 1976): 12–44.

40. The official church statement on abortion appeared in *Priesthood Bulletin*, June 1972, pp. 2–3, and was quoted in Coombs, "The LDS Church," 23–24.

41. For graphic representation of the relationship between Mormon and non-Mormon birth rates, see Bush, "Birth Control Among the Mormons," 23.

42. One example of such modification was the decision to introduce optional Relief Society lessons to encourage participation of younger, unmarried women who had ceased active participation in the more traditional family-centered programs.

43. Gottlieb and Wiley, *America's Saints*, 213, observe, "The issue of women's roles remains central to the future of the church."

44. Peter Steinfels, "Mormons Drop Rites Opposed by Women," *New York Times*, May 3, 1990, pp. Al, A13. Also see articles in *Arizona Republic*, Apr. 28, 1990; *Salt Lake Tribune*, Apr. 29, 1990; and *Los Angeles Times*, May 5, 1990.

45. Helen Candland Stark, Oral History, Interview by Jessie L. Embry, 1977, in the James Moyle Oral History Program, LDS Archives, 28.

12. A "PERMANENT REVOLUTION"?

1. This conclusion explores and expands upon some of the issues originally considered in Foster, *Religion and Sexuality*, chap. 6.

2. Many earlier studies of these groups have labeled them as utopian and hence, by definition, committed to static perfection. In fact, these groups considered themselves millenarian not utopian. They emphasized a concept of perfection as a continuing process of development, both in theological and social terms.

3. Karl Marx and Friedrich Engels labeled these groups "utopian socialists" in the *Communist Manifesto* (1848) to contrast their approach to the supposedly "scientific socialism" that they were propounding. Also see Friedrich Engels, *Socialism: Utopian and Scientific* (New York: International, 1935).

4. A succinct summary and interpretation of the different varieties of Puritanism is presented in Alan Simpson, *Puritanism in Old and New England* (Chicago: Univ. of Chicago Press, 1955). Kenneth A. Lockridge, *A New England Town, the First Hundred Years: Dedham, Massachusetts, 1636–1736* (New York: Norton, 1970), treats one New England town as utopian in much the same sense that the antebellum millennialists might be described as utopian. A summary of research on New England Puritanism is found in Francis J. Bremer, *The Puritan Experiment* (New York: St. Martin's, 1976).

5. For the religious context of antebellum America, useful starting points are Sidney E. Mead, *The Lively Experiment: The Shaping of Christianity in America* (New York: Harper & Row, 1963); Winthrop S. Hudson, *Religion in America* (New York: Charles Scribner's Sons, 1965); Sydney E. Ahlstrom, *A Religious History of the*

American People (New Haven: Yale Univ. Press, 1972); Bernard A. Weisberger, *They Gathered at the River: The Story of the Great Revivalists and Their Impact on America* (Chicago: Quadrangle, 1966) 6; Hatch, *Democratization of American Christianity;* and Cross, *Burned-over District.*

6. Joseph Smith's 1831 revelation criticizing the Shakers is printed in his *History of the Church,* 1:167–69, and a more detailed attack on women exercising any formal leadership role in the church is presented, ibid., 4:577–81.

7. For an overview of some of these trends, see Carl N. Degler, *At Odds: Women and the Family in America from the Revolution to the Present* (New York: Oxford Univ. Press, 1980).

8. For perspectivews on the shift toward "Victorian" attitudes, see Haller and Haller, *Physician and Sexuality in Victorian America;* Nissenbaum, *Sex, Diet and Debility;* Ronald G. Walters, ed., *Primers for Prudery: Sexual Advice to Victorian America* (Englewood Cliffs, N.J.: Prentice-Hall, 1974); and Altherr, ed., *Procreation or Pleasure.*

9. Noyes, *Male Continence,* 9.

10. Perhaps the best discussion of the Victorian ideal as it relates to groups such as the Shakers, Oneida Perfectionists, and Mormons is Jeffrey, "Family as a Utopian Retreat from the City."

11. This idea, which is also developed in O'Dea, *The Mormons,* was first called to my attention in 1971 by Melvyn Hammarberg in a paper he presented on Mormonism as a "revitalization movement." Also see Lawrence Foster, "Between Heaven and Earth: Mormon Theology of the Family in Comparative Perspective," *Sunstone* 7 (July–Aug. 1982): 6–13; and Lawrence Foster, "A Personal Odyssey: My Encounter with Mormon History," *Dialogue* 16 (Autumn 1983): 87–98.

12. As quoted in Persons, "Christian Communitarianism," 139.

13. George Peter Murdock, *Ethnographic Atlas* (Pittsburgh: Univ. of Pittsburgh Press, 1967). Of Murdock's sample, 193 out of 234 societies held polygamy as the ideal.

14. Somewhat ironically, anti-Mormons provided the Mormon church with inestimable assistance in furthering the group's eventual rapid growth by forcing Mormonism to give up the practice of polygamy at the end of the nineteenth century.

15. Wallace, "Revitalization Movements."

16. Interpretations of the Shakers and feminism by Desroche, *American Shakers,* and Kitch, *Chaste Liberation,* are conceptually intriguing but factually misleading because of their reliance on late nineteenth-century Shaker liberals as if they were representative of normative Shaker belief.

17. White and Taylor, *Shakerism,* 21.

18. Ibid., 405. Crossthwaite, " 'A White and Seamless Robe,' " 188–89, notes that Frederick Evans in his famous "Autobiography of a Shaker" described the Shakers as a community "where 'Woman's Rights' are fully recognized, by first giving her a Mother in Deity to explain and protect them; where equal suffrage for men

and women, and equal participation in the government of an order founded by a woman, was an inevitable necessity." Yet, Crossthwaite points out, as I have here, that Evans, like White and Taylor, ultimately saw women's true rise in status only within the Shaker communities under Shaker discipline.

19. Jean E. Friedman, *The Enclosed Garden: Women and Community in the Evangelical South, 1830–1900* (Chapel Hill: Univ. of North Carolina Press, 1985).

SELECTED BIBLIOGRAPHY

THIS BIBLIOGRAPHY includes a substantial, but necessarily incomplete, selection of sources dealing with (1) American social and religious history, (2) communitarianism, and the three groups analyzed in this study. In addition to citing most of the published sources mentioned in the notes of this book (and all sources cited more than once), this bibliography cites additional primary and secondary published sources on these three groups and their context. In some cases, sources could be listed under several headings so readers may need to check in more than one location to find the citation. Because of the large number of articles and dissertations, only those most directly relevant to this book have been cited. Manuscript sources are cited in the notes but not in the bibliography. Major manuscript repositories that provided background for this study are indicated in the acknowledgments. For an analytical introduction to the major works relevant to this study see the notes for chapter 1. To save space, this bibliography abbreviates *Dialogue: A Journal of Mormon Thought* as *Dialogue,* and *Brigham Young University Studies* as *BYU Studies.*

SOCIAL AND RELIGIOUS HISTORY

AHLSTROM, SIDNEY E. *A Religious History of the American People.* New Haven: Yale Univ. Press, 1972.

ALTHERR, THOMAS L., ed. *Procreation or Pleasure: Sexual Attitudes in American History.* Malabar, Fla.: Krieger, 1983.

ARIÈS, PHILIPPE. *Centuries of Childhood: A Social History of Family Life.* Translated by Robert Baldick. New York: Vintage, 1962.

BACON, MARGARET HOPE. *Mothers of Feminism: The Story of Quaker Women in America.* New York: Harper & Row, 1986.

BARKER-BENFIELD, GRAHAM J. *The Horrors of the Half-Known Life: Male Attitudes Toward Women and Sexuality in Nineteenth-Century America.* New York: Harper & Row, 1976.

———. "The Spermatic Economy: A Nineteenth-Century View of Sexuality." *Feminist Studies* 1 (1972): 45–74.

BARKUN, MICHAEL. *Crucible of the Millennium: The Burned-over District of New York State in the 1840s.* Syracuse, N.Y.: Syracuse Univ. Press, 1986.

———. *Disaster and the Millennium.* New Haven: Yale Univ. Press, 1974.

BARTELL, GILBERT D. *Group Sex: An Eyewitness Report on the American Way of Swinging.* New York: New American Library, 1971.

BEDNAROWSKI, MARY FARRELL. "Outside the Mainstream: Women's Religion and Women Religious Leaders in Nineteenth-Century America." *Journal of the American Academy of Religion* 48 (1980): 207–31.

BELLAH, ROBERT N., AND FREDERICK E. GREENSPAHN, eds. *Uncivil Religion: Interreligious Hostility in America.* New York: Crossroad, 1987.

BELLAH, ROBERT N., et al. *Habits of the Heart: Individualism and Commitment in American Life.* New York: Harper & Row, 1986.

BERG, BARBARA J. *The Remembered Gate: Origins of American Feminism: The Woman and the City, 1800–1860.* Ithaca, N.Y.: Cornell Univ. Press, 1978.

BERTHOFF, ROWLAND. *An Unsettled People: Social Order and Disorder in American History.* New York: Harper & Row, 1971.

BLOCH, RUTH M. "Untangling the Roots of Modern Sex Roles: A Survey of Four Centuries of Change." *Signs: Journal of Women in Culture and Society* 4 (1978): 237–52.

BONOMI, PATRICIA U. *Under the Cope of Heaven: Religion, Society, and Politics in Colonial America.* New York: Oxford Univ. Press, 1986.

BOYER, PAUL, and STEPHEN NISSENBAUM. *Salem Possessed: The Social Origins of Witchcraft.* Cambridge, Mass.: Harvard Univ. Press, 1974.

BRANCA, PATRICIA. "Image and Reality: The Myth of the Idle Victorian Woman." In Mary Hartman and Lois W. Banner, eds., *Clio's Consciousness Raised: New Perspectives on the History of Women*, pp. 179–91. New York: Harper & Row, 1974.

BREMER, FRANCIS J. *The Puritan Experiment.* New York: St. Martin's, 1976.

BROWN, PETER. *The Body and Society: Men, Women, and Sexual Renunciation in Early Christianity.* New York: Columbia Univ. Press, 1988.

BROWN, SLATER. *The Heyday of Spiritualism.* New York: Pocket Books, 1972.

BURRIDGE, KENELM. *New Heaven, New Earth: A Study of Millenarian Activities.* New York: Schocken, 1969.

BUSHMAN, RICHARD L. *From Puritan to Yankee: Character and Social Order in Connecticut, 1690–1775.* Cambridge, Mass.: Harvard Univ. Press, 1967.

CALHOUN, ARTHUR. *A Social History of the American Family.* 3 vols. Cleveland: Arthur Clark, 1918.

CHAFE, WILLIAM H. *Women and Equality: Changing Patterns in American Culture.* New York: Oxford Univ. Press, 1977.

CLARK, CLIFFORD E., JR. "Domestic Architecture as an Index to Social History: The Romantic Revival and the Cult of Domesticity in America, 1840–1870." *Journal of Interdisciplinary History* 7 (1976): 33–56.

CLIGNET, REMI. *Many Wives, Many Powers: Authority and Power in Polygynous Families.* Evanston, Ill.: Northwestern Univ. Press, 1970.

CLINTON, CATHERINE. *The Other Civil War: American Women in the Nineteenth Century.* New York: Hill & Wang, 1984.

COGAN, FRANCES B. *All-American Girl: The Ideal of Real Womanhood in Mid-Nineteenth-Century America.* Athens: Univ. of Georgia Press, 1989.

COHEN, CHARLES LLOYD. *God's Caress: The Psychology of the Puritan Religious Experience.* New York: Oxford Univ. Press, 1986.

COHN, NORMAN. *The Pursuit of the Millennium: Revolutionary Millenarians and Mystical Anarchists of the Middle Ages.* Rev. and enlarged ed. New York: Oxford Univ. Press, 1970.

CONRAD, SUSAN PHINNEY. *Perish the Thought: Intellectual Women in Romantic America, 1830–1860.* New York: Oxford Univ. Press, 1976.

COONTZ, STEPHANIE. *The Social Origins of Private Life: A History of American Families, 1600–1900.* New York: Verso, 1988.

COTT, NANCY F. *The Bonds of Womanhood: "Women's Sphere" in New England, 1790–1835.* New Haven: Yale Univ. Press, 1977.

———. "Passionlessness: An Interpretation of Victorian Sexual Ideology, 1790–1850." *Signs: Journal of Women in Culture and Society* 4 (1978): 219–36.

COTT, NANCY F., and ELIZABETH H. PLECK, eds. *A Heritage of Their Own: Toward a New History of American Women.* New York: Simon & Schuster, 1979.

CROSS, WHITNEY R. *The Burned-over District: The Social and Intellectual History of Enthusiastic Religion in Western New York, 1800–1850.* Ithaca, N.Y.: Cornell Univ. Press, 1950.

DAVIES, JOHN D. *Phrenology: Fad and Science, a Nineteenth Century Crusade.* New Haven: Yale Univ. Press, 1969.

DAVIS, DAVID BRION. *From Homicide to Slavery: Studies in American Culture.* New York: Oxford Univ. Press, 1986.

DAVIS, KENNETH RONALD. *Anabaptism and Asceticism: A Study in Intellectual Origins.* Scottdale, Pa.: Herald, 1974.

DEGLER, CARL. *At Odds: Women and the Family in America from the Revolution to the Present.* New York: Oxford Univ. Press, 1980.

———. "What Ought to Be and What Was: Women's Sexuality in the Nineteenth Century." *American Historical Review* 79 (1979): 1467–90.

D'EMELIO, JOHN, and ESTELLE B. FREEDMAN, *Intimate Matters: A History of Sexuality in America.* New York: Harper & Row, 1989.

DEMOS, JOHN. *Entertaining Satan: Witchcraft and the Culture of Early New England.* New York: Oxford Univ. Press, 1982.

———. *A Little Commonwealth: Family Life in Plymouth Colony.* New York: Oxford Univ. Press, 1970.

———. *Past, Present, and Personal: The Family and the Life Course in American History.* New York: Oxford Univ. Press, 1986.

———. "Underlying Themes in the Witchcraft of Seventeenth-Century New England." *American Historical Review* 75 (1970): 1311–26.

DITZION, SIDNEY. *Marriage, Morals, and Sex in America: A History of Ideas.* New York: Bookman Associates, 1953.

DIXON, WILLIAM HEPWORTH. *New America.* 6th ed. 2 vols. London: Hurst & Blackett, 1867.

DOUGLAS, ANNE. *The Feminization of American Culture.* New York: Knopf, 1977.

DRAKE, FREDERICK C. "Witchcraft in the American Colonies, 1647–62." *American Quarterly* 20 (Winter 1968): 694–725.

DUBLIN, THOMAS. *Women at Work.* New York: Columbia Univ. Press, 1979.

DUBOIS, ELLEN CAROL. *Feminism and Suffrage: The Emergence of an Independent Woman's Movement, 1848–1869.* Ithaca, N.Y.: Cornell Univ. Press, 1980.

ECKENSTEIN, LINA. *Women Under Monasticism: Chapters on Saint Lore and Convent Life Between A.D. 500 and A.D. 1500.* Cambridge: Cambridge Univ. Press, 1986.

ELIADE, MIRCEA. *Shamanism: Archaic Techniques of Ecstasy.* New York: Pantheon, 1970.

ELKINS, STANLEY M. *Slavery: A Problem in American Institutional and Intellectual Life.* 3d ed. rev. Chicago: Univ. of Chicago Press, 1976.

ELSON, RUTH MILLER. *Guardians of Tradition: American Schoolbooks of the Nineteenth Century.* Lincoln: Univ. of Nebraska Press, 1964.

ENGELS, FRIEDRICH. *Origin of the Family, Private Property, and the State: In the Light of the Researches of Lewis H. Morgan.* 1884. Reprint. New York: International Publishers, n.d.

————. *Socialism: Utopian and Scientific.* New York: International, 1935.

EPSTEIN, BARBARA LESLIE. *The Politics of Domesticity: Women, Evangelism, and Temperance in Nineteenth Century America.* Middletown, Conn.: Wesleyan Univ. Press, 1981.

ERIKSON, KAI T. *Wayward Puritans: A Study in the Sociology of Deviance.* New York: Wiley, 1966.

FARRAGHER, JOHN MACK. *Women and Men on the Overland Trail.* New Haven: Yale Univ. Press, 1979.

FELDBERG, MICHAEL. *The Turbulent Era: Riot and Disorder in Jacksonian America.* New York: Oxford Univ. Press, 1980.

FESTINGER, LEON, HENRY W. REICKEN, and STANLEY SCHACHTER. *When Prophecy Fails: A Social and Psychological Study of a Modern Group That Predicted the Destruction of the World.* New York: Harper & Row, 1963.

FILLER, LOUIS. *The Crusade Against Slavery, 1830–1860.* New York: Harper & Row, 1963.

FISCHER, CHRISTINE, ed. *Let Them Speak for Themselves: Women in the American West, 1849–1900.* Hamden, Conn.: Archon, 1977.

FISCHER, DAVID HACKETT. *Albion's Seed: Four British Folkways in America.* New York: Oxford Univ. Press, 1989.

FOUCAULT, MICHEL. *The History of Sexuality.* Volume 1: *An Introduction.* New York: Pantheon, 1978.

FREEDMAN, ESTELLE B. "Sexuality in Nineteenth-Century America: Behavior, Ideology, and Politics." *Reviews in American History* 10 (Dec. 1983): 192–215.

FREUD, SIGMUND. *Civilization and Its Discontents.* Translated by Joan Riviere. Garden City, N.Y.: Doubleday, n.d.

————. *Selected Papers on Hysteria and Other Psychoneuroses.* Translated by A. A. Brill. New York: Journal of Nervous and Mental Diseases, 1912.

FRIEDMAN, JEAN E. *The Enclosed Garden: Women and Community in the Evangelical South, 1830–1900.* Chapel Hill: Univ. of North Carolina Press, 1985.

GAGER, JOHN G. *Kingdom and Community: The Social World of Early Christianity.* Englewood Cliffs, N.J.: Prentice-Hall, 1975.

GAUSTAD, EDWIN S., ed. *The Rise of Adventism: Religion and Society in Mid-Nineteenth-Century America.* New York: Harper & Row, 1974.

GENOVESE, EUGENE D. *Roll, Jordan, Roll: The World the Slaves Made.* New York: Vintage, 1972.

GILLIGAN, CAROL. *In a Different Voice: Psychological Theory and Women's Development.* Cambridge, Mass.: Harvard Univ. Press, 1982.

GLOCK, CHARLES Y., and ROBERT N. BELLAH, eds. *The New Religious Consciousness.* Berkeley: Univ. of California Press, 1976.

GORDON, LINDA. *Woman's Body, Woman's Right: A Social History of Birth Control in America.* New York: Penguin, 1977.

GORDON, MICHAEL, ed. *The American Family in Social-Historical Perspective.* 3d ed. New York: St. Martin's, 1983.

GREVEN, PHILIP J., JR. *Four Generations: Population, Land, and Family in Colonial Andover, Massachusetts.* Ithaca, N.Y.: Cornell Univ. Press, 1970.

GRISWOLD, ROBERT L. "Law, Sex, Cruelty, and Divorce in Victorian America, 1840–1900." *American Quarterly* 38 (Winter 1986): 721–45.

GROSS, ROBERT A. *The Minutemen and Their World.* New York: Hill & Wang, 1976.

GROSSBERG, MICHAEL. *Governing the Hearth: Law and the Family in Nineteenth-Century America.* Chapel Hill: Univ. of North Carolina Press, 1985.

GUARNERI, CARL, and DAVID ALVAREZ, eds. *Religion and Society in the American West: Historical Essays.* Lanham, Md.: Univ. Press of America, 1987.

HADFIELD, J. A. *Dreams and Nightmares.* Baltimore: Penguin, 1954.

HALLER, JOHN S., and ROBIN M. HALLER. *The Physician and Sexuality in Victorian America.* Urbana: Univ. of Illinois Press, 1974.

HALTTUNEN, KAREN. *Confidence Men and Painted Women: A Study of Middle Class Culture in America, 1830–1870.* New Haven: Yale Univ. Press, 1982.

HANSEN, CHADWICK. *Witchcraft at Salem.* New York: New American Library, 1969.

HARE, E. H. "Masturbatory Insanity: The History of an Idea." *Journal of Mental Science* 108 (Jan. 1962): 1–21.

HARTMAN, MARY, and LOIS W. BANNER, eds. *Clio's Consciousness Raised: New Perspectives on the History of Women.* New York: Harper & Row, 1974.

HATCH, NATHAN O. *The Democratization of American Christianity.* New Haven: Yale Univ. Press, 1989.

HERSH, BLANCHE GLASSMAN. *The Slavery of Sex: Female Abolitionists in America.* Urbana: Univ. of Illinois Press, 1978.

HIGHAM, JOHN. *From Boundlessness to Consolidation: The Transformation of American Culture, 1848–1860.* Ann Arbor: William L. Clements Library, 1969.

HIMES, NORMAN. *Medical History of Contraception.* 1936. Reprint. New York: Schocken, 1970.

HINER, N. RAY, and JOSEPH M. HAWES, eds. *Growing Up in America: Children in Historical Perspective.* Urbana: Univ. of Illinois Press, 1985.

HOWARD, GEORGE ELLIOTT. *A History of Matrimonial Institutions, Chiefly in England and the United States.* 3 vols. Chicago: Univ. of Chicago Press, 1904.

HUDSON, WINTHROP S. *Religion in America.* New York: Charles Scribner's Sons, 1965.

JAMES, WILLIAM. *The Varieties of Religious Experience.* 1902. Reprint. New York: New American Library, 1958.

JARVIE, I. C. *The Revolution in Anthropology.* Chicago: Regnery, 1969.

JEFFREY, JULIE ROY. *Frontier Women: The Trans-Mississippi West, 1840–1880.* New York: Hill & Wang, 1979.

JEFFREY, KIRK. "The Family as a Utopian Retreat from the City: The Nineteenth Century Contribution." In Sallie TeSelle, ed., *The Family, Communes, and Utopian Societies,* pp. 21–41. New York: Harper & Row, 1972.

JENSEN, JOAN M. *Loosening the Bonds: Mid-Atlantic Farm Women, 1750–1850.* New Haven: Yale Univ. Press, 1986.

JOHNSON, CHARLES A. *The Frontier Camp Meeting: Religion's Harvest Time.* Dallas: Southern Methodist Univ. Press, 1955.

JOHNSON, CURTIS D. *Islands of Holiness: Rural Religion in Upstate New York, 1790–1860.* Ithaca, N.Y.: Cornell Univ. Press, 1989.

JOHNSON, PAUL E. *A Shopkeeper's Millennium: Society and Revivals in Rochester, New York, 1815–1837.* New York: Hill & Wang, 1978.

JUDAH, J. STILLSON. *The History and Philosophy of the Metaphysical Movements in America.* Philadelphia: Westminster, 1967.

KARLSEN, CAROL F. *The Devil in the Shape of a Woman: Witchcraft in Colonial New England.* New York: Norton, 1987.

KERBER, LINDA K. *Women of the Republic: Intellect and Ideology in Revolutionary America.* Chapel Hill: Univ. of North Carolina Press, 1980.

KERR, HOWARD, and CHARLES L. CROW, eds. *The Occult in America: New Historical Perspectives.* Urbana: Univ. of Illinois Press, 1983.

KETT, JOSEPH F. *Rites of Passage: Adolescence in America, 1790 to the Present.* New York: Basic Books, 1977.

KINSEY, ALFRED C., WARDELL POMEROY, and CLYDE MARTIN. *Sexual Behavior in the American Male.* Philadelphia: Saunders, 1948.

KINSEY, ALFRED C., WARDELL POMEROY, CLYDE MARTIN, and P. H. GEBBHARD. *Sexual Behavior in the American Female.* Philadelphia: Saunders, 1953.

KOEHLER, LYLE. *A Search for Power: The "Weaker Sex" in Seventeenth-Century New England.* Urbana: Univ. of Illinois Press, 1970.

KUHN, THOMAS S. *The Structure of Scientific Revolutions.* 2d ed., enlarged. Chicago: Univ. of Chicago Press, 1970.

LA BARRE, WESTON. "Materials for a History of Studies of Crisis Cults: A Bibliographic Essay." *Current Anthropology* 12 (Feb. 1971): 3–44.

LAND, GARY, ed. *Adventism in America: A History.* Grand Rapids, Mich.: Eerdmans, 1986.

LANTERNARI, VITTORIO. *The Religions of the Oppressed: A Study of Modern Messianic Cults.* Translated by Lisa Sergio. New York: New American Library, 1965.

LEA, HENRY CHARLES. *The History of Sacerdotal Celibacy in the Christian Church.* New York: Russell & Russell, 1957.

LERNER, GERDA. *The Majority Finds Its Past: Placing Women in History.* New York: Oxford Univ. Press, 1979.

LEVACK, BRIAN P. *The Witch-Hunt in Early Modern Europe.* London: Longman, 1989.

LEVY, BARRY. *Quakers and the American Family: British Settlement in the Delaware Valley.* New York: Oxford Univ. Press, 1988.

LEWIS, I. M. *Ecstatic Religion: An Anthropological Study of Spirit Possession and Shamanism.* Baltimore: Penguin, 1971.

LOCKRIDGE, KENNETH A. *A New England Town, the First Hundred Years: Deadham, Massachusetts, 1636–1736.* New York: Norton, 1970.

LUDLUM, DAVID. *Social Ferment in Vermont, 1791–1850.* New York: Columbia Univ. Press, 1939.

LYSTRA, KAREN. *Searching the Heart: Women, Men, and Romantic Love in Nineteenth-Century America, 1830–1900.* New York: Oxford Univ. Press, 1989.

MACFARLANE, A. D. J. *The Origins of English Individualism: The Family, Property, and Social Transition.* Oxford: Blackwell, 1978.

———. *Witchcraft in Tudor and Stuart England: A Regional and Comparative Study.* London: Routledge & Kegan Paul, 1970.

McGLOUGHLIN, WILLIAM G. *Modern Revivalism: Charles Grandison Finney to Billy Graham.* New York: Ronald, 1959.

———. *Revivals, Awakenings, and Reform: An Essay on Religion and Social Change in America, 1607–1977.* Chicago: Univ. of Chicago Press, 1978.

McGREGOR, J. F., and BARRY REAY, eds. *Radical Religion in the English Revolution.* New York: Oxford Univ. Press, 1984.

MARTY, MARTIN E. *Pilgrims in Their Own Land: 500 Years of Religion in America.* New York: Penguin, 1984.

MARX, LEO. *The Machine in the Garden: Technology and the Pastoral Ideal in America.* New York: Oxford Univ. Press, 1968.

MATHEWS, LOIS KIMBALL. *The Expansion of New England: The Spread of New England Settlement and Institutions to the Mississippi River, 1620–1865.* Boston: Houghton Mifflin, 1909.

MATTHEWS, GLENNA. *"Just a Housewife": The Rise and Fall of Domesticity in America.* New York: Oxford Univ. Press, 1987.

MEAD, SIDNEY E. *The Lively Experiment: The Shaping of Christianity in America.* New York: Harper & Row, 1963.

MECHLING, JAY. "Advice to Historians on Advice to Mothers." *Journal of Social History* 9 (1975): 44–63.

MELDER, KEITH. "Women's High Calling: The Teaching Profession in America, 1830–1860." *American Studies* 13, no. 2 (1972): 19–32.

MELTON, J. GORDON. "Spiritualization and Reaffirmation: What Really Happens When Prophecy Fails?" *American Studies* 26 (Fall 1985): 17–29.

MELTON, J. GORDON, and ROBERT L. MOORE. *The Cult Experience: Responding to the New Religious Pluralism.* New York: Pilgrim, 1982.

MESICK, JANE L. *The English Traveler in America, 1785–1835.* New York: Columbia Univ. Press, 1922.

MEYERS, MARVIN. *The Jacksonian Persuasion: Politics and Belief.* Stanford: Stanford Univ. Press, 1960.

MILLER, PERRY. *Errand into the Wilderness.* New York: Harper & Row, 1964.

———. *The New England Mind: From Colony to Province.* Boston: Beacon, 1961.

MINTZ, STEVEN, and SUSAN KELLOGG. *Domestic Revolutions: A Social History of American Family Life.* New York: Free Press, 1988.

MOHR, JAMES C. *Abortion in America: The Origins and Evolution of National Policy.* New York: Oxford Univ. Press, 1978.

MOORE, R. LAURENCE. *Religious Outsiders and the Making of Americans.* New York: Oxford Univ. Press, 1986.

MORANTZ-SANCHEZ, REGINA MARKELL. *Sympathy and Science: Women Physicians and American Medicine.* New York: Oxford Univ. Press, 1985.

MORGAN, EDMUND S. *The Puritan Family: Religion and Domestic Relations in Seventeenth Century New England.* New ed., rev. and enlarged. New York: Harper & Row, 1966.

MYERS, SANDRA L. *Westering Women and the Frontier Experience, 1800–1915.* Albuquerque: Univ. of New Mexico Press, 1982.

NISSENBAUM, STEPHEN. *Sex, Diet, and Debility in Jacksonian America: Sylvester Graham and Health Reform.* Westport, Conn.: Greenwood, 1980.

NORTON, MARY BETH. *Liberty's Daughters: The Revolutionary Experience of American Women, 1750–1800.* Boston: Little, Brown, 1980.

NUMBERS, RONALD L., and JONATHAN M. BUTLER, eds. *The Disappointed: Millerism and Millenarianism in the Nineteenth Century.* Bloomington: Indiana Univ. Press, 1987.

OAKLEY, ANN. *Woman's Work: The Housewife, Past and Present.* New York: Vintage, 1976.

PAGELS, ELAINE. *Adam and Eve and the Serpent.* New York: Random House, 1988.

PARKER, GAIL, ed. *The Oven Birds: American Women on Womanhood, 1820–1920.* New York: Anchor, 1972.

PESSEN, EDWARD. "The Egalitarian Myth and American Social Reality: Wealth, Mobility, and Equality in the Era of the Common Man." *American Historical Review* 76 (1971): 989–1034.

———. *Jacksonian America: Society, Personality, and Politics.* Homewood, Ill.: Dorsey, 1969.

POTASH, P. JEFFREY. *Vermont's Burned-over District: Patterns of Community Development and Religious Activity, 1761–1850.* New York: Carlson, 1991.

PRUDE, JONATHAN. *The Coming of the Industrial Order: Town and Factory Life in Rural Massachusetts, 1810–1860.* Cambridge: Cambridge Univ. Press, 1983.

PUNSHON, JOHN. *Portrait in Grey: A Short History of the Quakers.* London: Quaker Home Service, 1984.

RABB, THEODORE K., and ROBERT I. ROTBERG, eds. *The Family in History: Interdisciplinary Essays.* New York: Harper & Row, 1974.

RADIN, PAUL. *The Trickster: A Study in American Indian Mythology.* New York: Schocken, 1972.

REAY, BARRY. *The Quakers and the English Revolution.* New York: St. Martin's, 1985.

RICHARDS, LEONARD. *"Gentlemen of Property and Standing": Anti-Abolitionist Mobs in Jacksonian America.* New York: Oxford Univ. Press, 1970.

RILEY, GLENDA. *Inventing the American Woman: A Perspective on Women's History.* Arlington Heights, Ill.: Davidson, 1987.

ROSENBERG, CHARLES E., ed. *The Family in History.* Philadelphia: Univ. of Pennsylvania Press, 1973.

———. "Sexuality, Class and Role in 19th Century America." *American Quarterly* 25 (May 1973): 131–54.

ROSENBERG, ROSALIND. *Beyond Separate Spheres: Intellectual Roots of Modern Feminism.* New Haven: Yale Univ. Press, 1982.

ROSSI, ALICE, ed. *The Feminist Papers: From Adams to De Beauvoir.* New York: Bantam, 1973.

ROTHMAN, DAVID J. *The Discovery of the Asylum: Social Order and Disorder in the New Republic.* Boston: Little, Brown, 1971.

ROTHMAN, ELLEN K. *Hands and Hearts: A History of Courtship in America.* Cambridge, Mass.: Harvard Univ. Press, 1987.

ROURKE, CONSTANCE. *Trumpets of Jubilee.* New York: Harcourt, Brace & World, 1963.

RUETHER, ROSEMARY RADFORD, and ROSEMARY SKINNER KELLER, eds. *Women and Religion in America: The Nineteenth Century.* New York: Harper & Row, 1981.

RYAN, MARY P. *Cradle of the Middle Class: The Family in Oneida County, New York, 1790–1865.* Cambridge: Cambridge Univ. Press, 1981.

SANDEEN, ERNEST R. *The Roots of Fundamentalism: British and American Millenarism, 1800–1930.* Chicago: Univ. of Chicago Press, 1961.

SARGANT, WILLIAM. *Battle for the Mind: A Physiology of Conversion and Brainwashing.* Garden City, N.Y.: Doubleday, 1957.

———. *The Mind Possessed: A Physiology of Possession, Mysticism, and Faith Healing.* New York: Penguin, 1975.

SCHWARTZ, GARY. *Sect Ideologies and Social Status.* Chicago: Univ. of Chicago Press, 1970.

Scott, Anne Firor. *The Southern Lady: From Pedestal to Politics, 1830–1930*. Chicago: Univ. of Chicago Press, 1970.

Scott, Donald M., and Bernard Wishy, eds. *America's Families: A Documentary History*. New York: Harper & Row, 1982.

Sears, Hal D. *The Sex Radicals: Free Love in High Victorian America*. Lawrence: Regents Press of Kansas, 1977.

Simpson, Alan. *Puritanism in Old and New England*. Chicago: Univ. of Chicago Press, 1955.

Sinclair, Andrew. *The Emancipation of the American Woman*. New York: Harper & Row, 1966.

Sklar, Kathryn Kish. *Catharine Beecher: A Study in American Domesticity*. New Haven: Yale Univ. Press, 1973.

Smith, Daniel Scott. "Family Limitation, Sexual Control, and Domestic Feminism in Victorian America." In Mary Hartman and Lois W. Banner, eds., *Clio's Consciousness Raised: New Perspectives on the History of Women*, pp. 119–36. New York: Harper & Row, 1974.

Smith, Daniel Scott, and Michael S. Hindus. "Premarital Pregnancy in America, 1640–1971: An Overview and Interpretation." *Journal of Interdisciplinary History* 5 (1975): 537–70.

Smith-Rosenberg, Carroll. *Disorderly Conduct: Visions of Gender in Victorian America*. New York: Oxford Univ. Press, 1986.

———. "The Female World of Love and Ritual: Relations Between Women in Nineteenth Century America." *Signs: Journal of Women in Culture and Society* 1 (Autumn 1975): 1–29.

———. "The Hysterical Woman: Sex Roles and Role Conflict in 19th-Century America." *Social Research* 39 (Winter 1972): 652–78.

Steinberg, Stephen. *The Ethnic Myth: Race, Ethnicity, and Class in America*. New York: Atheneum, 1981.

Taylor, William R. *Cavalier and Yankee: The Old South and the American National Character*. New York: Braziller, 1961.

Thomas, John L. "Romantic Reform in America, 1815–1865." *American Quarterly* 17 (Winter 1965): 657–81.

Thomas, Keith. *Religion and the Decline of Magic: Studies in Popular Belief in Sixteenth and Seventeenth Century England*. New York: Charles Scribner's Sons, 1971.

Thrupp, Sylvia L., ed. *Millennial Dreams in Action: Studies of Revolutionary Religious Movements*. New York: Schocken, 1970.

Toqueville, Alexis de. *Democracy in America.* 2 vols. Translated by George Lawrence. Edited by J. P. Mayer. Garden City, N.Y.: Doubleday, 1969.

Turner, Victor W. *The Ritual Process: Structure and Anti-Structure.* Chicago: Aldine, 1969.

Tuveson, Ernest Lee. *Redeemer Nation: The Idea of America's Millennial Role.* Chicago: Univ. of Chicago Press, 1968.

Tyler, Alice Felt. *Freedom's Ferment: Phases of American Social History from the Colonial Period to the Outbreak of the Civil War.* New York: Harper & Row, 1962.

Ulrich, Laurel Thatcher. *Good Wives: Image and Reality in the Lives of Women in Northern New England, 1650–1750.* New York: Oxford Univ. Press, 1983.

Van Gennep, Arnold. *The Rites of Passage.* Translated by Monika B. Vizedom and Gabrielle L. Caffee. Chicago: Univ. of Chicago Press, 1960.

Vann, Richard T. *The Social Development of English Quakerism, 1655–1755.* Cambridge, Mass.: Harvard Univ. Press, 1969.

Veith, Ilza. *Hysteria: The History of a Disease.* Chicago: Univ. of Chicago Press, 1965.

Vinovskis, Maris A. *Fertility in Massachusetts from the Revolution to the Civil War.* New York: Academic Press, 1981.

Wallace, Anthony F. C. *The Death and Rebirth of the Seneca.* New York: Vintage, 1972.

———. "Revitalization Movements." *American Anthropologist* 58 (Apr. 1956): 264–81.

———. *Rockdale: The Growth of an American Village in the Early Industrial Revolution.* New York: Norton, 1978.

Walters, Ronald G. *American Reformers, 1815–1860.* New York: Hill & Wang, 1978.

———. *The Antislavery Appeal: American Abolitionism After 1830.* New York: Norton, 1978.

———, ed. *Primers for Prudery: Sexual Advice for Victorian America.* Englewood Cliffs, N.J.: Prentice-Hall, 1974.

Warner, Marina. *Alone of All Her Sex: The Myth and Cult of the Virgin Mary.* New York: Pocket Books, 1976.

Weisman, Richard. *Witchcraft, Magic, and Religion in 17th-Century Massachusetts.* Amherst: Univ. of Massachusetts Press, 1984.

WELTER, BARBARA. "The Cult of True Womanhood, 1820–1860." *American Quarterly* 18 (Summer 1966): 151–74.

———. *Dimity Convictions: The American Woman in the Nineteenth Century*. Athens: Ohio State Univ. Press, 1976.

———. "The Feminization of American Religion, 1800–1860." In William L. O'Neill, ed., *Insights and Parallels: Problems and Issues in American History*. Minneapolis: Burgess, 1973.

WOLOCH, NANCY. *Women and the American Experience*. New York: Knopf, 1984.

WORSLEY, PETER. *The Trumpet Shall Sound: A Study of "Cargo" Cults in Melanesia*. 2d enlarged ed. New York: Schocken, 1968.

ZARETSKY, IRVING I., and MARK P. LEONE, eds. *Religious Movements in Contemporary America*. Princeton: Princeton Univ. Press, 1974.

ZIKMUND, BARBARA BROWN. "The Feminist Thrust of Sectarian Christianity." In Rosemary Radford Ruether and Eleanor McLaughlin, eds., *Women of Spirit: Female Leadership in the Jewish and Christian Traditions*, pp. 206–24. New York: Simon & Schuster, 1979.

ZUCKERMAN, MICHAEL. *Peaceable Kingdoms: New England Towns in the Eighteenth Century*. New York: Knopf, 1970.

COMMUNITARIAN STUDIES

ALBERTSON, RALPH. "Survey of Mutualistic Communities in America." *Iowa Journal of History and Politics* 34 (Oct. 1936): 375–444.

ALDELFER, E. G. *The Ephrata Commune: An Early American Counterculture*. Pittsburgh: Univ. of Pittsburgh Press, 1985.

ANDELSON, JONATHAN G. "The Gift to Be Single: Celibacy and Religious Enthusiasm in the Community of True Inspiration." *Communal Societies* 5 (1985): 1–32.

ARMYTAGE, W. H. G. *Heavens Below: Utopian Experiments in England, 1560–1960*. Toronto: Univ. of Toronto Press, 1961.

ARNDT, KARL J. R. *George Rapp's Harmony Society, 1785–1847*. Rev. ed. Rutherford, N.J.: Fairleigh Dickinson Univ. Press, 1972.

BARKUN, MICHAEL J. "Communal Societies as Cyclical Phenomena." *Communal Societies* 4 (1984): 35–48.

BARTHEL, DIANE L. *Amana: From Pietist Sect to American Community*. Lincoln: Univ. of Nebraska Press, 1984.

BERGER, BENNETT M. *The Survival of a Counterculture: Ideological Work and Everyday Life Among Rural Communards.* Berkeley: Univ. of California Press, 1981.

BESTOR, ARTHUR E. *Backwoods Utopias: The Sectarian Origins and Owenite Phase of Communitarian Socialism in America, 1663–1829.* 2d enlarged ed. Philadelphia: Univ. of Pennsylvania Press, 1970.

———. "Patent-Office Models of the Good Society: Some Relationships Between Social Reform and Westward Expansion." *American Historical Review* 43 (1953): 505–26.

BOROWSKI, KAROL. *Attempting an Alternative Society: A Study of the Renaissance Movement in the U.S.A.* Norwood, Pa.: Norwood, 1984.

CALVERTON, VICTOR F. *Where Angels Dared to Tread: Socialist and Communist Utopian Colonies in the United States.* New York: Bobbs Merrill, 1941.

CARPENTER, DELBURN. "The Radical Pietists: Celibate Communal Societies Established in the United States Before 1820." Ph.D. diss., Univ. of Northern Iowa, 1972.

CLARK, ELMER T. *Small Sects in America.* Nashville: Abingdon, 1949.

CONKIN, PAUL K. *Two Paths to Utopia: The Hutterites and the Llano Community.* Lincoln: Univ. of Nebraska Press, 1964.

CUMMINGS, MICHAEL S. "Democratic Procedure and Community in Utopia." *Alternative Futures: The Journal of Utopian Studies* 3 (Fall 1980): 35–57.

DARE, PHILIP N. *American Communes to 1860: A Bibliography.* New York: Garland, 1990.

DIXON, WILLIAM HEPWORTH. *Spiritual Wives.* 2 vols. Philadelphia: Lippincott, 1868.

DURNBAUGH, DONALD F. "Work and Hope: The Spirituality of Radical Pietist Communitarians." *Church History* 39 (Mar. 1970): 72–90.

EGBERT, DONALD DREW, and STOW PERSONS, eds. *Socialism and American Life.* 2 vols. Princeton: Princeton Univ. Press, 1952. The second volume is a descriptive and critical bibliography by T. D. SEYMOUR BASSETT.

ELMEN, PAUL. *Wheat Flour Messiah: Eric Jansson of Bishop Hill.* Carbondale: Southern Illinois Univ. Press, 1976.

FAIRFIELD, RICHARD. *Communes USA: A Personal Tour.* Baltimore: Penguin, 1972.

FELLMAN, MICHAEL. *The Unbounded Frame: Freedom and Community in Nineteenth-Century American Utopianism.* Westport, Conn.: Greenwood, 1973.

FOGARTY, ROBERT S. *All Things New: American Communes and Utopian Movements, 1860–1914.* Chicago: Univ. of Chicago Press, 1990.

———. "Communal History in America." *Choice* 10 (June 1973): 578–90.

———. *Dictionary of American Communal and Utopian History.* Westport, Conn.: Greenwood, 1980.

———. *The Righteous Remnant: The House of David.* Kent, Ohio: Kent State Univ. Press, 1981.

FOSTER, LAWRENCE. *Religion and Sexuality: Three American Communal Experiments of the Nineteenth Century.* New York: Oxford Univ. Press, 1981. Reprinted in a paperbound edition, with identical pagination, as *Religion and Sexuality: The Shakers, the Mormons, and the Oneida Community.* Urbana: Univ. of Illinois Press, 1984.

FRENCH, DAVID, and ELENA FRENCH. *Working Communally: Patterns and Possibilities.* New York: Russell Sage Foundation, 1975.

GARDNER, HUGH. *The Children of Prosperity: Thirteen Modern American Communes.* New York: St. Martin's, 1978.

GOLLIN, GILLIAN LINDT. *Moravians in Two Worlds: A Study of Changing Communities.* New York: Columbia Univ. Press, 1967.

GUARNERI, CARL J. "Importing Fourierism to America." *Journal of the History of Ideas* 43 (Oct.–Dec. 1982): 581–94.

———. *The Utopian Alternative: Fourierism in Nineteenth-Century America.* Ithaca, N.Y.: Cornell Univ. Press, 1991.

———. "Who Were the Utopian Socialists? Patterns of Membership in American Fourierist Communities." *Communal Societies* 5 (1985): 65–81.

GUTEK, GERALD, and PATRICIA GUTEK. *Experiencing America's Past: A Travel Guide to Museum Villages.* New York: Wiley, 1986.

HARRISON, JOHN F. C. *Quest for the New Moral World: Robert Owen and the Owenites in Britain and America.* New York: Charles Scribner's Sons, 1969.

———. *The Second Coming: Popular Millenarianism, 1780–1850.* New Brunswick, N.J.: Rutgers Univ. Press, 1979.

HAYDEN, DOLORES. *Seven American Utopias: The Architecture of Communitarian Socialism, 1790–1975.* Cambridge, Mass.: MIT Press, 1976.

HINDS, WILLIAM ALFRED. *American Communities and Co-operative Colonies.* Chicago: Kerr, 1908.

HINE, ROBERT V. *California's Utopian Colonies.* New Haven: Yale Univ. Press, 1966.

HOLLOWAY, MARK. *Heavens on Earth: Utopian Communities in America.* 2d ed. New York: Dover, 1966.

HOSTETLER, JOHN A. *Amish Society.* 3d ed., rev. Baltimore: Johns Hopkins Univ. Press, 1981.

———. *Hutterite Society.* Baltimore: Johns Hopkins Univ. Press, 1974.

JACKSON, DAVE, and NETA JACKSON. *Living Together in a World Falling Apart.* Carol Stream, Ill.: Creation House, 1974.

JEROME, JUDSON. *Families of Eden: Communes and the New Anarchism.* New York: Seabury, 1974.

JOHNSON, CHRISTOPHER. *Utopian Communism in France: Cabet and the Icarians, 1839–1851.* Ithaca, N.Y.: Cornell Univ. Press, 1974.

KANTER, ROSABETH. *Commitment and Community: Communes and Utopias in Sociological Perspective.* Cambridge, Mass.: Harvard Univ. Press, 1972.

———, ed. *Communes: Creating and Managing the Collective Life.* New York: Harper & Row, 1973.

KEPHART, WILLIAM M. *Extraordinary Groups: An Examination of Unconventional Life-Styles.* 3d ed. New York: St. Martin's, 1986.

KERN, LOUIS J. *An Ordered Love: Sex Roles and Sexuality in Victorian Utopias—the Shakers, the Mormons, and the Oneida Community.* Chapel Hill: Univ. of North Carolina Press, 1981.

KINKADE, KATHLEEN. *A Walden Two Experiment: The First Five Years of Twin Oaks Community.* New York: Morrow, 1973.

KOLMERTEN, CAROL A. *Women in Utopia: The Ideology of Gender in the American Owenite Communities.* Bloomington: Indiana Univ. Press, 1990.

KRIYANANDA, SWAMI (DONALD WALTERS). *Cooperative Communities: How to Start Them and Why.* Nevada City, Calif.: Ananda, 1968.

LAUER, ROBERT H., and JEANETTE LAUER. *The Spirit and the Flesh: Sex in Utopian Communities.* Metuchen, N.J.: Scarecrow, 1983.

LEWARNE, CHARLES. *Utopias on Puget Sound.* Seattle: Univ. of Washington Press, 1975.

MCLAUGHLIN, CORINNE, and GORDON DAVIDSON. *Builders of the Dawn: Community Lifestyles in a Changing World.* Walpole, N.H.: Stillpoint, 1985.

MANUEL, FRANK E., and FRITZIE P. MANUEL. *Utopian Thought in the Western World.* Cambridge, Mass.: Harvard Univ. Press, 1979.

MELTON, J. GORDON. *Biographical Dictionary of American Cult and Sect Leaders*. New York: Garland, 1986.

―――― . *The Encyclopedia of American Religions*. 3d ed. Detroit: Gale, 1989.

―――― . *Encyclopedic Handbook of Cults in America*. New York: Garland, 1986.

MELVILLE, KEITH. *Communes in the Counter Culture: Origins, Theories, Styles of Life*. New York: Morrow, 1972.

MILLER, TIMOTHY. *American Communes, 1860–1960: A Bibliography*. New York: Garland, 1990.

MUNCY, RAYMOND LEE. *Sex and Marriage in Utopian Communities: 19th-Century America*. Bloomington: Indiana Univ. Press, 1973.

NORDHOFF, CHARLES. *The Communistic Societies of the United States: From Personal Visit and Observation*. New York: Harper & Bros., 1875.

NOYES, JOHN HUMPHREY. *History of American Socialisms*. Philadelphia: Lippincott, 1870.

OAKES, LEN. *Inside Centrepoint: The Story of a New Zealand Community*. Takapuna, Auckland, New Zealand: Benton Ross, 1986.

OVED, YAACOV. *Two Hundred Years of American Communes*. New Brunswick, N.J.: Transaction, 1988.

PALGI, MICHAL, JOSEPH BLASI, MENACHEM ROSNER, and MARILYN AFIR, eds. *Sexual Equality: The Israeli Kibbutz Tests the Theories*. Norwood, Pa.: Norwood, 1982.

PEASE, WILLIAM, and JANE PEASE. *Black Utopia: Negro Communal Experiments in America*. Madison: State Historical Society of Wisconsin, 1963.

PERSONS, STOW. "Christian Communitarianism in America," in Donald Drew Egbert and Stow Persons, eds., *Socialism and American Life*, 1:125–51. 2 vols. Princeton: Princeton Univ. Press, 1952.

PETERS, VICTOR. *All Things Common: The Hutterian Way of Life*. New York: Harper & Row, 1971.

PITZER, DONALD E. "Collectivism, Community and Commitment: America's Religious Communal Utopias from the Shakers to Jonestown." In Peter Alexander and Roger Gill, eds., *Utopias*, pp. 119–35. London: Duckworth, 1984.

―――― , ed. *America's Communal Utopias*. Madison: Univ. of Wisconsin Press, in press.

POPENOE, CHRIS, and OLIVER POPENOE. *Seeds of Tomorrow: New Age Communities That Work*. San Francisco: Harper & Row, 1984.

RIGBY, ANDREW. *Alternative Realities: A Study of Communes and Their Members*. London: Routledge & Kegan Paul, 1974.

ROBERTS, RON. *The New Communes*. Englewood Cliffs, N.J.: Prentice-Hall, 1971.

ROZEN, FRIEDA S., et al. *Communal Life*. New Brunswick, N.J.: Transaction, 1987.

RUETHER, ROSEMARY RADFORD. "Women in Utopian Movements." In Rosemary Radford Ruether and Rosemary Keller, eds., *Women and Religion in America: The Nineteenth Century*, pp. 46–53. New York: Harper & Row, 1981.

SCHNEIDER, HERBERT W., and GEORGE LAWTON. *A Prophet and a Pilgrim: Being the Incredible History of Thomas Lake Harris and Lawrence Oliphant*. New York: Columbia Univ. Press, 1942.

SEARS, HAL D. *The Sex Radicals: Free Love in High Victorian America*. Lawrence: Regents Press of Kansas, 1977.

SESSLER, JACOB JOHN. *Communal Pietism Among Early American Moravians*. New York: Holt, 1933.

SHAMBAUGH, B. M. H. *Amana That Was and Amana That Is*. Iowa City: State Historical Society of Iowa, 1932.

SHI, DAVID E. *The Simple Life: Plain Living and High Thinking in American Culture*. New York: Oxford Univ. Press, 1985.

SPURLOCK, JOHN CALVIN. "Anarchy and Community at Modern Times, 1851–1863." *Communal Societies* 3 (1983): 29–47.

———. *Free Love: Marriage and Middle-Class Radicalism in America, 1825–1860*. New York: New York Univ. Press, 1988.

STEPHAN, KAREN H., and G. EDWARD STEPHAN. "Religion and the Survival of Utopian Communities." *Journal for the Scientific Study of Religion* 12 (Mar. 1973): 89–100.

SWIFT, LINDSAY. *Brook Farm: Its Members, Scholars, and Visitors*. New York: Macmillan, 1900.

TAYLOR, BARBARA. *Eve and the New Jerusalem: Socialism and Feminism in the Nineteenth Century*. New York: Pantheon, 1983.

TESELLE, SALLIE, ed. *The Family, Communes, and Utopian Societies*. New York: Harper & Row, 1972.

TIGER, LIONEL, and JOSEPH SHEPHER. *Women in the Kibbutz*. New York: Harcourt Brace Jovanovich, 1975.

VEYSEY, LAURENCE. *The Communal Experience: Anarchist and Mystical Counter-Cultures in America*. New York: Harper & Row, 1973.

WAGNER, JON. "Sexuality and Gender Roles in Utopian Communities: A Critical Survey of Scholarly Work." *Communal Societies* 6 (1986): 172–88.

———. "Success in Intentional Communities: The Problem of Evaluation." *Communal Societies* 5 (1985): 89–100.

———, ed. *Sex Roles in Contemporary American Communes.* Bloomington: Indiana Univ. Press, 1982.

WEBBER, EVERETT. *Escape to Utopia: The Communal Movement in America.* New York: Hastings House, 1959.

WEISBROD, CAROL. *The Boundaries of Utopia.* New York: Pantheon, 1980.

WEISBROT, ROBERT. *Father Divine: The Utopian Evangelist of the Depression Era Who Became an American Legend.* Boston: Beacon, 1983.

WHITWORTH, JOHN MCKELVIE. *God's Blueprints: A Sociological Study of Three Utopian Sects.* London: Routledge & Kegan Paul, 1975.

WISBEY, HERBERT A., JR. *Pioneer Prophetess: Jemima Wilkinson, the Publick Universal Friend.* Ithaca, N.Y.: Cornell University Press, 1964.

ZABLOCKI, BENJAMIN. *Alienation and Charisma: A Study of Contemporary American Communes.* New York: Free Press, 1980.

———. *The Joyful Community: An Account of the Bruderhoff, A Communal Movement Now in Its Third Generation.* New York: Penguin, 1971.

ZICKLIN, GILBERT. *Countercultural Communes: A Sociological Perspective.* Westport, Conn.: Greenwood, 1983.

SHAKERS: Primary Publications

AVERY, GILES B. *Autobiography.* East Canterbury, N.H.: N.p., 1891.

BATES, PAULINA. *The Divine Book of Holy and Eternal Wisdom.* New Lebanon, N.Y.: United Society Called "Shakers," 1849.

BEAR, HENRY B. *Henry B. Bear's Advent Experience.* Whitewater, Ohio: N.p., n.d.

BLINN, HENRY CLAY. *The Manifestation of Spiritualism Among the Shakers, 1837–1847.* East Canterbury, N.H.: N.p., 1899.

BROWN, THOMAS. *An Account of the People Called Shakers: Their Faith, Doctrines, and Practice.* Troy, N.Y.: Parker & Bliss, 1812.

DUNLAVY, JOHN. *The Manifesto, or, A Declaration of the Doctrine and Practice of the Church of Christ.* Pleasant Hill, Ky.: P. Bertrand, 1818.

DYER, MARY MARSHALL. *A Portraiture of Shakerism.* Concord, N.H.: For the Author, 1822.

——— . *The Rise and Progress of the Serpent from the Garden of Eden to the Present Day.* Concord, N.H.: For the Author, 1847.

ELKINS, HERVEY. *Fifteen Years in the Senior Order of Shakers.* Hanover, N.H.: Dartmouth Press, 1853.

EVANS, FREDERICK W. *Autobiography of a Shaker, and Revelation of the Apocalypse.* Mt. Lebanon, N.Y.: F. W. Evans, 1869.

——— . *New England Witchcraft and Spiritualism.* N.p., 1881.

——— . *Tests of Divine Inspiration; or, The Rudimental Principles by Which True and False Revelation, in All Eras of the World, Can Be Unerringly Discriminated.* New Lebanon, N.Y.: United Society Called Shakers, 1853.

GREEN, CALVIN, and SETH Y. WELLS. *A Summary View of the Millennial Church or United Society of Believers (Commonly Called Shakers).* Albany: Packard & Van Benthuysen, 1823.

HASKETT, WILLIAM J. *Shakerism Unmasked.* Pittsfield, Mass.: The Author, 1828.

LAMSON, DAVID. *Two Years' Experience Among the Shakers.* West Boyleston, Mass.: The Author, 1848.

McNEMAR, RICHARD. *The Kentucky Revival, or, A Short History of the Late Extraordinary Outpouring of God in the Western States of America.* Cincinnati: John W. Browne, 1807.

MEACHAM, JOSEPH. *A Concise Statement of the Principles of the Only True Church, Together with a Letter from James Whittaker to His Natural Relations in England, Dated Oct. 9th, 1785.* Bennington, Vt.: Haswell & Russell, 1790.

Millennial Praises, Containing a Collection of Gospel Hymns, in Four Parts. Compiled by Seth Y. Wells. Hancock, Mass.: J. Tallcott, 1812.

The Other Side of the Question. [Compiled by Richard McNemar et al.] Cincinnati: Looker, Reynolds, 1819.

RATHBUN, DANIEL. *A Letter from Daniel Rathbun, of Richmond in the County of Berkshire, to James Whittacor, Chief Elder of the Church, Called Shakers.* [Springfield, Mass.: N.p., 1785?]

RATHBUN, REUBEN. *Reasons Offered for Leaving the Shakers.* Pittsfield, Mass.: N.p., 1800.

RATHBUN, VALENTINE. *An Account of the Matter, Form, and Manner of a New and Strange Religion, Taught and Propagated by a Number of Europeans, Living in a Place Called Nisqueunia, in the State of New-York.* Providence, R.I.: Bennett Wheeler, 1781.

STEWART, PHILEMON. *A Holy, Sacred and Divine Roll and Book.* Canterbury, N.H.: United Society, 1843.

TAYLOR, AMOS. *A Narrative of the Strange Principles, Conduct, and Character of the People Known by the Name of Shakers.* Worcester, Mass.: The Author, 1782.

Testimonies of the Life, Character, Revelations, and Doctrines of Our Ever Blessed Mother Ann Lee, and the Elders with Her. [Edited by Rufus Bishop and Seth Y. Wells.] Hancock, Mass.: J. Tallcott & J. Deming, Junrs., 1816.

WEST, BENJAMIN. *Scriptural Cautions Against Embracing a Religious Scheme, Taught by a Number of Europeans.* Hartford, Conn.: Basil Webster, 1783.

WHITE, ANNA, and LEILA S. TAYLOR. *Shakerism: Its Meaning and Message.* Columbus, Ohio: Fred J. Heer, 1904.

WHITSON, ROBLEY EDWARD, ed. *The Shakers: Two Centuries of Spiritual Reflection.* New York: Paulist Press, 1983.

YOUNGS, BENJAMIN SETH. *The Testimony of Christ's Second Appearing; Containing a General Statement of All Things Pertaining to the Faith and Practice of the Church of God in This Latter Day.* Lebanon, Ohio: John McClean, 1808.

SHAKERS: Secondary Publications

ANDREWS, EDWARD DEMING. *The Community Industries of the Shakers.* Albany: State Univ. of New York Press, 1933.

———. *The Gift to Be Simple: Songs, Dances and Rituals of the American Shakers.* New York: Dover, 1962.

———. *The People Called Shakers: A Search for the Perfect Society.* New enlarged ed. New York: Dover, 1963.

ANDREWS, EDWARD DEMING, and FAITH ANDREWS. *Visions of the Heavenly Sphere: A Study in Shaker Religious Art.* Charlottesville: Univ. Press of Virginia, 1969.

———. *Work and Worship: The Economic Order of the Shakers.* Greenwich, Conn.: New York Graphic Society, 1974.

BAINBRIDGE, WILLIAM SIMS. "The Decline of the Shakers: Evidence from the United States Census." *Communal Societies* 4 (1984): 19–34.

———. "Shaker Demographics, 1840–1900: An Example of the Use of U.S. Census Enumeration Schedules." *Journal for the Scientific Study of Religion* 21 (1982): 352–65.

BREWER, PRISCILLA J. "The Demographic Features of the Shaker Decline, 1787–1900." *Journal of Interdisciplinary History* 15 (1984): 31–52.

———. " 'Numbers Are Not the Thing for Us to Glory In': Demographic Perspectives on the Decline of the Shakers." *Communal Societies* 7 (1987): 25–35.

———. *Shaker Communities, Shaker Lives.* Hanover, N.H.: Univ. Press of New England, 1986.

CAMPBELL, D'ANN. "Women's Life in Utopia: The Shaker Experiment in Sexual Equality Reappraised, 1810–1860." *New England Quarterly* 51 (Mar. 1978): 23–38.

CROSSTHWAITE, JANE F. " 'A White and Seamless Robe': Celibacy and Equality in Shaker Art and Theology." *Colby Library Quarterly* 25 (Sept. 1989): 188–98.

DESROCHE, HENRI. *The American Shakers: From Neo-Christianity to Pre-Socialism.* Translated and edited by JOHN K. SAVACOOL. Amherst: Univ. of Massachusetts Press, 1971.

FOSTER, LAWRENCE. "Had Prophecy Failed?: Contrasting Perspectives of the Millerites and Shakers." In Ronald L. Numbers and Jonathan M. Butler, eds., *The Disappointed: Millerism and Millenarianism in the Nineteenth Century,* pp. 173–88. Bloomington: Indiana Univ. Press, 1987.

———. "Shaker Spiritualism and Salem Witchcraft: Social Perspectives on Trance and Possession Phenomena." *Communal Societies* (1985): 176–93.

GARRETT, CLARKE. *Spirit Possession and Popular Religion: From the Camisards to the Shakers.* Baltimore: Johns Hopkins Univ. Press, 1987.

GORDON, BEVERLY. *Shaker Textile Arts.* Hanover, N.H.: Univ. Press of New England, 1980.

HORGAN, EDWARD R. *The Shaker Holy Land: A Community Portrait.* Harvard, Mass.: Harvard Common Press, 1982.

HUMEZ, JEAN MCMAHON, ed. *Gifts of Power: The Writings of Rebecca Jackson, Black Visionary, Shaker Eldress.* Amherst: Univ. of Massachusetts Press, 1981.

Johnson, Theodore E. *Hands to Work and Hearts to God: The Shaker Tradition in Maine*. Brunswick, Me.: Bowdoin College Museum of Art, 1969.

Kitch, Sally L. *Chaste Liberation: Celibacy and Female Cultural Status*. Urbana: Univ. of Illinois Press, 1989.

MacLean, John Patterson. *A Bibliography of Shaker Literature*. Columbus, Ohio: F. J. Heer, 1905.

———— . *Shakers of Ohio: Fugitive Papers Concerning the Shakers of Ohio, with Unpublished Manuscripts*. Columbus, Ohio: F. J. Heer, 1907.

———— . *A Sketch of the Life and Labors of Richard McNemar*. Franklin, Ohio: Printed for the Author by the *Franklin Chronicle*, 1905.

Marini, Stephen A. *Radical Sects of Revolutionary New England*. Cambridge, Mass.: Harvard Univ. Press, 1982.

Melcher, Marguerite Fellows. *The Shaker Adventure*. Princeton: Princeton Univ. Press, 1941.

Morse, Flo. *The Shakers and the World's People*. New York: Dodd, Mead, 1980.

Neal, Julia. *By Their Fruits: The Story of Shakerism in South Union, Kentucky*. Chapel Hill: Univ. of North Carolina Press, 1947.

Nickless, Karen K., and Pamela J. Nickless. "Trustees, Deacons, and Deaconesses: The Temporal Role of the Shaker Sisters, 1820–1890." *Communal Societies* 7 (1987): 16–24.

Patterson, Daniel W. *The Shaker Spiritual*. Princeton: Princeton Univ. Press, 1979.

Piercy, Carolyn B. *The Valley of God's Pleasure: A Saga of the North Union Shaker Community*. New York: Stratford House, 1951.

Pike, Kermit J. *A Guide to Shaker Manuscripts in the Library of the Western Reserve Historical Society*. Cleveland: Western Reserve Historical Society, 1974.

Proctor-Smith, Marjorie. *Women in Shaker Community and Worship: A Feminist Analysis of the Uses of Religious Symbolism*. Lewiston, N.Y.: Mellen, 1985.

Richmond, Mary L. *Shaker Literature: A Bibliography*. 2 vols. Hanover, N.H.: Univ. Press of New England, 1977.

Rohman, Eric. "Words of Comfort, Gifts of Love: Spirit Manifestations Among the Shakers, 1837–1845." B.A. thesis, Antioch College, 1971.

Rosenblum, Naomi. "The Church Family at Canterbury: An Age-Based Demographic Study of a Shaker Family." In David R. Starbuck and

Margaret Supplee Smith, eds., *Historical Survey of Canterbury Shaker Village*, pp. 190–214. Boston: Boston Univ. Press, 1979.

ROURKE, CONSTANCE. "The Shakers." In Rourke, *The Roots of American Culture and Other Essays*, pp. 195–237. Edited by Van Wyck Brooks. New York: Harcourt, Brace, 1942.

SASSON, DIANE. *The Shaker Spiritual Narrative*. Knoxville: Univ. of Tennessee Press, 1983.

SEARS, CLARA ENDICOTT, comp. *Gleanings from Old Shaker Journals*. Boston: Houghton Mifflin, 1916.

SPRIGG, JUNE. *By Shaker Hands*. New York: Knopf, 1975.

STEIN, STEPHEN J. "Community, Commitment, and Practice: Union and Order at Pleasant Hill in 1834." *Journal of the Early Republic* 8 (Spring 1988): 45–68.

WILLIAMS, RICHARD E. *Called and Chosen: The Story of Mother Rebecca Jackson and the Philadelphia Shakers*. Metuchen, N.J.: Scarecrow, 1981.

WISBEY, HERBERT A., JR. *The Sodus Shaker Community*. Lyons, N.Y.: Wayne County Historical Society, 1982.

YOUNGERMAN, SUZANNE. " 'Shaking Is No Foolish Play': An Anthropological Perspective on the American Shakers—Person, Time, Space, and Dance Ritual." Ph.D. diss., Columbia Univ., 1983.

ONEIDA: Primary Publications

Bible Communism: A Compilation of the Annual Reports and Other Publications of the Oneida Association and Its Branches. Brooklyn, N.Y.: Office of the *Circular*, 1853.

The Circular. Brooklyn and Oneida, N.Y.: 1851–64.

DIXON, WILLIAM HEPWORTH. *New America*. Philadelphia: Lippincott, 1867.
———. *Spiritual Wives*. 2 vols. Philadelphia: Lippincott, 1868.

EASTMAN, HUBBARD. *Noyesism Unveiled: A History of the Self-Styled Perfectionists; with a Summary View of Their Leading Doctrines*. Brattleboro, Vt.: By the Author, 1849.

ELLIS, JOHN B. *Free Love and Its Votaries; or American Socialism Unmasked*. New York: United States Publishing Co., 1870.

ESTLAKE, ALLAN [ABEL EASTON]. *The Oneida Community: A Record of an Attempt to Carry Out the Principles of Christian Unselfishness and Scientific Race Improvement*. London: George Redway, 1900.

First Annual Report of the Oneida Association. Oneida Reserve, N.Y.: Leonard, 1849.

Handbook of the Oneida Community, Containing a Brief Sketch of Its Present Condition, Internal Economy and Leading Principles. No. 2. Oneida, N.Y.: Oneida Community, 1871.

Handbook of the Oneida Community, 1875. Oneida, N.Y.: Office of the Oneida Circular, 1875.

Handbook of the Oneida Community, with a Sketch of Its Founder and an Outline of Its Constitution and Development. Wallingford, Conn.: Office of the Circular, 1867.

Mutual Criticism. Oneida, N.Y.: Office of the American Socialist, 1876.

NOYES, CORINNA ACKLEY. *The Days of My Youth.* Kenwood, N.Y.: The Mansion, 1960.

NOYES, GEORGE WALLINGFORD, ed. *John Humphrey Noyes: The Putney Community.* Oneida, N.Y.: By the Author, 1931.

────── , ed. *Religious Experience of John Humphrey Noyes, Founder of the Oneida Community.* New York: Macmillan, 1923.

NOYES, JOHN HUMPHREY. *The Berean: A Manual for the Help of Those Who Seek the Faith of the Primitive Church.* Putney, Vt.: Office of the Spiritual Magazine, 1847.

────── . "Bible Argument Defining the Relations of the Sexes in the Kingdom of Heaven." In *First Annual Report of the Oneida Association,* pp. 27–35. Oneida Reserve, N.Y.: Leonard, 1849.

────── . *Confessions of John H. Noyes. Part I: Confession of Religious Experience, Including a History of Modern Perfectionism.* Oneida Reserve, N.Y.: Leonard, 1849. Part II was never published.

────── . *Dixon and His Copyists: A Criticism of the Accounts of the Oneida Community in "New America," "Spiritual Wives" and Kindred Publications.* Wallingford, Conn.: Oneida Community, 1872.

────── . *The Doctrine of Salvation from Sin, Explained and Defended.* Putney, Vt.: By the Author, 1843.

────── . *Essay on Scientific Propagation.* Oneida, N.Y.: Oneida Community, 1872.

────── . *History of American Socialisms.* Philadelphia: Lippincott, 1870.

────── . *Home Talks by John Humphrey Noyes.* Edited by Alfred Barron and George Noyes Miller. Vol. 1. Oneida, N.Y.: Oneida Community, 1875. Only Vol. 1 was published.

————. *Male Continence*. Oneida, N.Y.: Office of the *Oneida Circular,* 1872.

————. *Salvation from Sin: The End of the Christian Faith.* Wallingford, Conn.: Oneida Community, 1866.

————. *Slavery and Marriage, A Dialogue: Conversation Between Judge North, Major South, and Mr. Free Church.* Oneida, N.Y.: Oneida Community, 1850.

————. *"The Way of Holiness." A Series of Papers Formerly Published in the Perfectionist, at New Haven.* Putney, Vt.: J. H. Noyes, 1838.

NOYES, PIERREPONT B. *A Godly Heritage.* New York: Rinehart, 1958.

————. *My Father's House: An Oneida Boyhood.* New York: Farrar & Reinhart, 1937.

NOYES, THEODORE R. *Report on the Health of Children in the Oneida Community.* Oneida, N.Y.: N.p., 1878.

RICH, JANE KINSLEY, and NELSON M. BLAKE, eds. *A Lasting Spring: Jessie Catherine Kinsley, Daughter of the Oneida Community.* Syracuse, N.Y.: Syracuse Univ. Press, 1983.

Second Annual Report of the Oneida Association: Exhibiting Its Progress to February 20, 1850. Oneida Reserve, N.Y.: Leonard, 1850.

Third Annual Report of the Oneida Association: Exhibiting Its Progress to February 20, 1851. Oneida Reserve, N.Y.: Leonard, 1851.

WORDEN, HARRIET M. *Old Mansion House Memories.* Oneida, N.Y.: N.p., 1950.

ONEIDA: Secondary Publications

ACHORN, ERIK. "Mary Cragin: Perfectionist Saint." *New England Quarterly* 28 (1955): 490–518.

BARKUN, MICHAEL. "The Visionary Experiences of John Humphrey Noyes." *Psychohistory Review* 16 (Spring 1988): 313–34.

————. " 'The Wind Sweeping Over the Country': John Humphrey Noyes and the Rise of Millerism." In Ronald L. Numbers and Jonathan M. Butler, eds., *The Disappointed: Millerism and Millenarianism in the Nineteenth Century,* pp. 153–72. Bloomington: Indiana Univ. Press, 1987.

CARDEN, MAREN LOCKWOOD. *Oneida: Utopian Community to Modern Corporation.* Baltimore: Johns Hopkins Univ. Press, 1969.

DALSIMER, MARLYN HARTZELL. "Women and Family in the Oneida Community, 1837–1881." Ph.D. diss., New York University, 1975.

DE MARIA, RICHARD. *Communal Love at Oneida: A Perfectionist Vision of Authority, Property, and Sexual Order.* New York: Mellen, 1978.

FOGARTY, ROBERT S. "Oneida: A Utopian Search for Religious Security." *Labor History* 14 (Spring 1973): 202–27.

————. "The Oneida Community, 1848–1880: A Study in Conservative Christian Utopianism." Ph.D. diss., Univ. of Denver, 1968.

FOSTER, LAWRENCE. "Free Love and Feminism: John Humphrey Noyes and the Oneida Community." *Journal of the Early Republic* 1 (Summer 1981): 165–83.

————. "The Psychology of Free Love in the Oneida Community." *Australasian Journal of American Studies* 5 (Dec. 1986): 14–26.

————. "The Rise and Fall of Utopia: The Oneida Community Crises of 1852 and 1879." *Communal Societies* 8 (1988): 1–17.

HOEHN, RICHARD A. "The Kingdom Goes Joint Stock: Learning from Oneida 100 Years Later." *Christian Century,* Jan. 28, 1981, pp. 77–80.

KEPHART, WILLIAM M. "Experimental Family Organization: An Historico-Cultural Report on the Oneida Community." *Journal of Marriage and Family Living* 25 (Aug. 1963): 261–71.

KERN, LOUIS J. "Ideology and Reality: Sexuality and Women's Status in the Oneida Community." *Radical History Review* 20 (Spring/Summer 1979): 181–205.

McGEE, ANITA NEWCOMB. "An Experiment in Stirpiculture." *American Anthropologist* 4 (Oct. 1891): 319–25.

MANDELKER, IRA L. *Religion, Society, and Utopia in Nineteenth-Century America.* Amherst: Univ. of Massachusetts Press, 1984.

NOYES, HILDA HERRICK, and GEORGE WALLINGFORD NOYES. "The Oneida Community Experiment in Stirpiculture." Scientific Papers of the Second International Congress of Eugenics, 1921. *Eugenics, Genetics, and the Family,* 1: 374–86. Baltimore: Williams & Wilkins, 1923.

OLIN, SPENCER C., JR. "Bible Communism and the Origins of Orange County." *California History* 58 (Fall 1979): 220–33.

————. "The Oneida Community and the Instability of Charismatic Authority." *Journal of American History* 67 (1980): 285–300.

PARKER, ROBERT ALLERTON. *A Yankee Saint: John Humphrey Noyes and the Oneida Community.* New York: G. P. Putnam's Sons, 1935.

ROBERTSON, CONSTANCE NOYES. "The Oneida Community." *New York History* (Apr. 1949): 131–50.

——. *Oneida Community: The Breakup, 1876–1881.* Syracuse, N.Y.: Syracuse Univ. Press, 1972.

——, ed. *Oneida Community: An Autobiography, 1851–1876.* New York: Syracuse Univ. Press, 1970.

SANDEEN, ERNEST R. "John Humphrey Noyes as the New Adam." *Church History* 40 (Mar. 1971): 82–90.

SIBLEY, MULFORD Q. "Oneida's Challenge to American Culture." In JOSEPH J. KWIAT and MARY C. TURPIE, eds., *Studies in American Culture,* pp. 41–62. Minneapolis: Univ. of Minnesota Press, 1959.

TEEPLE, JOHN B. *The Oneida Family: Genealogy of a 19th Century Perfectionist Commune.* Oneida, N.Y.: Oneida Community Historical Committee, 1984.

THOMAS, ROBERT DAVID. "The Development of a Utopian Mind: A Psychoanalytic Study of John Humphrey Noyes, 1828–1869." Ph.D. diss., State Univ. of New York at Stony Brook, 1973.

——. "John Humphrey Noyes and the Oneida Community: A 19th-Century American Father and His Family." *Psychohistory Review* 6 (Fall-Winter 1977–78): 68–87.

——. *The Man Who Would Be Perfect: John Humphrey Noyes and the Utopian Impulse.* Philadelphia: Univ. of Pennsylvania Press, 1977.

VAN DE WARKER, ELY. "Gynecological Study of the Oneida Community." *American Journal of Obstetrics and Diseases of Women and Children* 17 (Aug. 1884): 755–810.

WAYLAND-SMITH, ELLEN. "The Status and Self-Perception of Women in the Oneida Community." *Communal Societies* 8 (1988): 18–53.

WELLS, LESTER G. *The Oneida Community Collection in the Syracuse University Library.* Syracuse, N.Y.: Syracuse Univ. Library, 1961.

WYATT, PHILIP R. "John Humphrey Noyes and the Stirpicultural Experiment." *Journal of the History of Medicine and Allied Sciences* 31 (Jan. 1976): 55–66.

MORMONS: Primary Publications

Affidavits and Certificates Disproving the Statements and Affidavits Contained in John C. Bennett's Letters. Nauvoo, Ill.: N.p., Aug. 31, 1842.

BENNETT, JOHN C. *The History of the Saints: or, an Exposé of Joe Smith and Mormonism.* Boston: Leland & Whiting, 1842.

BRIGGS, JASON. *The Basis of Brighamite Polygamy: A Criticism upon the (So-Called) Revelation of July 12th, 1843.* Plano, Ill.: Reorganized Church of Jesus Christ of Latter Day Saints, [1875].

BROOKS, JUANITA, ed. *On the Mormon Frontier: The Diary of Hosea Stout, 1844–1861.* 2 vols. Salt Lake City: Univ. of Utah Press, 1964.

———, ed. *Not by Bread Alone: The Journal of Martha Spence Heywood, 1850–1856.* Salt Lake City: Utah State Historical Society, 1978.

BURTON, RICHARD F. *City of the Saints, and Across the Rocky Mountains to California.* 1861. Reprint. New York: Knopf, 1963.

CANNON, DONALD Q., and LYNDON W. COOK, eds. *Far West Record.* Salt Lake City: Deseret, 1983.

CLAYTON, WILLIAM. *Clayton's Secret Writings Uncovered.* Salt Lake City: Modern Microfilm, 1982.

CLELAND, ROBERT GLASS, and JUANITA BROOKS, eds. *A Mormon Chronicle: The Diaries of John D. Lee, 1848–1876.* 2 vols. San Marino, Calif.: Huntington Library, 1955.

Complainant's Abstract of Pleading and Evidence in the Circuit Court of the United States, Western District of Missouri, Western Division at Kansas City. The Reorganized Church of Jesus Christ of Latter Day Saints, Complainant, vs. The Church of Christ at Independence, Missouri . . . Lamoni, Iowa: Herald, 1893. This work is most commonly cited as *Abstract of the Temple Lot Case.*

CROCHERON, AUGUSTA JOYCE. *Representative Women of Deseret.* Salt Lake City: J. C. Graham, 1884.

EHAT, ANDREW F., and LYNDON W. COOK, eds. *The Words of Joseph Smith.* Provo: Religious Studies Center, Brigham Young Univ., 1980.

ELLSWORTH, S. GEORGE, ed. *Dear Ellen: Two Mormon Women and Their Letters.* Salt Lake City: Univ. of Utah Library, 1974.

FAULRING, SCOTT H., ed. *An American Prophet's Record: The Diaries and Journals of Joseph Smith.* Salt Lake City: Signature, 1989.

FORD, THOMAS. *History of Illinois.* 1854. Reprint. Chicago: S. C. Griggs, 1859.

FROISETH, JENNIE ANDERSON, ed. *The Women of Mormonism, or, The Story of Polygamy as Told by the Victims Themselves.* Introduction by Frances E. Willard. Detroit: C. G. Paine, 1882.

GREGG, THOMAS. *History of Hancock County, Illinois.* Chicago: Charles C. Chapman, 1880.

GUNNISON, JOHN W. *The Mormons, or, Latter-day Saints, in the Valley of the Great Salt Lake.* Philadelphia: Lippincott, Grambo, 1852.

HALL, WILLIAM. *The Abominations of Mormonism Exposed.: Containing Many Facts and Doctrines Concerning that Singular People, During Seven Years' Membership with Them from 1840 to 1847.* Cincinnati: Published for the Author by I. Hart, 1852.

HARDY, JOHN. *History of the Trial of Elder John Hardy, Before the Church of Latter Day Saints in Boston, for Slander, in Saying That G. J. Adams, S. Brannan and William Smith Were Licentious Characters.* Boston: Conway, 1844.

HARRISON, PAUL. *An Extract of Grand Selections from a Manuscript Entitled The Peace Maker: By the Great Mormon Prophet, J. Smith, Wherein Is Contained all the Secrets of Mormonism in Relation to the Vows of Marriage, Polygamy, Spiritual Wives, Whoredom, Adultery, Fornication, Rapes, Concubinage, Virginity, Etc., Etc.* Manchester, Eng.: Printed for P. Harrison by J. Leach, 1850. The only copy of this pamphlet known to be still extant is held in the Coe Collection of the Beinecke Library at Yale Univ., New Haven, Conn.

HAVEN, CHARLOTTE. "A Girl's Letters from Nauvoo." *Overland Monthly* 16 (Dec. 1890 and Feb. 1891): 616–38, 645–51.

HEDRICK, GRANVILLE. *The Spiritual Wife System Proven False; and the True Order of Church Discipline.* Bloomington, Ind.: W. E. Foote's Power Press, 1856.

HOWE, EBER D. *Mormonism Unvailed [sic]; or a Faithful Account of That Singular Imposition and Delusion from Its Rise to the Present Time.* Painesville, Ohio: By the Author, 1834.

HYDE, JOHN, JR. *Mormonism: Its Leaders and Designs.* New York: W. P. Fetridge, 1857.

JACOB, UDNEY H. *An Extract, from a Manuscript Entitled The Peace Maker, or the Doctrines of the Millennium: Being a Treatise on Religion and Jurisprudence. Or a New System of Religion and Politicks [sic].* Nauvoo, Ill.: J. Smith, Printer, 1842.

JENSEN, JULIAETTA BATEMAN. *Little Gold Pieces: The Story of My Mormon Mother's Life.* Salt Lake City: Stanway, 1948.

JENSON, ANDREW. "Plural Marriage." *Historical Record* 6 (May 1887): 219–34.

JESSEE, DEAN C. "Early Accounts of Joseph Smith's First Vision." *BYU Studies* 9 (Spring 1969): 275–94.

————, ed. *Letters of Brigham Young to His Sons.* Salt Lake City: Deseret, 1974.

————. *The Personal Writings of Joseph Smith.* Salt Lake City: Deseret, 1984.

JOHNSON, BENJAMIN F. *My Life In Review.* Independence, Mo.: Zion's Printing and Publishing Company, 1947.

KRAUT, OGDEN. *Jesus Was Married.* 2d rev. ed. N.p., 1970.

LEBARON, VERLAN M. *The LeBaron Story.* Lubbock, Tex.: Keels, 1981.

LEE, JOHN D. *Mormonism Unveiled; or The Life and Confessions of the Mormon Bishop, John D. Lee.* Edited by W. W. Bishop. St. Louis: Bryan, Brand, 1877.

LEWIS, CATHERINE. *Narrative of Some of the Proceedings of the Mormons; Giving an Account of Their Iniquities, with Particulars Concerning the Training of the Indians by Them, Describing of the Mode of Endowment, Plurality of Wives, &c., &c.* Lynn, Mass.: By the Author, 1848.

MERRILL, MELISSA [pseud.]. *Polygamist's Wife.* Salt Lake City: Olympus, 1975.

MULDER, WILLIAM, and A. RUSSELL MORTENSEN, eds. *Among the Mormons: Historic Accounts by Contemporary Observers.* New York: Knopf, 1958.

Nauvoo Expositor, June 7, 1844.

OLNEY, OLIVER H. *The Absurdities of Mormonism Portrayed.* Hancock County, Ill.: N.p., 1843.

[PRATT, BELINDA MARDEN.] *Defence of Polygamy by a Lady of Utah, in a Letter to Her Sister in New Hampshire.* [Salt Lake City: N.p., 1854.]

PRATT, ORSON. *The Bible and Polygamy. Does the Bible Sanction Polygamy? A Discussion Between Prof. Orson Pratt . . . and Rev. J. P. Newman . . . 1870, To Which Are Added Three Sermons on the Subject by Prest. George A. Smith, and Elders Orson Pratt and George Q. Cannon.* Salt Lake City: Deseret News, 1877.

————. "Celestial Marriage." *Journal of Discourses* 1 (1854): 53–66. This first official public defense of Mormon plural marriage was initially printed, without any title, in the *Deseret News* Extra for September 14, 1852.

————. *The Seer.* Washington, D.C., and Liverpool: S. W. Richards, 1853–54.

PRATT, PARLEY P. *The Autobiography of Parley Parker Pratt, One of the Twelve Apostles of the Church of Jesus Christ of Latter-day Saints.* Edited by Parley P. Pratt, Jr. New York: Russell Brothers, 1874.

————. "Celestial Family Organization." *Prophet* 1 (Mar. 1, 1845): 1–2.

————. *Marriage and Morals in Utah: An Address Written by Parley P. Pratt . . . Read in Joint Session of the Legislature in the Representatives Hall, Fillmore City, Dec. 31, 1855.* Liverpool: Orson Pratt, 1856.

ROBINSON, EBINEZER. "Items of Personal History of the Editor." *Return*, vols. 1–3. Davis City, Iowa, 1889–91.

SHEEN, JOHN K. *Polygamy, or the Veil Lifted.* York, Neb.: N.p., 1889. Includes polygamy extracts allegedly from William Smith's no longer extant 1844 manuscript *The Elder's Pocket Companion.*

SHOOK, CHARLES A. *The True Origin of Mormon Polygamy.* Cincinnati: Standard, 1914.

SHORT, DENNIS R. *For W⊘Men Only: The Lord's Law of Obedience.* Salt Lake City: Dennis R. Short, 1977.

SMITH, EMMA HALE. "Last Testimony of Sister Emma." *Saint's Herald* 36 (Oct. 1, 1879): 289–90.

SMITH, JOSEPH, JR. *A Book of Commandments, for the Government of the Church of Christ, Organized According to Law, on the 6th of April, 1830.* Zion [Independence, Mo.]: W. W. Phelps, 1833.

————. *Book of Mormon: An Account Written by the Hand of Mormon, Upon Plates Taken from the Plates of Nephi.* Palmyra, N.Y.: E. B. Grandin, For the Author, 1830.

————. *Doctrine and Covenants of the Church of Latter Day Saints: Carefully Selected from the Revelations of God and Compiled by Joseph Smith, Junior, Oliver Cowdery, Sidney Rigdon, Frederick G. Williams [Presiding Elders of Said Church].* Kirtland, Ohio: F. G. Williams, 1835.

————. *History of the Church of Jesus Christ of Latter-day Saints: Period 1.* Edited by Brigham H. Roberts. 6 vols. 2d ed. rev. Salt Lake City: Deseret, 1948.

————. *The Pearl of Great Price: Being a Choice Selection from the Revelations, Translations, and Narratives of Joseph Smith, First Prophet, Seer, and Revelator to the Church of Jesus Christ of Latter-day Saints.* Liverpool: F. D. Richards, 1851.

SMITH, JOSEPH, III. *Joseph Smith III and the Restoration.* Edited by Mary Audentia Smith Anderson. Independence, Mo.: Herald, 1952.

SMITH, JOSEPH F., JR. [Joseph Fielding Smith]. *Blood Atonement and the Origin of Plural Marriage: A Discussion.* Salt Lake City: Deseret News, 1905.

SMITH, LUCY MACK. *Biographical Sketches of Joseph Smith, the Prophet, and His Progenitors for Many Generations.* Liverpool: For Orson Pratt by S. W. Richards, 1853.

SMITH, WILLIAM. *William Smith on Mormonism.* Lamoni, Iowa: Herald, 1883.

SNOW, ELIZA R. *Biography and Family Record of Lorenzo Snow.* Salt Lake City: Deseret News, 1884.

SOLOMON, DOROTHY ALLRED. *In My Father's House: An Autobiography.* New York: Franklin Watts, 1984.

SPENCER, ORSON. *Patriarchal Order, or Plurality of Wives!* Liverpool: S. W. Richards, 1853.

STEAD, J. D. *Doctrines and Dogmas of Brighamism Exposed.* Independence, Mo.: Reorganized Church of Jesus Christ of Latter Day Saints, 1911.

STENHOUSE, FANNY. *"Tell It All": The Story of a Life's Experience in Mormonism.* Hartford, Conn.: A. D. Worthington, 1875.

STENHOUSE, T. B. H. *The Rocky Mountain Saints; A Full and Complete History of the Mormons.* New York: D. Appleton, 1873.

STRANG, JAMES J. *Book of the Law of the Lord.* Saint James, Mich.: Royal Press, 1856.

STRANG, MARK A., ed. *The Diary of James J. Strang: Deciphered, Transcribed, Introduced and Annotated.* East Lansing: Michigan State Univ. Press, 1961.

TANNER, ANNIE CLARK. *A Mormon Mother: An Autobiography.* Salt Lake City: Published by the Tanner Trust Fund, Univ. of Utah Library, 1983.

TAYLOR, JOHN. *Three Nights' Public Discussion Between the Revds. C. W. Cleve, James Robertson, and Philip Cater, and Elder John Taylor, of the Church of Jesus Christ of Latter-day Saints at Boulogne-sur-Mer, France.* Liverpool: John Taylor, 1850.

TULLIDGE, EDWARD WHEELOCK. *The Women of Mormondom.* New York: [Tullidge and Crandall], 1877.

WHITMER, DAVID. *An Address to All Believers in Christ.* Richmond, Mo.: By the Author, 1887.

WHITNEY, HELEN MAR KIMBALL. *Plural Marriage as Taught by the Prophet Joseph. A Reply to Joseph Smith, Editor of the Lamoni (Iowa) "Herald."* Salt Lake City: Juvenile Instructor Office, 1882.

———. "Scenes and Incidents at Nauvoo." *Woman's Exponent,* Mar. 15, 1882–Jan. 1, 1883.

————. *Why We Practice Plural Marriage.* Salt Lake City: Juvenile Instructor Office, 1884.

WHITNEY, ORSON F. *Life of Heber C. Kimball.* Salt Lake City: Kimball Family, 1888.

WOODRUFF, WILFORD. *Wilford Woodruff's Journal.* 9 vols. Midvale, Utah: Signature, 1983–85.

WYL, DR. W. [Wilhelm Ritter von Wymetal]. *Joseph Smith, the Prophet, His Family and Friends: A Study Based on Facts and Documents.* Salt Lake City: Tribune, 1886.

MORMONS: Secondary Publications

ALEXANDER, THOMAS G. *Mormonism in Transition: A History of the Latter-day Saints, 1890–1930.* Urbana: Univ. of Illinois Press, 1986.

ALLEN, JAMES B. *Trials of Discipleship: The Story of William Clayton, a Mormon.* Urbana: Univ. of Illinois Press, 1987.

ALLEN, JAMES B., and GLEN M. LEONARD. *The Story of the Latter-day Saints.* Salt Lake City: Deseret, 1976.

ANDERSON, C. LEROY. *For Christ Will Come Tomorrow: The Saga of the Morrisites.* Logan: Utah State Univ. Press, 1981.

ANDERSON, LAVINA FIELDING. "Ministering Angels: Single Women in Mormon Society." *Dialogue* 16 (Autumn 1983): 59–72.

ARRINGTON, LEONARD J. *Brigham Young: American Moses.* New York: Knopf, 1985.

————. "Early Mormon Communitarianism: The Law of Consecration and Stewardship." *Western Humanities Review* 7 (Autumn 1953): 341–69.

————. "The Economic Role of Pioneer Mormon Women." *Western Humanities Review* 9 (Spring 1995): 145–64.

————. *Great Basin Kingdom: An Economic History of the Latter-day Saints, 1830–1900.* Cambridge, Mass.: Harvard Univ. Press, 1958.

————. "Rural Life Among Nineteeth-Century Mormons: The Women's Experience." *Agricultural History* 58 (July 1984): 239–62.

ARRINGTON, LEONARD J., and DAVIS BITTON. *The Mormon Experience: A History of the Latter-day Saints.* New York: Knopf, 1979.

ARRINGTON, LEONARD J., FERAMORZ Y. FOX, and DEAN L. MAY. *Building the City of God: Community and Cooperation Among the Mormons.* Salt Lake City: Deseret, 1976.

ARRINGTON, LEONARD J., and JON HAUPT. "Intolerable Zion: The Image of Mormonism in Nineteenth Century American Literature." *Western Humanities Review* 22 (Summer 1968): 243–60.

———. "The Missouri and Illinois Mormons in Ante-bellum Fiction." *Dialogue* 5 (Spring 1970): 37–50.

AVERY, VALEEN TIPPETTS. "Insanity and the Sweet Singer: A Biography of David Hyrum Smith, 1844–1904." Ph.D. diss., Northern Arizona Univ., 1984.

———. "Irreconcilable Differences: David H. Smith's Relationship with the Muse of Mormon History." *Journal of Mormon History* 15 (1989): 3–14.

AVERY, VALEEN TIPPETTS, and LINDA KING NEWELL. "The Lion and the Lady: Brigham Young and Emma Smith." *Utah Historical Quarterly* 48 (Winter 1980): 81–97.

BACHMAN, DANEL W. "New Light on an Old Hypothesis: The Ohio Origins of the Revelation on Eternal Marriage." *Journal of Mormon History* 5 (1978): 19–32.

———. "A Study of the Mormon Practice of Plural Marriage Before the Death of Joseph Smith." M.A. thesis, Purdue Univ., 1975.

BAER, HANS A. *Recreating Utopia in the Desert: A Sectarian Challenge to Modern Mormonism.* Albany: State Univ. of New York Press, 1988.

BEECHER, MAUREEN URSENBACH. "The Eliza Enigma: The Life and Legend of Eliza R. Snow." *Dialogue* 11 (Spring 1978): 30–43.

———. "Women at Winter Quarters." *Sunstone* 8 (July–Aug. 1983): 26–39.

———. "Women's Work on the Mormon Frontier." *Utah Historical Quarterly* 49 (Summer 1981): 276–90.

BEECHER, MAUREEN URSENBACH, and LAVINA FIELDING ANDERSON, eds. *Sisters in Spirit: Mormon Women in Historical and Cultural Perspective.* Urbana: Univ. of Illinois Press, 1987.

BEECHER, MAUREEN URSENBACH, LINDA KING NEWELL, and VALEEN TIPPETTS AVERY. "Emma, Eliza, and the Stairs." *BYU Studies* 22 (Winter 1982): 87–96.

BENNETT, RICHARD E. *Mormons at the Missouri, 1846–1852: "And Should We Die. . ."* Norman: Univ. of Oklahoma Press, 1987.

BENNION, LOWELL "BEN." "The Incidence of Mormon Polygamy in 1880: 'Dixie' Versus Davis Stake." *Journal of Mormon History* 11 (1984): 27–42.

BENNION, SHERILYN COX. "Enterprising Ladies: Utah's Nineteenth-Century Women Editors." *Utah Historical Quarterly* 49 (Summer 1981): 291–304.

———. "The *Woman's Exponent*: Forty-two Years of Speaking for Women." *Utah Historical Quarterly* 44 (1976): 222–39.

BITTON, DAVIS. *Guide to Mormon Diaries and Autobiographies.* Provo: Brigham Young Univ. Press, 1977.

———. "Mormon Polygamy: A Review Article." *Journal of Mormon History* 4 (1977): 101–18.

———. "Mormons in Texas: The Ill-Fated Lyman Wight Colony." *Arizona and the West* 2 (Spring 1969): 5–26.

BITTON, DAVIS, and MAUREEN URSENBACH BEECHER, eds. *New Views of Mormon History: Essays in Honor of Leonard J. Arrington.* Salt Lake City: Univ. of Utah Press, 1987.

BRADFORD, MARY LYTHGOE, ed. *Mormon Women Speak: A Collection of Essays.* Salt Lake City: Olympus, 1982.

BRADLEY, MARTHA S. "Changed Faces: The Official LDS Position on Polygamy, 1890–1990." *Sunstone* 14 (Feb. 1990): 26–33.

BRINGHURST, NEWELL G. *Brigham Young and the Expanding American Frontier.* Boston: Little, Brown, 1986.

———. *Saints, Slaves, and Blacks: The Changing Place of Black People Within Mormonism.* Westport, Conn.: Greenwood, 1981.

BRODIE, FAWN M. *No Man Knows My History: The Life of Joseph Smith, the Mormon Prophet.* 2d ed. rev. New York: Knopf, 1971.

BROOKS, JUANITA. *John Doyle Lee: Zealot—Pioneer Builder—Scapegoat.* Glendale, Calif.: Arthur H. Clark, 1961.

———. *The Mountain Meadows Massacre.* Norman: Univ. of Oklahoma Press, 1962.

BUERGER, DAVID JOHN. "The Fullness of the Priesthood: The Second Anointing in Latter-day Saint Theology and Practice." *Dialogue* 16 (Spring 1983): 10–44.

BUNKER, GARY L., and DAVIS BITTON. *The Mormon Graphic Image, 1834–1914: Cartoons, Caricatures, and Illustrations.* Salt Lake City: Univ. of Utah Press, 1983.

BURGESS-OLSON, VICKY. "Family Structure and Dynamics in Early Utah Mormon Families, 1847–1885." Ph.D. diss., Northwestern Univ., 1975.

———, ed. *Sister Saints.* Provo: Brigham Young Univ. Press, 1978.

BUSH, LESTER E., JR. "Birth Control Among the Mormons: Introduction to an Insistent Question." *Dialogue* 10 (Autumn 1976): 12–44.

————. "Mormonism's Negro Doctrine: An Historical Overview." *Dialogue* 18 (Spring 1973): 11–68.

BUSH, LESTER E., JR., and ARMAND L. MAUSS, eds. *Neither White nor Black: Mormon Scholars Confront the Race Issue in a Universal Church.* Midvale, Utah: Signature, 1984.

BUSHMAN, CLAUDIA, ed. *Mormon Sisters: Women in Early Utah.* Cambridge, Mass.: Emmeline, 1976.

BUSHMAN, RICHARD L. *Joseph Smith and the Beginnings of Mormonism.* Urbana: Univ. of Illinois Press, 1984.

CAMPBELL, EUGENE E. *Establishing Zion: The Mormon Church in the American West, 1847–1869.* Salt Lake City: Signature, 1988.

CAMPBELL, EUGENE E., and BRUCE L. CAMPBELL. "Divorce Among Mormon Polygamists: Extent and Explanations." *Utah Historical Quarterly* 46 (Winter 1978): 4–23.

CANNON, CHARLES A. "The Awesome Power of Sex: The Polemical Campaign Against Mormon Polygamy." *Pacific Historical Review* 43 (Feb. 1974): 61–82.

CANNON, KENNETH, II. "Beyond the Manifesto: Polygamous Cohabitation Among LDS General Authorities After 1890." *Utah Historical Quarterly* 46 (Winter 1978): 24–36.

CARTER, KATE B. *Denominations That Base Their Teachings on Joseph Smith, the Mormon Prophet.* Salt Lake City: Daughters of the Utah Pioneers, 1969.

CASTERLINE, GAIL FARR. " 'In The Toils' or 'Onward for Zion': Images of the Mormon Woman, 1852–1890." M.A. thesis, Utah State Univ., 1974.

COOK, LYNDON W. *The Revelations of the Prophet Joseph Smith.* Provo: Seventy's Mission Bookstore, 1981.

DAVIS, DAVID BRION. "The New England Origins of Mormonism." *New England Quarterly* 16 (June 1953): 147–68.

————. "Some Themes of Counter-Subversion: An Analysis of Anti-Masonic, Anti-Catholic, and Anti-Mormon Literature." *Mississippi Valley Historical Review* 47 (Sept. 1960): 205–24.

DAVIS, INEZ SMITH. *The Story of the Church.* Independence, Mo.: Herald, 1938.

DE PILLIS, MARIO S. "The Development of Mormon Communitarianism, 1826–1846." Ph.D. diss., Yale Univ., 1960.

———. "The Quest for Religious Authority and the Rise of Mormonism." *Dialogue* 1 (Spring 1966): 68–88.

———. "Social Sources of Mormonism." *Church History* 37 (Mar. 1968): 50–79.

DERR, JILL MULVAY. "Eliza R. Snow and the Woman Question." *BYU Studies* 16 (Winter 1976): 29–39.

———. "Woman's Place in Brigham Young's World." *BYU Studies* 18 (Spring 1978): 377–95.

EHAT, ANDREW F. "Joseph Smith's Introduction of Temple Ordinances and the 1844 Mormon Succession Question." M.A. thesis, Brigham Young Univ., 1982.

EMBRY, JESSIE L. *Mormon Polygamous Families: Life in the Principle.* Salt Lake City: Univ. of Utah Press, 1987.

ESSHOM, FRANK. *Pioneers and Prominent Men of Utah, Comprising Photographs—Genealogies—Biographies.* Salt Lake City: Utah Pioneers, 1913.

EVANS, VELLA NEIL. "Mormon Women and the Right to Wage Work." *Dialogue* 23 (Winter 1990): 45–61.

FLAKE, CHAD, ed. *A Mormon Bibliography, 1830–1930: Books, Pamphlets, Periodicals, and Broadsides Relating to the First Century of Mormonism.* Salt Lake City: Univ. of Utah Press, 1978.

FLANDERS, ROBERT B. "The Mormons Who Did Not Go West: A Study of the Emergence of the Reorganized Church of Jesus Christ of Latter Day Saints." M.A. thesis, Univ. of Wisconsin, 1954.

———. *Nauvoo: Kingdom on the Mississippi.* Urbana: Univ. of Illinois Press, 1965.

FOSTER, LAWRENCE. "Between Heaven and Earth: Mormon Theology of the Family in Comparative Perspective." *Sunstone* 7 (July–Aug. 1982): 6–13.

———. "Career Apostates: Reflections on the Works of Jerald and Sandra Tanner." *Dialogue* 17 (Summer 1984): 35–60.

———. "Cults in Conflict: New Religious Movements and the Mainstream Religious Tradition in America." In Robert N. Bellah and Frederick E. Greenspahn, eds., *Uncivil Religion: Interreligious Hostility in America,* pp. 185–204. New York: Crossroad, 1987.

———. "First Visions: Personal Reflections on Joseph Smith's Religious Experience." *Sunstone* 8 (Sept.–Oct. 1983): 39–43.

———. "From Frontier Activism to Neo-Victorian Domesticity: Mormon Women in the Nineteenth and Twentieth Centuries." *Journal of Mormon History* 6 (1979): 3–21.

————. "James J. Strang: The Prophet Who Failed." *Church History* 50 (June 1981): 181–92.

————. "A Little-Known Defense of Polygamy from the Mormon Press in 1842." *Dialogue* 9 (Winter 1974): 21–34.

————. "New Perspectives on the Mormon Past: Reflections of a Non-Mormon Historian." *Sunstone* 7 (Jan.–Feb. 1982): 41–45.

————. "A Personal Odyssey: My Encounter with Mormon History." *Dialogue* 16 (Autumn 1983): 87–98.

————. "Polygamy and the Frontier: Mormon Women in Early Utah." *Utah Historical Quarterly* 50 (Summer 1982): 268–89.

————. " 'Reluctant Polygamists': The Strains and Challenges of the Transition to Polygamy in a Prominent Mormon Family." In Carl Guarneri and David Alvarez, eds., *Religion and Society in the American West: Historical Essays*, pp. 131–52. Lanham, Md.: Univ. Press of America, 1987.

[FULTON, GILBERT A., JR.] *The Most Holy Principle.* 4 vols. Murray, Utah: Gems, 1970–75.

GATES, SUSA YOUNG, and LEAH D. WIDTSOE, *The Life Story of Brigham Young.* New York: Macmillan, 1930.

————. *Women of the "Mormon" Church.* Salt Lake City: Deseret News, 1926.

GODFREY, KENNETH. "Causes of Mormon Non-Mormon Conflict in Hancock County, Illinois, 1839–1846." Ph.D. diss., Brigham Young Univ., 1967.

GODFREY, KENNETH, AUDREY M. GODFREY, and JILL MULVAY DERR. *Women's Voices: An Untold History of the Latter-day Saints, 1830–1900.* Salt Lake City: Deseret, 1982.

GOODYEAR, IMOGENE. "Joseph Smith and Polygamy: An Alternative View." *John Whitmer Historical Association Journal* 4 (1984): 16–21.

GOTTLIEB, ROBERT, and PETER WILEY. *America's Saints: The Rise of Mormon Power.* New York: Harcourt Brace Jovanovich, 1986.

GREGORY, THOMAS. "Sydney Ridgon: Post-Nauvoo." *BYU Studies* 21 (Winter 1981): 51–67.

GROESBECK, C. JESS. "The Smiths and Their Dreams and Visions: A Psycho-Historical Study of the First Mormon Family." *Sunstone* 12 (Mar. 1988): 22–29.

HAMPSHIRE, ANNETTE P. *Mormonism in Conflict: The Nauvoo Years.* New York: Mellen, 1985.

HANSEN, KLAUS J. "The Making of King Strang: A Re-Examination." *Michigan History* 46 (Sept. 1962): 201–19.

———. *Mormonism and the American Experience.* Chicago: Univ. of Chicago Press, 1981.

———. *Quest for Empire: The Political Kingdom of God and the Council of Fifty in Mormon History.* East Lansing: Michigan State Univ. Press, 1967.

HEATON, TIM B. "Four Characteristics of the Mormon Family: Contemporary Research on Chastity, Conjugality, Children, and Chauvinism." *Dialogue* 20 (Summer 1987): 101–14.

HEEREN, JOHN, DONALD B. LINDSAY, and MARYLEE MASON. "The Mormon Concept of Mother in Heaven: A Sociological Account of Its Origins and Development." *Journal for the Scientific Study of Religion* 23 (1984): 396–411.

HILL, DONNA. *Joseph Smith: The First Mormon.* Garden City, N.Y.: Doubleday, 1977.

HILL, MARVIN S. *Quest for Refuge: The Mormon Flight from American Pluralism.* Salt Lake City: Signature, 1989.

———. "The Role of Christian Primitivism in the Origin and Development of the Mormon Kingdom, 1830–1844." Ph.D. diss., Univ. of Chicago, 1968.

———. "Secular or Sectarian History? A Critique of *No Man Knows My History.*" *Church History* 33 (Mar. 1974): 78–96.

———. "The Shaping of the Mormon Mind in New England and New York." *BYU Studies* 9 (Spring 1969): 351–72.

HILL, MARVIN S., and JAMES B. ALLEN, eds. *Mormonism and American Culture.* New York: Harper & Row, 1972.

HOWARD, RICHARD P. "The Changing RLDS Response to Mormon Polygamy: A Preliminary Analysis." *John Whitmer Historical Association Journal* 3 (1983): 14–29.

———. *Restoration Scriptures: A Study of Their Textual Development.* Independence, Mo.: Reorganized Church of Jesus Christ of Latter Day Saints, 1969.

HULETT, JAMES EDWARD, JR. "Social Role and Personal Security in Mormon Polygamy." *American Journal of Sociology* 45 (Jan. 1940): 542–53.

———. "The Social Role of the Mormon Polygamous Male." *American Sociological Review* 8 (June 1943): 279–87.

———. "The Sociological and Social Psychological Aspects of the Mormon Polygamous Family." Ph.D. diss., Univ. of Wisconsin, 1939.

IRVING, GORDON. "The Law of Adoption: One Phase of the Mormon Concept of Salvation, 1830–1900." *BYU Studies* 14 (Spring 1974): 291–314.

————. "The Mormons and the Bible in the 1830s." *BYU Studies* 13 (Summer 1973): 473–88.

IVINS, STANLEY S. "Notes on Mormon Polygamy." *Western Humanities Review* 10 (Summer 1956): 229–39.

JENSON, ANDREW. *Encyclopedic History of the Church of Jesus Christ of Latter-day Saints.* Salt Lake City: Deseret News, 1941.

————. *The Historical Record: A Monthly Periodical Devoted Exclusively to Historical, Biographical, Chronological and Statistical Matters.* 9 vols. Salt Lake City, 1882–90.

————. *Latter-day Saint Biographical Encyclopedia.* 4 vols. Salt Lake City: Andrew Jenson History Co., 1901–36.

JOHNSON, JEFFREY OGDEN. "Determining and Defining 'Wife': The Brigham Young Households." *Dialogue* 20 (Fall 1987): 57–70.

JOHNSON, SONIA. *From Housewife to Heretic.* Garden City, N.Y.: Doubleday, 1981.

KIMBALL, STANLEY B. *Heber C. Kimball: Mormon Patriarch and Pioneer.* Urbana: Univ. of Illinois Press, 1981.

KUNZ, PHILLIP R., ed. *The Mormon Family.* Provo: Brigham Young Univ. Press, 1977.

LARSEN, HERBERT RAY. " 'Familism' in Mormon Social Structure." Ph.D. diss., Univ. of Utah, 1954.

LARSON, ANDREW KARL. *Erastus Snow: The Life of a Missionary and Apostle of the Early Mormon Church.* Salt Lake City: Univ. of Utah Press, 1971.

LARSON, GUSTIVE O. *The "Americanization" of Utah for Statehood.* San Marino, Calif.: Huntington Library, 1971.

LAUNIUS, ROGER D. *Joseph Smith III: Pragmatic Prophet.* Urbana: Univ. of Illinois Press, 1988.

————. "Methods and Motives: Joseph Smith III's Opposition to Polygamy, 1860–90." *Dialogue* (Winter 1987): 105–20.

LEONE, MARK P. *Roots of Modern Mormonism.* Cambridge, Mass.: Harvard Univ. Press, 1979.

LeSUEUR, STEPHEN C. *The 1838 Mormon War in Missouri.* Columbia: Univ. of Missouri Press, 1987.

LINDSEY, ROBERT. *A Gathering of Saints: A True Story of Money, Murder, and Deceit.* New York: Simon & Schuster, 1988.

LOGUE, LARRY M. *A Sermon in the Desert: Belief and Behavior in Early St. George, Utah.* Urbana: Univ. of Illinois Press, 1988.

————. "A Time of Marriage: Monogamy and Polygamy in a Utah Town." *Journal of Mormon History* 11 (1984): 3–26.

LYMAN, EDWARD LEO. *Political Deliverance: The Mormon Quest for Utah Statehood.* Urbana: Univ. of Illinois Press, 1986.

McKIERNAN, F. MARK. *The Voice of One Crying in the Wilderness: Sidney Rigdon, Religious Reformer, 1793 to 1876.* Lawrence, Kans.: Coronado, 1971.

McKIERNAN, F. MARK, ALMA R. BLAIR, and Paul M. Edwards, eds., *The Restoration Movement: Essays in Mormon History.* Lawrence, Kans.: Coronado, 1973.

McMURRIN, STERLING M. *The Theological Foundations of the Mormon Religion.* Salt Lake City: Univ. of Utah Press, 1965.

MADSEN, CAROL CORNWALL. " 'Remember the Women of Zion': A Study of the Editorial Content of the *Woman's Exponent,* a Mormon Women's Journal." M.A. thesis, Univ. of Utah, 1977.

MADSEN, CAROL CORNWALL, and DAVID J. WHITTAKER. "History's Sequel: A Source Essay on Women in Mormon History." *Journal of Mormon History* 6 (1980): 123–45.

MAY, DEAN L. "The Making of Saints: The Mormon Town as a Setting for the Study of Cultural Change." *Utah Historical Quarterly* 15 (Winter 1977): 75–92.

————. *Utah: A People's History.* Salt Lake City: Univ. of Utah Press, 1987.

MEHR, KAHLILE. "Women's Response to Plural Marriage." *Dialogue* 18 (Fall 1985): 84–97.

MULDER, WILLIAM. *Homeward to Zion: The Mormon Migration from Scandinavia.* Minneapolis: Univ. of Minnesota Press, 1957.

MUSSER, JOSEPH WHITE. *Celestial or Plural Marriage: A Digest of the Mormon Marriage System as Established by God through the Prophet Joseph Smith.* Salt Lake City: N.p., 1944.

NELSON, LOWRY. *The Mormon Village: A Pattern and Technique of Land Settlement.* Salt Lake City: Univ. of Utah Press, 1952.

NEWELL, LINDA KING. "Emma Hale Smith and the Polygamy Question." *John Whitmer Historical Association Journal* 4 (1984): 3–15.

————. "The Emma Smith Lore Reconsidered." *Dialogue* 17 (1984): 87–100.

————. "The Historical Relationship of Mormon Women and the Priesthood." *Dialogue* 18 (Fall 1985): 21–32.

NEWELL, LINDA KING, and VALEEN TIPPETTS AVERY. *Mormon Enigma: Emma Hale Smith—Prophet's Wife, "Elect Lady," Polygamy's Foe.* Garden City, N.Y.: Doubleday, 1984.

————. "New Light on the Sun: Emma Smith and the *New York Sun* Letter." *Journal of Mormon History* 6 (1979): 23–35.

NOALL, CLAIRE. *Intimate Disciple: A Portrait of Willard Richards, Apostle to Joseph Smith—Cousin of Brigham Young.* Salt Lake City: Univ. of Utah Press, 1957.

OAKS, DALLIN H., and MARVIN S. HILL. *Carthage Conspiracy: The Trial of the Accused Assassins of Joseph Smith.* Urbana: Univ. of Illinois Press, 1975.

O'DEA, THOMAS F. "Mormonism and the Avoidance of Sectarian Stagnation: A Study of Church, Sect, and Incipient Nationality." *American Journal of Sociology* 60 (Nov. 1954): 285–93.

————. *The Mormons.* Chicago: Univ. of Chicago Press, 1957.

PACE, D. GENE. "Wives of Nineteenth-Century Mormon Bishops: A Quantitative Analysis." *Journal of the West* 21 (Apr. 1982): 49–57.

PETERSEN, LAMAR. *Hearts Made Glad: The Charges of Intemperance Against Joseph Smith the Mormon Prophet.* Salt Lake City: The Author, 1975.

PHILLIPS, EMMA M. *33 Women of the Restoration.* Independence, Mo.: Herald, 1970.

POLL, RICHARD D. "The Mormon Question Enters National Politics, 1850–1856." *Utah Historical Quarterly* 25 (Apr. 1957): 117–31.

————. "Nauvoo and the New Mormon History: A Bibliographic Survey." *Journal of Mormon History* 5 (1978): 105–23.

————, et al. *Utah's History.* Provo: Brigham Young Univ. Press, 1978.

QUAIFE, MILO M. *The Kingdom of Saint James: A Narrative of the Mormons.* New Haven: Yale Univ. Press, 1930.

QUINN, D. MICHAEL. *Early Mormonism and the Magic World View.* Salt Lake City: Signature, 1987.

————. "Latter-day Saint Prayer Circles." *BYU Studies* 19 (Fall 1978): 79–105.

————. "LDS Church Authority and New Plural Marriages, 1890–1904." *Dialogue* 18 (Spring 1985): 9–105.

————. "The Mormon Succession Crisis of 1844." *BYU Studies* 16 (Winter 1976): 187–233.

————. "Organizational Development and Social Origins of the Mormon Hierarchy, 1832–1932: A Prosopographical Study." M.A. thesis, Univ. of Utah, 1973.

QUIST, JOHN. "Polygamy Among James Strang and His Followers." *John Whitmer Historical Association Journal* 9 (1989): 31–48.

RICH, RUSSELL. *Those Who Would Be Leaders (Offshoots of Mormonism)*. Provo: Extension Publications, Division of Continuing Education, Brigham Young Univ., 1967.

ROBERTS, BRIGHAM H. *A Comprehensive History of the Church of Jesus Christ of Latter-day Saints, Century I*. 6 vols. Provo: Brigham Young Univ. Press, 1965.

————. *Studies of the Book of Mormon*. Edited with an Introduction by Brigham D. Madsen. Urbana: Univ. of Illinois Press, 1985.

SCHINDLER, HAROLD. *Orrin Porter Rockwell: Man of God, Son of Thunder*. Salt Lake City: Univ. of Utah Press, 1966.

SCOTT, LYN, and MAUREEN URSENBACH BEECHER. "Mormon Women: A Bibliography in Process, 1977–1985." *Journal of Mormon History* 12 (1985): 113–28.

SESSIONS, GENE A. *Mormon Thunder: A Documentary History of Jedediah Morgan Grant*. Urbana: Univ. of Illinois Press, 1982.

SHEPHERD, GORDON, and GARY SHEPHERD. *A Kingdom Transformed: Themes in the Development of Mormonism*. Salt Lake City: Univ. of Utah Press, 1984.

SHIELDS, STEVEN L. *Divergent Paths of the Restoration*. 3d ed, rev. and enlarged. Bountiful, Utah: Restoration Research, 1982.

————. *The Latter Day Saint Churches: An Annotated Bibliography*. New York: Garland, 1987.

SHIPPS, JAN. *Mormonism: The Story of a New Religious Tradition*. Urbana: Univ. of Illinois Press, 1985.

————. "The Principle Revoked: A Closer Look at the Demise of Plural Marriage." *Journal of Mormon History* 11 (1984): 65–78.

————. "The Prophet Puzzle: Suggestions Leading Toward a More Comprehensive Interpretation of Joseph Smith." *Journal of Mormon History* 1 (1974): 4–20.

SHORT, DENNIS R. *Questions on Plural Marriage, with a Selected Bibliography and 1600 References*. Salt Lake City: Dennis R. Short, 1975.

SILLITOE, JOHN, ed. *From Cottage to Market: The Professionlization of Women's Sphere*. Salt Lake City: Utah Women's History Association, 1983.

SILLITOE, LINDA, and ALLEN ROBERTS. *Salamander: The Story of the Mormon Forgery Murders.* Salt Lake City: Signature, 1988.

SMITH, JAMES E., and PHILIP R. KUNZ. "Polygyny and Fertility in Nineteenth-Century America." *Population Studies* 30 (1976): 465–80.

SMITH, JOSEPH, III, and HEMAN C. SMITH. *The History of the Reorganized Church of Jesus Christ of Latter Day Saints.* 6 vols. Independence, Mo.: Herald, 1951–70.

SONNE, CONWAY B. *Saints on the Seas: A Maritime History of Mormon Migration, 1830–1890.* Salt Lake City: Univ. of Utah Press, 1983.

SPENCER, CLARISSA YOUNG, and MABEL HARMER. *Brigham Young at Home.* Salt Lake City. Deseret News, 1947.

STANLEY, REVA [REVA HOLDWAY SCOTT]. *A Biography of Parley P. Pratt, the Archer of Paradise.* Caldwell, Idaho: Caxton, 1937.

TANNER, JERALD, and SANDRA TANNER. *The Changing World of Mormonism.* Chicago: Moody, 1980.

——— . *Joseph Smith and Polygamy.* Salt Lake City: Modern Microfilm, n.d.

——— . *Mormonism—Shadow or Reality?* Enlarged ed. Salt Lake City: Modern Microfilm, 1972.

TAYLOR, SAMUEL W. *Nightfall at Nauvoo.* New York: Macmillan, 1971. Fictionalized account of Nauvoo.

TERRY, KEITH CALVIN. "The Contribution of Medical Women During the First Fifty Years in Utah." M.A. thesis, Brigham Young Univ., 1964.

TINNEY, THOMAS MILTON. "The Royal Family of the Prophet Joseph Smith, Junior, First President of the Church of Jesus Christ of Latter-day Saints." Typescript, 1973. Available in the Utah State Historical Society Library and in the University of Utah Library Special Collections.

TURNER, RODNEY. *Women and the Priesthood.* Salt Lake City: Deseret, 1972.

VAN NEST, ALBERT J. *A Directory to the 'Restored Gospel' Churches.* Evanston, Ill.: Institute for the Study of American Religion, 1983.

VAN NOORD, ROGER. *King of Beaver Island: The Life and Assassination of James Jesse Strang.* Urbana: Univ. of Illinois Press, 1988.

VAN WAGONER, RICHARD S. *Mormon Polygamy: A History.* Salt Lake City: Signature, 1986.

——— . "Sarah M. Pratt: The Shaping of an Apostate." *Dialogue* 19 (Summer 1986): 69–99.

WARENSKI, MARILYN. *Patriarchs and Politics: The Plight of the Mormon Woman.* New York: McGraw-Hill, 1980.

WASPE, ILEEN ANN. "The Status of Women in the Philosophy of Mormonism from 1830 to 1845." M.A. thesis, Utah State Univ., 1942.

WERNER, MORRIS ROBERT. *Brigham Young.* New York: Harcourt, Brace, 1925.

WHALEN, WILLIAM J. *The Latter-day Saints in the Modern Day World: An Account of Contemporary Mormonism.* Rev. ed. Notre Dame, Ind.: Univ. of Notre Dame Press, 1967.

WHITE, JEAN BICKMORE. "Dr. Martha Hughes Cannon: Doctor, Wife, Legislator, Exile." In Vicky Burgess-Olson, ed., *Sister Saints,* pp. 383–97. Provo: Brigham Young Univ. Press, 1978.

WHITE, O. KENDALL, JR. *Mormon Neo-Orthodoxy: A Crisis Theology.* Salt Lake City: Signature, 1987.

WHITTAKER, DAVID J. "Early Mormon Polygamy Defenses." *Journal of Mormon History* 11 (1984): 43–64.

WHITTAKER, DAVID J., and CAROL C. MADSEN. "History's Sequel: A Source Essay on Women in Mormon History." *Journal of Mormon History* 6 (1979): 123–45.

WINN, KENNETH H. *Exiles in a Land of Liberty: Mormons in America, 1830–1846.* Chapel Hill: Univ. of North Carolina Press, 1989.

YOUNG, KIMBALL. *Isn't One Wife Enough? The Story of Mormon Polygamy.* New York: Holt, 1954.

———. "Sex Roles in Polygamous Mormon Families." In Theodore M. Newcomb and Eugene L. Hartly, eds., *Readings in Social Psychology,* pp. 373–83. New York: Holt, 1947.

INDEX

345

Utopianism and Communitarianism
LYMAN TOWER SARGENT AND GREGORY CLAEYS
Series Editors

This new series offers historical and contemporary analyses of utopian literature, communal societies, utopian social theory, broad themes such as the
treatment of women in these traditions, and new editions of fictional works
of lasting value for both a general and a scholarly audience.
Other titles in the series include:

The Concept of Utopia. Ruth Levitas
Low Living and High Thinking: Modern Times, New York, 1851–1864.
Roger Wunderlich
Unveiling a Parallel. Alice Ilgenfritz Jones and Ella Merchant

WOMEN, FAMILY, AND UTOPIA
was composed in 11 on 13 Goudy Old Style on a Mergenthaler Linotron
by BookMasters, Inc.;
with display type in Goudy Cursive by Dix Type;
printed by sheet-fed offset on 50-pound, acid-free Antique Cream,
Smyth-sewn and bound over binder's boards in Joanna Arrestox B
and notch bound with paper covers printed in 2 colors
by Maple-Vail Book Manufacturing Group, Inc.
and published by
SYRACUSE UNIVERSITY PRESS
SYRACUSE, NEW YORK 13244-5160

886 3